RIGHTING MISCARRIAGES OF JUSTICE?

Ten years of the Criminal Cases Review Commission

Laurie Elks

JUSTICE – advancing access to justice, human rights and the rule of law

JUSTICE is an independent law reform and human rights organisation. It works largely through policy-orientated research; interventions in court proceedings; education and training; briefings, lobbying and policy advice. It is the British section of the International Commission of Jurists (ICJ).

JUSTICE is a charity (registered charity 1058580). We rely on the help of our members and supporters for the funds to continue our work.

For more information visit www.justice.org.uk.

JUSTICE, 59 Carter Lane, London EC4V 5AQ
Tel: +44 (0)20 7329 5100
Fax: +44 (0)20 7329 5055
E-mail: admin@justice.org.uk
www.justice.org.uk

© JUSTICE 2008
ISBN 978 0 907247 45 6
Designed by Adkins Design
Printed by Hobbs the Printers Ltd

Extract from Criminal Appeal Act 1995 (C35) is reproduced under the terms of Crown Copyright policy guidance issued by HMSO.
Article on page 269 © Guardian News & Media Ltd 2004, reproduced with permission.

JUSTICE is grateful to the Law Society Charity for its support of this publication.

Contents

Biography of author

Laurie Elks first worked in the NGO sector, including teaching for Voluntary Services Overseas in Nigeria, and as a welfare rights worker for the Child Poverty Action Group. After qualifying as a solicitor in 1980, he spent over 15 years as a commercial lawyer – where he was a partner at Nabarro – specialising in corporate and regulatory work.

In 1997, Laurie took up appointment as one of the founding members of the Criminal Cases Review Commission, acting as a decision maker in many of the cases discussed in this book, as well as acting as caseworker on a number of high-profile cases. At the Commission, he assumed responsibility for training Commission Members and staff on the implications of Court of Appeal decisions in cases referred to it by the Commission. This work has formed the basis of the present study. He also had considerable involvement in developing the decision-making processes of the Commission. He is also a member of the Competition Commission.

Laurie has lived in Hackney for over 35 years and has been involved in a wide range of community activities, including as founder of the Lee Valley Association. He is a director of Hackney Historic Buildings Trust and acts as custodian of St Augustine's Tower – Hackney's oldest building.

Foreword

On 1 April 1997, the Criminal Cases Review Commission took over responsibility for the review of alleged miscarriages of justice in England and Wales and Northern Ireland. The Commission was set up following the recommendation of the Royal Commission on Criminal Justice – the Runciman Commission – which proposed that review of alleged miscarriages should be transferred from the Home Office to an independent non-departmental public body.[1] The establishment of the Commission was warmly welcomed by JUSTICE, which had campaigned for such an independent body for many years.

The Commission took over some 300 files from the Home Office and the Northern Ireland Office – including many hoary old cases which the Home Office had deferred sine die as 'too difficult' – but none of the Home Office's procedures or personnel. This was not a case where departmental functions were transferred as a 'going concern' into a new agency – the Commission started with carte blanche, establishing its procedures and policies, and indeed its defining ethos, from scratch.

The governing body of the new Commission consisted of a Board of 15 Commission Members, of whom I was one. Much suspicion attached to the fact that the Chairman, Sir Frederick Crawford, was a declared freemason and that four of the members had a police or prosecution background. It was suggested darkly in some quarters that the Commission might prove to be *worse* than the Home Office in dealing with miscarriage cases.[2] Most of the sceptics – but by no means all – would now agree that the Commission's achievements have surpassed their expectations.

The purpose of this study is to provide an accessible summary of the outcome of the Commission's referrals during its first ten years. I was a member of the Commission for all but the last three months of this ten-year period and had some personal involvement in about one-third of the cases discussed in this study. I also provided regular training to my fellow Commission Members and to Case Review Managers about the outcome of the Commission's referrals during this period. I hope that this will provide some valuable raw material to enable readers to judge what the Commission has (and has not) achieved during this period and to measure the outcome of the Commission's endeavours against prior expectations.

I am intensely aware that I have had very little to say about the 96 per cent of cases that come to the Commission but are *not* referred. The Commission has been the subject of considerable criticism for the way in which it deals with rejected applications. It has been widely commented, in particular, that there is no obvious explanation for the fact that the Commission's rate of referral runs consistently at about one half of the rate of referrals made by the Scottish Criminal Cases Review Commission (SCCRC). The SCCRC has a broadly similar (although not identical) remit, but some eight per cent of applications – twice the proportion of CCRC cases – are referred.[3] Other criticisms of the Commission relate to the failure to interview more than a small proportion of applicants;[4] to the insufficiency of communication with applicants and their representatives; and to alleged deficiencies of investigation, among other matters.

It would be the height of conceit on the part of the Commission, or its former members, to say that there is nothing in any of these criticisms and I do not do so. However, the purpose of my study is not to dissect the working methods or the effectiveness of the Commission but to characterise the cases that *have* been referred. This may be a matter of particular interest to members and supporters of JUSTICE, which campaigned tirelessly under its first Secretary, Tom Sargent, to bring the Commission (or something like it) into being. The JUSTICE campaign was forged when the criminal justice system was vastly different from today, when modern protections for suspects were lacking, and when the use of 'verballing' and other means to secure unjust convictions was all too common. The Commission has played an important role in resolving miscarriages from that period, but the great majority of its referrals have been of convictions that have occurred since the Police and Criminal Evidence Act 1984 and modern standards of disclosure were introduced. I hope that the discussion of the Commission's cases will help to bring into focus some of the modern issues concerning miscarriages of justice.

The concept of an 'unsafe'[5] conviction has been something of a moving target over this period as the Court of Appeal (Criminal Division) (henceforth the Court)[6] has developed its jurisprudence (sometimes in direct response to Commission referrals) and has conducted an occasionally clamorous and public 'dialogue'[7] with the Commission about the wisdom of some of its referrals. The early chapters of this book deal with this dialogue, and developments of the legal test of safety that have affected the Commission's remit. As will be apparent from these chapters, the issue of what should or should not constitute a safe conviction has attracted the interest of politicians in recent years. In 2007, the government brought forward measures in the Criminal Justice and Immigration

Bill to restrict appeals based either upon legal technicalities or upon post-trial changes of the law. The background to these proposals is discussed in detail in chapters 2 and 7 but, in brief, both proposed measures that appeared designed to cut down the effective scope of the Commission's jurisdiction. In the outcome, the government has pursued its proposal for providing judges with a discretion to disregard post-trial changes of law but has abandoned its proposals to restrict appeals based on legal technicalities. It remains to be seen whether the changes will have any significant impact upon the Commission's referrals or their outcome.

In preparing this study, I have considered all of the judgments on Commission referrals handed down by the Court up to 1 April 2007 – the tenth anniversary of the Commission's inception. I have also taken account of a small number of cases decided since then which appear to me to be particularly significant or which will assist understanding as to where the law presently stands. I have made some reference in this study to the great majority of the decisions made on Commission referrals in this ten-year period, excepting only a small number of outlying cases which appear either not to raise any points of wider interest or to replicate other cases to which reference has been made. However, I have not been able to do any kind of justice to the complexity of the cases or (in many cases) to the range of issues raised by the Commission's referrals. I hope that readers will go to the judgments themselves for a fuller understanding of the issues where required.

I would particularly like to thank John Wagstaff – who has been a legal adviser to the Commission since its inception – for assistance on many points in the preparation of this book. I would like to thank the inexhaustible former Commissioner, Tony Foster, my wife June Harben, and Sally Ireland, Roger Smith and Beverley Slaney at JUSTICE – who have reviewed the manuscript. I also thank my former colleagues, Alastair MacGregor, Angela Flower, Ralph Barrington, Sally Berlin and Esther Parker Duber who have assisted me on specific points, and Paul Taylor and Henry Blaxland QC who have commented on some of the chapters. I am also grateful for an illuminating discussion with Lord Garry Runciman.

I would also like to thank all of my past and present colleagues at the Commission for great comradeship. I would particularly like to thank Ralph Barrington for teaching me so much about the investigation and reinvestigation of crime and Sir Frederick Crawford, the first Chairman of the Commission, who persuaded the government to appoint a surprisingly nonconformist first cohort of Commissioners and created such a positive working ethos at the Commission.

I unreservedly exonerate everyone who has helped me of any responsibility for errors of fact, interpretation and judgment. The views I have expressed are my own and neither the Commission nor JUSTICE bears any responsibility for any of them. This work has taken account of legal developments up to 15 July 2008.

Laurie Elks
August 2008

Note on case references

I have listed the Commission's cases discussed in this study, which are referred to in bold text, in the tables that follow (see Appendices 1-5), together with the case reference where available. Non-Commission cases are italicised in the text and are referenced in endnotes. However, I have also listed the non-Commission cases that have been cited repetitively in a separate table (see Appendix 6).

Commission cases have been referred to and indexed by name or initial. The names used for this study do not necessarily correspond with the full case names in the official record. In particular, a number of the cases were decided as part of multi-party appeals (including some co-appellants whose cases were not referred by the Commission). Where there has been more than one Commission referral of appellants having the same (or almost identical) names I have added first names.

A full listing of the judgments on the Commission's Court of Appeal cases may be found on the Commission's website, which is at www.ccrc.gov.uk. The Commission has recently taken down the judgments from its website but a link is provided to the British and Irish Legal Information Institute (Bailii) database which can be accessed directly at http://www.bailii.org/. Cases may be searched by citation by clicking on 'case law search' on the home page. The Bailii database is free to all users and contains the great majority of the judgments resulting from Commission referrals both in England and Wales and in Northern Ireland. The majority of the judgments (including some judgments not available from Bailii) may also be found on the *Casetrack* database at www.casetrack.com (which is available to subscribers).

Where cases are not freely accessible, it may be possible to obtain copies for bona fide research purposes. Application may be made to one of the Commission's legal advisers and in some cases subscribers to the *Casetrack* database may be able to obtain copies of judgments by application to the 'Case Detective'. Some particularly sensitive cases, such as those containing informant details, are unlikely to be made available from any source and, indeed, I have not provided case references for those cases.

The judgments on the Commission's referral of summary cases are not available on any public database and indeed the majority of these decisions have not been the subject of lengthy formal judgments. The Commission's legal advisers may in some cases be able to assist with enquiries made for research purposes.

The Commission's referral documents – its Statements of Reasons – are not made available by the Commission. In some cases, applicants or their legal advisers may be willing to release the Statement of Reasons. The solicitors who have acted for applicants may be identified in many cases from the archive press releases, which can be accessed through the 'news' tab on the Commission's website.

Notes

1. *Report of the Royal Commission on Criminal Justice* Cm 2263, HMSO, London, 1993.
2. See, for instance, *New Crime Law, Old Police Culture* in the *Independent* 1 April 1997 at http://findarticles.com/p/articles/mi_qn4158/is_19970401/ai_n14116515. Had the Commission's early critics seen the Home Office files bequeathed to the Commission they might have realised that this suggestion was even more hurtful than they intended!
3. The rejoinder is sometimes made on the Commission's behalf that the referral rate for Northern Ireland cases at some 15 per cent is in turn about twice the referral rate in Scotland, but that may reflect the particularities of the criminal justice system in the Province – as discussed in chapter 13.
4. In contrast with the SCCRC, which interviews *all* applicants.
5. See s2 Criminal Appeal Act 1968 as amended.
6. The Court is responsible for hearing appeals against convictions and sentences passed by Crown Courts in England and Wales.
7. The 'dialogue' is one-sided in the sense that the Commission's referral documents – its Statements of Reasons – are not in the public domain, whereas the Court's judgments generally are.

Chapter 1 - The Commission's origins and powers

The requirement for the Commission

The need for effective redress for victims of miscarriages of justice has been pursued by JUSTICE from its very inception 50 years ago. Two committees of JUSTICE, which reported as long ago as 1964[1] and 1968,[2] highlighted the many practical difficulties faced by petitioners seeking review of wrongful convictions and the lack of any adequate machinery for dealing with miscarriages of justice.

Responsibility for review of miscarriages formerly lay with the Home Secretary who, under the terms of s17 Criminal Appeal Act 1968, had power to refer alleged cases of miscarriage to the Court of Appeal if he 'thought fit' to do so.[3] A small unit of the Home Office, named C3, was responsible for investigating miscarriage cases. Referrals of suspected miscarriages ran at an average of some ten per year in the years preceding the establishment of the Commission. In general, the Home Office refused to take a proactive stance in investigating allegations of miscarriage and referred cases only when served with clear-cut evidence of miscarriage. It was left to under-resourced voluntary bodies, drawing on the pro bono efforts of lawyers, and supported by a small number of broadcasters and journalists, to bring miscarriages to light. JUSTICE was at the forefront of these activities, dealing with some 200-300 applications to review allegations of miscarriage in each year, most from serving prisoners.

The campaign for an effective and independent machinery for review of miscarriages achieved increasing prominence in the 1980s, at a time when there was rising awareness of the inadequacies and the hazards of the criminal prosecution process and when many of the most important procedural safeguards now available to defendants did not exist. In particular:

- There was no requirement for recording of police interviews before the Police and Criminal Evidence Act 1984 (henceforth PACE) came into force on 1 January 1986. Great numbers of convictions were based upon police evidence that the prisoner had confessed to the crime, with no proper safeguards against the 'verballing' of defendants by police officers.

- The rights of defendants to legal advice in the police station, and of young and vulnerable defendants to the support of an 'appropriate adult', were sketchy and unclear until the coming into effect of PACE.

- The prosecution had scant obligations to disclose material capable of undermining its case.[4] This situation did not change significantly until the *Judith Ward* case,[5] decided in 1992.

In addition to the want of such basic procedural safeguards, there was formerly a much poorer appreciation of the flaws that might exist in an apparently watertight prosecution case. By way of example, it was only in the 1970s, following the case of *Turnbull*,[6] that the courts adopted the practice of warning juries of the possibility of mistaken identification evidence, particularly in 'fleeting glance' situations. Similarly, it was little appreciated until the case of *Confait*[7] that it was possible that completely innocent defendants could have confessed to crimes with which they had no connection. And it was only when the work of Professors MacKeith and Gudjonsson became known in the 1980s that there was any appreciation of the fact that there were some vulnerable suspects who would be particularly susceptible to confessing to crimes put to them by police officers. These matters were all of concern to JUSTICE in the years leading up to the establishment of the Commission. They have all now been resolved, in the sense that in modern trials juries would normally be exposed to the uncertainties that exist in the evidence before reaching their verdicts.

Other matters cited by JUSTICE in its early reports have a more familiar and contemporary ring. A report entitled *Miscarriages of Justice,* prepared by a committee chaired by a retired Court of Appeal judge, Sir George Waller, was published in 1989. It referred to inadequate pre-trial preparation by solicitors, and inadequate preparation by trial counsel due to late returned briefs, as important causes of miscarriages of justice. These are issues that continue to arise in criminal trials and, indeed, they have been exacerbated by the progressive strangulation of criminal legal aid by successive governments.

It is interesting to note the 'top five' causes of miscarriages of justice noted by the Waller Committee:

1. wrongful identification;

2.   false confession;

3.   perjury by a co-accused or other witness;

4.   police misconduct, usually in the allegation of a 'verbal confession' which, it is claimed, was never made, or the planting of incriminating evidence;

5.   bad trial tactics.

The establishment of the Commission

It is unlikely that these hardy perennial issues would have led to reform had the criminal justice system not been assailed by a series of catastrophic wrongful convictions in the 1970s, many of them related to terrorist crimes. These cases illustrate the fact (unchanged to this day) that crimes which create the greatest public outrage are particularly susceptible to giving rise to miscarriages because of the extreme pressure upon police to identify the culprits. The defects of these convictions were gradually unravelled over the succeeding years with revelations of false police testimony about 'contemporaneous' confessions, re-writing of documents, non-disclosure and unreliable scientific forensic evidence. High-profile convictions subsequently quashed over the period 1989 to 1992 included those of the *Guildford Four*,[8] *the Maguire Seven*[9] and the *Birmingham Six*,[10] each involving allegations of responsibility for terrorist offences and each supported by confessions secured by illegitimate and/or violent police tactics.

The concern raised by such cases was magnified by the intransigence of the Court of Appeal in recognising the dangers of wrongful convictions. This was particularly apparent in the second appeal of the Birmingham Six, decided in 1988 following reference by the Home Secretary. Giving judgment upholding the convictions, Lord Justice Lane famously remarked (in the face of compelling evidence of an unsafe conviction) that 'the longer this case has gone on, the more convinced this court has become that the verdict of the jury ... was correct'. It was directly following the quashing of the convictions of the Birmingham Six in 1990, after a further reference by the Home Secretary, that the government announced the establishment of the Royal Commission on Criminal Justice under the chairmanship of Lord Runciman, with the reform of the arrangements for the review of miscarriages of justice at the centre of its terms of reference.

Runciman – as widely anticipated – recommended that responsibility for review of allegations of miscarriages of justice should pass to an independent body, referred to as the 'Criminal Cases Review Authority'. The rationale for this independent authority is set out with great brevity and clarity in the Report of the Runciman Commission,[11] the great majority of whose recommendations were subsequently given legislative effect.

The salient features of the proposed authority, and the Runciman Commission's reasons for proposing them, can be summarised as follows.

Independence

Responsibility for reviewing alleged miscarriages was to be entrusted to a body independent of ministerial influence. The Runciman Commission, drawing upon the report of Sir John May in his second report on the notorious *Maguire* case,[12] considered that there was a systemic constitutional difficulty in entrusting the review of miscarriages to the executive branch of government. The Home Office – said to be mindful of the doctrine of separation of powers – was unwilling either to refer cases upon the view that the Court of Appeal had reached the wrong decision, or to carry out investigations to establish whether applicants had been wrongfully convicted. The Runciman Commission concluded that it was 'neither necessary nor desirable' that the Home Secretary should continue to hold this responsibility and laid stress upon the independence of the new Authority.

Relationship with the Court of Appeal and the jury system

In the light of the notorious miscarriages of justice, and the somewhat abject performance of the Court of Appeal in cases such as the Birmingham Six appeal, there was strong support from JUSTICE and others for the establishment of a determinative body to deal with miscarriage cases outside the normal criminal appellate system. The Runciman Commission rejected this approach. It emphasised that the Authority should be wholly independent of the Court in determining the scope and extent of its investigations but the end process, 'when an investigation is completed whose results the Authority believes should be considered by the Court of Appeal', would be that the matter should be referred to be determined by the Court of Appeal in the normal way. This recommendation, which places the Criminal Cases Review Commission (the Commission) into an effectively subordinate relationship with the Court of Appeal, was given effect in the Criminal Appeal Act 1995 establishing the Commission.

A consequence of the relationship proposed by Runciman was that any new evidence or argument raised by the Commission's investigation would ultimately be received and evaluated by the Court of Appeal. It was (and is) a matter within the discretion of the Court of Appeal whether or not it is 'necessary or expedient in the interests of justice'[13] to receive new evidence. It, therefore, followed from the Runciman recommendations that any evidence to be reviewed by the new Authority had to be considered from the perspective of whether or not the Court of Appeal would be prepared to receive it. Most importantly, any system for reviewing miscarriages that leaves the ultimate decision to the Court of Appeal necessarily operates within the parameters of the Court's assumptions. Central among those assumptions is that the Court should be extremely hesitant to substitute its own judgment of the facts for the verdict of the jury, which has had the benefit of seeing and hearing the witnesses give evidence. This necessarily has a profound impact upon the way in which the Commission investigates and considers evidence. Whatever view the Commission takes of a particular case, its determination must always focus upon the question of whether the evidence and the arguments available are sufficient to give rise to the real possibility that the Court of Appeal – ever respectful of the jury's role – will quash the conviction.

Constitution of the Commission

The Runciman Commission proposed an Authority consisting of several members serving under a chairman who should be chosen 'for his or her personal qualities rather than any particular qualifications or background'. Members should be a mixture of lawyers and lay persons who would bring to bear 'several points of view', and the model of a single ombudsman was explicitly rejected. The first cohort of Commissioners was highly diverse, including, inter alia, a former Chief Constable; a former County Council Chief Executive; and a psychiatrist, as well as members with backgrounds in the City, the civil service, the professions, academia and industry.[14] Decisions to refer are required by the Act to be made by a committee of not less than three members[15] and it is, therefore, inescapably the case that the Commission has many possible 'constitutions' – depending upon the members deciding a particular case – as does the Court of Appeal itself. The Commission is, nevertheless, a collegiate body and its approach and ethos is defined by its output of referred cases; by its extensive archive of published policy statements and memoranda;[16] and in other public documents, such as the annual report delivered to the Secretary of State.[17]

Wider role of the Commission

The Runciman Commission's report considered the principal causes of miscarriage and its recommendations dealt, inter alia, with late returned briefs; prosecution pre-trial disclosure; organisation of forensic science facilities; the availability of psychiatric advice; and support for suspected persons. The Runciman Commission proposed that the new Authority would have responsibility for dealing with specific allegations of miscarriage on an individual casework basis, but would also maintain an overview of the causes and the 'state' of miscarriages in the light of the continuing development of the criminal justice system. Their report stated:

> we think it important that the Authority should also be able to draw attention in its [Annual] Report to general features of the criminal justice system which it has found unsatisfactory in the course of its work and to make any recommendations for change which it thinks fit.

The Authority was not, therefore, seen as merely a body for resolving miscarriages post hoc, but also as a way of helping to ensure the continuous review of the adequacy of the criminal justice system in preventing miscarriages.

The Commission's powers to refer convictions and sentences

The Commission came into being on 1 April 1997. Its powers and duties are set out in the Criminal Appeal Act 1995 (the 1995 Act). The sections of the 1995 Act referring to the Commission are reproduced in Appendix 7. The scope of the Commission's remit is set out at sections 9 to 12 of the 1995 Act:

- Section 9 provides that the Commission may at any time refer the conviction or sentence of a person convicted on indictment in England and Wales.

- Section 10 provides the like power to refer the conviction or sentence of a person convicted on indictment in Northern Ireland.

- Section 11 provides that the Commission may at any time refer the conviction or sentence of a person convicted summarily in England and Wales.

- Section 12 provides the like power to refer the conviction or sentence of a person convicted summarily in Northern Ireland.

As a result of the Armed Forces Act 2006, the Commission's jurisdiction will also extend to convictions by Courts Martial and by the Service Civilian Court. The commencement date for this extension of the Commission's jurisdiction is not yet known.

Section 13 sets out the test for referral:

(1) *A reference of a conviction, verdict, finding or sentence shall not be made under any of sections 9 to 12 unless—*

    (a) *the Commission consider that there is a real possibility that the conviction, verdict, finding or sentence would not be upheld were the reference to be made,*

    (b) *the Commission so consider—*

        (i) *in the case of a conviction, verdict or finding, because of an argument, or evidence, not raised in the proceedings which led to it or on any appeal or application for leave to appeal against it, or*

        (ii) *in the case of a sentence, because of an argument on a point of law, or information, not so raised, and*

    (c) *an appeal against the conviction, verdict, finding or sentence has been determined or leave to appeal against it has been refused.*

(2) *Nothing in subsection (1)(b)(i) or (c) shall prevent the making of a reference if it appears to the Commission that there are exceptional circumstances which justify making it.*

The following points should be noted:

The test of safety

Section 13 makes no reference to 'miscarriages of justice'. In carrying out its primary role of reviewing Crown Court convictions, the Commission's determination is whether there is a real possibility that the Court of Appeal would quash the conviction as 'unsafe'.[18] A conviction may be found unsafe due to new evidence establishing that a miscarriage has occurred, or on other more juridical grounds. This is discussed at some length in chapter 2.

The corresponding provisions of the Scottish legislation read quite differently, providing that the SCCRC may refer a case (to the High Court in Scotland) if it believes:

(a) that a miscarriage of justice may have occurred; and

(b) that it is in the interests of justice that a reference should be made.[19]

The government of the day argued (and would appear to be entitled to be believed) on this point that the difference of wording was not intended to connote any difference of philosophic approach – rather the fact that each Commission would be embedded within the criminal justice system applying in its own jurisdiction. As the test in England and Wales (and Northern Ireland) for quashing convictions is one of *safety*, the referring body inevitably is required to apply that criterion in deciding which cases to refer.

The new evidence or argument test

A referral of a conviction requires (unless exceptional circumstances apply) argument or evidence not previously raised in trial or appellate proceedings. The legislative scheme, therefore, rests firmly on the premise that the Commission (like the Home Secretary before it) will be concerned principally with cases that raise some genuinely new issue. Inevitably, this nicety is not necessarily understood by applicants, and a very high proportion of the applications rejected by the Commission fail because they raise no material new matters. That said, the Runciman Committee had been critical in its report of the reluctance of the Court of Appeal to quash verdicts in cases of genuine 'lurking doubt' stating simply that:

> *Where ... on reading the transcript and hearing argument the Court of Appeal has a serious doubt about the verdict it should exercise its powers to quash.*

And it was critical, too, of the Home Secretary's reluctance to refer convictions in the absence of new evidence. There is, therefore, a power reserved to the Commission to refer even in the absence of new evidence if it considers that there are exceptional circumstances justifying the making of a reference. Quite apart from the no-new-evidence cases covered by this 'exceptional circumstances' provision, the Commission from time to time encounters cases where there is a smidgen of new evidence overlying profound concerns about the probative force of the 'old' evidence. Convictions where there is a pervasive sense of unease – but little or no new evidence – have been quite problematical for the Commission. Some of these cases are discussed at chapter 5.

The requirement for a previous appeal

The 1995 Act requires that referrals may not be made of either conviction or sentence absent a previous appeal against conviction or sentence (as the case may be) unless there are 'exceptional circumstances which justify making [a reference]'. The Commission has generally taken a liberal view of the exceptional circumstances provision. If the failure to pursue any good appeal points appears to be due to reasons beyond the responsibility of the applicant, then provided the new evidence or argument meets the 'real possibility' test, the Commission will generally refer. By way of example, the Commission would be likely to consider the use of the exceptional circumstances provision justified in the following circumstances:

- the new referral issue is based upon an argument on a point of law that was unknown on the general understanding of the law at the time of trial;

- the referral issue was not taken at trial or appeal due to the deficient advice of defence counsel; or

- new evidence is put forward that was not available at trial – for instance, evidence undisclosed by the prosecution prior to trial or evidence now available due to advances of scientific techniques.

'No appeal' applications are currently screened on a preliminary basis by a Commissioner[20] and if it appears that there is a significant point for the Commission to consider, the matter will be allocated for review in the normal way. The Commission's relatively liberal approach to no appeal cases has run into some contention with the Court of Appeal in 'change-of-law' cases which are discussed at chapter 7.

A power – not a duty – to refer

The language of sections 9-12 refers throughout to the *power* of the Commission, not a duty, to refer cases that satisfy the referral test of section 13. There are a variety of situations in which the Commission would deem it inappropriate to refer even when the section 13 test is satisfied. Some such cases are straightforward. For example, in a case where an applicant has been convicted on one indictment of (say) 20 offences, the Commission would be unlikely to refer because of a technical fault affecting a conviction for one of the lesser offences on the indictment, if all the other offences (and the sentence passed) would be unaffected. A referral in such a case would confer no meaningful benefit either upon the applicant or the interests of justice generally. On the other hand, cases involving the use of discretion to refer in change-of-law cases have become extremely problematical. This is discussed at chapter 7.

Powers of investigation

The Commission's powers to conduct in-house investigations are underpinned by section 17 of the 1995 Act, which gives the Commission power to call for material from any public body. The Commission's power to call for documents overrides any duties of confidentiality to which those public bodies may be subject. The powers are used routinely to require papers from the police and prosecution, the Courts Service, the Forensic Science Service, local authority social services authorities, health authorities and the Criminal Injuries Compensation Authority and – more occasionally – from a wide range of other public bodies. The Commission's powers to require production of material are sometimes met with disbelief and occasionally resistance on the part of officials of the bodies concerned,[21] but the Commission is insistent in the exercise of its powers to obtain information where required for the purpose of its investigations.

The Commission has a general duty, provided by the case of *Hickey*,[22] to disclose to appellants information that would be helpful to them to make their best case for referral. Public bodies called on to disclose confidential information to the Commission sometimes express anxiety that this information will find its way into the hands of the appellant. Such concern would extend, for example, to confidential and sensitive social services material, and also to information that could reveal the identity of informants or disclose covert surveillance procedures operated by the police. There are somewhat complex provisions at section 25 of the 1995 Act limiting the Commission's power to disclose information obtained from public bodies without consent, but the Commission in any event takes great care to use its powers of disclosure responsibly, within the framework of its obligations as set out in the *Hickey* judgment.

There was for some time disagreement between the Commission and the Home Office as to whether the Commission's section 17 powers extended to intercept information obtained by law enforcement agencies and covered by the Regulation of Investigatory Powers Act 2000 (RIPA). The Home Office took the view that the Commission's power to require disclosure of information under section 17 had been overridden by the terms of RIPA generally preventing the disclosure of intercept evidence. The Home Office has now indicated that it accepts that the Commission's section 17 powers extend to the provision of such information.

There are also occasional disagreements as to whether a particular organisation is or is not a public body[23] and problems have arisen, for instance, in some historic sex abuse cases where care homes run by voluntary agencies have been able to resist disclosure of information since they are not 'public bodies'.[24] The problem does not exist in Scotland where private bodies are subject to the same duty to disclose information as public bodies. The Commission has pressed the Home Office[25] to consider sponsoring an amendment of the law to bring private bodies within the scope of the duty of disclosure.

Appointment of investigating officers

The Commission also has power under section 19 of the 1995 Act to require the appointment of an Investigating Officer (IO) by and at the expense of the public body that investigated the offence. The Commission's (non-exhaustive) list of criteria for requiring the appointment of an IO is set out as follows in a Formal Memorandum which may be found on the Commission's website:

1. Where the scale and nature of the inquiry suggest it is appropriate to use police resources.

2. Where the nature of the inquiry is such that police expertise is considered essential.

3. Where there are grounds to suspect that a police officer, or other person involved in an official capacity in the investigation of offences or the prosecution of offenders, has committed an offence such as perjury and/or perverting the course of justice.

4. Where there are grounds to suspect that a person, who is not involved in an official capacity in the investigation of offences or the prosecution of offenders, has committed a serious offence in such circumstances that if there were to be sufficient evidence there is a real possibility that the person would be prosecuted.

Most IO appointments are made for an amalgam of considerations that do not fit neatly within one or other of the above categories. Ground 1 connotes the fact, simply, that the Commission's resources would be unduly stretched by taking on large-scale investigations, particularly where the locus of inquiries is far from the Commission's offices in Birmingham. Ground 4 arises because it is not uncommon that, where in-depth investigations are required, there is a possibility that other possible offences or offenders may need to be investigated. For instance, there may be a question whether other individuals have been guilty of or complicit in the commission of the offence(s) under investigation, or a possibility that witnesses who gave evidence at trial have been guilty of perjury or perversion of the course of justice. Where the investigations may take the form of a fresh criminal investigation (entailing the possible questioning of suspects under caution) those investigations can only be pursued by a police officer.

The Commission may require the IO to be appointed from an outside force which has not been involved in the original investigation of the crime. The Formal Memorandum lists (again non-exhaustively) reasons for considering the appointment of an officer from another force:

- Where there are grounds to suspect that a police officer involved in the original investigation has committed an offence such as perjury and/ or perverting the course of justice.

- Where there is concern that the appointment of an IO from the police force which conducted the original investigation would not be seen as impartial.

- Where the response from the police force conducting the original investigation is such that there are grounds for concern that any inquiries made by an IO from that police force may not be satisfactorily completed.

In its first ten years, the Commission required the making of 33 IO appointments in cases involving review of convictions. All but one of the appointments have been made by the Chief Constable of the investigating police force; the remaining appointment was made by Her Majesty's Customs and Excise (HMCE). In all 33 cases, the IO appointed has been a police officer.[26] The Commission has made a decision to refer in 16 cases and not to do so in 13.[27] Of the 33 IO appointments, 18 have been of officers from an outside force and 15 from the original investigating force.

The foregoing statistics show that the use of IOs occurs very much by exception, the vast majority of the investigations being conducted by the Commission in-house – albeit with the assistance of outside forensic experts as required. This contrasts very much with the Home Office's practice – it maintained no significant resources for investigation and, therefore, relied heavily upon the police.

The use of the police is a matter which has attracted suspicion on the part of some campaigning groups. The Commission's own perception has been that police investigations have generally been effective and thorough and there have been cases (**Blackwell** – discussed at chapter 9 – is a conspicuous example) where the police have identified important lines of enquiry beyond those stipulated or foreseen by the Commission in making the initial appointment. The Commission supervises the police enquiries carried out on its behalf through its investigations advisers – one being a former Detective Superintendent and the other a former Detective Chief Superintendent. It also requires reports to be submitted in draft so that the Commission can address any points of concern (including any requirement for further work to resolve the relevant issues) before the report is finalised. The high rate of referrals resulting from IO investigations in any event provides support for the conclusion that IO investigations do not take place to cover up wrongdoing, as some critics of the Commission have supposed.[28]

The most significant problem has generally been maintaining a satisfactory momentum to enquiries, as IOs have had to deal with other competing priorities imposed by their own forces. In one case, the IO was appointed as Senior Investigating Officer in a very large murder enquiry mid-way through his IO assignment – leading to a lengthy hiatus in the work done for the Commission. In another enquiry, the Commission's investigations have been bogged down in collateral disciplinary issues, bringing momentum to a virtual halt. Whilst it would be unrealistic to say that every IO's investigation has been of equal quality, the Commission has been satisfied that it can direct investigations effectively and has never felt the temptation to set up an in-house investigation force comparable with that of the Independent Police Complaints Commission.

Despite this generally positive experience, there will inevitably remain some concern about 'police on police' investigations. It has already been indicated that, where the police conduct of the original investigation is under question, the IO will be appointed from an outside force. Even so it is possible that a police on police investigation might 'pull its punches' and the Commission, in supervising the investigation at second hand, will not necessarily be aware that this is the case. Allegations to this effect have been made in one high-profile enquiry – **Steele, Whomes and Corry.**[29] The Commission cannot provide any absolute assurance that this will not happen but can minimise the risk by active supervision of the IO's investigation and by making it consistently clear that investigations should be objective and thorough. The Commission has been extremely fortunate in the appointment of its first two investigations advisers and – in my personal judgment – has been always concerned to ensure that IO investigations are carried out thoroughly. It remains important, however, that where concerns about the thoroughness of IO investigations are expressed, these should be taken seriously by the Commission.

Amendments to the 1995 Act introduced by the Criminal Justice Act 2003

Two significant changes affecting the Commission were introduced by the 2003 Act

Section 315 – Limitation of appeal grounds in cases referred by the Commission

Prior to the 2003 Act, a reference by the Commission launched an appeal but there was no requirement for the appellant to limit himself or herself to the grounds of appeal identified by the Commission (or even to adopt the Commission's grounds at all). There were many instances (the case of **Bamber,** discussed at chapter 4, being a good example), where the Commission referred on quite narrow and specific grounds but the ensuing appeal raised large numbers of further matters. Section 315 now provides that in respect of all appeals resulting from referrals made after 4 April 2005 the appeal may not be pursued on a ground which is not related to any reason given by the Commission for making the reference, unless leave is obtained from the Court to put forward further (unrelated) grounds of appeal.

Section 315 poses quite knotty issues for the Commission and for applicants. If the Commission refers only on the 'best point', the appellant is put to the burden of satisfying the Court that he or she should be allowed to develop other grounds of appeal. Conversely, if the Commission pursues lesser (or less fathomable) points in an application, it may unduly delay the referral to the detriment of the applicant. Section 315 in any event puts the onus on the Commission to maintain some degree of communication with applicants and their advisers if it is considering putting forward a 'best point' referral and dispensing with other matters which it considers to be either more difficult or of lesser importance. A Formal Memorandum, which can be accessed through the Commission's website, sets out in some detail the considerations and the policies which the Commission brings to bear in such cases.

Section 313 – Extension of power of the Court to order investigations by the Commission

Section 15 of the 1995 Act permits the Court of Appeal to direct the Commission to carry out investigations to enable it to resolve any matters of fact which the Court considers necessary in order to resolve an appeal. As originally drafted, the power of the Court to order such an investigation only arose after it had given leave to appeal. Since the Court's view of the factual issues very often determines its decision whether or not to grant leave, the Commission's role in assisting the Court arose at a very late stage and was infrequently used. Section 313 enables the Court to require the Commission to carry out investigation at an earlier stage – when the Court is considering whether or not to grant leave. This amendment was requested by the Court, which considered that the Commission's assistance would be more useful at this earlier stage. The amendment has increased the number of section 15 directions as shown below.

Calendar year	No of s15 directions	Directions issued at leave to appeal stage
1997	2	N/A
1998	2	N/A
1999	1	N/A
2000	0	N/A
2001	1	N/A
2002	2	N/A
2003	2	N/A
2004	3	N/A
2005	3	3
2006	7	5
2007	11	5

A number of section 313 cases have entailed investigation of alleged irregularities in the deliberations of the jury. In at least[30] one case, *Tyrell and Fisher*,[31] the Court has given judgment allowing the appeals in consequence of matters arising from the Commission's jury investigations. It might be noted that the seeking of the amendment of section 15 by the Court, and its increasing use to refer matters for investigation by the Commission, constitute something of a vote of confidence on the part of the Court in the Commission's investigative processes.

Amendment by Armed Forces Act 2006

The 1995 Act does not permit the Commission to review convictions or sentences passed by Courts Martial. This is to be revised by virtue of the provisions of the Armed Forces Act 2006, which will enable the Commission to review convictions made by the Courts Martial and the Service Civilian Court and will also permit those courts to order an investigation by the Commission in terms parallel to section 15. The proposal that the Commission's powers of review be extended to Courts Martial was first put to the Home Office by the Commission some years ago and has been acceded to only after very lengthy reflection. No commencement date for this extension of the Commission's jurisdiction has been set. It is understood that the Commencement Order will preclude review of convictions preceding commencement which would exclude the Commission from reviewing, for instance, the many contentious military verdicts dating from the First World War.

Organisation of the Commission

This book is not intended to be a study of the *organisation* of the Commission. The Commission's processes and methods of working have been described at great length in its successive annual reports.[32] The Commission uses a process of triage to segment cases with a view to dealing rapidly with the most straightforward cases and applying its resources most effectively to cases requiring in-depth investigation. The current processes of the Commission are quite fully described in the 2006-7 annual report, which can be obtained through the Commission's website. The website also provides detailed information (through the 'publications' tab) on various aspects of the Commission's casework procedures.

Notes

1. *Criminal Appeals,* 1964, Stevens and Sons.
2. *Home Office Reviews of Criminal Convictions,* 1968, Stevens and Sons.
3. S17 Criminal Appeal Act 1968.
4. Guidelines on the prosecution's duties of disclosure issued by the Attorney General in December 1981 ([1982] 1 All ER 734), were regarded as the most authoritative description of the prosecution's obligations prior to the *Judith Ward* case.
5. [1993] 1 WLR 619.
6. (1976) 63 Cr App R 132.
7. *R v Lattimore and Others* (1976) 62 Cr App R 53. In the *Confait* case, three young men were convicted in 1972 of murder and arson on the basis of their uncorroborated confessions. Their

convictions were subsequently quashed by the Court of Appeal in 1975 following a public campaign on their behalf. They had originally been refused leave to appeal. The subsequent inquiry into the case, conducted by Sir Henry Fisher, criticised the police but concluded that the three men had probably committed the crimes. Three years later, as a result of further new evidence, the Attorney General repudiated the Inquiry's findings and declared the men innocent.

8. *R v Richardson and Others*, The *Times*, 20.10.89.
9. *R v Maguire and Others* (1992) 94 Cr App R 133.
10. *R v McIlkenny and Others* (1991) 93 Cr App R 287.
11. *Report of the Royal Commission on Criminal Justice* Cm 2263, HMSO, London, 1993.
12. *Return to an address of the Honourable, the House of Commons dated 3 December 1992 for a report of the inquiry into the circumstances surrounding the convictions arising out of the bomb attacks in Guildford and Woolwich in 1974 2nd report on the Maguire case*, HC 296, 1992-93.
13. S23 Criminal Appeal Act 1968.
14. The Commission membership has subsequently become very much more legal. Only two current members of the Commission – David Jessel, a journalist, and Ian Nichol, an accountant – do not have a legal background.
15. There has only been one committee, a committee of five convened to consider the case of James **Hanratty**, consisting of *more* than three members.
16. See in particular the very extensive casework policies and procedures published on the Commission's website at www.ccrc.gov.uk.
17. The Secretary of State for this purpose was the Home Secretary for the whole of the ten-year period covered by this study but, following the demerger of the criminal justice functions of the Home Office, is now the Secretary of State for Justice.
18. The Court of Appeal has had since 1968 the option of ordering a retrial of appellants whose convictions are quashed. The Commission's statutory responsibilities do not require it to consider the possibility that the Court will order a retrial and, in general, the Commission has not done so.
19. S194C Criminal Procedure (Scotland) Act 1995 (as inserted by s25 Crime and Punishment (Scotland) Act 1997).
20. The members of the Commission were formerly referred to as 'Commission Members' but are now referred to within the Commission as 'Commissioners' and this term is used henceforth.
21. For an explanation of the Commission's powers, designed to reassure such officials, see [2000] *Journal of Local Government Law Issue 2*.
22. *R v Secretary of State for the Home Department ex p Hickey and Others (No 2)* [1995] 1 All ER 489.
23. The BBC for instance – which has resisted disclosure of information on the basis that it is not a public body.
24. This is further discussed at chapter 9. Voluntary care homes which may have unwittingly employed staff guilty of sex abuse offences are sometimes unwilling to open their records to the Commission for fear that any information could subsequently be used against them in civil compensation claims.
25. But any response will now be a matter for the Ministry of Justice.
26. There have been a number of IO appointments which have entailed the re-investigation of HMCE prosecutions but, for a variety of reasons, the police have generally had a parallel role in the investigations and the police rather than HMCE have, therefore, been made subject to the requirement to appoint an IO. See for instance on this subject the brief discussion of the Operation Brandfield investigation of 'controlled delivery' cases in chapter 10.
27. Other IO cases are still ongoing.

28. The 'success' rate of IO cases is somewhat higher than the bare statistics outlined above suggest, as a number of the 15 IO cases which did not conclude in referral were cases where an IO was brought in purely to interview a witness under caution – not to conduct a substantive investigation of the case.

29. It is clear that in that case, some further matters came to light as a result of enquiries carried out by the appellants' legal team after the IO 'closed his books'. This case is subject at the time of writing to further review by the Commission following a re-application by Mr Whomes.

30. There may be others – the Commission has not kept systematic information on the ultimate outcome of its section 15 reports.

31. [2005] EWCA Crim 3678.

32. One might even say *inordinate* length. It is my personal view that the annual reports have generally been unduly inward looking documents and that these reports might usefully in the future pay greater attention to the wider role of the Commission as suggested by the Runciman Commission. This is further touched upon in the concluding chapter.

Chapter 2 - The meaning of safety

The Commission's central role is to identify and refer convictions which raise a 'real possibility' that they would be quashed if referred for appeal. Since the Court may *only* quash a conviction which it considers 'unsafe', the ultimate question for the Commission (in reviewing Crown Court convictions[1]) is whether the Court may find the conviction unsafe. As already noted, the term 'miscarriage of justice' appears nowhere in the 1995 Act. It has been suggested in some quarters that the Commission is not directly concerned with miscarriages of justice at all, but rather with the juridical concept of safety, which may be something completely different from the purposes for which the Commission was established. This is a somewhat complex subject which necessarily begins with a discussion of what is meant by an 'unsafe' conviction.

The statutory definition of safety

The test to be applied by the Court of Appeal in deciding whether or not to quash a conviction is set out in s2 Criminal Appeal Act 1968 (the 1968 Act). Before the law was amended by the 1995 Act, section 2 read as follows:

> *Except as provided by this Act, the Court of Appeal shall allow an appeal against conviction if they think -*
>
> > *(a)   that the [conviction] should be set aside on the ground that under all the circumstances of the case it is unsafe or unsatisfactory; or*
> >
> > *(b)   that the judgment of the court of trial should be set aside on the ground of a wrong decision of any question of law; or*
> >
> > *(c)   that there was a material irregularity in the course of the trial,*
>
> *and in any other case shall dismiss the appeal:*
>
> *Provided that the Court may, notwithstanding that they are of the opinion that the point raised in the appeal might be decided in favour of the appellant, dismiss the appeal if they consider that no miscarriage of justice has actually occurred.*

This test set out above was collapsed by the 1995 Act, which amended section 2 by substituting the following much simpler formulation:

> *Subject to the provisions of this Act, the Court of Appeal*
>
> > *(a)   shall allow an appeal against conviction if they think that the conviction is unsafe; and*
> >
> > *(b)   shall dismiss such an appeal in any other case.*

This simplified test has been the test that has been applied by the Court of Appeal and by the Commission throughout the ten-year period considered in this study. Prospectively, the test will be modified by the provisions of the Criminal Justice and Immigration Act 2008, which will be further considered in this chapter and in chapter 7 below.

The purpose of the amendment of section 2

Section 2 was amended on the recommendation of the Runciman Commission, which considered that the somewhat complex definition in the original 1968 Act was unnecessary and confusing, and in particular that the difference between 'unsafe' and 'unsatisfactory' was by no means clear. The report of the Runciman Commission stated:

> *In the view of the majority of us, the present grounds of appeal should be replaced by a single broad ground which would give the court sufficient flexibility to consider all categories of appeal as is the case in Scotland.*

It appears that the amendment was intended by the Runciman Commission to simplify the definition rather than to alter it. It was also confirmed by the then government to Parliament that there was no intention substantively to amend the test of safety. In moving the second reading of the Criminal Appeal Bill, the Home Secretary said of this section:

> *In substance, it restates the existing practice of the Court of Appeal and I am pleased to note that the Lord Chief Justice has already welcomed it.*[2]

In the Standing Committee, the Minister of State said:

> *The Lord Chief Justice and members of the senior judiciary have given the test a great deal of thought and they believe that the new test re-states the existing practice of the Court of Appeal.*[3]

As was noted in an influential article by the late Professor Sir John Smith:[4]

> *The importance of these reported statements is that, if the Court should consider that the new section is ambiguous and that it is necessary to resort to the debates, they will find that Parliament passed the clause on being assured that it restated existing practice; so that it is Parliament's intention that that practice should continue.*

In particular, although no longer explicitly stated, the proviso contained in the original section 2 – that notwithstanding any irregularity of proceedings the Court might uphold the conviction 'if they consider that no miscarriage of justice has actually occurred' – still effectively applies. This was stated in the case of *R v Graham and Others*[5] in which the Court said:

> *This new provision ... is plainly intended to concentrate attention on one question: whether in the light of any arguments raised or evidence adduced on appeal the Court of Appeal considers a conviction unsafe. If the court is satisfied despite any misdirection of law or any irregularity in the conduct of the trial or any fresh evidence, that the conviction is safe, the court will dismiss the appeal. But if, for whatever reason, the court concludes that the appellant was wrongly convicted of the offence charged or is left in doubt whether the appellant was rightly convicted of that offence or not, then it must of necessity consider the conviction unsafe. The court is then subject to a binding duty to allow the appeal.*

The most clear-cut case of an unsafe conviction is one where there is new evidence available to show that the convicted person did not commit the offence of which he or she has been convicted or at the very least to raise significant doubt that he or she did so. That is the sort of miscarriage of justice that was primarily in the minds of JUSTICE and others who campaigned for a change of the law; of the Runciman Commission; and of Parliament when debating the introduction of the 1995 Act. Much of what follows in this study is concerned with the consideration of fresh evidence – and the test applied by the Court to fresh evidence cases. However, given the test of safety which it is required to consider, the Commission very frequently deals with cases that turn on fresh legal argument rather than upon fresh evidence.

It is a somewhat contentious question whether there has been a miscarriage of justice in a case where, after the jury have found they are certain of the defendant's guilt, some procedural error is shown to have taken place but the evidence remains where it was at trial. This was emphasised when the government, in the shape of the then Home Secretary, John Reid, weighed in with heavy boots in a consultation paper entitled *Quashing Convictions*, published in 2006.[6] The tone of this paper can be grasped from Mr Reid's foreword:

> *We must, of course, ensure that we have an effective and robust appeals system so that those who are innocent have their convictions quashed. Equally, however, we must have a system that punishes the guilty and delivers justice for victims.*

> *It may come as a surprise to some that the existing law empowers the Court of Appeal to quash a conviction on purely procedural grounds even where the judges of that Court have no doubt the appellant is guilty. Such outcomes are damaging to public confidence in the criminal justice system. They may also put the public at further risk of crime.*

The government proposed reforming the law to restrict the quashing of convictions on appeal to cases of factual innocence, irrespective of any irregularities or even excess of executive power instrumental in securing the conviction. The Commission, in common with JUSTICE and many others, responded by pointing out the deficiencies of the Home Office's shallow and populist analysis of this issue.[7]

The government's determination to bring forward legislation was not daunted by the critical response to its proposals and, in 2007, it brought forward legislation, as part of the Criminal Justice and Immigration Bill, to amend section 2 with the intent of preventing the factually guilty succeeding in appeals on the basis of legal technicalities. The denouement of the government's attempts to change the law is described at the conclusion of this chapter. Before plotting the outcome of this debate, however, it may be helpful to consider the main kinds of 'no-new-evidence' cases considered by the Commission. These have been schematically divided here into three categories:

- Cases where convictions have been secured following procedural irregularities amounting (or at the very least arguably amounting) to abuse of executive power.

- Cases where convictions have been secured following procedural irregularities of a 'second order' and not entailing abuse of executive power.

- Cases where convictions have been secured following a trial in which there were errors or omissions in the judge's directions of law to the jury or summing up of the trial evidence.

Abuse of executive power cases

In *Chalkley*[8] the Court, led by Auld LJ, had to consider the application of the amended section 2 in a case where the defendant had pleaded guilty after it was ruled that illegally obtained tape recordings were admissible in evidence. The Court concluded that the amendment of the terminology of section 2 to remove any reference to an 'unsatisfactory' conviction had the effect that the Court had no power to quash the conviction due to a 'material irregularity' of this nature, provided that they were satisfied that the conviction was safe.

> *In our view, whatever may have been the use by the Court of the former tests of "unsatisfactor[iness]" and "material irregularity"… they are not available to it now, save as aids to determining the safety of a conviction. The Court has no power under the substituted Section 2(1) to allow an appeal if it does not think the conviction unsafe but is dissatisfied in some way with what went on at the trial.*

This formulation of the law of course begs the (key) question as to how far, and in what circumstances can 'irregularity' make the verdict of the jury 'unsafe' in a case where all the facts which were available to the jury as tribunal of fact remain unchanged.

The interpretation of the law in *Chalkley* was not followed in **Togher,** which was a Commission case, or in *Mullen,*[9] which was not. In **Togher**[10] the issue was whether very serious irregularities committed by Her Majesty's Customs and Excise (HMCE) vitiated the conviction of T and his co-defendants for serious drug smuggling offences. In brief, the defendants had pleaded guilty in a case where there had been both breaches of procedure and defaults in the discharge of the prosecution's duty of disclosure. The Court stated the general proposition that:

> *we consider that if a defendant has been denied a fair trial it will almost be inevitable that the conviction will be regarded as unsafe.*

But it added that the question of whether such irregularities made a conviction unsafe was a matter of fact and degree. The Court concluded that in the instant case:

> *the shortcomings on the part of the prosecution are not of the category of misconduct which would justify interfering with the defendants' freely entered pleas of guilty.*

And it upheld the appellants' convictions.

In *Mullen*, the irregularities had consisted of the wholly illegal abduction of the suspect from Zimbabwe by members of the Secret Intelligence Service who had knowingly bypassed legal extradition procedures. The Court stated that blatantly illegal conduct of this nature put the conviction beyond the pale of safety, irrespective of the weight of the evidence for conviction:

> *The conduct of the security services and police in procuring the unlawful deportation of the defendant in the manner which has been described represents, in the view of this court, a blatant and extremely serious failure to adhere to the rule of law with regard to the production of a defendant for prosecution in the English courts. The need to discourage such conduct on the part of those who are responsible for criminal prosecutions is a matter of public policy to which ... very considerable weight must be attached.*

And it quashed the conviction.

In another HMCE case, *Early and Others*[11] (widely known as the *London City Bond* case), customs officers had made heavy use of participating informants to build up the case for conviction but withheld this information from prosecuting counsel with the result that counsel (unintentionally) misled the trial judge about the role played by informants when making applications to the Court for material to be protected from disclosure by Public Interest Immunity (PII). Quashing the convictions the Court stated:

> *Judges can only make decisions and counsel can only act and advise on the basis of the information with which they are provided. The integrity of our system of criminal trial depends on judges being able to rely on what they are told by counsel and on counsel being able to rely on what they are told by each other. This is particularly crucial in relation to disclosure and PII hearings. ... Furthermore, in our judgment, if, in the course of a PII hearing or an abuse argument, whether on the voir dire or otherwise, prosecution witnesses lie in evidence to the judge, it is to be expected that, if the judge knows of this, or this court subsequently learns of it, an extremely serious view will be taken.* **It is likely that the prosecution case will be regarded**

> *as tainted beyond redemption, however strong the evidence against the defendant may otherwise be.* (Emphasis added)

Early was followed by a Commission referral, **Ghuman**, whose conviction was also quashed by the Court.

In both *Mullen* and *Early* there remained strong evidence of the factual guilt of the convicted persons but the Court concluded that the extent of the irregularities made it repugnant to the interests of justice to uphold their convictions. It is, therefore, clearly part of the remit of the Commission to consider cases where there has been significant irregularity of process. Indeed, where the irregularity first comes to light after the trial and first-time appeal, a referral by the Commission is the only means of bringing such cases back before the courts.[12] This theme has considerable resonance in the context of some of the Commission's customs cases, which are discussed in chapter 10.

The Home Office in its *Quashing Convictions* proposals took exception to the point of law in **Togher** and *Mullen*, arguing that the Court should consider only the guilt or innocence of the applicant and have no regard whatever to infractions of process – however grave – leading to conviction. As the Commission pointed out in its response to *Quashing Convictions,* it would represent a serious threat to what remains of the separation of powers in the United Kingdom if the judiciary were denied power to quash convictions which had been secured by illegal actions of the executive. The point was put more forcibly by Professor John Spencer of Cambridge University in responding to *Quashing Convictions* and also, as follows, in an article for *Justice of the Peace*:[13]

> *To remain the sort of society in which it is safe for the "law abiding majority" to live, the citizens of this country need to be protected not only from being blown to pieces by the likes of Mullen, but also from being convicted and sent to prison after outrageously illegal conduct by the police and the other agencies of the state. As the law stands at present, happily, they are. But if the Government succeeds in its attempt to "rebalance" the Criminal Appeal Act, this will no longer be the case.*

As will be seen, the government has now abandoned its proposals on this point.

'Second order' irregularities

The cases discussed in the previous section were characterised by gross violation of trial and/or pre-trial procedures, and the government's proposals in *Quashing Convictions* to put such cases beyond redress encountered very strong opposition. But what of 'second order' irregularities – errors of procedure or of process which cannot be characterised as 'gross violations' in the sense discussed above?

There are two preliminary points to make about such cases:

- First, it was clear under the old section 2 (preceding amendment by the 1995 Act), and adopting the terminology then in use, that such convictions might well be 'unsatisfactory' but it was open to the Court to apply the proviso and uphold the conviction where it considered that no miscarriage of justice had actually occurred. Since it appears settled that the redrafting of section 2 by the 1995 Act has not substantively altered its meaning, it follows from first principles that the Court – in determining whether a conviction is safe – can effectively apply the proviso in the same way as before.

- Second, irregularities in trial process are grist to the mill of learned counsel advising on the prospects of a first-time appeal. Indeed, given that first-time appeals have generally to be lodged within 28 days of conviction, there is rarely new evidence to consider. It is, therefore, errors either in the conduct of the trial or in the summing up which typically form the basis for such appeals. The number of purely procedural cases that reach the Commission, after passing through the filter of first-time appeals, should, therefore, be limited.

Two cases stand out among the 'material irregularity' convictions considered by the Commission. In **Clarke and McDaid**, the issue was whether the applicants' convictions were unsafe because the indictments against them were unsigned – in breach of the clear requirements of s2(1) Administration of Justice (Miscellaneous Provisions) Act 1933. The Commission felt bound to refer the convictions as the Court in *Morais*[14] had allowed an appeal on closely similar facts. In the event, by the time the appeals of Clarke and McDaid came to be considered, the Court of Appeal had effectively determined in *Ashton and Others*[15] that *Morais* was no longer good authority. In *Sekhon*,[16] a 2003 authority, the Court of Appeal stated:

We would expect a procedural failure only to result in a lack of jurisdiction if this was necessary to ensure that the criminal justice system served the interests of justice and thus the public or where there was at least a real possibility of the defendant suffering prejudice as a consequence of a procedural failure.

And in *Soneji*[17] the House of Lords in 2005 had approved the following dictum from an Australian authority:

... a court, determining the validity of an act done in breach of a statutory provision, may easily focus on the wrong factors if it asks itself whether compliance with the provision is mandatory or directory and, if directory, whether there has been substantial compliance with the provision. A better test for determining the issue of validity is to ask whether it was a purpose of the legislation that an act done in breach of the provision should be invalid.

In **Clarke and McDaid**, the Court concluded that:

the sea-change wrought by the decisions in Soneji *and* Sekhon *is that the court should concentrate in future on, first, the intention of Parliament (viz. was it intended that a procedural failure should render the proceedings invalid)* **and, second, the interests of justice and particularly whether the procedural failure caused any prejudice to any of the parties, such as to make it unjust to proceed further.** (Emphasis added)

The Court concluded that it would not serve the interests of justice to quash the convictions only because of defects in the indictment and the convictions were upheld.

This decision was, however, reversed on appeal to the House of Lords. The Law Lords did not dissent from the broad thrust of the Court of Appeal's reasoning. As Lord Carswell put it:

I see much attraction in the decision of the Court of Appeal, for the prevailing trend is in general against regarding procedural steps as mandatory requirements.

But their Lordships were unanimous in the opinion that the provisions of section 2(1), requiring due signature of the indictment, created a clear and unambiguous statutory requirement. Their Lordships noted that Parliament had had ample opportunity to repeal *Morais* (which was decided some 20 years ago) but had not done so.

Clarke and McDaid exemplifies the fact that the Court of Appeal may be pulled back by the House of Lords from time to time if it pursues a 'pragmatic' approach to legal technicalities to the extent of disregarding clear statutory language. As Lord Bingham put it:

> *The decisions in* R v Sekhon *and* R v Soneji *are valuable and salutary, but ... they do not warrant a wholesale jettisoning of all rules affecting procedure irrespective of their legal effect.*

Nevertheless it is probably fair to say that the trend of the case law against technicality, which the Court of Appeal characterised as a 'sea change', will continue to mark the Court of Appeal's approach in the majority of cases.

Compare the outcome in **Caley-Knowles** and **Jones**. The common feature of these two cases was that the judges (considering the evidence of guilt of the respective defendants to be incontrovertible) had directed a verdict of guilty without even permitting the jury members to retire to consider their verdict. **Jones** had been convicted of criminal damage after climbing on to the roof of Llandovery Town Hall to protest against the action of local councillors in granting planning permission for industrial development. As such, it was the kind of political case in which British juries occasionally deliver perverse verdicts to show their support for a fellow citizen who makes a stand against the acts of executive authorities.[18] The Commission in referring noted that the decision of the judge to withdraw the decision from the verdict of the jury might be considered particularly objectionable on that account. In any event, the judge's action did not stand with the subsequent decision of the House of Lords in *Wang*[19] that such a direction to convict should never be given.

Both convictions were quashed following referral. Reading the judgment of the Court, its reluctance to quash appears palpable and the particular concerns of the Commission about the political nature of the **Jones** case cut no ice with the Court (which made no reference to the point). The Court however concluded that:

Following clarification of the law in Wang, *this must, we think, be characterised as a significant legal misdirection or a material irregularity, even though the evidence of the appellant's guilt in each case was clear.*

The Commission was subsequently criticised by Lord Justice Judge for referring these two cases in his judgment in the case of **Cottrell and Fletcher.** This will be discussed in chapter 7.

One other 'procedural' case also merits mention. **Taylor (John Henry)** was convicted of larceny in 1962. His conviction was referred by the Commission and quashed in 1998. He had appeared before a much-feared Deputy Chairman of the London Quarter Sessions – 'Ossie' MacLeay – and had been unrepresented. The Commission concluded that he had been denied the opportunity to put forward a perfectly plausible defence case – and the Court's judgment, in suitably muted judicial language – appears to have accepted that this was the case.

The government in *Quashing Convictions* purported to be concerned about the number of appeals of guilty persons being allowed due to legal and procedural technicalities. However, it seems that section 2, as currently drafted, gives every scope to the Court to uphold convictions – material irregularities notwithstanding. The dictum of the Court of Appeal in **Clarke and McDaid,** referring to a 'sea change' in the approach taken by the Court to material irregularities, suggests that the Court will be very slow in the future to quash convictions on the basis of technical points – save where the technical flaw flies in the face of a clear legislative requirement – as the House of Lords concluded was the case in **Clarke and McDaid** itself.

The case of **Steele, Whomes and Corry** also illustrates this point. A key witness had sold his story to the media and the amount of royalties payable appeared likely to depend upon the outcome of the trial. Moreover, the Court accepted that the police might have known about and facilitated the witness's media contacts but had failed to make any disclosure of this matter. The Court stated that:

It is obvious that contacts and contracts between a witness and media interests in advance of a trial have a potential to engender injustice, especially when they are unknown to the defence at the time of trial and cannot be used in cross-examination of the witness.

So *in principle* this was a matter capable of affecting the safety of the conviction. The question for the Court, however, was whether it was persuaded that the verdict was *in practice* unsafe on the facts of the instant case. After a very full analysis, the Court concluded that the witness's credibility was not affected by the irregularities that had occurred, and it upheld the conviction.[20] The facts of this case are more fully discussed in chapter 3.

For the Commission's part, it will be clear from the decisions of the Court in cases, such as **Clarke and McDaid** and **Steele, Whomes and Corry,** that procedural irregularities do not equate with want of safety. The Commission must, therefore, bear in mind that in considering the ultimate question of safety, the Court will always carefully consider whether or not the fairness of the trial has been compromised by the irregularity in the proceedings. This will no doubt have a bearing on the number of procedural cases referred by the Commission in the future.

Summing up errors

Significant errors in the trial judge's summing up of the law or facts should generally be picked up by counsel in advising upon a first-time appeal. In principle, therefore, absent changes in the relevant law over the supervening period, the Commission is unlikely to refer many cases upon the basis of a defective summing up. In the case of **Davis, Rowe and Johnson,** one of the Commission's early referrals, the Court considered whether the test to be applied in the case of misdirection (or omission to give a required direction) by the trial judge had been altered by the revision of section 2. The Court adopted the dictum in an old case, *Stirland v DPP:*[21]

> *When the transcript [of the summing up] is examined it is evident that no reasonable jury, after a proper summing up, could have failed to convict the appellant on the rest of the evidence to which no objection could be taken. There was, therefore, no miscarriage of justice, and this is the proper test to determine whether the proviso ... should be applied.*[22]

The Court concluded, applying the passage in *Graham,* quoted above, that the amendment of section 2 had not altered the position as set out in *Stirland.*

The Court more recently formulated its approach to this issue in response to the Commission's reference of **Boyle and Ford.** In this case, the Commission referred the convictions due to misdirections given to the jury on the approach they should take in deciding whether to draw adverse inferences from the fact that the defendants had relied on matters at trial that they had failed to mention when being questioned by police following arrest. The Court accepted that there had been some misdirections but, upholding the convictions, it very plainly sought to pass a message to the Commission as to the approach it should take:

> Each case depends on its own circumstances. The essential question is whether any misdirection identified has caused an injustice and whether the Court of Appeal is satisfied that the verdict was safe. In reaching a decision as to the safety of the verdict it may assist to analyse first how the case was left to the jury by virtue of the direction given and then second to analyse how it would have been left to the jury if a proper direction had been given. The court should then assess, whether having regard to the jury's verdict on the direction as given, the jury would have been bound to convict if a proper direction had been given.

The approach to summing up errors is, therefore, to focus not so much upon the error in the summing up but upon the impact of the misdirection (or non-direction) upon the deliberations of the jury.

Most of the Commission's referrals based upon summing up points have been change-of-law cases, that is to say cases where the interpretation of the law has changed since the trial with the result that a summing up that was impeccable when given could, following subsequent legal authorities, be characterised as defective. Where the required form of summing up changes (as a result of case law) it is the normal practice of the Judicial Studies Board (JSB) to amend the relevant model direction in the handbook issued to judges. So, for instance, a model direction contained in the 2000 edition of the JSB handbook may be deficient when measured against the requirements set out in the 2004 edition.

The problem that this may cause can be illustrated by reference to the directions required to be given to juries about the circumstances in which they may draw an adverse inference from the fact that the defendant either (i) has elected not to give evidence at trial or (ii) has relied on information in his or her defence at trial which he or she could have – but did not – volunteer when being interviewed by police. The relevant statutory provisions are ss34-35 Criminal Justice and Public Order Act 1994.[23] The model directions require trial judges to warn juries of the matters they need to consider before drawing an adverse inference, and a leading authority, **Cowan**, sets out five 'essential elements' of a section 35 direction to the jury.[24]

There have been eight referrals considered by the Court in the period covered by this study in which misdirections under sections 34-35 have been at the heart of the referral grounds – **Allan (Richard Roy)** and **Beckles**, which were quashed, and **Adetoro**, **Boyle and Ford**, **Bromfield**, **Howell**, **Lowe** and **Whitehead**, which were upheld. Section 34 points were also raised unsuccessfully in the grounds of appeal (albeit not by the Commission itself) in the appeals of **Benn and Benn** and **Steele, Whomes and Corry**.

Beckles illustrates why a misdirection may be important. B was arrested on suspicion of attempted murder and before being interviewed by police he saw his solicitor and gave a detailed and exculpatory (and also plausible) account of events. His solicitor (it was not disputed) advised B to give a 'no comment' interview to police and B followed this advice. At trial, B gave essentially the same account that he had given to his solicitor but had not given when interviewed by police. The judge told the jury that they could draw an adverse inference from the fact that B had not given his trial account to the police when he had had the chance to do so (leaving it open to the jury to conclude that B's trial account was 'late invention'). The trial judge failed to warn the jury in the required terms that if they were satisfied that B had said nothing to the police because he had been genuinely relying upon legal advice,[25] they should not draw the adverse inference. B's case was referred by the Commission[26] and, allowing the appeal, the Court (Woolf LCJ) stated:

> the fact is that the drawing of adverse inferences was left to [the jury], and in an unsatisfactory manner. Such inferences can give added strength to the Crown's case against a Defendant. It can tip the balance from being not sure of the Crown's case to being sure. It can give confirmation of the jury's preference for the Crown's case, of which (without that confirmation) they might not have been sure. It is impossible to say whether the jury would have reached the same conclusion were it not for this element in their deliberations. And if the jury drew a further adverse inference from the failure of the Appellant to call his solicitor to explain the advice which she had given, this could have had a significant effect on the verdicts at which they arrived ... In our judgment it follows that the convictions are unsafe.

Beckles illustrates the positive case for referring a conviction on the basis of a summing up deficiency. It is certainly arguable that some – at least – of the other referrals have been narrowly technical and the Court in **Boyle and Ford** gave the Commission somewhat negative feedback about such referrals, deprecating the fact that in that case the Commission had raised a summing up issue which counsel had not seen fit to raise in advising on the grounds of a first-time appeal:

> *We are troubled as to what should be the right approach of the Court of Appeal in a case such as the present. We follow the argument based on the absolutist approach. But if an absolutist approach must be adopted in all cases where a misdirection is <u>now</u> identified in respect of cases where it has never previously been suggested that a trial was unfair, or a conviction unsafe, that would seem to leave it open to appellants on the advice of lawyers to bring before the CCRC cases where permission to appeal out of time might not have been given. It is relevant, as it seems to us, in considering a s.34 case, and indeed this case, to recognise that all the points taken as to the inadequacy of the direction, are points taken in other cases. In other words it is important to recognise that it was open to the appellants in this case to take the points now taken, if anyone had thought of them at the trial or immediately after the trial, if it were thought that there was force in any argument that the trial had been unfair.*

> *We believe that an absolutist approach, **particularly to a reference**, is not called for. Each case depends on its own circumstances. The essential question is whether any misdirection identified has caused an injustice and whether the Court of Appeal is satisfied that the verdict was safe.*
> (The underlining emphasis is the Court's; the bold emphasis is the author's)

And the Court went so far as to say that it should, perhaps, have declined to allow the appeal in **Beckles** if in fact the point of law had not been raised by counsel in advising upon the first-time appeal.[27]

Boyle and Ford was followed in **Lowe**. The Court noted that – holding the summing up up against the most recent edition of the JSB guidelines – a number of valid criticisms could be made of the way the judge instructed the jury. On the other hand, the Court noted:

- Experienced counsel could have ventilated these issues either at trial or at first-time appeal but had not done so.

- Although the judge had failed to give a specific and required direction that L had been entitled to remain silent in police interview, the jury could not have been left in any doubt of this point having heard the summing up as a whole.

- The failure of L to answer questions in interview formed only a small part of the prosecution case.

- The evidence against L and his co-defendant was 'overwhelming'.

And it upheld L's conviction.

The Court took another swipe at a summing up point raised in the appeal of **Steele, Whomes and Corry**. In this appeal, counsel took the point (which had not been part of the Commission's grounds for referral) that the section 34 direction (in a trial which took place in 1996) did not comply with the requirements of the most recent edition of the JSB handbook issued prior to the appeal – which was heard in 2006. Dismissing the appeals, the Court noted that the application of what was – at the time of trial – a new statutory provision had inevitably undergone some change and deprecated 'an unduly technical approach'. The Court went back to a dictum of Lord Lane in 1978:

> The provisions of many modern statutes are so complex that their interpretation is in a constant state of development and refinement; earlier convictions are not rendered unsafe simply because the law has moved on in the meantime. In Mitchell (1977) 65 Cr. App. R 185, at p 189 Lane LJ said:
>
> > "It should be clearly understood, and this Court wants to make it even more abundantly clear, that the fact there has been an apparent change in the law or, to put it more precisely, that previous misconceptions about the meaning of a statute have been put right, does not afford a proper ground for allowing an extension of time in which to appeal against conviction".
>
> ... [This] approach, ... was endorsed by Lord Bingham CJ in Hawkins [1997] 1 Cr. App. R. 234 at page 240:
>
> > "It is plain, as we read the authorities, that there is no inflexible rule on this subject, but the general practice is plainly one which sets its face against the re-opening of convictions in such circumstances. Counsel submits – and in our judgment correctly

> *submits – that the practice of the Court has in the past, in this and comparable situations, been to eschew undue technicality and ask whether any substantial injustice has been done."*

The Court delivered a similarly dusty response in giving recent judgment on the Commission's referral of **R (M)**. R had been convicted of sexual offences against his stepdaughters and the issue in the referral and the subsequent appeal was the correctness of the judge's direction as to how the jury should evaluate 'recent complaint' evidence.[28] The Commission approached leading trial counsel, who agreed that there had been a misdirection and that the point could have been (but was not) raised in the first-time appeal. Dismissing the appeal, the Court concluded: (i) that the jury had been adequately directed to consider whether they believed the evidence of the complainants, and in the circumstances any deficiencies of the recent complaint direction were immaterial; and (ii) although counsel conceded that the recent complaint point is one that could have been properly brought at the first-time appeal, 'we are not at all surprised that [he] found nothing defective in this respect in the summing-up when he conducted the appeal in the year 2000'. In both this case and **Boyle and Ford** the Commission was clearly being warned off coming up with technicalities that learned counsel had either not thought of or not pursued.

It would not be correct to conclude from the foregoing that the Court will never quash a conviction referred by the Commission due to a summing up error, as the following cases show:

Smith (Donald Denzil)
The case against S (possession of Class A drugs) was put on the basis that he had been in possession of drugs found (i) in his car and (ii) at premises with which he was associated. The judge omitted to give the jury a required '*Brown*' direction to the effect that where the jury are presented with a prosecution case in which there are two different scenarios, each capable of proving guilt, the jury must all agree (or the requisite majority must agree) that the defendant is guilty of one or other 'scenarios' – they could not convict in the present case if some jurors were sure that S had been in possession of the drugs in the car, and others that he had been in possession of the drugs in the flat. The Court, noting that Mr Smith had served his sentence, added 'had it not been the case ... we would unhesitatingly have ordered a retrial'.

Popat

Various deficiencies were noted in the summing up but, in particular, a deficient warning about the dangers of mistaken identification. In this case, P had a substantial period of his sentence still to run and a retrial was ordered.[29]

Howard

H was convicted as one of a gang who had committed a street robbery. He was convicted on identification evidence by the victim, who said that H had physically attacked him. H admitted that he had been in the company of others involved in the robbery both previously and later on the same day but denied presence when the robbery took place. There were in fact three possibilities to be considered by the jury: (i) he had been a physical assailant; (ii) he had been present as part of the gang but not directly involved in the robbery; (iii) he had not been present.

The judge directed the jury thus:

> As to robbery, somebody committed robbery that night. What the defendants say is "not us". If you are involved in a joint enterprise, you know perfectly well what is afoot and if somebody else does it then you are equally guilty. That is common sense and good law. But as to the robbery, somebody committed the robbery that night. Robbery is simply taking something which does not belong to you with violence in order to achieve the objective and either immediately before or at the time of the taking there is violence by you or by somebody else, you knowing perfectly well what that person is about.

The Court noted:

> That direction on the law, whilst perfectly adequate in the circumstances to explain to the jury what an offence of robbery was, was in our judgment wholly inadequate to explain to them the somewhat difficult concept of joint enterprise.

And it added:

> This court is always reluctant to be critical of judges who are economical in the way that they sum up, but nonetheless it has to be recognised that a proper summing-up must have a number of important ingredients, and one

is that it gives adequate directions to the jury on the law so that they can deal with any finding of fact that they make.

And when the jury sent a note asking 'can the defendant be found guilty of robbery when he knowingly went with the others and knew they were going to commit the offence?' the judge compounded his error by simply replying 'yes', ignoring both Crown and defence counsel's urging to explain the elements of joint enterprise.

Howard reflects a situation that is not so very uncommon: a relatively minor case, a judge in a hurry, and a slipshod direction. Such cases very rarely reach the Commission because they are picked up at the first-time appeal[30] and, as noted, the Court has in any event taken a somewhat stuffy attitude to summing up points raised by the Commission which have not been previously raised by counsel. The case shows that (subject to what follows) such cases may be 'successfully' referred by the Commission albeit not – one feels – in a great many cases.

The government rides in

The Court's responses to the cases discussed in this chapter illustrate the broad brush approach allowed by the existing formulation of the test of safety, in which the Court balances the competing considerations of the weight of evidence of guilt, on the one hand, and the extent (and impact) of any irregularity, on the other. At one end of the spectrum, extreme instances of executive abuse, as in *Mullen,* will outweigh any amount of evidence of guilt. At the other, lesser irregularities give way before powerful evidence of guilt. There has been a strong tide of recent authority against allowing appeals on the basis of anything other than grave irregularities of process.

The government concluded, however (and apparently without any prompting from the judiciary), that the courts needed a helping hand in stemming the flow of appeals by the plainly guilty. In *Quashing Convictions,* it proposed amending section 2 either (i) to restore the law to the pre-1995 test (on the rather mysterious, and plainly wrong, presumption that the law had been substantively changed by the 1995 Act) or (ii) to introduce a blanket provision to prevent appeals succeeding where the Court believed the appellant guilty, even in the case of clear illegality of prosecution conduct such as had occurred in *Mullen.* The government in *Quashing Convictions* made plain its view that there was no degree of executive illegality or abuse which should stand in the way of the conviction of the guilty, a proposition which would have required the re-writing of many school and university textbooks on British constitutional law and history. This initiative was part of the 'rebalancing' agenda then being promoted by Tony Blair (and discussed in the final chapter), in which it was supposed that the securing of better redress for the victims of crime necessarily required the curtailment of the rights of suspects and defendants.

Quashing Convictions had the unusual effect of uniting respondents – including the judiciary, the Criminal Bar and the Law Society, the Commission, and legal pressure groups including JUSTICE and Liberty – in condemning the proposals as unnecessary and constitutionally dangerous. The first response of the Home Office to this criticism was to dishonour its commitment to publish a summary of the responses on its website.[31] In June 2007, the Ministry of Justice (which had assumed responsibility for the relevant policy area from the Home Office in the previous month) brought forward the Criminal Justice and Immigration Bill, Part 4 of which was substantially based on the *Quashing Convictions* proposals.[32] Subsequently however, the Ministry published a summary of the responses to *Quashing Convictions*.[33] The foreword to this summary conceded that:

> Although the Consultation Paper made clear that the Government was seeking views about how, not whether, the test for quashing convictions should be changed, most legal respondents expressed the view that no reform is needed. They argued that the current test works satisfactorily and it is only in the most exceptional cases that the Court of Appeal quashes the conviction of a plainly guilty appellant.

The government also came up with a 'compromise' proposal at the committee stage of the bill proposing the addition of a new section 2(1A) and 1(B) of the 1995 Act which would have read as follows:

> 2(1) Subject to the provisions of this Act, the Court of Appeal—

> (a) shall allow an appeal against conviction if they think that the conviction is unsafe; and

> (b) shall dismiss such an appeal in any other case.

> (1A) For the purposes of subsection (1)(a), the conviction is not unsafe if the Court think that there is no reasonable doubt about the appellant's guilt.

(1B) Subsection (1A) does not require the Court to dismiss the appeal if they think that it would seriously undermine the proper administration of justice to allow the conviction to stand.

1(A), clearly, was intended to give effect to the *Quashing Convictions* proposal to block the appeals of the factually guilty, whilst (1B) was presented as a saving to enable the Court to allow appeals in cases, such as *Mullen*, where the executive had played fast and loose with the 'proper administration of justice'. The proposals still remained open to the objection, however, that they were pointless since the judiciary had already substantially developed the test of safety to the point that the legislation was purportedly designed to achieve. In the committee stage, a Liberal member, David Heath, was moved to remark that the Lord Chancellor had been unable to come up with a single concrete example of a case in which the discretion available to the court was not sufficient to deal with the supposed mischief.[34] Finally, on 5 March 2008, the government announced that it was abandoning its proposal in the interests of making progress in bringing the bill into law.[35]

This retreat leaves unaffected the clauses brought forward by the government to restrict appeals mounted on the basis of changes of law between the date of trial and appeal. These clauses were introduced as a postscript to the *Quashing Convictions* debate and will be discussed in chapter 7.

Final reflections

Whilst the *Quashing Convictions* debate has ultimately proved to be something of an irrelevance, the general trend of the law outlined in this chapter clearly presents an interesting and difficult challenge to the Commission. The weight of recent authority has been so strongly against referrals on 'technical' legal matters that the Commission has inevitably to reflect on referrals of convictions which would have self-evidently satisfied the 'real possibility' test earlier in its existence. There is also a danger that the Court will overreact to future referrals to the extent that any referral based upon a legal or summing up point is tarred by its provenance and by the presumption that the 'lay' Commission is constitutionally incapable of identifying any meritorious legal point that wise and learned counsel failed to pursue at trial or appeal. This is the sort of approach that can perpetuate miscarriages of justice. There is also a real danger that the Court in this kind of rebarbative mood will disdain even serious infractions of process identified by the Commission. The Commission will need to select issues and cases for referral with care, but without fear, recognising that in a small number of instances the proper administration of justice will require it to bring cases of serious irregularity unflinchingly to the Court's attention.

Notes

1. The position is entirely different in respect of *summary* convictions – as chapter 12 seeks to show.

2. *Hansard*, vol 256, para 24, 6 March 1995.

3. Standing Committee B, col 26, 21 March 1995.

4. [1995] *Crim LR* 920.

5. [1997] 1 Cr App R 302.

6. In the interests of accuracy, it must be added that the full title of the consultation paper is as follows: *Quashing Convictions. Report of a review by the Home Secretary, Lord Chancellor and Attorney General.* It may be found at www.cjsonline.gov.uk/downloads/application/pdf/quashing_convictions_consult.pdf.

7. The Commission's response can be ordered or downloaded from its website at www.ccrc.gov.uk/publications/publications_get.asp. The response of JUSTICE entitled *Response to OCJR consultation Quashing Convictions: Report of a review by the Home Secretary, Lord Chancellor and Attorney General* may be found at www.justice.org.uk/images/pdfs/quashingconvictions.pdf. The response of Liberty may be found at www.liberty-human-rights.org.uk/pdfs/policy06/quashing-convictions.pdf.

8. [1998] QB 848.

9. [1999] 2 Cr App R 143.

10. **Togher** was referred by the Commission but essentially upon the instruction of the Court of Appeal.

11. [2003] 1 Cr App R 288.

12. It is of course also open to the government in such cases to set up an ad hoc judicial enquiry, as occurred in the *Matrix Churchill* case.

13. 14 October 2006, 170 *JP* 790-793.

14. (1988) 87 Cr App R 9.

15. [2006] EWCA Crim 794.

16. [2003] 1 WLR 1655.

17. [2005] 3 WLR 303.

18. Remarkably, this point was borne out after Mr Jones staged a further rooftop protest (on the same issue) at Swansea Town Hall. In February 2008, he was acquitted by a jury of a charge of criminal damage. A spokesman for Carmarthenshire County Council described the verdict as 'beyond belief' and it seems clear that the jury was expressing sympathy for his protest. See http://news.bbc.co.uk/1/hi/wales/south_west/7232500.stm for a news report on this case.

19. [2005] UKHL 9.

20. As already noted, this case has been the subject of a further application to the Commission.

21. [1944] AC 315 at p321.

22. The Court here applied the proviso to the Criminal Appeal Act 1907, which was in terms similar to the proviso in the 1968 Act.

23. S34 deals with the drawing of inferences from the defendant's reliance at trial upon facts which he or she failed to mention at police interview; s35 deals with the inferences which may be drawn from the defendant's failure to give evidence at trial.

24. [1996] 1 Cr App R 1.

25. It should be appreciated that in all of these 'inferences-from-silence' cases, a distinction is to be drawn between a defendant's genuinely *relying upon* solicitor's advice on the one hand and *sheltering behind* such advice on the other.

26. The case had had a long prior legal journey via the European Court of Human Rights. A description of this journey, and the legal issues raised, is beyond the scope of this study.

27. This particular comment epitomises the Court at its most rebarbative and illogical. To suggest that because counsel failed to take a meritorious point at trial or appeal, the Commission should be prevented from doing so is perverse and contrary to the purpose of the legislation. Perhaps the Court is suggesting that learned counsel, being infallible, never overlooks a meritorious point and that – by definition – if the Commission pursues a point which counsel failed to pursue, it must be a bad point. The Runciman Commission, whose report led to the establishment of the Commission, recognised that counsel sometimes make errors and it would be well if the Court accepted this fact too – even when it is the 'lay' Commission which has the temerity to draw attention to the point. Finally, it might be added that in the case of **Beckles**, the point which inspired the Commission's referral was a matter extensively litigated through the European Court of Human Rights with the result that the legal merit of the issue was clearer by the time of the Commission's referral than it had been at the time of trial or first-time appeal.

28. That is to say, evidence from a number of witnesses that the stepdaughters had complained about R's conduct not very long after the offences were said to have occurred.

29. The summing up points that led to the quashing of the conviction were matters raised by learned counsel representing P at his appeal following referral by the Commission and were not directly raised by the Commission itself. A cynic might suspect that had the same summing up points been raised by the Commission, they would have been less respectfully considered by the Court.

30. For reasons that are not entirely clear, counsel did not advise in this case that the misdirection could be raised as a ground of appeal and Mr Howard did not originally appeal.

31. This commitment was made pursuant to Cabinet Office guidelines on consultation.

32. This first version of the bill did, however, contain a very limited saving to the effect that the new law should not require the Court to dismiss an appeal where to do so would be 'incompatible with the appellant's [European] Convention Rights'– a saving that would have possibly covered an extreme *Mullen* type situation.

33. This can be found at http://www.justice.gov.uk/news/announcement_081007b.htm.

34. For a summary of the Parliamentary response to the proposals see the House of Commons Library research paper 07/93 at
http://www.parliament.uk/commons/lib/research/rp2007/rp07-093.pdf.

35. See http://www.publications.parliament.uk/pa/ld200708/ldhansrd/text/80227-0002.htm#08022765000076. The government was anxious to have co-operation from opposition parties in supporting new provisions restraining the Prison Officers Association from taking industrial action.

Chapter 3 - The approach to fresh evidence (1) – Pendleton and after

In discussing the juridical concept of 'safety', chapter 2 has concentrated upon the Commission's more 'legalistic' referrals. This should not, however, divert attention from the Commission's main purpose. The review of fresh evidence lies at the heart of the Commission's functions. The Commission's power to refer a conviction, it should be remembered, generally arises 'because of an argument, or evidence, not raised in the proceedings which led to it or on any appeal or application for leave to appeal against it'.[1] In its referrals to the Court over the first ten years, the Commission has, perhaps, been preoccupied with fresh *argument* (sometimes of a recondite nature) somewhat more than its advocates might have hoped, and with fresh *evidence* somewhat less. Nevertheless, many of the clearest miscarriages of justice referred by the Commission have been cases where there has been fresh evidence to show that the jury convicted on a misleading, incomplete or simply wrong view of the relevant facts.

A central concern of JUSTICE and others – in pressing for a change of the law – was the restrictive approach taken by the Court of Appeal in exercising its power to receive fresh evidence, the Court being only too ready to assume that the fresh evidence should have been adduced by the defence at the time of trial. In a paper issued following the publication of the Runciman Commission's report, JUSTICE stated as follows:[2]

> There is clearly a consensus that what is considered as fresh evidence should no longer be subject to the restrictive approach adopted by the Court of Appeal in the past. Our view is that although the Court is entitled to seek and take account of any explanation why evidence which was available was not adduced at trial, this should not be the determining factor; the test must be a broad one of whether the evidence goes to the safety of the conviction ... The same test should be applicable to new evidence put forward in an application to the CCRA.

The last sentence was particularly pertinent in the light of the approach frequently taken by the Home Office in reviewing alleged miscarriages. Adopting a 'heads we win, tails you lose' approach, the Home Office were apt to say to applicants bringing forward new evidence that they did not consider that the Court of Appeal would be willing to receive fresh evidence, as it should have been advanced at trial. Conversely, where there was no new evidence, the Home Office reasoned that there was nothing for them to consider.

The difficulty of weighing up new evidence has scarcely been dispelled by the Commission's taking over responsibility for reviewing miscarriages of justice. In a great many cases the Commission deals with applications based on new evidence which is trivial, peripheral, or unbelievable; or which is based upon a completely inconsistent version of events from that put forward at trial. The Commission has, therefore, to sort the wheat from a considerable quantity of chaff.[3] The point can be illustrated by two cases which are, in the author's opinion, among the most misconceived referrals ever made by the Commission.

In **Rowe (Michael)**, R was convicted of robbing the store premises where he had previously worked, on strong recognition evidence of former colleagues. (The evidence was that the masked figure conducting a 'stick-up' was so obviously R that it took them some time to be convinced that he wasn't playing a practical joke.) R's account of his movements on that day only strengthened the case against him. The robber had made his way out through a fire door which was regularly used by smokers working at the premises stepping outside for a cigarette. There were 13 fingerprints of uncertain age on this door of which the police had managed to match 10 with past or present staff members, leaving three unaccounted for.[4] The Commission referred on the basis that this information, if disclosed, could have promoted the argument that one of the unaccounted fingerprints might have been that of the true robber. The Court stated:

> Adopting the words used by Lord Cross in Stafford and Luvaglio ... *the fresh evidence, although relevant and credible, adds so little to the weight of the defence case as compared with the weight of the prosecution case that a doubt induced by the fresh evidence would not be a reasonable doubt, so we leave the conviction standing, and dismiss the appeal.*

It is submitted that the approach of the Court in this case was right and sensible.

And in **Hakala**, of which more anon, the Commission referred on the basis of ESDA evidence[5] to show that police interview notes taken when H confessed to two crimes of rape had been to some degree re-written, the possible inference being that police might have invented or altered the details of the confession to strengthen the prosecution case. The difficulty with this line of reasoning was that H, at trial, had accepted that the confession statements used against him had been made and had been correctly recorded. His case, at trial, was that the confession statements, although made, were in fact wholly untrue. In dismissing the appeal, Lord Justice Judge thundered:

> The trial process is not a tactical game. Under the rules which govern every trial at any given stage in the evolution of the criminal justice process, forensic steps taken by one side, or the other, carry forensic consequences. None of the tactical decisions appropriate to meet contemporary rules are predicated on the basis that any witness, and in particular any defendant who chooses to exercise his right to give evidence, is somehow entitled to depart from the fundamental requirement that his evidence should be truthful evidence. As a corollary, the opportunity for the defendant to give his evidence is provided at his trial, and that is where he must take it.

> In this appeal ... we are being asked to ignore the oral testimony given by Hakala to the jury which convicted him and simultaneously to find that two police officers, whose evidence was unchallenged, indeed accepted by him, some 15 years ago, were or may have been, guilty of gross misconduct. The present Reference does not sufficiently address these problems.

It is impossible to resist the observation that the referral was poorly judged.[6]

Contrast, at the other extreme, the case of **Mulcahy**, convicted of a shop robbery after he was picked out on identity parade by the shop assistant, Miss L, who had witnessed the raid. Following M's trial and unsuccessful appeal, a bin liner at the shop premises was found to bear a fingerprint matching that of another man whose description closely matched that given by Miss L, including having a gold tooth, of which she had made particular mention. M's conviction was readily quashed in the face of such an obvious case of mistaken identity.

Between these two extremes, there have been many cases, much more difficult than either **Michael Rowe** or **Hakala**, where the Court has rejected appeals based upon new evidence referrals. The Court's reasoning and approach in such cases will be discussed in this chapter.

Righting miscarriages of justice?

The statutory test

The test for receipt of new evidence is at s23 Criminal Appeal Act 1968, which now reads (following amendment by the 1995 Act) as follows:

(1) *For the purposes of this Part of this Act the Court of Appeal may, if [they] think it necessary or expedient in the interests of justice ... receive any evidence which was not adduced in the proceedings from which the appeal lies.*

(2) *The Court of Appeal shall, in considering whether to receive any evidence, have regard in particular to -*

   (a) *whether the evidence appears to the court to be capable of belief;*

   (b) *whether it appears to the court that the evidence may afford any ground for allowing the appeal;*

   (c) *whether the evidence would have been admissible in the proceedings from which the appeal lies on an issue which is the subject of the appeal; and*

   (d) *whether there is a reasonable explanation for the failure to adduce the evidence in those proceedings.*

The Runciman Commission made three recommendations with respect to the admission of new evidence:

- In considering whether to receive fresh evidence the Court of Appeal should take a broad approach to the questions whether the fresh evidence was available at the time of trial and, if it was, whether there was a reasonable explanation for the failure to adduce it then or for any subsequent departure by a witness from the evidence given at trial.

- Where an appeal is based on alleged error by trial lawyers, the test to be applied should not be whether there was 'flagrantly incompetent advocacy', but whether the particular decision, whether reasonable or unreasonable, caused a miscarriage of justice.

- The test for receiving fresh evidence should be whether it is 'capable of belief'. (The previous requirement was that the evidence sought to be admitted must have been 'likely to be credible'.)[7]

The amendment of section 23 by the 1995 Act broadly gave effect to the Runciman proposals. It is plain that the Court has an overriding discretion to receive new evidence when it is 'necessary or expedient in the interests of justice' to do so and that the criteria set out at section 23(2)(a)–(d) are only matters to be taken into account by the Court in exercising its overriding discretion. There have been numerous exegeses by the Court of Appeal designed to clarify the section 23 test, but the following – from the judgment of Lord Bingham in the Administrative Court in **R v Criminal Cases Review Commission ex p Pearson** – sets out the position as well as any:

> The Court of Appeal is not precluded from receiving fresh evidence if the conditions in subsection (2)(a), (b), (c) and (d) or any of them are not satisfied, but the Court would for obvious reasons be unlikely to receive evidence which did not appear to it to be capable of belief, or which did not appear to it to afford any ground for allowing the appeal, or which would not have been admissible in the trial court. The Court of Appeal would ordinarily be less ready, and in some cases much less ready, to receive evidence which the appellant had failed without reasonable explanation to adduce at the trial, since receipt of such evidence on appeal tends to subvert our system of jury trial by depriving the decision-making tribunal of the opportunity to review and assess the strength of that fresh evidence in the context of the case as a whole, and retrials, although sometimes necessary, are never desirable. On any application to the Court of Appeal to receive fresh evidence under section 23 in an appeal against conviction, the question which the Court of Appeal must always ask itself is this: having regard in particular to the matters listed in subsection (2), does the Court of Appeal think it necessary or expedient in the interests of justice to receive the new evidence? In exercising its statutory discretion to receive or not to receive fresh evidence, the Court of Appeal will be mindful that its discretion is to be exercised in accordance with the statutory provision and so as to achieve, in the infinitely varying circumstances of different cases, the objective for which the discretion has been conferred. The exercise of this discretion cannot be circumscribed in a manner which fails to give effect to the statute or undermines the statutory objective, which is to promote the interests of justice; the Court will bear in mind that the power in section 23 exists to safeguard defendants against the risk and consequences of wrongful conviction.

This formulation articulates the obstacles that have to be surmounted in bringing forth fresh evidence whilst recognising the ultimate discretion of the Court to do as it thinks just. The position was expressed in similar terms by the Privy Council in *Benedett and Labrador*:[8]

> ... *the discretionary ... power to receive fresh evidence represents a potentially very significant safeguard against the possibility of injustice. The Court's discretionary power is one to be exercised if, after investigation of all the circumstances, the court thinks it is necessary or expedient in the interests of justice to do so.*

The Commission's task

In practice, the Commission – in any new evidence case – is bound to ask itself the section 23 question – 'would the Court receive the evidence?' as a milestone to asking the ultimate question – 'is there any real possibility that the new evidence will cause the Court to quash the conviction?' If this were not in any event obvious, the running order of the Commission's deliberations is set out in the **Pearson** judgment:

> *In a case which is likely to turn on the willingness of the Court of Appeal to receive fresh evidence, the Commission must also make a judgment how, on all the facts of a given case, the Court of Appeal is likely to resolve an application to adduce that evidence under section 23, because there could in such a case be no real possibility that the conviction would not be upheld were the reference to be made unless there were also a real possibility that the Court of Appeal would receive the evidence in question. Thus, in a conviction case of this kind, the first task of the Commission is to judge whether there is a real possibility that the Court of Appeal would receive the evidence. The Commission has, in effect, to predict how the Court of Appeal is likely to answer the question which arises under section 23, as formulated above. In a conviction case depending on the reception of fresh evidence, the Commission must ask itself a double question: do we consider that if the reference is made there is a real possibility that the Court of Appeal will receive the fresh evidence? If so, do we consider that there is a real possibility that the Court of Appeal will not uphold the conviction? The Commission would not in such a case refer unless it gave an affirmative answer to both questions.*

This task may appear to put the Commission in an invidious position. It is set up by the 1995 Act as the 'gatekeeper' entrusted with ensuring that suspected miscarriages of justice are properly reviewed, yet it is also required to shut out appeals if it reaches the judgment that the Court of Appeal will not receive the evidence. The Commission can only square this circle by remembering at all times the primacy of the 'interests of justice' referred to in section 23(1) and in the *Benedett and Labrador* judgment. If there is new evidence which raises a genuine possibility of a miscarriage of justice, the Commission should recognise a real possibility that the Court of Appeal will be prepared to receive it. However the Court of Appeal – at the end of the day – decides to deal with new evidence, the Commission should certainly not bar the progress of potentially meritorious applications on the basis of section 23 considerations, and I am not aware of any cases where it has done so.

The Court's approach to new evidence – the road to Pendleton

In appeals where new evidence is tendered – and passes the section 23 threshold of admissibility – there are two quite distinct approaches of principle that the Court can take in appraising this evidence.

At one extreme lies the 'primacy of the jury' approach. This approach would emphasise that the jury is the sole arbiter of fact in a criminal trial. If new evidence deserves to be admitted, it would be a usurpation of the jury's function for the Court of Appeal to decide how it would have influenced the outcome of the jury's deliberations. If in any doubt whatsoever about the impact that the new evidence would have had upon the jury, the Court should quash the verdict, whilst also considering whether to remit the conviction for retrial (if retrial is practicable). At the other extreme lies the proposition that the Court of Appeal's function is to decide whether or not the conviction is *safe* and the only way to deal with new evidence is for the Court to weigh it up and make up its mind whether it feels uneasy about the conviction.[9]

In practice, the Court has generally adopted a formulation somewhere between these two extremes. In the leading authority – the House of Lords' judgment in *Stafford and Luvaglio*[10] – Lord Dilhorne set out the approach to be adopted by the Court of Appeal:

> It would, in my opinion, be wrong for the Court [of Appeal] to say: "In our view this evidence does not give rise to any reasonable doubt about the guilt of the accused. We do not ourselves consider that an unsafe or unsatisfactory verdict was returned but as the jury who heard the case might conceivably have taken a different view from ours, we quash the conviction" for Parliament has, in terms, said that the court should only quash a conviction

> *if, there being no error of law or material irregularity at the trial, "they think"*
> *the verdict was unsafe or unsatisfactory. ... If the court has no reasonable*
> *doubt about the verdict, it follows that the court does not think that the jury*
> *could have one; and,* **conversely, if the court says that a jury might in**
> **the light of the new evidence have a reasonable doubt, that means**
> **that the court has a reasonable doubt.** (Emphasis added)

This formulation essentially remains good law, albeit it has become subject to a number of glosses as a result of **Pendleton** and subsequent authorities.

The correct approach to new evidence was the issue raised when the Commission's referral of **Pendleton** was considered by the Court of Appeal. P was convicted in 1986 of a murder committed some 15 years earlier. He had been intensively interviewed by police officers, pre-PACE, over two days and without the presence of a solicitor, and confessed to the murder. This confession was a central plank of the prosecution case. There was much else put forward by the prosecution to persuade the jury that they could rely upon the credibility of the confession but – as cases like **Fell** (discussed in chapter 6) show – the view taken of supporting evidence may be very different once it is conceded that the confession is worthless. The conviction was referred on the basis of fresh evidence from Professor Gudjonsson[11] that, having regard to P's vulnerability, the confession was unreliable. Upholding the conviction, the Court of Appeal stated:

> *We assess the reliability of the admissions made in interview on their own*
> *merits and also having regard to the additional material. If, notwithstanding*
> *a provisional view as to their reliability, there was additional extraneous*
> *material which cast doubt on their reliability, that could affect the safety of*
> *the verdict. Nothing in the additional material, in our judgment, casts doubt*
> *upon the admissions made. ... Not only does the material canvassed at the*
> *trial and the additional material canvassed upon the hearing of this appeal*
> *fail to cast doubt upon the reliability of the admissions, it provides other*
> *substantial evidence of the guilt of the appellant. ... We have no doubt that*
> *the conviction was safe.*

The Court's decision was appealed to the House of Lords upon the certified question:

> *Where, on an appeal against conviction, the Court of Appeal receives fresh*
> *evidence under section 23 of the Criminal Appeal Act 1968, in determining*

the safety of the conviction, is the court confined to answering the question, might a reasonable jury have acquitted the appellant had they heard the fresh evidence?

The House of Lords unanimously allowed the appeal and quashed the conviction, but the judgments contained a marked diversity of approach to the certified question. Giving the majority opinion supported by three other Noble Lords, Lord Bingham stated:

... the test advocated by counsel in Stafford *and by Mr Mansfield in this appeal does have a dual virtue ... First, it reminds the Court of Appeal that it is not and should never become the primary decision-maker. Secondly, it reminds the Court of Appeal that it has an imperfect and incomplete understanding of the full processes which led the jury to convict. The Court of Appeal can make its assessment of the fresh evidence it has heard, but save in a clear case it is at a disadvantage in seeking to relate that evidence to the rest of the evidence which the jury heard. For these reasons it will usually be wise for the Court of Appeal,* **in a case of any difficulty**, *to test their own provisional view by asking whether the evidence, if given at the trial, might reasonably have affected the decision of the trial jury to convict. If it might, the conviction must be thought to be unsafe.* (Emphasis added)

The minority opinion of Lord Hobhouse gave a different emphasis:

Unless and until the Court of Appeal has been persuaded that the verdict of the jury is unsafe, the verdict must stand. Nothing less will suffice to displace it. A mere risk that it is unsafe does not suffice: the appellant has to discharge a burden of persuasion and persuade the Court of Appeal that the conviction is unsafe. It is ironic that the appellant has, under the banner "the supremacy of the jury", sought to undermine that supremacy and the finality of the jury's verdict.

The mere production on a later appeal of additional evidence which would have been admitted at the trial had it then been adduced demonstrates no unsafety of the verdict. It merely raises for the consideration of the Court of Appeal the question whether the Court of Appeal thinks that, taking into account the new evidence, the verdict has become unsafe ... the Court of Appeal will have to look at the new evidence tendered and, if it thinks fit, listen to the witnesses giving it orally and being cross-examined, as happened in the Court of Appeal in the present case, in order to decide whether or not

> *it thinks that the conviction is unsafe. The admission of the evidence in the Court of Appeal in no way prejudges or forecloses this question: s.23(2) refers to evidence which appears to the court to be 'capable of belief and which "may" afford a ground' for allowing an appeal.*

Lord Hobhouse's opinion plainly proposes to give freer rein to the Court of Appeal to form its own judgment of the weight that should be given to the new evidence without being unduly burdened by concern as to how a hypothetical jury would have approached it.

Returning to the majority view, **Pendleton** did not necessarily alter the existing law – it expressly affirmed the leading authority of *Stafford and Luvaglio*. However, it served an important role in reminding the Court of Appeal to stand back in cases of 'any difficulty' and consider what doubts the jury might have had. This is a point of great importance in Commission cases. The Commission carries out a retrospective review, sometimes years after the event. There is clearly no opportunity either to assail the jury with the new evidence or to revisit with the jury the weight that it gave to the other evidence in the case. The Commission has to make its own judgment as to whether the new evidence carries the case into the realms of 'any difficulty' as discussed by Lord Bingham.

The exercise is one which requires particular intellectual clarity and honesty. It is all too easy, on the one hand, to deduce from the jury's guilty verdict that every aspect of the prosecution case was proved to the jury beyond a smidgen of doubt; that every prosecution witness was wholly credible; that every corroborative aspect of the prosecution case was considered to be significant. If that approach is taken the new evidence has to confront a wall of incontrovertible and proven evidence of the appellant's guilt. Adopting the approach of Lord Hobhouse, this places a very heavy burden upon new evidence to satisfy the 'real possibility' test. At the other extreme, without due evaluation of the strength of the prosecution case at trial, it would be only too easy to assume that any new piece of evidence, however insubstantial, *might* have tipped the balance of the jury's deliberations.

It was thought at first that **Pendleton** would have a significant impact upon the approach of the Court of Appeal in new evidence cases and its impact is apparent in two historic cases referred by the Commission and quashed following **Pendleton**.

In **Cooper and McMahon,** the famous Luton Post Office Murder case, it had long been clear that there were profound flaws in the prosecution case which the jury (which gave its verdict in 1971) could not have appreciated. To put the matter very briefly, the Crown's case rested heavily on the evidence of an informer, Mathews. Mathews' evidence was said to have been untrue by an associate, called Edwards, at an appeal in 1973, which resulted in the quashing of the conviction of the appellants' co-accused, named Murphy. The Home Secretary referred the convictions to the Court of Appeal in 1975 and again in 1976 due to concerns about Mathews' evidence, but the Court on both appeals upheld the convictions on the basis that *they* believed that Mathews had been telling the truth. The two men were released by the Home Secretary in 1980 because of the 'widely felt sense of unease' about the safety of their convictions. Their case was among the many inherited by the Commission from the Home Office. The new evidence considered by the Commission mostly replicated matters raised in the unsuccessful appeals that had followed the Home Secretary's references, with some limited new matters. The Commission nevertheless referred. Quashing the convictions, the Court stated:

> We, with the distinct advantage and benefit of the decision of the House of Lords in Pendleton *in 2001, respectfully disagree with the Court of Appeal's assessment in 1975. If the jury at the trial had had the benefit of Edwards' evidence exculpating Murphy, we accept that it would have been directed by the trial judge that such evidence was also relevant to the jury's assessment of the truthfulness of Mathews, not only in respect of Murphy, but also in respect of Cooper and McMahon. In our opinion it is impossible to say that such evidence would have made <u>no</u> impact on the jury in respect of Mathews' veracity when considering Cooper and McMahon. On the contrary, it might have made a heavy impact.*

> In 1976 Mathews gave evidence before a differently constituted Court of Appeal. He roundly asserted that there was no question of mistake in his identification of Murphy, Cooper or McMahon. The Court explained why Murphy's appeal had been allowed, and went on to consider the evidence from Mathews. It found that "he was clearly telling the truth". The Court did not hear Edwards although it is fair to point out that (a) he had previously been found to have been an honest and credible witness and (b) the Court of Appeal in 1976 was anxious and would have been prepared to listen to any witness whom the court or the defence had wished to call. Nevertheless, it is the submission of Mr Emmerson that the Court of Appeal in fact conducted the very exercise which Pendleton, *many years later,*

said was impermissible. If Edwards was to the Court of Appeal in 1973 a credible witness, it was not permissible for the Court of Appeal in 1976 to say that they believed Mathews. For, he submitted, that was deciding the very matter which in Pendleton *in 2001 it was made clear the Court of Appeal could not decide, namely the guilt or innocence of the defendant.* (Emphasis in the original)

Pendleton was also cited in another historic case, **Mills and Poole**; the convoluted history of this case will be referred to shortly. Citing Lord Bingham's majority speech, Kennedy LJ said:

It is clear from his reasoning that in those cases where the answer to the question, safety or unsafety, is not immediately clear, the Court may have to ask itself, for example, whether and to what extent the jury relied on a particular piece of evidence in convicting an accused and how their decision might reasonably have been affected if they had known what the Court now knows.

In a nutshell, although **Pendleton** represented no wholly new point of law, it could potentially tip the balance of the Court of Appeal's approach – perhaps most especially in older miscarriage cases. It required the Court to consider carefully the impact of the new evidence, and not adopt as a starting point the presumption that the jury's verdict showed that the Crown had made out an incontrovertible case at trial.

The road from Pendleton

The Court of Appeal had an early opportunity to serve its own gloss on **Pendleton** in the unfortunate referral of **Hakala**. This would not, it is submitted, have been a case of 'any difficulty' in the sense referred to in Lord Bingham's judgment, as H's acceptance that he had confessed to the crimes in police interviews would surely have led any hypothetical jury to give little or no weight to fresh evidence that there had been some (limited) rewriting of the interview notes. However, Judge LJ also took the opportunity to clarify **Pendleton**:

In Pendleton *itself, Lord Bingham's conclusion that it was not possible to be sure of the safety of the conviction followed an analysis of the fresh evidence in its factual context. The judgment in "fresh evidence" cases will inevitably therefore continue to focus on the facts before the trial jury, in order to ensure that the right question - the safety, or otherwise, of the conviction - is answered. It is integral to the process that if the fresh evidence is disputed,*

> *this court must decide whether and to what extent it should be accepted or rejected, and if it is to be accepted, to evaluate its importance, or otherwise, relative to the remaining material which was before the trial jury: hence the jury impact test. Indeed, although the question did not arise in Pendleton, the fresh evidence adduced by the appellant, or indeed the Crown, may serve to confirm rather than undermine the safety of the conviction. Unless this evaluation is carried out, it is difficult to see how this court can perform ... its statutory responsibility in a fresh evidence case, and exercise its "power of review to guard against the possibility of injustice".*

Hakala has been much cited since – indeed this authority and Lord Hobhouse's minority speech are now frequently cited by the Court of Appeal in preference to Lord Bingham's speech for the majority in **Pendleton**. This 'post-**Pendleton**' approach was applied in the very shocking judgment of the Privy Council in *Dial and Dottin*,[12] a 'death row' case heard on appeal from the Court of Appeal in Trinidad and Tobago. The new evidence consisted of undisputed information that a critical identification witness, named Shawn, had given lying testimony at trial. The appeal was dismissed by a 3-2 majority, Lord Bingham being in the majority.[13] Lord Browne, giving the judgment of the majority, stated:

> *Wherever fresh evidence establishes that a material prosecution witness has told a lie, the question arising for the Appeal Court's determination is whether that realistically places the appellant's guilt in reasonable doubt - whether, in other words, the verdict is now to be regarded as unsafe. That necessarily must depend upon **all** the evidence in the case. However barefaced the lie and however central to the prosecution case the witness who told it, the Court of Appeal is bound in law to address that question. Even in a case of capital murder it cannot be right to allow an appeal, without more, simply on the basis that the State's main witness has later been shown to have told an outright lie.*

> *The Court is not in such circumstances exonerated from undertaking its analytical task. And if it remains sure of the appellant's guilt and upholds his conviction, the Court is not thereby to be regarded as having deprived the appellant of due process.* (Emphasis in the original)

The correct legal approach, said Lord Browne, was as follows:

> *In the Board's view the law is now clearly established and can be simply stated as follows. Where fresh evidence is adduced on a criminal appeal it*

is for the Court of Appeal, assuming always that it accepts it, to evaluate its importance in the context of the remainder of the evidence in the case. If the Court concludes that the fresh evidence raises no reasonable doubt as to the guilt of the accused it will dismiss the appeal. The primary question is for the Court itself and is not what effect the fresh evidence would have had on the mind of the jury. That said, if the Court regards the case as a difficult one, it may find it helpful to test its view "by asking whether the evidence, if given at the trial, might reasonably have affected the decision of the trial jury to convict" (Pendleton at p83, para 19). The guiding principle nevertheless remains that stated by Viscount Dilhorne in Stafford (at p906) and affirmed by the House in Pendleton:

> "While ... the Court of Appeal and this House may find it a convenient approach to consider what a jury might have done if they had heard the fresh evidence, the ultimate responsibility rests with them and them alone for deciding the question [whether or not the verdict is unsafe]."

The decision was the subject of powerful dissenting judgments from Lord Steyn and Lord Hutton, both of whom suggested that the approach taken by the majority conflicted with the majority view in **Pendleton**.

More recently, in the decision following the Commission's referral of **L (Stuart)**, a division of the Court of Appeal under Moses LJ went one stage further and appeared to stand the Court's judgment in **Pendleton** on its head. L was convicted of sexual offences against his niece, JR. JR's established mendacity was such that the head of the local office of the Crown Prosecution Service took the unprecedented step of commending L's application to the Commission. Part of the new evidence affecting the assessment of JR's veracity was contained in an NSPCC file which the jury had not been told about. The Court concluded, however, that they could be sure that JR's evidence against L was true and they were not detained by 'jury impact':

> It must be emphasised that the task of this court is not primarily focussed on the question whether the disclosure of the file would have had an effect on the jury's consideration. As to that there can be little doubt. But, as ... R v Pendleton ... emphasises, the task of this court is to consider whether, in the light of the fresh evidence, the conviction is unsafe.

If the approach described by Moses LJ were correct, it would seem that the Court of Appeal has re-interpreted **Pendleton** from emphasising the requirement to consider carefully the question of jury impact to discounting entirely the jury impact of the new evidence – an adventurous approach to higher judicial authority!

The current state of play

The post-Pendleton view of new evidence, as expressed in *Dial and Dottin,* appears to be currently in the ascendancy, although the Court continues from time to time to adopt the more liberal view of the law expressed by Lord Bingham. An excellent recent illustration is the Northern Ireland case of **MacDermott and McCartney**, the facts of which are set out in chapter 13. In that case, the new evidence, on the one hand, was relatively slender but the evidence that had given rise to the conviction was by any standards troubling. The Court cited the formulations of both Lord Bingham and Lord Hobhouse and quashed the convictions.

However, in other cases, **Pendleton** has been relied upon by the Court in upholding convictions in the face of new evidence. **Probyn** is perhaps an unexceptionable case where the Court found that the new evidence failed the jury impact test. The issue in this case was whether P had pushed the victim (his wife) in her car into the River Severn (as asserted by the Crown) or whether she had driven the car into the river (as argued by the defence). The case was referred on the basis of new evidence from an accident reconstruction expert, whose analysis of debris found on the riverbank gave some support to the case that the car had entered the river at a greater speed than P could have achieved by pushing it. In upholding the conviction, the Court analysed the very formidable evidence to support the Crown's case against P which, it felt, entirely overbore any doubts which might have arisen in the jury's mind had they heard the new expert evidence. The Court bore in mind that the issue sought to be put in doubt by the new evidence was also one which had been very fully ventilated at trial:

> *It is in our view relevant to look at the issue to which the fresh evidence relates and to consider the extent to which that issue was before the jury at the trial and the impact the fresh evidence may have had on that issue.*

It is hard to argue with the Court's application of **Pendleton** on the facts of this case.

Much more contentious is the case of **Steele, Whomes and Corry** – the much discussed Rettendon Range Rover case. At trial, the lynchpin of the prosecution case was the testimony of Darren Nicholls, whose evidence was that he had driven S and W to and from the place where three of their associates had been shot, and that S and W had admitted to the killings. There was some corroborating evidence (such as cell phone triangulation evidence) but without the evidence of N, there was little to corroborate. The convictions were referred on new evidence that N had had contacts with the media prior to trial, that he had sold his story, and appeared to have the prospect of receiving more for his story if the defendants were convicted than if they were acquitted. There was also evidence put forward at the appeal that police guarding N at the relevant time (N was on remand for other offences and was being held in protective custody as an informer) might have colluded with N in allowing him to slip away from prison to meet his literary representatives in order to negotiate a book contract.

Against this evidence, the Court set out the considerable evidence which, they considered, showed that N had been telling the truth:

> we turn to the central question identified in Pendleton, namely "whether the conviction is safe and not whether the accused is guilty". It seems to us that the following matters are of particular significance ...

And then, after conducting a lengthy analysis of N's evidence:

> For all these reasons, we have come to the firm conclusion that what has been established about Nicholls' contacts with the media does not undermine the safety of the convictions of the appellants.

It must be acknowledged that – in this instant case – the Court made quite a formidable case on the facts for its conclusion that N's undisclosed contacts with the media did not mean that his account should be doubted. Nevertheless, one is left with an uneasy view that where the Court of Appeal forms a clear and definite view as to the rights and wrongs of a conviction there can be a degree of circularity in the reasoning which leads the Court to depreciate the significance of the new evidence. It is hard not to recall (again) the infamous words of Lord Lane giving judgment in 1988 upholding the conviction of the Birmingham Six,[14] a case which led ultimately to the establishment of the Commission. It is this 'closed' mental approach against which the House of Lords counseled in **Pendleton.**

Pendleton and non-disclosure

A matter which exercised the Commission in its early days was whether the approach to new evidence would differ in a case where the new evidence relied upon in support of an application was known to the prosecution at the time of trial but not disclosed. The non-availability of the evidence in such cases could be laid directly at the door of the prosecution, and the question was whether any abuse of process or kindred considerations should place non-disclosed evidence on a higher plane than other new evidence in considering the safety of a conviction. At the inception of the Commission in 1997, the leading non-disclosure cases of *Ward*[15] and *Keane*,[16] in which the Court had been much exercised by prosecution non-disclosure, were relatively recent. As the Court put it in *Ward*:

> *Non-disclosure is a potent source of injustice and even with the benefit of hindsight, it will often be difficult to say whether or not an undisclosed item of evidence might have shifted the balance or opened up a new line of defence.*

It now seems clear (i) that the Court does not consider that there are any special considerations to be applied in deciding whether to receive and how to evaluate evidence consisting of material that was undisclosed at trial, and (ii) that the jury impact test is likely to be applied in the same way to undisclosed as to other new information. In **Underwood**, a case which concerned the non-disclosure of previous convictions of an important prosecution witness, the Court stated:

> *... it cannot be the case that if an important witness's convictions are not disclosed, the conviction must inevitably be quashed. As Lord Bingham said later in* Pendleton *... it is for this court to determine whether the conviction is unsafe and in any case of difficulty to test its provisional view by asking whether the new evidence (here the previous convictions) if given at the trial might reasonably have affected the decision of the trial jury to convict.*

Reflections

As the legal deconstruction of **Pendleton** has continued, there seems some danger that the wheel has come full circle and that the approach of Lord Lane in the Birmingham Six case will once again represent the mainstream approach of the Court of Appeal. It should be added that the Court of Appeal seems to be anxious to stress that the gloss on **Pendleton**, as set out in **Hakala** and *Dial and Dottin*, represents a correct understanding of the law. In a letter to the Commission's chairman, Graham Zellick,[17] Judge LJ drew attention to the Privy

Council's judgment in *Dial and Dottin*, concluding by saying 'I did ... wonder whether a personal letter to you might encourage some further thoughts about fresh evidence cases'. It should be added that this personal letter was tendered as a more discreet way of providing guidance to the Commission than through the public medium of a formal judgment.

Professor Zellick in his reply stated as follows:

> *You were quite right to point out that we have fallen into the habit of habitually citing* Pendleton *as if that were the last word on the subject, which it clearly is not. I have had produced for me material on our system which shows that we are aware of the Privy Council's decision in* Dial and Dottin *and, indeed, your own judgment in* Hakala ... *which is cited approvingly by the Board.*

> *I am assured that my colleagues have been applying the correct test and asking the right question, but I can see that the citing of the particular passage in* Pendleton *hardly inspires confidence that that is indeed the case.*

> *We are therefore taking steps to rectify this. The only problem with that is that there is a school of thought here that decisions of the Privy Council cannot in any way supersede the magisterial words of the very same Law Lords when sitting in the House! Unfortunately, that view seems to have been given some cogency by a recent case in which the Court of Appeal has reserved judgment to deal with that very point (following the Privy Council's recent decision in* Holley). *I hope their ruling will be robust!*

He continued:

> *The only other observation I would make is that I wonder whether there really is a material difference between the view advanced in* Pendleton *and the different formulation found in* Dial and Dottin.

This response might be read as implying an acceptance on the Commission's part that the majority judgment in **Pendleton** should no longer be taken, as Professor Zellick put it, as 'the last word on the subject'. It should be added, however, that the Commission has not adopted any formal position on this matter, and if steps were indeed taken to 'rectify' the Commission staff's understanding of the law I, as a member of the Commission, was never made aware of them.

In any event, it would seem that – from the Commission's perspective – the judicial reaction to **Pendleton** needs to be viewed from a balanced perspective. To repeat, the key words in Lord Bingham's judgment were:

> It will usually be wise for the Court of Appeal, **in a case of any difficulty**, to test their own provisional view by asking whether the evidence, if given at the trial, might reasonably have affected the decision of the trial jury to convict. (Emphasis added)

Clearly, it is incumbent on the Commission to make its own thoroughgoing analysis of the warp and weft of the evidence before concluding whether the case is one of 'any difficulty' that merits referral. The careful analyses of the evidence contained in the judgments in **Probyn** and in **Steele, Whomes and Corry** are instructive in showing the manner in which the Court will conduct such an exercise. It is not unreasonable for the Commission to decline to refer a conviction on the basis of new evidence, should it be the case that reflection and analysis will show beyond reasonable question that the evidence would have made no impact upon the jury.

Conversely, if in the context of the prosecution and defence cases at trial, the new evidence *might* have drawn the jury up short so to speak – to reflect whether they could be certain of the prosecution case – then that is surely a case of 'difficulty'. The Commission should refer such cases and analyse carefully in its Statement of Reasons why the case is considered to be difficult. Where necessary, the Commission's investigation and its reasoning will need to assail the 'closed' assumption that the entirety of the prosecution evidence must have been accepted without doubt by the jury, and articulate why, viewing the case as a whole, the new evidence might support the conclusion that the conviction is unsafe. If this exercise is carried out rigorously, and on the basis of careful analysis of the facts, then appeals based on such referrals should not fall foul of the more illiberal approach referred to above.

The danger for the Commission is that it will be influenced by the decisions in **Hakala** and *Dial and Dottin*, and by the feedback it has received from the Court in cases such as **Steele, Whomes and Corry**, to use its gatekeeper role to bar the progress of applications based upon evidence which it predicts the Court of Appeal will view negatively. The difficulty (if such it is) is expressed as follows in a letter to the writer from counsel who has been much concerned in miscarriage cases:

> *What I find most infuriating is that whilst the Commission clearly has to predict the [Court's] approach, it has before it two acceptable approaches ... I feel that the Commission is occasionally (and increasingly so) timid in refusing to refer cases that would fall within the jury impact test.*

I cannot – on the basis of my own experience – endorse the view that the Commission has become 'increasingly timid' (as opposed to increasingly rigorous) due to the post-**Pendleton** jurisprudence. However, it would seem impracticable to put such a hypothesis to scientific test, and it is possible that the Commission may have become more timid (as a result of the post-**Pendleton** jurisprudence) without adopting an explicit policy to that effect or even necessarily appreciating that its approach has been changing.

What the Commission should not do is run scared of judicial attitudes expressed in cases such as *Dial and Dottin*. Its duty, as gatekeeper, is to view the impact of the new evidence realistically but also expansively. If there is sensible basis to conclude that the new evidence exceeds the 'any difficulty' threshold, then the Commission should refer, leaving it to the adversarial proceedings of the Court of Appeal to resolve whether or not the conviction is unsafe.

Notes

1. S13(1)(b)(i) Criminal Appeal Act 1995.
2. JUSTICE discussion paper, *Remedying Miscarriages of Justice*, September 1994.
3. As noted in chapter 1, the Commission uses a system of triage to identify cases which require relatively little investigative effort and which can be resolved quickly – leaving the Commission's resources to be concentrated on cases raising significant investigative issues.
4. There had been many temporary workers – mostly students – working at the store over previous Christmas periods and it was impossible to trace all former members of staff.
5. ESDA stands for Electrostatic Detection Apparatus. It is used to detect and to assist in the decipherment of indented impressions of handwriting on paper.
6. Note also a slightly similar (early) case referred by the Commission – **Such**. S had made an incriminating admission to a medical practitioner at trial and the case was referred on the basis of evidence in the prosecution files to show that S had been intoxicated at the time – potentially affecting the reliability of the self-incriminating statement. The Court of Appeal noted that at trial S had denied making the incriminating statement. Since the defence had chosen to deny the incriminating statement (as opposed to disputing its reliability) the Court did not think that this new evidence assisted S and it upheld the conviction.
7. In an entertaining but somewhat tongue in cheek analysis, the late Professor Sir John Smith doubted whether, semantically, this alteration of the law was actually a relaxation. 'Credible' means nothing more than 'capable of belief', so changing the test from 'likely to be credible'

to 'capable of belief' meant changing the test from 'likely to be credible' to 'credible' – which made the new test more demanding and not less! That was, however, clearly not the intention of the amendment and it is generally understood to signify a relaxation of the test.

8. [2003] 1 WLR 1545 (PC).

9. In a private conversation, a senior judge referred to those who incline towards the first view as 'idealistic' and those who favour the second as 'highly pragmatic'.

10. [1974] AC 878.

11. Gísli Gudjónsson is Professor of Forensic Psychology at the Institute of Psychiatry, King's College London. He is an internationally renowned authority on suggestibility and false confessions and his evidence has figured in many of the Commission's referrals.

12. [2005] UKPC 4.

13. In a private conversation, a senior judge has suggested that this is evidence that Lord Bingham has repented of his speech in **Pendleton**.

14. 'As has happened before in References by the Home Secretary to this court, the longer this hearing has gone on the more convinced this court has become that the verdict of the jury was correct.' (See chapter 1.)

15. [1993] 1 WLR 619.

16. [1994] 1 WLR 746.

17. Both this letter and Professor Zellick's reply were provided to JUSTICE pursuant to a Freedom of Information Act request.

Chapter 4 - The approach to fresh evidence (2) – expert evidence

At the time when JUSTICE and others were campaigning for an independent miscarriage authority, the issue of wrong or questionable expert evidence loomed very much less than now as a prospective cause of miscarriages. In Kate Malleson's longitudinal study of Court of Appeal decisions, commissioned by Runciman,[1] only two out of 300 appeals involved the tendering of fresh expert evidence, both appeals being dismissed. In the Waller Report – *Miscarriages of Justice*, published by JUSTICE in 1989 – problems associated with forensic expert evidence are scarcely mentioned at all.

It cannot be said, however, that problems occasioned by expert evidence were then unknown. The outcry about the Cleveland sex abuse cases was centred upon the very questionable techniques, in particular the reflex anal dilatation test, used by certain experts to ascertain sexual abuse. And in a number of the most high-profile terrorist cases – including the *Birmingham Six*, the *Maguire Seven* and *Judith Ward* cases – the prosecution case had relied significantly on evidence from a discredited Home Office forensic scientist, Dr Frank Skuse. In the *Birmingham Six* case, it will be remembered, an important issue raised at appeal was that traces of nitroglycerine found on the defendants could have been due to contact with playing cards, rather than explosives, as the prosecution asserted.

That said, it is clear that the need for experts to approach forensic issues with care, with circumspection, with humility and with an absence of preconceived notions is a matter that was very much less appreciated then than now. It is instructive, for instance, to note the instructions issued by the Court of Appeal in the case of Sally **Clark** to pathologists investigating suspicious deaths:

> It is desirable, however, that we should first set out our clear understanding of how a pathologist will approach a case of suspicious death. In the first place, he will obtain information about the circumstances of the death. This may, in some cases, involve a visit to the body in situ before it is removed to the mortuary. It will almost inevitably involve receiving information from the investigating officers. This will include any version of the circumstances emanating from witnesses and any possible explanation advanced by any suspect. Although the suggestion has been made that the

obtaining of such information may be undesirable, we have no doubt that this is wrong. The initial post mortem is critical to any conclusion as to the cause of death. Amongst the questions the pathologist will want to answer are whether any competing explanations for the death are consistent with his findings. The very act of carrying out the post mortem examination will alter the condition of parts of the body and to learn only after examination of explanations that have been advanced runs the risk that the best evidence to confirm or contradict the explanation may no longer be available. A competent pathologist will not assume that any one of the explanations for death advanced is necessarily the correct explanation but in considering the range of possibilities, he will have specific regard to evidence consistent with or contradictory of such explanations. It is, of course, important that the pathologist records such information so that any one else can understand any matter that he may have had in mind in conducting the examination.

These general observations are followed by detailed rules of guidance dealing with matters such as the obtaining of microscopic samples and photographs. This guidance might now be regarded by the most experienced forensic practitioners as a statement of the obvious. It was given by the Court, however, both because practice had been so widely deficient in the past and because the dangers of insufficient forensic procedures were, even at the time of the judgment in 2002, considered to be insufficiently appreciated by some members of the profession.

By contrast, there is now a level of criticism of expert evidence which at times approaches a feeding frenzy. Particular interest arises when an expert, such as Professor Roy Meadows (who famously opined in the Sally **Clark** case that there were odds of 73 million to one against two cases of sudden infant death syndrome (SIDS) in one family), is seen to fall from grace.[2] Professor Meadows' case occasioned general vilification not only of the fallen expert, but of the forensic discipline he represented and expert witnesses in general.

The response of the Court of Appeal

The Court of Appeal has sensed great danger to the administration of justice (and in particular the state of its own lists) from undue elevation of new expert evidence as a potential ground of appeal. The first concern addressed by the Court has been the mounting on appeal of an improved expert case – the 'bigger and better' expert, so to speak. In the much cited case of *Steven Jones*[3] the Court considered the application of section 23 of the 1968 Act to applications for the admission of fresh expert evidence on appeal. The Court referred to 'the crucial obligation on a defendant in a criminal case to advance his whole defence and any evidence on which he relies before the trial jury' adding:

He is not entitled to hold evidence in reserve and then seek to introduce it on appeal following conviction. While failure to give a reasonable explanation for failure to adduce the evidence before the jury is not a bar to reception of the evidence on appeal, it is a matter which the Court is obliged to consider in deciding whether to receive the evidence or not.

The Court has in the past accepted that section 23 may apply to expert evidence, and we would not wish to circumscribe the operation of a statutory rule enacted to protect defendants against the risk of wrongful conviction. But it seems unlikely that the section was framed with expert evidence prominently in mind. ... Expert witnesses, although inevitably varying in standing and experience, are interchangeable in a way in which factual witnesses are not. It would clearly subvert the trial process if a defendant, convicted at trial, were to be generally free to mount on appeal an expert case which, if sound, could and should have been advanced before the jury. If it is said that the only expert witness in an established field whose opinion supports a certain defence was unavailable to testify at the trial, that may be thought (save in unusual circumstances) to reflect on the acceptability of that opinion.

The Court has also expressed concern that expert evidence given at trial should not be raked over in a manner that impinges upon the sovereign exercise by the jury of its function of reaching a verdict on the evidence. In Angela Cannings,[4] a SIDS case which followed closely upon Sally **Clark**, the Court in quashing the convictions commented upon the difficulty faced by the jury in choosing between conflicting expert opinions in a case involving sudden infant death. These dicta were interpreted in some quarters as implying that the Court accepted as a general proposition that where the jury would have had difficulty in deciding between competing expert testimony, their verdict might be considered unsafe. That point might be considered particularly relevant in a complex field such as brain injury. The Court was swift to put paid to that interpretation in two linked judgements on SIDS, Donna **Anthony** (which was a Commission case) and *Kai-Whitewind*[5] (which was not). In *Kai-Whitewind* the Court stated:

In the context of disputed expert evidence, on analysis, what was required in this case was no different to that which obtains, for example, when pathologists disagree about the cause of death in a case of alleged strangulation. An argument whether the hyoid bone was fractured before death (supporting the conclusion of strangulation) or whether it occurred post mortem, perhaps during the course of the autopsy itself (which would discount strangulation), is commonplace. More important, it does not alter the fact that the hyoid bone was fractured. And even if the experts disagree about whether it was indeed fractured, that is a question for the jury. Cannings does not produce the result that it follows from an argument between experts that the issue whether the fracture occurred before or after death, or whether there is a fracture at all, is not appropriate for the jury's consideration. Evidence of this kind must be dealt with in accordance with the usual principle that it is for the jury to decide between the experts, by reference to all the available evidence, and that it is open to the jury to accept or reject the evidence of the experts on either side.

In *Kai-Whitewind*, the Court was also keen to dispose of the notion that, if the defence expert evidence goes off badly at trial, this is a matter which will lead it to intervene:

The fact that the expert chosen to give evidence by the defence did not give his evidence as well as it was hoped that he would, or that parts of his evidence were exposed as untenable ... thereby undermining confidence in his evidence as a whole, does not begin to justify the calling of further evidence, whether to provide "substantial enhancement" of the unsatisfactory earlier evidence, or otherwise. Where expert evidence has been given and apparently rejected by the jury, it could only be in the rarest of circumstances that the court would permit a repetition, or near repetition of evidence of the same effect by some other expert to provide the basis for a successful appeal. If it were otherwise the trial process would represent no more, or not very much more than what we shall colloquially describe as a "dry run" for one or more of the experts on the basis that, if the evidence failed to attract the jury at trial, an application could be made for the issue to be revisited in this court. That is not the purpose of the court's jurisdiction to receive evidence on appeal.

In expressing itself in these terms, the Court clearly sought to warn off appeals mounted on the premise that the prosecution forensic evidence might have been less watertight than the jury had been led to believe. However, as ever in cases where the Court has issued somewhat stern guidelines about its general approach, it has been willing to exercise pragmatic exceptions in cases where it has the sense that the jury's verdict is unsafe. In *Jones*, for example, having set out its general presumption against receiving improved expert evidence, it elected to do so in that instant case and allowed the appeal.[6]

The task for the Commission

Bearing in mind the Court's approach, the Commission has to establish whether, in any specific case, fresh expert opinion should be sought and whether any new expert evidence resulting from its investigations is likely to carry weight with the Court in the event of referral. In reviewing the expert case, the Commission is often better placed than defence lawyers at trial for at least three reasons:

- Although the Commission has always sought to obtain value for money, it is not financially constrained to the same extent as legally-aided defendants in selecting experts and commissioning forensic work.

- The Commission can ask the expert to review the totality of the expert evidence, including the expert testimony at trial.

- The Commission has developed a database of leading experts and its instructions are generally considered prestigious. It is, therefore, generally able to call upon the most experienced experts. This luxury is not always available to defence lawyers.

In addition, the Commission's retrospective review can plainly call upon any developments of expert understanding since the date of trial. Nevertheless, in approaching fresh expert evidence, the Commission has been subject to two distinct criticisms from lawyers representing applicants.

First, it has been suggested that the Commission has been somewhat intimidated in some cases by the Court's approach – as indicated in particular in *Jones* – and has wrongly concluded that the Court would refuse to receive improved expert evidence on the basis of 'finality of trial' considerations. If the Commission has, indeed, adopted that approach – rejecting expert evidence that significantly improves upon the expert case at trial – that would be a serious criticism. As already noted, the Court has always been prepared to admit pragmatic exceptions to its expressed general presumption against receiving improved expert evidence. Where, therefore, the expert case presented to the Commission is significantly better in relation to the material issues than the expert case at trial then (unless there is evidence of intentional failure to put up at trial the expert case now relied upon) it would seem to be an invidious (and probably wrong) application of the 'real possibility' test for the Commission to conclude without more that the Court would not receive it.

The second criticism levelled against the Commission is that it has been too ready to reject expert cases put to it on the basis of its own judgment of the 'jury impact' of such cases. It is certainly true that the Commission has in the past rejected expert cases which appear to be inconsequential – and no doubt will continue to do so in the future. The Commission may, for instance, decline to refer a new expert case on any one (or more) of the following grounds:

- The expert case is not essentially different from the expert case at trial.

- The expert case now relied upon was known at trial but a tactical decision was made to use the expert evidence to cross-examine the Crown expert rather than to put the defence expert in the witness box. (This decision is sometimes made on the ground that, if called, the expert would be bound to concede matters highly damaging to the defence in cross-examination.)

- The expert case – taken at its highest – could make no meaningful inroads upon the prosecution case.

- The expert case promotes a factual account different from the factual account relied upon at trial. (**Hakala**, discussed in chapter 3 and **Wooster**, discussed below, are cases in point.)

- The expert case put up to the Commission is clearly incompetent.

This list is by no means exhaustive. The Commission has been subject to judicial review applications asserting that the Commission should have referred on the basis of new expert evidence, but to date no application made on such grounds has succeeded. It goes without saying that the Commission's decisions on such matters must always be made with care, and bearing in mind the Court's willingness to make pragmatic exceptions to its general practice.

Expert evidence referrals considered by the Court

All of the cases referred by the Commission primarily on expert evidence matters are considered in this study. Note that expert evidence referrals based upon coerced/compliant confessions are considered in chapter 6 whilst referrals based on 'psychological' defences to charges of murder are considered separately in chapter 8. Leaving those cases aside for the present, the Commission's expert evidence referrals have been considered within the following categories:

- Convictions quashed following Commission referral in which the competence of trial expert evidence has been a central issue.

- Other new expert evidence cases quashed following referral by the Commission.

- New expert evidence cases upheld following reference by the Commission.

- Cases where new expert evidence has been rejected by the Court of Appeal as inadmissible.

The important case of Barry **George**, convicted of the murder of the television presenter, Jill Dando, stands somewhat outside any of these categories. Although his case was decided outside the ten-year period covered by this study, it will be considered in some detail.[7]

Convictions quashed following Commission referral in which the competence of trial expert evidence has been a central issue
SIDS cases
In Sally **Clark** and Donna **Anthony**, to which reference has already been made, a central issue was the misleading evidence of Professor Roy Meadows as to the statistical improbability of multiple SIDS deaths in one family (and see also on the same point the non-Commission case of Angela *Cannings*). The case of **Clark** raised a number of other matters (including serious non-disclosure) and her conviction would almost certainly have been quashed even in the absence of concerns about Professor Meadows' evidence. By contrast, **Anthony** is a case where, even though the Court felt that there was considerable extraneous evidence to support the jury's verdict, the introduction of the misleading and discredited statistical evidence provided substantially self-standing grounds for allowing the appeal.

Following the judgments of the Court in Sally **Clark** and *Cannings*, there was widespread concern expressed that these cases might represent only the tip of the iceberg of wrongful convictions following cot deaths. In consequence, the Attorney General announced a general inquiry into 258 cases (later raised to

297) where parents had been convicted of killing their children – and which featured the evidence of expert witnesses, including Professor Roy Meadows. The Attorney General finally identified 28 cases meriting further investigation.[8] Six of these have been the subject of application to the Commission, including the case of Donna **Anthony** whose case was referred and quashed, and **Gore** whose conviction for infanticide was referred by the Commission but was upheld by the Court in June 2007. The remaining four cases were investigated by the Commission but not referred.[9] This will no doubt appear to be a somewhat paltry outcome, given the strength of criticism expressed of Professor Meadows and the number of cases covered by the Attorney General's initial enquiries. However, it should be noted that expert evidence is uncontentious in most cases, even where the expert himself (or the expert approach used) has subsequently become the subject of criticism; the very limited outcome of the Attorney General's review must be understood with this point in mind.

Pathology

In **Boreman and Byrne**, the issue was whether, in a murder trial, the jury could be certain that the victim's death was due to injuries inflicted by the defendants or whether it was possible that death had been due to a fire for which the defendants may not have been responsible. Dr Michael Heath, a pathologist, gave evidence that the injuries were the operative cause of death. Dr Heath's conclusions were subject to forceful criticism in a new expert report obtained by the Commission and, moreover, Dr Heath's professional standing and competence had been more generally criticised in several other cases. The Commission and the Court both concluded that on the 'jury impact' test, whilst the jury *might* have concluded, irrespective of Dr Heath's evidence, that they were sure of the case against the defendants, the evidence given by Dr Heath might have 'tipped the balance' and the convictions were quashed.[10]

Note also the cases of **Nicholls** and **Wickens** which are discussed in chapter 8.

Interpretation of sexual injury

In all the cases below expert evidence concerning the state of the complainant's vagina or anus was tendered in support of allegations of sexual assaults. All the convictions were quashed following referral by the Commission.

In **F (Reginald)**, the complainant gave evidence that she had been regularly penetratively assaulted by her father from the age of 12 and over many years. The case only came to court at a time when the complainant was adult and – by her own evidence – had had a sexual relationship of a short duration. Expert evidence was given at trial by a relatively inexperienced doctor that she could establish from vaginal examination that the complainant had had regular sexual intercourse over a period of some years. The trial expert's conclusion was said to be without any basis by more experienced experts who gave evidence at appeal.

In **B (Kevin)**, expert evidence was given, inter alia, by Dr Camille de San Lazaro that features of the complainant's anus supported his allegations of buggery. Dr San Lazaro's professional methods and objectivity had been subsequently subjected to strong criticism in a libel case, *Lillie and Reed v Newcastle City Council*.[11] The Court concluded that the medical evidence at trial had been 'superficial'. The Court also noted the concession made by the prosecution that 'if we were to take the view that at the trial the evidence of Dr San Lazaro formed a significant part of the prosecution case then the Crown would be in difficulty in resisting this appeal'.

C (Martin) was convicted of rape of his very young daughter. There was expert evidence at trial from a doctor who examined the complainant some three years *after* C had been ejected from the complainant's household, at which point he had ceased to have the opportunity to commit the offences. The expert's gynaecological examination supported the conclusion that the young complainant (who had still then not reached the age of puberty) had at some previous time been sexually penetrated. The jury was not told that an earlier examination by the same doctor had found that the complainant had then been a virgin. This earlier examination had also taken place *after* C had ceased to have any opportunity of contact with the complainant. It, therefore, provided the most powerful evidence that penetration had first occurred between the dates of the two examinations and at a time when C was no longer 'on the scene'. The report of this earlier examination had been withheld from the defence and the Court.[12]

In **B (David)**, there had been evidence at trial that the complainant had been sexually penetrated. A more thorough examination, which had been carried out following B's conviction, concluded without reservation that the complainant was a virgin. Unfortunately, the detailed facts of this somewhat shocking case are not set out in the Court's very brief judgment.

Facial mapping

Facial mapping is an immensely contentious technique in which images which do not lend themselves to recognition (such as indistinct CCTV stills) are analysed to establish whether there is an expert case that the blurred image is of the defendant. Facial mapping evidence is generally based upon a 'compare and contrast' between the blurred CCTV image of the malefactor and a clear and reliable image of the defendant. Comparison is made of matters such as the relative size and position of features of the face and head in order to gauge the degree of similarity. The technique can never be used to say with certainty whether the blurred image is that of the defendant and expert opinion can only be properly expressed with degrees of confidence. There has been widely expressed concern that some experts fail to make sufficient allowance for the limitations of the technique in giving evidence. In **Bacchus**, the Crown's expert facial mapping witness had been accepted by the Crown as unreliable and the appeal was not contested.

Auditory recognition

In **O'Doherty**, expert evidence was given at trial that it was 'highly probable' that the defendant's voice was the same as the voice of a man who had called the 999 service, admitting to a serious assault. The expert's opinion was based upon auditory recognition. Her conclusions and her methods were attacked by expert witnesses at the appeal following referral using digital voice recognition techniques. Allowing the appeal, the Northern Ireland Court of Appeal stated that:

> in the present state of scientific knowledge no prosecution should be brought in Northern Ireland in which one of the planks is voice identification given by an expert which is solely confined to auditory analysis.

Interpretation of machine controls

In **Jenkinson**, patients at a hospital had been subjected to injury due to interference with the controls of a ventilation machine. The case against J rested substantially upon expert evidence that examination of the controls showed that they had been tampered with at times when J had been on shift. Expert evidence obtained by the Commission showed that this expert opinion was entirely baseless, a view which the trial expert himself eventually accepted. Again, the Court's very brief judgment fails to set out the shocking facts of this case.

Explosives

In **Assali**, the appellant was convicted of making explosives contrary to s4 Explosive Substances Act 1883. Expert evidence was given by Dr Fereday to rebut the evidence of the defendant (who owned and managed an electronics factory) that the timer devices were designed for innocent purposes. The defence at trial was unable to contest this evidence, as the only expert they could find deferred to the conclusions of Dr Fereday. Subsequently, Dr Fereday's evidence and approach had been discredited in another case, *Berry*,[13] and Dr Fereday's methods in Mr Assali's case were also criticised in the expert reports obtained by the Commission. The Crown did not contest the appeal.

Forensic methodology
In **P (Christopher Scott)**, there was evidence to suggest that there might have been cross-contamination or confusion between vaginal swabs and anal swabs. The defendant admitted vaginal intercourse which he said was consensual and denied anal intercourse. The anal swabs were adduced to prove that anal intercourse had occurred but the jury were unaware of the possibility of cross-contamination or confusion. The expert accepted that this might have occurred and the appeal was not contested.

Other new expert evidence cases quashed following referral by the Commission
DNA cases
Surprisingly, only two convictions were quashed in the first ten years of the Commission's existence on the basis of DNA evidence. It should be added that there have been a number of other cases – including the famous case of **Hanratty** – where DNA tests carried out by the Commission have been supportive of the safety of applicants' convictions.

In **Shirley**, S was convicted in 1988 of rape and murder. One of the four planks against S was that old-fashioned blood grouping tests upon semen swabs from the victim's vagina showed a match with S (but also with 23 per cent of the population at large). DNA tests arranged by the Commission of exhibits retained by the Forensic Science Service proved conclusively that the semen was not attributable to S (and it appeared not very likely that the victim had had any recent intercourse with anyone apart from the rapist). The Crown resisted the appeal, unsuccessfully arguing that the remaining planks of the evidence still provided a powerful case against S.

In **Otoo**, O, who was a law student, appeared an unlikely perpetrator of a petrol station robbery but he was sunk by the match between indentations in his training shoes and a footprint made in a flower bed by the robber in the course of his getaway. O's account that he had been forced to swap footwear with another person appeared to be a cock-and-bull story, but modern DNA testing established that DNA extracted from bodily fluids impregnating the insole of the trainers matched the person named by O as having forced him to swap footwear.

Bloodspatter

In the much discussed case of Sion **Jenkins**, a major issue at trial was whether microscopic droplets of the victim's blood found on J's clothing must have been caused by his inflicting the fatal injuries; J's case was that the bloodspattering must have occurred when he tended to the dying victim after she had been assaulted by some other person. The case was referred by the Commission on other grounds, but was quashed by the Court on the basis of new forensic evidence providing support for the possibility that if J's account that he tended the victim as she lay dying were true, the force of exhalation through her nose could have caused the bloodspattering – a possibility which the Crown's experts had rejected at trial. The case is notable for the fact that a new (and decisively better) expert case was mounted on appeal, notwithstanding that great effort and expense had been mounted by both sides in exploring this aspect of the forensic case at trial.

Expert evidence as to the cause of bloodstaining also featured in the appeal of Stephen **Downing**, who was convicted of murder in 1974. In a report prepared for the Crown at the time of trial, the prosecution expert, Mr Lee, stated the opinion that bloodstains found on D's clothes:

> ... might well be described as a textbook example of the pattern of blood staining which might be expected on the clothing of the assailant in a wounding such as that which [the victim] suffered.

The case was referred by the Commission partly on the basis of criticism of this evidence (but principally on other grounds). Experts for both the Crown and D agreed at appeal that Mr Lee's evidence was effectively worthless, D's expert stating that:

> the blood staining is equally consistent with the appellant's account in evidence that he had contact with the deceased only after she had been seriously injured, as it was with his guilt of the offence.

The Court concluded that the expert evidence at trial should be entirely discounted.

Fingerprints

In **McNamee**, the appeal issue was the reliability of expert evidence that a thumbprint linked to certain explosives used by terrorists could be matched to M's thumbprint. The Court heard the evidence of no fewer than 14 fingerprint experts, much of whose evidence concerned the changes in the conventional wisdom as to the number of matching characteristics required to establish a fingerprint match.

ESDA[14]

In **Gorman and McKinney**, a Northern Ireland case, convictions were quashed on the basis of ESDA evidence to show that notes taken by police officers who had interviewed the suspects had been re-written, rebutting the officers' claim that the notes were entirely contemporaneous. The notes had been adduced to support the case that the defendants had confessed to the offences. The significance of the ESDA evidence was that the convictions of G and M rested heavily on the credibility of the interviewing officers' narrative accounts of the police interviews. The ESDA evidence threw strong doubt upon the credibility of their accounts.

In a further Northern Ireland case, **Boyle**, the facts and the conclusions of the Court were extremely similar and **Gorman and McKinney** was cited and followed. Both these cases are described more fully in chapter 13.

Forensic linguistics

In **Brown (Robert)**, a 1977 conviction was based in part on a confession statement which was said to have been of the defendant's own composition. The referral was based partly on linguistic analysis by Professor Coulthard, who concluded that the statement was produced, at least in part, by a process of questioning by police officers and answers from the appellant being converted into a monologue ostensibly emanating from the appellant. This significantly undermined the officers' account of the course of the interview (which was pre-PACE and unrecorded). Evidence to similar effect from Professor Coulthard was also given some weight by the Court in the case of Derek **Bentley.**

Note, by contrast, **Burton,** where the Court declined to receive the evidence of Professor Coulthard because – in the context in which the evidence was tendered – it went only to the credit of an undercover police officer and was inadmissible for that purpose.

Evidence relating to limitations of human memory

In the case of **H (J)**, the conviction of H for sexual offences against his daughter was quashed largely on the basis of evidence from Professor Conway that detailed information contained in the complainant's accounts of events when she was four years old greatly exceeded what she could have remembered from such a young age and that her accounts must therefore have been confabulated. The case is discussed in greater detail in chapter 9.

Evidence relating to reliability of witnesses

In **MacKenney and Pinfold**, the convictions of the appellants of six murders were quashed on the basis of expert psychiatric evidence (Dr Somekh) that the main prosecution witness, Childs, was subject to a personality disorder which made his evidence wholly unreliable. At the original trial in 1980, the trial judge had ruled (and the Court of Appeal upheld in 1983) that evidence to similar effect as to Childs' lack of reliability was inadmissible. The ruling by the trial judge had followed the case of *Toohey* v *Metropolitan Police Commissioner*[15] where it was held (in broad terms) that the reliability of a witness was a matter for the jury's commonsense assessment and not a matter for expert evidence. On the appeal which followed referral by the Commission, the Court considered that *Toohey* is now applied less restrictively and, therefore, Dr Somekh's evidence should be received. The Court concluded that Childs' evidence should be regarded as worthless in the light of Dr Somekh's evidence and the convictions were quashed.

Shaken Baby Syndrome (SBS)

The case of **Faulder**, which was referred by the Commission, was considered by the Court in a leading judgment, **Harris, Rock, Cherry and Faulder**, along with three other (non-Commission) SBS cases. There was (and remains) intense scientific debate concerning the inferences as to causation that can be safely drawn from certain forms of brain damage suffered by very young children. Putting it briefly, the kinetic energy leading to such damage could, in principle, be caused by shaking, hitting or falling. The conventional wisdom (as to when it is possible to say with confidence that injuries were due to shaking) had been strongly challenged by experts (Professors Whitwell and Geddes) who considered that some deaths said by other experts to have been due to shaking could have been caused by falling accidents. The Court of Appeal heard evidence from 37 experts (deploying a variety of scientific techniques) and its judgment runs to 275 paragraphs.[16] At the conclusion of reading this judgment, it is hard to dissent from the view expressed by the Commission's chairman,

Professor Zellick, that such cases put an extraordinary test upon the scientific understanding of randomly selected juries.

In **Faulder's** case, the Crown's position at trial was that the victim, N, suffered brain damage[17] due to shaking by his father, F; F's evidence was that N had been injured by a fall. The lead crown expert witness was Dr San Lazaro, whose objectivity had been subjected to severe criticism in the *Lillie and Reed* case as noted above. Her evidence at F's trial appears from the transcript to have been given in somewhat emotive terms. At appeal, the Crown, somewhat outrageously, abandoned its expert case that the jury had safely concluded that N was injured due to *shaking,* but argued that the conviction was safe on the basis of fresh expert evidence that it could now be equally safely concluded that N had been injured due to *hitting.* The Court allowed the appeal and its concluding paragraph is worth quoting:

> *... we are struck in this appeal by the very radical change in the Crown case; the jury considered one case, shaking, yet that case is now rejected and we have been asked to consider a totally different allegation of multiple blows to the head. During the summing up at trial the jury were told that Dr San Lazaro was "very, very experienced" and "specialises in child protection and abuse" cases. They were also reminded that Dr San Lazaro had said "I am as certain as you can be in medicine" in her opinion that this was a shaking injury. This "certain" opinion from the Crown's principal witness is now rejected by Crown experts who are equally firm in their own opinion. We have to consider the evidence in its totality, both at trial and before us. There are, as we have observed, now five different explanations put forward by experts for N's injuries.*

In F's appeal, the convictions of Harris and Cherry were also quashed whilst Rock's conviction was reduced from murder to manslaughter. Following the appeal verdict, the Attorney General reconsidered a number of shaken baby cases which had been considered in the previous review that followed the *Cannings* case. In the outcome he advised the solicitors of three defendants convicted of murder due to shaking that it might be appropriate for the safety of their clients' convictions to be considered further by the Court of Appeal. One of these three applied to the Commission and his case was not referred, the others have not (at time of writing) made any application.

There has been a postscript to this case in the judgment on the recent non-Commission appeal of *Holdsworth*.[18] The Crown's case at trial was that evidence of the prosecution medical witnesses proved that the victim had been killed by H (who was babysitting him at the relevant time) by blunt force head injury, causing cerebral oedema. At appeal, in the face of contrary medical evidence, Crown Counsel argued that the circumstantial evidence created an unanswerable case that H had killed the victim, irrespective of the scientific evidence albeit this had not been the Crown's position at trial. The Court noted the developing scientific understanding of head injury and stated:

> Conclusions of medical experts on the cause of an injury or death necessarily involve a process of deduction, that is inferring conclusions from given facts based on other knowledge and experience. But particular caution is needed where the scientific knowledge of the process or processes involved is or may be incomplete. As knowledge increases, today's orthodoxy may become tomorrow's outdated learning. Special caution is also needed where expert opinion evidence is not just relied upon as additional material to support a prosecution but is fundamental to it.

H's appeal was allowed and a retrial was ordered.[19]

Attention Deficit Hyperactivity Disorder

In **Friend**, the defendant, Billy Joe Friend, was aged 14 when tried for murder – he was considered to have a mental age of eight, although (perhaps unfortunately for him) he looked older than his chronological age. The killing had been committed by his older brother, Ned, whom Billy Joe had called in to sort out an altercation between friends. The case against Billy Joe rested on the doctrine of joint enterprise and there were some difficult questions about Billy Joe's intent in fetching Ned, and his foresight of violence, which might have taxed a more intellectually able defendant called upon to give evidence but were certainly well over Billy Joe's head. Application was made under s35(1)(b) Criminal Justice and Public Order Act 1994 that although Billy Joe was fit to stand trial, his mental condition made it *undesirable* for him to give evidence and, therefore, no adverse inference should be drawn if he declined to do so. The judge rejected the application and, after Billy Joe was not put up to give evidence, the judge directed the jury that it was open to them to draw an adverse inference from the fact that he had not done so.

The conviction was quashed following referral by the Commission on the basis of abundant new evidence that Billy Joe suffered from Attention Deficit Hyperactivity Disorder (ADHD), supporting the conclusion that he would have been unable to follow trial proceedings and it should not have been left to the jury to draw an adverse inference from his failure to give evidence. There were also related issues about the admissibility of evidence from police interviews. ADHD had not been argued at trial. The Court noted:

> The understanding of ADHD has, on the expert evidence before us, significantly increased since the date of trial. Through no fault of the appellant or his advisers or anyone, the nature and extent of the appellant's problem was not fully appreciated at trial, as it now has been.

Friend is a good example of new evidence based upon developments of scientific understanding since trial. It is the view of Professor Gudjonsson,[20] who was involved in this case, that ADHD may also be relevant to the safety of other convictions of child defendants.

New expert evidence cases upheld following reference by the Commission
In several other cases, convictions referred by the Commission on the basis of new expert evidence have been upheld by the Court of Appeal. The Court's reasons for doing so are outlined briefly below. Of the cases listed below the greater number were referred quite early in the Commission's existence and, upon reflection, some of these earlier referrals possibly appear naïve. Subsequently, as discussed below, the Commission has undoubtedly 'raised its game' in expert evidence cases, having absorbed the lessons of cases such as **Hakala**, **Bamber**, **Maloney** and **Wooster**. This may possibly result in fewer expert evidence cases going forward from the Commission, but it should also mean that those cases referred on the basis of expert evidence are more strongly and robustly argued than in the past – which should not be a bad outcome for the Commission's applicants.

ESDA
In **Hakala**, the Court rejected an appeal based on new ESDA evidence. The facts of this case have been previously referred to at chapter 3.

DNA
In **Bamber**, the jury had to consider whether B had shot five members of his family, as argued by the Crown, or whether, as contended by the defence, B's sister, Sheila Caffell (SC), might have shot the other four victims before turning the gun on herself. The prosecution contended that a sound moderator (silencer) had been used and traces of blood on the silencer were found by the blood grouping tests then available to have been compatible with SC's blood grouping but with none of the other victims. It was part of the prosecution case

that if the silencer was contaminated with SC's blood when SC was shot, it was physically impossible that SC could also have been the person who pulled the trigger. The case was referred by the Commission on the basis of DNA evidence to show that the blood on this silencer could not have derived from SC but could have come from one of the other victims. The scientific case that the scenario contended by the defence was a physical impossibility was, therefore, undermined.

In an immensely detailed judgment[21] the Court of Appeal discounted the significance of the new DNA evidence principally on the ground that there was every possibility that the DNA findings obtained by the Commission were due to the contamination of exhibits – the forensic scientists at the time having no notion of the sensitivity that DNA testing would in the future provide or of the extent of safeguards required to guard against contamination. The Court also reached its conclusion having regard to its 'take' on the whole of the evidence which, being strongly inculpatory of B, would inevitably have affected the weight that any jury would give to forensic evidence which (once the possibility of contamination was taken into account) it considered to be tenuous. The Commission was not criticised by the Court in its judgment, but the judgment caused considerable reflection within the Commission that the rejoinder to the arguments raised by the DNA evidence – which had come out very clearly at the appeal – had not been considered by the Commission in making reference. Whilst it would be going much too far to say that the referral of **Bamber** was misconceived, it is a case which has led the Commission to 'raise its game' in making forensic assessment of the significance of new scientific evidence.

Firearms
Cleeland concerned an appellant who was convicted of murder by the use of an antique firearm. The conviction was referred on the basis of new expert evidence criticising the evidence of the trial firearms expert, Mr McCafferty. In a highly complex case, the Court considered whether, applying the **Pendleton** jury impact test, the case was one of 'any difficulty' within the formulation of Lord Bingham. The nub of the Court's conclusion was as follows:

> In all the circumstances therefore, it does not seem to us that the undoubted error as to the choking of the left hand barrel which Mr McCafferty made in his examination and report upon the G&M shotgun submitted to him casts any real doubt upon the validity of his evidence that the fatal shot could have been fired from the left hand barrel of that gun. [It is to be noted that the effect of his evidence never went further than that.] Accordingly, even if

that error had been corrected when the evidence was placed before the jury, it seems to us quite impossible to hold that the totality of the evidence both old and new, would have led the jury to come to a different verdict. Certainly, the revelation of that error does not lead us to conclude that the conviction is unsafe upon that ground.

Accident reconstruction

Maloney and **Probyn** were both convicted of murders, which they were said to have attempted to conceal by staged car accidents. Both cases were referred on the basis of new accident reconstruction expert evidence, which added some weight to the respective defendants' accounts and (in M's case) included criticism of the main Crown accident reconstruction witness.

In **Maloney**, the Court not only upheld the conviction but declined to receive the new expert evidence, reasoning that the evidence could have been adduced at trial and, in any event, would make no impact on the strength of the Crown's case. The Court stated:

> *The material test for the Court ... in considering whether to "receive" the [new] evidence ... is whether ... "it may afford any ground for allowing the appeal", that is, for holding the conviction to be unsafe. The issue of unsafety ... is one for the Court in the light of the evidence before the jury and the proposed fresh evidence; see R v. Trevor [1998] Crim L.R. 652. The issue is not whether the Court considers, in the light of the proposed fresh evidence, that a jury might conceivably have reached a different decision if it had heard it. So, the Commission and the Court should beware against adopting, consciously or unconsciously, a train of thought that unless they can be certain the jury would have convicted had they heard the proffered fresh evidence, the conviction must be unsafe. However, the Court, in a case of any difficulty should usually "test their own provisional view by asking whether the evidence, if given at the trial, might reasonably have affected the decision of the jury to convict" – "the jury impact test"; see R v. Pendleton, per Lord Bingham of Cornhill at paras. 18 – 19, and R v. Hanratty, at para. 93, citing the judgment of Judge LJ in R v. Hakala [2002] EWCA Crim 730 at para. 11.*

It is hard to argue with the Court's approach on the facts of M's case, and this was by no means one of the Commission's finest referrals.

Probyn – previously mentioned in chapter 3 – was a case where the issue was whether or not P had pushed the victim in her car into the River Severn. In applying **Pendleton**, the Court emphasised the overwhelmingly formidable evidence to support the Crown's case, notwithstanding that the new expert evidence gave some limited additional support to Mr P's case.

Banknote contamination

In **Benn and Benn**, the issue was the reliability of expert evidence that traces of cocaine found on banknotes handled by the defendants supported the case that they had been guilty of cocaine importations. There were issues both concerning the possibility of innocent contamination and concerning the statistical inferences drawn by the prosecution witnesses. The soundness of the methods used by the prosecution experts (MSA Limited) had been the subject of virulent and even vitriolic debate but, in **Benn and Benn** and in another (non-Commission) case, *Compton*,[22] the Court found itself profoundly unimpressed with the appellants' expert witness. This appeal failed, therefore, in large measure, due to concern about the quality of the new expert evidence.

Ligatures

In both **Gilfoyle** and **Kavanagh**, a central issue in the appeals was new evidence to support the possibility that the respective victims might have died due to self-strangulation rather than murder. In **Gilfoyle**, the new evidence was provided by a ligature expert and in **Kavanagh**, the new evidence was provided by pathologists. In both cases, the Court considered that the new evidence shifted the weight of the overall evidence very little from where it had been at trial.

Pathological evidence re fractures

There was a similar outcome in **Fannin**. F was convicted of murder, death being due to punching injuries – F contended that he had not intended serious bodily harm. The conviction was referred on the basis of pathological evidence (Dr West) offering fresh theories as to the cause of fractures to the victim's skull and supporting the conclusion that the blow had not been as hefty as the jury had been led to believe. The Court (pre-**Pendleton**) put this new evidence in context and upheld the conviction:

> There was also the eyewitness evidence of Mr Georghiades, who said it lifted
> [the victim] off the ground, "an extremely powerful punch", unlike anything
> he had ever seen before, and the evidence of Mr Lewis, who also said that
> he had never seen a punch like it. Those descriptions were put to Dr West,
> who said that there was nothing in the medical evidence to cast doubt upon

them. It follows that even if Dr West's evidence had been before the jury,
they would still have been bound to find that, as Dr West accepted, this
appellant delivered a powerful blow. He was a professional boxer who may
or may not have had an accurate appreciation of his own strength, but that
was something fully canvassed at the trial.

Scene of crime evidence

In **May**, the referral and appeal were based on new expert evidence casting
doubt on the sufficiency of the work done by the Scenes of Crime Officers. In
a much criticised judgment, the Court deprecated the significance of the new
scene of crime evidence and also adopted a somewhat indulgent view of the
shortcomings of the scene of crime evidence tendered at trial.

Cell phone triangulation evidence

In **Steele, Whomes and Corry**, a secondary ground of referral was 'enhanced'
cell phone triangulation evidence. S and W had given evidence as to their
movements and whereabouts at the time that the offences had taken place.
The convictions were referred on other grounds (discussed in chapter 2) but
the Commission also gave some very limited weight to fresh evidence from the
trial telecommunications expert to bolster the case that cell phone triangulation
evidence supported the defendants' account of their movements. The Court
felt that, although the evidence was more detailed in some respects than it had
been at trial, it added nothing of substance to the defence case, and declined to
receive the evidence.

Ballistics

In **Wooster**, W was convicted of the murder of the victim with a revolver. He
had shot at the victim's car as it made its way from a quarry where W had been
'larking about' and showing off his gun. The Commission referred on the basis
of the evidence of a ballistics expert (Dr Renshaw) who estimated that the car in
which the victim had been travelling when shot was 185 yards distant when the
shot was fired and considered that the trajectory of the bullet would have fallen
over this distance. This supported the case that W had aimed above the car
and could not have meant to shoot to kill. This was thought to strengthen W's
case that the shooting was a tragic case of horseplay having fatal consequences,
justifying a verdict of manslaughter rather than murder. The trouble was that –
as in **Hakala** – the expert case did not go with W's evidence at trial:

> *... the proposition that the car was 185 yards away or so does not fit with*
> *the appellant's own account. The appellant's own account was that he fired*

down. That was the way he exculpated himself. He did not seek to exculpate himself by saying that he fired over the car or that he fired when it was a long distance away. It seems to us, in those circumstances, that the evidence of Dr Renshaw is evidence which, if it was called before a jury, would clearly have had no effect upon the jury's deliberations, for the reasons that we have given. In those circumstances … we do not consider that it is appropriate to receive that evidence and accordingly that ground of appeal falls away.

As with **Hakala**, it is probably fair to say that the Commission would not today refer a case on the basis of an expert case so clearly inconsistent with the defence trial evidence.

New expert evidence rejected by the Court of Appeal as inadmissible

In a small number of cases, new expert evidence in Commission cases has been treated by the Court as inadmissible. Of such cases perhaps the most contentious is **Smith (Allen)**, who was convicted of rape. It was common ground that S had accepted an invitation to the complainant's home and that intercourse had taken place, the only issue in dispute being consent. The case was referred and the appeal was argued on the basis of evidence given by psychiatrists (Cordess and Swann) that the complainant suffered enduring histrionic personality disorder, which was said to have had 'a direct effect on her credibility when she makes accusations and also on her ability to give honest testimony'. There was also material from social services files to corroborate the doctors' conclusions. Having heard the evidence of the psychiatric witnesses, the Court held that:

> *neither witness gave evidence tending to show that, by reason of mental disability, the complainant was incapable of giving reliable evidence, or that her capacity to give reliable evidence was substantially impaired on the one matter in dispute, namely consent*

and that, following the authorities of *Toohey*[23] and *MacKenney (No 1)*,[24] the evidence was inadmissible. It might be noted in passing that – pace the Court's reasoning – the issue raised by the new evidence was not necessarily whether it was *impossible* for the complainant to give reliable evidence but whether, in a case which relied on the jury's assessment of her credibility, the jury might have taken a different view of her evidence. Note also that the Court has subsequently effectively overruled *MacKenney (No 1)* in the appeals of **MacKenny and Pinfold** (see chapter 3) which followed a later reference by the Commission.

Barry George

G was convicted of murder, the case against him consisting of four elements, namely (i) his appearance at the scene of the murder some hours after it took place; (ii) his lies in police interview; (iii) his considerable attempts to create a false alibi and (iv) a single speck of firearm discharge residue (FDR) found in his coat pocket when examined approximately one year later. The weight to be attached to the FDR evidence was a major issue at trial and appeal, but in brief, both trial judge and the Court of Appeal at the first-time appeal concluded that 'the FDR evidence was capable of supporting the Prosecution case and that its weight was a matter for the jury'.

In fact, the forensic significance of the FDR particle had been subject to keen internal debate within the Forensic Science Service (FSS), but this had not been disclosed to the jury. The forensic results were analysed prior to trial by an FSS scientist named Dr Evett, who was developing a technique called 'Case Assessment and Interpretation'. Put very briefly, Dr Evett considered the FDR evidence in the light of the alternative hypotheses: (i) that Mr George had committed the murder and that that accounted for the FDR particle found in his pocket a year later and (ii) he had not committed the murder but the microscopic FDR particle had got into his coat pocket in some other (unknown) way. He considered that both propositions were more or less equally unlikely and, therefore, depreciated the significance of the FDR evidence. Dr Evett discussed his conclusions with his colleague, Mr Keeley, who later gave evidence for the prosecution at G's trial, but Mr Keeley made no reference to Dr Evett's reservations in giving his trial evidence.

Subsequently, Dr Evett's methodology was largely adopted by the FSS, which issued new guidelines in 2006 on 'the assessment, interpretation and reporting of firearms chemistry cases'. These guidelines noted:

> Whilst the presence of residue in the environment is considered to be extremely rare, persons who associated with firearms users might unknowingly and unwittingly pick up the odd particle of residue. This is the so called 'lifestyle' issue. There has been an increasing trend for investigators to gather intelligence information and look for any incriminating evidence against a suspect and to use this as part of the bad character evidence. Casework experience of searching through whole wardrobes of clothes shows that single particles are occasionally detected.

> *Single particles present a particular problem being the smallest detectable amount of residue it is possible to find. A single particle is defined as one particle found on an item or group of items from a single source, e.g. samples and clothing from a suspect all taken at the same time.*

> *Unfortunately, it is not possible to say when or how single particles were deposited. It cannot be determined if they are the last remains of some prior association with firearms, or whether they have been deposited quite recently from some lightly contaminated source.*

The Commission, having regard to Dr Evett's reservations, and the issues raised by the guidelines, commissioned a report from two further experts – Dr Moynehan and Miss Shaw. In the conclusions of their report they stated:

> *In our opinion, it would be just as likely that a single particle of discharge residue would have been recovered from the pocket of Mr George's coat whether or not he was the person who shot Ms Dando nearly a year previously. Consequently, we consider that the FDR findings in this case would be reported as inconclusive with regard to the issue of whether or not Mr George shot Ms Dando.*

This new evidence did not come wholly out of the blue. The defence experts at trial had strongly urged upon the jury the possibility of innocent contamination, but this had been resisted as extremely unlikely by the prosecution expert, who failed to discuss the fact that the first hypothesis (ie that the FDR particle could be linked to the shooting a year before) was essentially no less unlikely. At the second appeal which followed the Commission's reference the same prosecution experts conceded this point. As the Court's judgment notes:

> *In that respect their evidence at the trial was in marked conflict with the evidence that they have given to this court with the result that the jury did not have the benefit of a direction that the possibility that the FDR had come from the gun that killed Miss Dando was equally as remote as all other possibilities and thus, on its own, entirely inconclusive. In the light of the way in which Mr Keeley now puts the matter, we have no doubt that the jury were misled upon this issue.*

Applying the **Pendleton** test, the Court quashed G's conviction but ordered a retrial.

Some reflections

There has been enormous tabloid interest in the reliability of expert evidence, given added impetus by cases such as Sally **Clark** and, more recently, the salt-poisoning case of *Gay and Gay*,[25] who were found not guilty following retrial in March 2007. Much of the discussion has been unenlightening, taking the form of ad hominem attacks on individuals, such as Professor Meadows. Unfortunately, despite its intensive efforts, the proceedings and reports of the House of Commons Select Committee on Science and Technology[26] have not carried the debate very much further.

Based upon the Commission's experience over ten years, the following contributions to this expert evidence debate are offered for consideration:

1. There is great variation in the effective probative value of expert evidence put forward in criminal trials. At one extreme, there are scientific disciplines, such as DNA, where expert evidence can (generally) be adduced with great certainty and precision. At the other extreme, there are disciplines, such as facial mapping, auditory recognition and (in many cases) fingerprinting and sexual injury, where expert opinions can be highly judgmental.[27] Whilst scrupulous experts adopt highly modulated language to express degrees of certainty of opinion, it is not at all clear that juries get any great assistance in considering how useful the particular field of expert evidence is likely to be in deciding whether or not they can be certain of the defendant's guilt. Indeed, it is in the nature of the adversarial system of trial that prosecution and defence trade in certainties rather than nuances. It is impossible to avoid the conclusion that, in many cases, juries do not fully appreciate the areas of doubt and uncertainty that may exist.

2. There is a particular danger in complex medical or scientific cases that prosecution witnesses can present their hypotheses with excessive certainty. The case of **Faulder**, referred to above, is particularly striking. The prosecution case at trial was that the victim was beyond question the victim of *shaking* injuries, but the Crown was no less emphatic at appeal that the injuries were due to *hitting*. It is hard to resist the inference that the reservations about the shaking hypothesis were likely to have been available to the Crown, but these reservations were either not articulated or were expressly excluded by its expert witnesses at trial.

3. The case of Barry **George** is an extreme, but not necessarily uncommon example of the issue described at 2 above. In that case, faced with the alternative hypotheses (i) that the FDR particle found in Mr George's pocket was probative of guilt and (ii) that it was not, the prosecution expert put forward only the first hypothesis. This is a situation that can also arise in quite different areas of forensic science (for instance when experts opine whether or not irregularities of a child's sexual organs are or are not probative of abuse). It may be the case that the Crown expert sees his or her job as stating the case for the probative hypothesis, leaving it to the defence expert – and the adversarial process – to point out the opposite point of view. The George case exemplifies the fact that in the outcome juries may be misled about the weight and significance of the forensic case.

4. The difficulties outlined above have promoted the suggestion, expressed among others by Professor Zellick and by members of the House of Commons Select Committee on Science and Technology, that there may be merit in removing particularly complex matters of scientific evidence from the purview of juries. As noted above, the Court made somewhat light of these difficulties in its judgment in *Kai-Whitewind*.

5. There is an unhealthy 'trendiness' in the expert evidence debate. At the time of writing, there has been great interest in infant pathology cases following **Clark**, *Cannings, Gay and Gay* and other cases. Some years ago, the focus of interest (following the Cleveland controversy) was upon dubious diagnoses of sexual assault – a matter which now receives very little attention. Yet there have been sexual cases considered by the Commission in which evidence has been questionable and attitudes entrenched. Emphasis on the most current 'scandal' can lead to loss of wider perspective in this debate.

6. In sexual injury cases, particularly those affecting children, there is a danger that experts' detachment can be affected by concern for complainants. It is clearly right to suppose that the great majority of children who complain of sexual assaults do so truthfully and naturally doctors' primary concern is to protect such complainants as victims. Doctors giving evidence at criminal trials may, in some cases, have had previous involvement in making decisions about the legal care of the complainant.[28] It is arguable that such prior involvement

might affect the subsequent evidence – at least to the extent of excluding the articulation of degrees of uncertainty that can attach to the interpretation of sexual injury.[29] Moreover, doctors may end up recycling the child's complaint as expert evidence – the 'history', ie the fact that the child has complained, being presented by the doctor as evidence of the truth of the complaint – the case of **F (Reginald)** being a case in point.

7. New disciplines at the frontiers of forensic science afford dangers as well as opportunities in establishing where the truth lies. Note has already been made of **Bacchus**, which concerned facial mapping, and **O'Doherty**, which concerned auditory voice recognition. Facial mapping is a particularly contentious area. There is an expert school of thought that facial recognition is a complex psychological process and that facial mapping, by concentrating on measurable aspects of physiognomy, is a positively misleading technique. A moderate view in this debate is that facial mapping *can* be useful, so long as the limitations of this evidence are accepted by those giving it. It is not at all clear that this always happens in practice.

Note should also be made in this context of the use of ear print evidence, which was accepted as admissible by the Court of Appeal in the case of *Dallagher*.[30] The Court noted in that case:

> It is essential that our criminal justice system should take into account modern methods of crime detection. ... There are no closed categories where such evidence may be placed before a jury. It would be entirely wrong to deny to the law of evidence the advantages to be gained from new techniques and new advances in science.

That being the case, the reliability of ear prints as a forensic technique, nevertheless, remains extremely contentious. Subsequent to the period covered by this study, the Commission referred the case of Mark **Kempster** on the basis of new expert evidence criticising ear print evidence deployed by the Crown at trial. Giving judgment, the Court agreed that 'ear print comparison is capable of providing [identification evidence]' whilst noting the dangers of misinterpretation of such evidence. In K's case, the Court considered that the ear print match could not be assumed with the confidence asserted by the prosecution expert, Miss McGowan, notwithstanding that the latter had 'stuck to her guns' in giving evidence on appeal. The Court quashed the conviction that rested on this evidence. The report of the case nicely illustrates the possible hazards of over-confident reliance on novel forensic techniques.

There has also been recent controversy about a further 'frontier' technique employed by the Crown – DNA profiling using Low Copy Number (LCN) techniques. The technique is explained as follows in a Fact Sheet issued by the Forensic Science Service:[31]

> Since its implementation in the early 1980s, DNA profiling has developed rapidly to become more discriminating and more sensitive. Since 1999 The Forensic Science Service® (FSS®) has offered a specialist service that has had a major impact on police investigations for not only the most serious current crimes, but also those that happened decades ago.

> DNA Low Copy Number (DNA LCN) is an extension of the routine SGM Plus® profiling technique and enables scientists to produce DNA profiles from samples expected to contain very few cells, even if they are too small to be visible to the naked eye. Initially used for the most serious crime cases, the technique is now also used to help police investigating crimes such as burglaries and thefts. More recently the FSS has been called in to carry out DNA LCN testing in international cases, where standard DNA testing has failed to get a result.

> The main application of this technique is to target areas on items where it is believed that an offender may have transferred DNA through touch, like the residue believed to have come from cells such as skin or sweat, left in a fingerprint. DNA LCN profiles have also been successfully generated from items such as discarded tools, matchsticks, weapon handles and grabbed clothing.

> Given its increased sensitivity, DNA LCN can be a particularly useful tool for investigating serious crimes where other profiling techniques have been exhausted or when options for forensic evidence appear to be limited. For example, when there is a very small amount of material present.

LCN evidence was tendered by the Crown as a major part of the evidence against Sean *Hoey*,[32] the Omagh bombing case, which was heard in Northern Ireland by a Diplock judge, Mr Justice Weir. In acquitting the defendant, the judge (who was required to give reasons for his verdict) made forceful criticisms of the LCN evidence. This prompted a review by the Crown Prosecution Service of the use of this technique and an announcement by the Association of Chief Police Officers that it was suspending the use of LCN testing pending the outcome of the CPS review. After a brief period, the CPS announced that it 'had not seen anything to suggest that any current problems exist with LCN' and had approved the resumption of the use of this technique.[33]

A fuller *Review of the Science of Low Template DNA Analysis*, commissioned by the Forensic Science Regulator, was published in April 2008 by a team of distinguished forensic scientists led by Professor Brian Caddy.[34] The review validated the technique and rightly emphasised the importance of proper funding for the development of forensic knowledge. However, it also made numerous recommendations with respect to procedures and the training of the police and the forensic scientists. The report noted that 'developing aspects of evidence interpretation are still on-going' and that 'the challenges in terms of statistical interpretation of the data and in communicating them to a largely innumerate criminal justice system should not be under-estimated'. It recommended that scientific findings based upon this technique should always be presented with appropriate caveats.

The report may well be seen as something of a primer for the assessment and validation of other novel forensic techniques in the future. It is striking that it has taken the verdict of a Diplock judge to bring about this searching and welcome review.

8. Similar dangers arise where a scientific speciality is established but scientific understanding is developing. This was recognised by the Court in *Holdsworth* – discussed above – where the Court noted that 'today's orthodoxy may become tomorrow's outdated learning'. It is particularly important that scientific experts, on all sides, should be prepared to accept that their expert opinions may not be the last word on the subject. As the Court has recognised, both in **Faulder** and in *Holdsworth*, it is helpful for the criminal justice system to establish

novel systems of case management in such cases, so that expert witnesses can meet before trial to clarify the points of agreement and dispute between them.

9. The process of recognition and regulation of forensic disciplines lags behind practice. There have been strenuous efforts at self-regulation through the Council for the Registration of Forensic Practitioners (CRFP) but a scheme for voluntary registration has obvious limitations both in terms of the scope of sanctions and the extent of coverage. At the time of writing, the highly contentious area of facial mapping is not, for instance, within the scope of the CRFP scheme at all.[35] The government has now taken the initial step towards a statutory scheme of regulation with the appointment, in March 2008, of Andrew Rennison as the first Forensic Science Regulator.

10. It is important, on the other hand, to preserve due balance in the discussion of new and developing areas of forensic practice. There have been cases where relatively new forensic disciplines have assisted applicants to the Commission, such as forensic linguistics (**Brown (Robert)** and **Bentley**); analysis of memory (**H (J)** and **G (T)**), and consideration of the psychological characteristics of adolescents (**Blackburn** – discussed in chapter 6). It would be inconsistent to deprecate forensic techniques pursued by the Crown simply on grounds of novelty whilst pushing for novel techniques to assist the case of defendants.

11. The availability of best forensic advice to defendants is highly problematical for a number of reasons:

    •   Defence practitioners may come to a complex area of forensic knowledge with no notion as to what are the contentious issues or who the best experts are. The Crown will almost certainly have more experience of the expert field (and may well have engaged the most forensically experienced experts). There are no systematic means of identifying the most qualified experts and restrictions of legal aid may limit the time and resources available to defence solicitors in making appropriate enquiries.[36]

    •   There may be a shortage of experts who are practically in a position to make themselves available. In the medical field, for instance, new-style NHS contracts make it increasingly difficult for consultants to commit to giving evidence without booking leave. When trial fixtures collapse, remuneration is unlikely. Such mundane considerations can affect the practical ability of the defence to engage the experts it requires.

- Experts approached by defence lawyers to give evidence at trial may cover up their own inexperience (in the interest of earning professional fees) until exposed by cross-examination at trial.

12. The Court of Appeal approaches the expert evidence issue with a certain degree of detachment – and concern for the state of its own lists! It has pronounced in its own leading authorities:

- That – expert witnesses being interchangeable – it is only exceptionally the case that it should accede to fresh expert evidence on appeal on a matter previously canvassed at trial (*Steven Jones*).

- That conflicts of expert evidence, no matter how complicated, can always be left safely to be determined by the jury (*Kai-Whitewind, Gay and Gay*).

- That if the defence expert evidence goes off badly at trial, that is tant pis, but not a matter for the Court (*Kai-Whitewind*).

In this overall context, it would seem that the Commission's gatekeeper role is of particular importance. The Court having expressed its general attitude to expert evidence appeals, it would be easy for the Commission to avoid irritating the Court by declining to refer all but the clearest expert evidence cases. Such an approach would be misconceived. It is submitted that the Commission should not hesitate to refer where it considers that the defence expert case was 'muffed' for reasons outside the control of the defendant and to the detriment of the fairness of trial. If the Court of Appeal wishes to disdain the new evidence, that is a matter for it and not for the Commission. On the other hand, insubstantial expert evidence cases, or **Hakala**-type cases (where the expert case runs contrary to the factual scenario put forward by the defence at trial), are unlikely, in the view of this author, to merit referral.

Notes

1. Kate Malleson, *A Review of the Appeal Process*, HMSO, 1993. Research Study No 17 carried out for the Royal Commission on Criminal Justice.
2. Professor Meadows was struck off the medical register by the General Medical Council following a case which centred on his evidence in the case of Sally **Clark**. Subsequently, he successfully appealed to the High Court against the decision of the GMC and was restored to the register.
3. [1997] 1 Cr App R 86.
4. [2004] EWCA Crim 01.
5. [2005] EWCA Crim 1092.
6. For another example *see Campbell* [1997] 1 Cr App R 199 where fresh evidence was introduced as to the effects of epilepsy. The Court issued an extremely firm (and much cited) pronouncement against new defences being mounted on appeal:

> This court has repeatedly underlined the need for defendants in criminal trials to advance their full defence before the jury and call any necessary evidence at that stage. It is not permissible to advance one defence before the jury and, when that has failed, to devise a new defence, perhaps many years later, and then seek to raise that defence on appeal.

However, having made this point, the Court agreed to receive the new evidence and allowed C's appeal.
7. Mr George's case has been ordered by the Court to be re-tried. At the time of writing, his re-trial is in progress and the Court has reminded journalists of the reporting restrictions attaching to the case.
8. The Commission was not involved in the Attorney General's review but some of the Commission's former Case Review Managers were engaged to assist the Attorney General in carrying out this review.
9. Of the remaining 22 cases, four who had not previously appealed applied directly to the Court of Appeal; the remainder either informed the Commission that they did not wish to pursue an application to the Commission or have not pursued an application, having been informed of the possibility of doing so.
10. A review was subsequently carried out by the Commission to ascertain whether any of its closed cases which had involved Dr Heath's evidence should be referred, but concluded there were none. Enquiry showed that the evidence of Dr Heath had been wholly uncontentious in the great majority of cases.
11. [2002] EWHC 1600 QB.
12. Notwithstanding that this earlier report provided the strongest case that C had been the victim of a miscarriage of justice, the doctor who had provided these reports bizarrely sought to resist its disclosure on grounds of patient confidentiality.
13. *R v Berry (No 3)* [1995] 1 WLR 7.
14. Electrostatic Detection Apparatus – see chapter 3, endnote 4.
15. [1965] AC 595.
16. Much of the evidence related to the application of biomechanics – described by the Court of Appeal as the 'application of traditional engineering principles to living organisms'.
17. The other three victims all died as a result of their injuries.
18. [2008] EWCA Crim 971.
19. Note also the recent civil case of *Lancashire County Council v D and E* [2008] EWHC 832 (Fam) which contains a lengthy review of the expert evidence issues raised by such cases.
20. Expressed in conversation with the author.
21. The Court of Appeal – very unusually – also issued a brief summary of its judgment which can be found through *Casetrack*.

22. [2002] EWCA Crim 2835.
23. [1965] AC 595.
24. (1983) 76 Cr App R 278.
25. [2006] EWCA Crim 820.
26. See http://www.publications.parliament.uk/pa/cm200405/cmselect/cmsctech/96/9602.htm.
27. This also applies to much psychiatric evidence – discussed in other chapters.
28. This was the case, for instance, in **Faulder**.
29. This was very much a concern of the late Dr James MacKeith, a distinguished forensic psychiatrist and founding member of the Commission, who made a great contribution to the Commission's analysis of many of the expert cases described in this study.
30. [2002] EWCA Crim 1903.
31. http://www.forensic.gov.uk/forensic_t/inside/news/documents/DNA_Low_Copy_Number_000.doc.
32. The judgment in this case may be viewed at http://business.timesonline.co.uk/tol/business/law/article3083217.ece.
33. See http://www.cps.gov.uk/news/pressreleases/101_08.html.
34. See http://police.homeoffice.gov.uk/publications/operational-policing/Review_of_Low_Template_DNA_1.pdf?view=Binary
35. The CRFP's register may be examined at www.crfp.org.uk.
36. The CRFP register is a helpful step in the right direction, but provides only bare details of the registered experts and does not give those searching the register any assistance in judging the extent of an expert's expertise or relevant experience.

Chapter 5 - The approach to fresh evidence (3) – further considerations

Fresh prosecution evidence

It has become clear from the jurisprudence of the Commission that the prosecution has broad scope to put forward fresh evidence on appeal. Fresh prosecution evidence will be considered for admissibility under section 23 of the 1968 Act, and weighed in account by the Court, in the same way as new defence evidence. The likelihood of the Crown seeking to add to its trial case is inherently greater in a Commission case, where the appeal may be heard some years after trial and at a time when scientific or other techniques may be more advanced than they were at the time of trial.

This issue came up first in **Craven**, heard in 2000. C was convicted of murder through a nightclub glassing. The identification case against C was not the strongest and there was a good deal of media interest in his case as a possible miscarriage of justice. The Commission referred the conviction because the Crown had failed to disclose the fact that a fingerprint was found on the broken glass which the Crown identified as the murder weapon and that that fingerprint was not from the appellant – a 'severe' case of non-disclosure by any standards. The Court (pre-**Pendleton**) deprecated the significance of this information, giving vent to doubt whether the Crown should have committed itself to the proposition that this glass had necessarily been the murder weapon and observing that the position of the fingerprint on the glass was inconsistent with its use as a weapon of attack. However, equally or more important was fresh evidence about a bloodstain on the shirt of one Storey – it being clear from eyewitness evidence that the person who had glassed the victim had also fought Storey. DNA evidence was obtained by the Commission,[1] which showed that there was only a one in a billion chance that the bloodstain did not come from C or a person related to him. The Court was clear that in deciding whether the conviction was safe, it should consider all the new evidence available to it in the round:

> We take the view that this court, empowered as it is under section 23 of the Criminal Appeal Act 1968 to consider the jury's verdict in the light of fresh evidence, should do so in the light of all the fresh evidence that is available to it. We are entitled, as it seems to us, to consider whether the material which was withheld could have affected the jury's verdict in the light of all

> *the facts now known to this court. If it could have done, the conviction would be unsafe. If, on the other hand, the material that has been withheld has not, on a proper analysis of the facts known to this court, undermined in any way the verdict of the jury, then the conviction will be safe.*

The conviction was, accordingly, upheld in the light of the new evidence. **Craven** was followed in **Hanratty**, where fresh evidence was available to the Crown by the time the case came to appeal that seminal fluid found on the knickers of the rape victim, Valerie Storie, could be linked by DNA testing[2] to Mr Hanratty.[3] The Court rejected submissions that it should decline to exercise its discretion under section 23 to receive the DNA evidence, reasoning that 'it would undermine the public's confidence in the justice system' if evidence that established the true facts were excluded from consideration.

It is hard to disagree with the Court's exercise of discretion on this point. The DNA evidence in both cases pointed very powerfully to the guilt of the appellants. In Hanratty's case, although the issue of contamination continues to be argued by some advocates of his innocence, the new evidence (which came to light in the course of an outstandingly detailed and painstaking investigation by the Commission)[4] has effectively laid to rest a very long-standing and anguished debate about one of the most contentious criminal cases of modern times.

It is harder to support the Court of Appeal when new evidence gives the Crown 'open season' to present an embellished or even totally different case. Notable in this respect is the case of **Faulder** discussed in chapter 4. In this case, the Court admitted without debate new expert evidence from four witnesses who – as the Court was ultimately moved to observe – put forward a 'radically changed case' as to how Mr Faulder had allegedly inflicted injuries to his baby son. Whether it is right to allow the Crown to use section 23 to put up a totally new expert case (after concluding that the expert case heard by the jury is no longer defensible) is questionable in the extreme.

Legal incompetence

In a number of referrals, a central issue has been whether the Court should accede to new evidence or argument on the ground that it was not adduced at trial due to legal incompetence.

This is an issue which greatly exercised JUSTICE and others in pressing for reform of the law. In the report of the Waller committee, prepared for JUSTICE (and referred to in chapter 1), legal errors were identified as one of the 'top five' causes of miscarriage of justice. The subject was also identified as one of concern in the research study carried out for the Runciman Commission by Kate Malleson,[5] which proposed, simpliciter, that 'the errors of a convicted person's legal advisers should constitute valid grounds of appeal'. The Runciman Commission was concerned that the Court of Appeal set too high a standard in requiring evidence of incompetence on the part of legal representatives as a basis for appeal. It recommended that the test for receipt of new evidence should be not 'whether there was "flagrantly incompetent advocacy" [but] whether the particular decision, whether reasonable or unreasonable, caused a miscarriage of justice' – an eminently fair proposition.

In the intervening years, the test of legal incompetence has been relaxed to some degree along the lines proposed by Runciman. In *Nangle*[6] the Court stated:

> *... in the light of the present requirement under the European Convention on Human Rights "flagrant incompetence" may no longer be the appropriate measure of when this Court will quash a conviction. What Article 6 requires in this context is that the hearing of the charges against an accused shall be fair. If the conduct of the legal advisers has been such that this objective is not met, then this Court may be compelled to intervene.*

The judgment comes across somewhat grudgingly and the Court actually found no operative unfairness in Mr Nangle's case:

> *We would add that since we have not been persuaded that such deficiencies as there may have been resulted in any unfairness to the appellant, nor yet imperilled the safety of his conviction, it is not strictly necessary for us to consider what level of incompetence would have to exist before the Court could be satisfied that there had been a relevant breach of the provisions of Article 6(1).*

It is clear from this and other cases that persuading the Court of Appeal to accept that even this lower threshold of incompetence has been exceeded in practice is no easy task.

Nangle was followed in *Thakrar*[7] where the Court stated that the question:

> *is whether the appellant received a fair trial or whether such a trial was prevented by the failings in preparation on the part of his solicitors. Such an issue is to be determined by considering the proceeding [sic] as a whole, as*

the jurisprudence of the European Court of Human Rights makes clear, and it follows that one cannot confine one's attention merely to the solicitor's preparations in isolation. As this court said in Nangle *... if the conduct of an accused's legal advisors has been such that the objective of a fair trial is not met, then this court may be compelled to intervene.*

The issue of legal incompetence has been immensely difficult for the Commission. As an essentially lay body, it has become clear that the Commission is liable to be distrusted or even resented by the Court of Appeal when it has the temerity to suggest that learned counsel has slipped up on the job. It is arguable that the Commission has been to some degree intimidated by the hostile approach of the Court of Appeal to referrals based upon allegations of legal incompetence (especially on the part of trial counsel).[8] When the Commission has sensed a miscarriage or unsafe conviction associated with counsel's performance, it has tended pragmatically to engineer the Statement of Reasons to stress concerns about the outcome and to skirt round any concerns about counsel's role.

It hardly needs to be stated that in the Commission's other interface – with applicants – assertions of legal incompetence loom very large indeed. It is probably fair to say that a majority of such claims are plainly incredible and defamatory. It is a question of spotting serious concerns among spurious assertions – nuggets in ordure.

The approach that is to be taken by the Commission to allegations of incompetence has been prescribed by the Court of Appeal in the case of **Moseley.** M's conviction was referred on the basis of expert evidence (Dr Holloway) to support the case that she may have had a defence to the charge of robbery due to psychological fragility which made her subject to duress on the part of her boyfriend (who had pleaded guilty to the offence). M's defence at trial had been non-participation. The case was not defended on the basis of duress as M had apparently made the choice (for whatever reason) not to blame her boyfriend for her offending behaviour, and it is hard to see this as a legal incompetence case. The Court of Appeal however, reading between the lines, saw things differently:

We are in effect being invited to conclude that somewhere in the process her legal advisors (a) failed in their duty to the appellant to obtain the information now advanced by her, and expert evidence of the quality now supplied by Dr Holloway and/or (b) decided that her full account should

> *not be presented to the jury, and that accordingly relevant evidence was omitted.*

And it criticised the Commission for failing to put the case to trial solicitors:

> *The appellant's former legal advisors have not, as far as we can ascertain, been invited to respond to the criticisms made of them. We cannot see any sound basis for concluding that there was any forensic neglect, let alone forensic neglect sufficient to justify interference by this Court.*

The Commission was directed that in any future case where legal incompetence was raised, the 'case to answer' should be put to solicitors and counsel.

> *When an appeal is brought under section 9 of the Criminal Appeal Act 1995, and assuming that there is good reason for believing that genuine questions arise, directly or indirectly, about the competence of an appellant's legal representation, whether before or during the trial, sufficient to form the basis for an appeal with a realistic prospect of success on this ground, the procedures which obtain when such issues are raised by new counsel apply equally when they are raised by the CCRC. We draw attention to* Doherty & McGregor *(1997) 2 Cr. App. R. 218, and the Bar Council Guidance on the topic which was approved by Lord Taylor CJ (Archbold B - 48). Sensibly applied, these procedures will enable, first, the Commission, and if the matter were then pursued, this Court, to know precisely what instructions had in fact been given by the client to counsel, not only in her proof, but also in conference, and whether counsel had improperly prevented the client from giving evidence about relevant matters.*

The Commission has rigorously applied this approach subsequently, but with a bruising outcome in a number of cases.

In **Day**, D was convicted of a murder which had taken place during a brawl. The facts were not entirely straightforward as (i) there had been two separate fights and a question about who had been involved in which fight; (ii) there were questions about the role of different participants in the fight leading to the victim's death; and (iii) there were issues of causation. The Court accepted that pre-trial preparation by D's solicitors had been incompetent. The mode of preparation of D's statements was described by the Court as 'wholly unsatisfactory' and a letter written by solicitors was said by the Court to have 'displayed a wholly incorrect attitude to the solicitor's role and responsibilities'.

One of the solicitors' many failings had been a failure to instruct leading counsel until just before the trial – two briefs having been returned by previously instructed counsel. At the last minute they succeeded in engaging immensely distinguished counsel, Roy Amlot QC (although, being engaged so late in the day, Mr Amlot had to absent himself for part of the trial leaving the matter with very inexperienced junior counsel). Mr Amlot saw Mr Day in conference on Friday and the trial commenced the following Monday. The Commission put it to Mr Amlot that – instructed so late and with no satisfactory statements taken from Mr Day – he had been practically unable to explore all the issues in evidence at the trial. Mr Amlot delivered a very robust defence of his performance, but the Commission remained concerned that deficiencies in the defence handling of the case pre-trial had, arguably, affected the direction of the trial and it referred the conviction. The Commission was concerned in particular that, however able, learned counsel was only practically in a position to base his strategy upon the material made available by his instructing solicitors, which in the present instance had by no means 'bottomed out' all the relevant issues.

The Commission, to its no great surprise, received a flea in its ear when the case came to appeal:

> The case was certainly a serious one, but it could not remotely be described as complicated or difficult. ... It would have been well within the competence of criminal advocates less experienced than Mr Amlot to deal with [the contentious] matters effectively within the time and under the conditions presented to Mr Amlot. Mr Amlot told us, as he had told the CCRC, that he was confident that he had been able properly to master the case before the trial ... In our view the CCRC underestimated the ability of any competent member of the Bar to master a brief well within the time available to Mr Amlot ... In our view, Mr Amlot conducted the case with skill and judgment. The appellant was fortunate to have secured his services.

Generally, the Court stated:

> While incompetent representation is always to be deplored ... it cannot **in itself** form a ground of appeal or a reason why a conviction should be found to be unsafe ... in order to establish lack of safety in an incompetence case the appellant has to go beyond the incompetence and show that the incompetence led to identifiable errors or irregularities in the trial, which themselves rendered the process unfair or unsafe. (Emphasis in original)

Howell also proved a bruising case for the Commission. H was convicted of wounding a fellow resident at the lodging house where both lived, his defence being that the victim had been the aggressor. Having given a 'no comment' interview in the police station, the jury were told that they could draw adverse inferences from the fact that he had not given the account of events he relied on at trial when he had had the opportunity to do so at the police station, the obvious inference being that his account was late invention.

In fact:

- Prior to his police station interview, H had made a detailed written statement to his solicitors very similar in terms to his trial evidence.

- He had been advised at the police station by a solicitor's clerk who had advised H to make no comment at the police interview and he had followed this advice.

- The solicitors had obtained a statement from H pre-trial saying that he did not wish to call the solicitor's clerk to give evidence about this advice.

H's statement was quoted in the Court of Appeal judgment:

> "I Jeffrey John Howell have carefully considered whether I want [AO] called as a witness in my defence.
>
> I do _not_ want him called.
>
> I fully realise that the court i.e. the prosecution and the judge in his summing-up will tell the jury that my 'no replies' can be held against me. Indeed Mr Rouch QC has actually read the terms of the direction out to me.
>
> But having considered the matter I remain of the view that I do not want him called. I fully realise the consequences of this decision."

The Commission experienced difficulty in obtaining an account from solicitors and counsel as to why H had been advised not to put in evidence the fact that his account was not late invention and that he had in fact given a clear and detailed consistent account before being interviewed by police. The lawyers' eventual explanation did not appear persuasive to the Commission which referred the conviction. However, when the matter came to appeal, the defence lawyers' account was accepted without reserve by the Court, which rejected H's appeal with 'utmost prejudice'.

In two cases, during the course of pre-referral iterations, counsel agreed with the Commission that they had omitted to argue a relevant matter. In **G (G)**, a case of historic sex abuse discussed in chapter 9, trial counsel (eventually) agreed that on the facts, he could have sought a stay of proceedings as an abuse of process (there being important matters of fact in contention that it was impossible to put to the test after so many years). The Court, nevertheless, found G's professional representation above reproach. The same thing happened in **R (M)** where trial counsel agreed that he had omitted to raise a matter concerning a misdirection at trial. Although counsel himself was prepared to accept that there had been an omission, the Court decided otherwise.

Another 'unsuccessful' referral based upon allegations of legal incompetence was **Hall (Philip)**, convicted of actual bodily harm in the course of an incident between two groups of young men in the car park of a public house. The Commission felt that there was considerable material to support the case that one of Hall's confederates, A, had committed the assault but that this had not been pursued at trial by defence solicitors or counsel. The less than fulsome memory of trial on the part of both solicitors and counsel sharpened the Commission's suspicions of incompetence. However, following referral, counsel assigned to represent H quickly concluded from H's defence statement that, whatever the true narrative account, H's stance at trial had clearly exonerated A of any responsibility. Upholding the conviction, the Court noted that any strategy to inculpate A would have been caught in a web of contradictions. This is a case which shows the necessity for the Commission to make a full analysis of allegations of legal incompetence taking account of the information and the statements actually available to counsel at the time of trial.

Legal incompetence has, however, been found an issue to justify quashing convictions in the following cases:

In **Hester**, a critical alibi witness was not called at trial. The Commission found clear evidence that H had given instructions that this witness be called but that there appeared to have been a breakdown of communication, as a result of which no arrangements were made by defence solicitors for the witness to be notified or attend trial. In this case, the defence solicitors were in a state of some chaos at the time and the Law Society had to intervene and take over the practice very shortly afterwards. On these unusual facts, the Commission felt that the non-calling of a key witness might have been due to factors genuinely beyond H's control. The conviction was referred and quashed.

In **Allen (Alexander)**,[9] the prosecution adduced two confession statements – one said to have been made by A after he had been subdued by police at the time of his arrest, and one said to have been made in the police custody cell. Both statements were taken in circumstances which breached PACE Codes of Practice. The Court, most unusually, considered on the facts that counsel had erred in failing to make application under s78 PACE for exclusion of the statements[10] – on the facts there was a good prospect that the statements would have been excluded had such application been made. The Court concluded that the failure to have the statements excluded might have influenced the outcome of the trial, and quashed A's conviction. This has been the only Commission case to date in which non-argumentation of a PACE point has led the Court to quash a conviction. The Court has generally been unamenable to such arguments: **Gerald** and **Iroegbu**, both upheld after somewhat similar arguments were raised, are cases in point.

In **W (CP)**, W, then aged 25, was convicted of the rape of the 15-year-old friend of his sister. W's evidence was that the complainant had taken the lead and pretended to be older than she was. The jury was aware that W's sister, aged 16, had been in the house at the time of the events but was not called to give evidence, from which they could only have sensibly assumed that her version of events would not have helped W. The sister had, in fact, made a very long statement corroborating (with considerable supporting detail) her brother's version of events, which defence counsel had described in a pre-trial advice as 'vital'. Counsel had changed her mind on learning that the Crown had possession of photographs of the sister in provocative poses, which she apparently feared could be produced to attack the sister's credibility as a witness.[11] The Court expressed great unwillingness to criticise counsel for her decision not to call the sister but decided she had been wrong and 'reluctantly' allowed the appeal.[12]

In **Kamara**, trial counsel was caught short when K's co-defendant, entirely unexpectedly, changed his plea to guilty in the middle of the trial. As the judgment states, 'the defence team was clearly at a disadvantage by this turn of events', which raised the question whether counsel had acted erroneously in failing to apply for a retrial. The judgment continues:

> *We consider it would be wrong to stigmatise Counsel's decision as gross incompetence or that the promptings of reason and good sense pointed the other way. Following the reasoning in* Clinton, *we have to consider the effect of that decision in the light of the circumstances then prevailing and what happened when the trial resumed.*

In the outcome, the Court considered that the devastating effect of this unforeseen development, and counsel's omission to make an application for a retrial, were matters which contributed to the Court's 'uneasiness' about the safety of the conviction.

Finally in **Adams (Andrew)**, there has been (at last) a case where a division of the Court of Appeal, led by Gage LJ, has been willing to follow through a properly detailed and critical reconstruction of the forensic preparation for a major criminal trial. The case was immensely complex, but in brief, A was convicted of a gangland murder in Newcastle, to a large extent on the evidence of an informant, named T, and in a case where an associate, called H, had previously been tried and acquitted. Trial was scheduled to start on 21 April 1993. Leading and junior counsel first instructed by A's solicitors had previously represented H. On 8 April, they returned their briefs due to conflict of interest as it had become apparent that the defence strategy would raise questions about H's involvement. New counsel (Menary QC and Fordham) were instructed on 16 April and the trial was deferred for just five days – to 26 April – to give them time to prepare for trial. Among the criticisms accepted by the Court were:

- It should have been foreseen that the first instructed counsel would have to drop out due to conflict of interest.

- In an immensely complicated case, new counsel had insufficient time to prepare (this was conceded at the appeal by solicitors and junior counsel but disputed by senior counsel).

- Important pre-trial preparatory work was not done. Inter alia, the police HOLMES database was not interrogated; discrepancies of timings in police evidence were not bottomed out; and important questions about the nature of the understanding between police and the crucial informant witness, T, were not considered or pursued.

The Court did not accept every criticism made of solicitors or counsel but dealt with the points raised on their respective merits. The Court considered the authority of **Day**, but ultimately recognised that this was a case of the 'double whammy' of insufficient pre-trial preparation and late-instructed counsel, a matter which had so little concerned the Court in **Day**. The Court summarised the matter as follows:

> *It was this deficiency in pre-trial preparation which caused the failures which we have identified. It would be unfair to blame Mr Fordham and Mr Menary alone for all these failures. We have no doubt that they did their best. We have also no doubt that they believed that everything that ought to have been done had been done. But in our judgment they underestimated the time needed to complete the work.*

> *It is difficult to conclude that the criticisms and failures which we have found in respect of any one of the individual topics were on their own sufficient to render the verdict unsafe but we are quite satisfied that taken together, cumulatively they were sufficient to render the verdict unsafe. Each of these topics was important.*

Day and **Adams** are a fine 'compare and contrast' in exhibiting the approach taken by the Court to such cases. It could possibly be argued that the Court came to the right conclusion in both cases. It is arguable that in **Day** the facts were not so complicated that an experienced QC could not master them over the weekend. However, it is also arguable that in the face of robust justification of his actions by very highly respected counsel, Mr Day's case did not receive particularly open-minded consideration by the Court.

It remains the case that concerns expressed prior to Runciman, for instance with respect to late-returned briefs and the late instruction of counsel, apply in equal measure today. On top of those concerns must be added concern about the remorseless squeeze on the legal aid budget for pre-trial defence work by solicitors and by junior counsel. It is plain that every aspect of defence work – from the review of unused material, to the interviewing of witnesses of fact, and the instruction and briefing of counsel and expert witnesses – may be jeopardised by cuts in legal aid funding. These are, of course, matters for politicians (and ultimately the electorate) to make up their minds upon, but the Court for its part should recognise that concerns about defence preparation are not always the product of applicants' artifice or the Commission's naïveté. The Commission, for its part, will need to continue to sift spurious allegations of legal incompetence and misfeasance out from those having real substance, and hold its nerve in referring cases of concern.

Witness retraction cases

Witness retraction cases are not without difficulty for the Commission. Such cases certainly (although the Commission has compiled no systematic data on the point) loom larger among applications than referrals. Retractions most often come from witnesses who remain in contact with the convicted person, or his or her family, and many retractions tendered to the Commission relate to allegations of intra-family sexual abuse. There is clearly potential scope for suborning of witnesses in such cases. Indeed, there have been cases when the Commission, interviewing a witness said to be keen to retract his or her trial evidence, has found the witness anxious to retract the retraction. It is impossible to escape the inference that some such persons have been leaned on to change their evidence.

On the other hand, the Commission would scarcely be doing its job if it failed to consider both sides of the story. Accusations of offences – perhaps most particularly allegations of abuse within families – may be the outcome where relationships break down in bitterness. In chapter 9, there is discussion of the cases of A (Derek) and of C (Martin); A was accused of the rape of his ex-girlfriend's daughter, and C of the rape of his natural daughter. In both cases, the accusations were closely linked in time to family break-up and the cases gave real basis for concern that the child might have been prevailed upon to make (or magnify) the allegations. The Commission has to tread warily indeed in such cases.

There are a number of practical considerations to point out.

First, the Commission does not, as a matter of normal practice, approach non-expert witnesses[13] to ask whether or not they stand by their trial evidence. If a witness has given an account of events under oath, the Commission does not inquire whether he or she stands by this account unless there is clear and specific reason to suspect that he or she may wish to change it. The unsupported assertion by an applicant that a witness has admitted giving lying evidence (and such assertions are often made) would not, without more, be generally considered sufficient reason to interview the witness. It would be unjustifiable – surely – if the Commission were in any sense routinely to interrogate witnesses as to whether they had been telling the truth at trial. It is interesting to note, in this context, the reaction of the Court of Appeal in Northern Ireland in **Walsh** – a rare instance where the Commission did go back to a witness of fact to discuss the truth of his evidence. The witness in the case was B, a British soldier, who gave important eyewitness evidence against W. A visit to the scene by the

Commission's caseworker showed strong grounds for belief that B's evidence could not have been correct.[14] B, when eventually interviewed, did indeed amend his trial account in a way which clearly affected the weight to be given to his evidence. The Court, however, appeared to doubt whether it had been right to re-interview B, stating:

> Unless there is some positive ground to suppose that evidence given was so suspect, we could not regard it as a desirable practice for witnesses to be re-interviewed after a trial by defendants' solicitors to see if their evidence has varied in any respect.

It is unclear whether or not the Court was criticising the Commission here[15] but it should be observed that B was, in fact, re-interviewed by police at the request of the Commission precisely because in this case there *was* positive reason to suspect the accuracy of the trial evidence.

Second, it is not uncommon for the retracting witness to be asked to make a statement by those acting for the applicant before the matter is presented to the Commission. Any such statement is almost certain to be the product of an interview carried out by a person with a prior view as to the desired outcome. By contrast, an interview carried out by or on behalf of the Commission should be dispassionate, neutral and rigorous. From the applicant's point of view, a retraction statement, which is the product of a testing and dispassionate interview, should be more useful than one which is the result of a 'soft' interview. This is also borne out by Court of Appeal case law, which has emphasised that a retraction statement must be 'of sufficient weight, cogency and relevance to displace the verdict of the jury' before the Court will give any weight to it – cogency often being the most pressing consideration in practice.[16]

Third, when witness retraction is in the air, there are important legal consequences to bear in mind. A statement by a witness that he or she has given untrue evidence is an admission to perjury. If a retraction of this kind is a possible outcome, the Commission will normally appoint a police officer to carry out the interview under caution. It may sometimes be possible to obtain a waiver of prosecution from the Crown Prosecution Service against a prospectively retracting witness, and this possibility is always considered by the Commission. However, if there is any realistic possibility that the investigations will lead to admission of perjury a police officer is (rightly) appointed to pursue the investigation of the matter.

Witness retractions have failed to carry weight with the Court of Appeal in the following cases:

P (Peter) was a case in which P was convicted of sexual offences against his stepdaughter, K, importantly corroborated by the evidence of her sister, A. The application to the Commission was based upon a retraction statement made by A. In a very careful analysis, the Commission considered that, notwithstanding some doubts, A's retraction evidence was sufficiently credible to merit referral. The Court, in a very painstaking analysis noted:

- A's credibility as a witness at the trial was enhanced by her obvious emotional instability/stress.

- A said that her false statement against P had been made due to physical intimidation and bullying by K and by her mother. For various reasons – analysing the history of the family relationships – the Court concluded that her account of the shifting family alliances did not 'add up'.

- A had stuck to her trial account for a long time afterwards – the account given in her retraction evidence (in terms of the changing dynamic of the family relationships) as to why she gave false evidence did not 'fit' with her previous adherence to her trial account.

- The version of events given by A in her retraction statement was uncannily similar to accounts given by P's wife in submissions to the Home Office (and which were said to have been given at a time when A was sticking to her trial account).

- Following a suicide attempt, A had given a very detailed account to psychiatrists of guilt she was carrying associated with family relationships – but she had never mentioned guilt about falsely accusing her father.

Probably, it can be fairly said that both the Commission's decision to refer and the Court's decision to uphold the conviction were well and fairly reasoned.

Ahmed (Ishtiaq) was a case in which a vital witness in a murder investigation had changed her account several times since trial. The Commission took the view that her inconsistency was itself a matter affecting her reliability. The alternative explanation was that her varying accounts had been given due to the fact that she had been strongly leaned on at various times by associates of the convicted person. The Court gave quite cogent reasons for upholding the conviction.

Witness retractions have led to convictions being quashed in the following cases:

Druhan is a case where the Court of Appeal might well have referred to 'lurking doubt', but avoided doing so. D was convicted of murder by arson. She was not the only candidate for the crime and the prosecution put some weight on the evidence of a witness, Fludgate. F provided a statement to police, and later gave evidence in similar terms at trial, that D had uttered threats to kill during an altercation in a nearby public house shortly before the offence was committed.

F was approached post-trial by journalists from the television programme, *Trial and Error.* As the Court's judgment put it:

> *In the course of his answers he did not accuse the police of putting words into his mouth, but did suggest that some of the language in his statement was not language which he would himself have used, and did suggest that he had been encouraged to put his evidence strongly against the appellant.*

He did not deny having been at the pub or having been witness to an ill-natured altercation, but the account he gave to journalists was a good deal more uncertain than his account at trial. The Court was to conclude:

> *When making his statement in 1988, and when testifying in 1989, we consider that Mr Fludgate acted in good faith and without any malicious or dishonest intention. But in significant respects we consider his description given at the trial of the scene in the public house to have been seriously exaggerated.*

Druhan is a case which illustrates the truism that where police have formed a clear view of a case there may be some straining for emphasis (or consistency) in the statements taken from witnesses. This may in turn affect the evidence subsequently·given at trial, at which time the witness's recollection of events, and his evidence-in-chief, may be coloured by the summary prepared by the police officer in the witness statement. It is the kind of case which, one suspects, proponents of the Commission expected to see more of: a nasty murder in which the police took a clear view of the culprit and possibly 'nuanced' the evidence of a key witness in a way which made the case look clearer than it was.[17]

M (EM) was a case where both mother and father and also the family's milkman were convicted of offences against two of M's seven children. The children subsequently retracted allegations against their mother.

A review of the social services file showed that social workers' involvement began with a complaint of inter-sibling abuse, escalated when a third child of the couple made (un-retracted) allegations that her stepfather was indecently assaulting her, and that once all seven children were taken into care they were repeatedly questioned by social workers who adopted protocols for questioning which would now be considered as leading and unsafe. The files also included applications to the Criminal Injuries Compensation Authority, which showed that the allegations by the children became so exaggerated that their credibility had to be doubted in the absence of supporting medical evidence.

The Court stated that the referral placed it in 'an almost irreconcilable dilemma' as it was impossible, at this distance (some 14 years after the allegations were made), to determine which version of events was the truth, but in those circumstances the convictions must be unsafe. The Court noted, however, that each case must be decided on its own facts, stressing that 'there may well be other cases ... where a court would conclude that the retractions were so unreliable as to have no effect on the safety of the conviction'.

The case of **B (David)** contains a somewhat similar history of children being subject to pressure to disclose sexual abuse after being removed from the family and placed in a foster home. In **B**'s case, the pressure upon the children to make allegations appears to have been intense. Unfortunately, the Court of Appeal's judgment – brief to a fault – failed to deal with this part of the referral case.

Unreliable witnesses

There have been a number of cases in which the Commission has referred on the basis of fresh evidence disclosing serious concerns about the reliability of witnesses. These will be summarised relatively shortly – many are discussed in greater detail elsewhere.

B (Ernest) and **O (Paul)** are both cases where the complainants in sexual abuse cases added to the allegation of sexual abuse, post trial, to an extent that strained credence to possible breaking point.

In **B**, the complainants (aged 11 and 13 at trial) had named five perpetrators of abuse, including their natural father, in the course of interviews which were disclosed to the defence. The older child, J, said in reply to a specific question that she had no further allegations to make. After B's conviction, J made a supplemental statement naming 18 further people who had allegedly sexually abused her (including – for the first time – her mother). The prosecution elected not to bring further charges on the basis of this statement. The Commission considered that the jury might have taken a different view of the allegations against B had they had a complete picture of the complainants' assertions. The Court, quashing the convictions, stated:

> We find ourselves in a thoroughly unsatisfactory state of mind at the conclusion of this hearing. We have no doubt that both J and C have been the victims of widespread abuse within what is highly likely to have been a paedophile ring in which many friends and neighbours were almost certainly involved ... However, for the reasons advanced by counsel, we consider that, had the allegations made in the post-trial interview been before the jury, or at least available to the defence, at the time of trial, it is quite impossible to say what course the trial would have followed. In particular, we suspect, the cases of [B] and [C] would have been assisted by reason of their relatively peripheral involvement.

In **O**, the complainant had (shortly after O was convicted) made two further allegations against different men, both of which she subsequently retracted. The Court felt that knowledge of these matters would have affected the jury's assessment of her reliability.

C (Anthony Mark) was convicted of the rape of his wife – the two were going through a somewhat acrimonious separation and the offence was said to have occurred when the two met to discuss the division of matrimonial assets. It appears from the record of trial that the complainant was possibly a somewhat histrionic witness. The Commission referred on the basis of evidence showing that the complainant had manifestly lied under oath in subsequent civil proceedings brought by an unpaid private investigator whom she had engaged to monitor her husband's movements. She had also lied in making claims for invalidity benefit when she had falsely said that she had been disabled by assaults committed by C. The Court – drawing an analogy with police misconduct witnesses – felt that subsequent misconduct on the part of a prosecution witness whose credibility was at the heart of the trial was an admissible matter and quashed the conviction.

In three cases, **P (Ricardo)**, **Brooke and Siddall**, and **M (EM)**, all sexual abuse convictions, the respective complainants' trial accounts of injuries caused by the convicted person were very considerably enhanced in subsequent applications to the Criminal Injuries Compensation Authority (CICA) resulting in substantially increased claims for compensation. In all three cases the unexplained discrepancies of the complainants' accounts were matters which the Court considered were relevant to their credibility and in **P** this was the sole matter of substance which led to the quashing of the convictions. Further details of **Brooke and Siddall** are given in chapter 9.

A (Derek) and **K (Jamie)** were both cases in which convictions were quashed on the basis of examination of social services files which contained material severely affecting the credibility of the respective complainants (and, in A's case, the complainant's mother) as witnesses of truth. These cases are discussed in chapter 9.

Blackwell, **Warren** and **K (Jason)** – also discussed in chapter 9 – are cases in which complainants in rape or indecent assault cases were shown by the Commission's investigation to be serial and unreliable complainants. Note also the case of **Burt**, who was convicted of a firearms offence, in large measure on the evidence of H. Burt's conviction was quashed without opposition on evidence that it had become apparent that H had given wholly false and fabricated evidence in another (unrelated) case.

MacKenney and Pinfold and **H (J)** and **G (T)** are cases which turned on fresh psychological evidence concerning the reliability of a key prosecution witness as a witness of truth. In each case, a key issue was the admissibility of such psychological evidence. **MacKenney and Pinfold** was a case in which a very liberal constitution of the Court under Woolf LCJ took a much more favourable view as to the admissibility of evidence of witness reliability than the division of the Court which decided the first-time appeal in 1983. See however, **Smith (Allen)** for a case decided against the applicant on somewhat comparable facts. These cases are all discussed in chapter 4.

By contrast, **McCann** is an instructive case where the Court of Appeal was unmoved by fresh evidence as to a witness's want of reliability. M was convicted of manslaughter, in part on the evidence of his sister, Bridget. The conviction was referred on the basis of a number of medical reports calling into question whether Bridget could be considered a reliable witness. In upholding the conviction, the Court referred to the fact that the jury had had ample evidence before them from which they could not but have concluded that Bridget was an immensely 'flaky' witness. The jury had been heavily warned about convicting in reliance on Bridget's evidence, and there had been much other evidence to convict M. In the circumstances, the Court did not consider that a further accretion of evidence as to Bridget's want of reliability affected the safety of the conviction.

Little or no new evidence cases/lurking doubt

Finally, we consider cases where new evidence is slender or non-existent; cases where the almost forbidden words 'lurking doubt' have arisen. Some preliminary observations on this important issue are required.

First, the phrase 'lurking doubt' became part of the appeal language in the case, dating from 1969, of *Cooper*,[18] in which Lord Widgery stated that the new test of safety introduced by the 1968 Act was not always simply a matter of weighing up the new evidence:

> *The court must in the end ask itself a subjective question, whether we are content to let the matter stand as it is, or whether there is not some lurking doubt in our minds which makes us wonder whether an injustice has been done. This is a reaction which may not be based strictly on the evidence as such; it is a reaction which can be produced by the general feel of the case as the Court experiences it.*

And it was treated as axiomatic in the debate up to and including Runciman that miscarriages of justice included cases where something had gone wrong, and the trial verdict felt troubling and unsafe, even where the new evidence was slender or non-existent. However, in more recent years the Court of Appeal has frequently expressed an aversion to appeals based upon 'lurking doubt', adopting the mantra that if a jury, having heard the evidence and having been properly directed by the trial judge, has harboured no 'lurking doubt' then it is no business of the Court to introduce any of its own. Indeed, in a case called *Farrow*[19] it was stated that 'the concept of lurking doubt [is] no part of the appeal language' following the adoption of the new simplified test of safety in the 1995 Act. Subsequently, the Court has drawn back to some degree from this position and accepted that lurking doubt is available in principle as a ground of appeal, whilst very rarely acceding to appeals based upon such arguments in practice.[20] Rightly or wrongly, the Commission for its part has steered clear of 'lurking doubt' as a free-standing ground for any of its references, recognising that it is desirable to anchor the existence of any such lurking doubt to some point of evidence that was not available, or not pursued, at trial.

Second, the government which brought in the 1995 Act was initially minded not to include no-new-evidence cases within the Commission's jurisdiction at all – on the assumption that the Commission's role was to review cases based upon new evidence or argument, not to re-open verdicts where the evidence had not changed. This was a view strongly opposed by JUSTICE and others. At a relatively late stage in the Parliamentary proceedings, the government conceded the point, permitting the Commission to refer convictions (but not sentences) in the absence of new evidence or argument if there were 'exceptional circumstances justifying reference'.

Third, the Court of Appeal has developed its own gloss on exceptionality. If the Commission may only in 'exceptional circumstances' refer a no-new-evidence case, the Court for its part has stated that it may only exceptionally quash such a conviction – an exception superimposed upon an exception. This was a matter expressed by the Court in **Thomas (Ian)**. T's case was referred on grounds of new evidence but the grounds of appeal developed by counsel following the Commission's reference substantially replicated matters raised unsuccessfully on T's behalf at the first-time appeal.[21] The Court stated:

> ... *in the absence of new argument or evidence, the proper exercise of the Court's power to depart from its previous reasoning or conclusions should, we believe, equally be confined to "exceptional circumstances"; see e.g. R v. Chard (1984) 78 Cr. App. R 106, per Lord Diplock at 113, under the former procedure of reference by the Home Secretary:*
>
> > *"... the Court that hears the reference will give weight to the previous judgment, from which it will be very slow to differ, unless it is persuaded that some cogent argument that had not been advanced at the previous hearing would, if it had been properly developed at such hearing, have resulted in the appeal against conviction being allowed."*

This dictum has been repeated in both **Mills and Poole** and **Stock**, of which more below. Accordingly, if the Commission is contemplating sending back a case in the absence of any telling new evidence, it needs to articulate exceptional circumstances why the Court might change its mind, as well as exceptional circumstances why the Commission should refer it.

All of these considerations came to a point in the much-litigated case of **Mills and Poole**. Put extremely briefly, the applicants having been convicted of murder, their first-time unsuccessful appeal raised the issues of (i) evidence of an eyewitness (Jukes) whose account of the fatal incident was favourable to the appellants, and (ii) conduct of the police (including one DI Gladding) in relation to investigation and disclosure. The case against the defendants much depended upon the credibility of a key witness, named Stadden. The case was covered by the Channel 4 Programme, *Trial and Error*, which criticised Gladding. Gladding then sued Channel 4 for comments made about him but judgment was given against him. The case then came to the Commission on the basis that matters raised by the Gladding libel action provided additional evidence about police misconduct. The Commission concluded that none of the points now being raised substantively added to the case that had been unsuccessfully argued at the first-time appeal and declined to refer. This decision was then challenged on judicial review. The Divisional Court upheld the rationality of the Commission's decision not to refer but the Court (Woolf LCJ) commented as follows:

> *Having given detailed consideration to the propriety and advisability of so doing we have come with hesitation to the conclusion in this case that we should express a view. Before expressing that view we feel it is right to point out that we would regard this course as one which should only rarely be adopted. Further, we would strongly discourage the Commission from lowering the threshold they set for a referral. It would be all too easy for the Commission to adopt the soft option and very readily refer, to the disadvantage of the other work waiting to be heard in the Court of Appeal. We congratulate the Commission for not falling into that temptation.*

> *The view which we express is that the Court of Appeal now could have a doubt about the safety of these convictions. In expressing that view we note the recent statement of Lord Bingham of Cornhill in* R v Pendleton *[2001] … that in considering whether to allow an appeal the Court of Appeal should "bear very clearly in mind the question for consideration is whether the conviction is safe not whether the accused is guilty".*

> *First of all in relation to Poole, there is only one witness who gave evidence that might be reliable in directly making him a party to the offence though we have not forgotten the telling nature of the deceased's injuries. The reliability of Miss Stadden's evidence and of her second statement might have been viewed differently in light of the full knowledge of the array of*

misconduct. Secondly, in relation to Mills, though again we bear in mind the telling nature of the injuries suffered by the deceased, his argument as to self-defence might have been viewed differently in the light of all the misconduct.

Although the Court of Appeal had the material to form their own view of D.I. Gladding's behaviour, the verdict of the jury in the libel action is damning condemnation of his conduct and that verdict was reached after a more detailed examination than would have been possible in the Court of Appeal when his conduct was only one of many issues before that Court. He was found guilty of perjury and perverting the course of justice in relation to this case. Any jury would be and, in our view, would rightly be, deeply influenced by this finding if they could have known of it. It just might have affected their view of Miss Stadden who was such a critical witness. The trouble with a senior officer behaving as D.I. Gladding has been found to have behaved is that a jury would find it difficult to be sure that there was not other misconduct for which he could have been responsible.

...

In expressing the views we have we do not suggest the Court of Appeal's previous decision can be faulted. We reject entirely the suggestion of bias as fanciful. ... But although the new material may not be that significant it can still be sufficient to tip the balance, from upholding the conviction to allowing an appeal.

It is entirely a matter for the Commission to decide what if any weight to attach to the views we have expressed. If the matter is to be reconsidered by them it is desirable this is done while the facts are still fresh in the Commission's mind.

This lengthy passage is quoted as demonstrating that some – at least – of the senior judiciary are willing to accept that it is proper for the Commission to use the referral procedure to enable the Court to have second thoughts where even very limited new material may tip the balance of the Court's reasoning. The metaphor of the see-saw is apt – a small shift of evidence can tip the balance from safety to unsafety.

The Commission – taking the hint from Lord Woolf's observations – reconsidered and referred the convictions, which were subsequently quashed by the Court of Appeal. The Court did not by any means buy into the broader see-saw argument. It emphasised that the Court could only exceptionally go back on a previous judgment, citing the passage in **Thomas** quoted above. Its decision to quash the conviction was based partly upon the impact of **Pendleton** and partly upon the convenient fiction that argument developed by leading counsel in the appeal that followed the Commission's referral represented a wholly new point unconsidered by the Court at the first-time appeal.[22] In allowing the appeal, the Court took some care to avoid creating a precedent that would encourage the Commission to refer no-new-evidence cases in the future.

Other 'little new evidence' cases

Mills and Poole apart, the Commission has never within the period of this study referred a case in the absence of significantly new evidence or on the basis, simpliciter, of lurking doubt. However, there have been a number of cases where the Commission has referred on the basis of relatively slender new evidence and the Court has subsequently quashed the convictions. A number of these cases were historic cases which were overhanging the Commission when it took over the unresolved caseload from the Home Office in 1997.

Cooper and McMahon is the clearest of these cases, to which reference has already been made. The main problematic aspects of the appellants' convictions, and in particular the enormous questions about the integrity of the key prosecution witness, Mathews, had been known since the 1970s. These questions had failed to move the Court of Appeal when considering previous appeals in 1975 and 1976. The Commission's reference raised some very limited new matters but the central issues were ones which had already been considered by the Court of Appeal. The Court at the conclusion of its judgment that followed the Commission's reference stated:

> So, as it seems to us, there are now a number of matters which can be described as causes for genuine concern, when evaluating the safety of these convictions.

These concerns were then listed – the old matters which had failed previously to carry weight with the Court admixed with the more limited new matters raised by the Commission. The Court concluded:

> For present purposes it is unnecessary to say that one of those matters, or any combination of them, is decisive. It is sufficient to say that in their

totality they persuade us that these convictions are no longer safe, and that the appeals against conviction must be allowed.

Brannan and Murphy concerned a gangland murder in Manchester with a large cast of witnesses. Conviction had taken place in 1992 but the Court of Appeal was prevailed upon at the first-time appeal in 1993 to hear a number of new witnesses. It rejected the evidence of the new witnesses and upheld the conviction. The key issue was whether at the moment of the killing the victim, Pollitt, had possessed and had been attempting to use a gun. There was some limited new witness evidence to support the Commission's referral but the critical issue was whether the jury at trial and the Court of Appeal at the first-time appeal had been right in rejecting the evidence about Pollitt's possession of a gun. The Court stated:

> *We accept that all the evidence now available has to be looked at as a whole, including the evidence at trial, that given at the 1993 appeal hearing and the fresh evidence produced before this court. The situation has altered since 1993. Both Murphy's evidence and Haslam's evidence at trial, and Brannan's evidence in 1993, may well have been discredited by factors which now appear to have been unjustified. There is a knock-on effect, as we have described, on the assessment of some of the other evidence given in 1993. When all the evidence now available about Pollitt's possession of a gun is put together, we find it impossible to say that a jury hearing such evidence would necessarily have come to the same conclusion.*
>
> *… our task is to consider whether these convictions are unsafe or not. Because of the way in which the issue of the gun became of central importance when the charges were left to the jury, we have concluded that the totality of the evidence now available on that topic, if given at trial, might reasonably have affected the decision of the jury to convict these two men. In those circumstances these convictions must be regarded as unsafe and therefore both appeals are allowed.*

In **MacKenney and Pinfold**, which has been discussed briefly in chapter 4, the Court was prepared to re-open an old case upon the basis of re-tendered evidence that the main prosecution witness was wholly unreliable. As already noted, the Court concluded that evidence of this matter was admissible, notwithstanding that the trial judge and the Court of Appeal at the appellants' first-time appeal had ruled otherwise. The Court stated:

In deciding whether a conviction is safe on a reference by the Criminal Cases Review Commission we have to have regard to the evidence that is properly available to us. If evidence was not admitted at an earlier trial because of the then approach to the admissibility of evidence we cannot ignore the evidence if it would be regarded as admissible and relevant today.

Broughton was a case where a man named Cahill had been injured in a knife attack on his doorstep in what appeared to be a clear case of mistaken identity. The prosecution of B for the offence was not pursued for over a year and the case that the assailant was in fact B was quite thin, so thin in fact that the Court of Appeal had been moved (most unusually) to say at the first-time appeal that 'this may be regarded as a case near to the borderline of cases which it might be unsafe to leave to the jury'.

The case was referred (not without some misgivings) on a relatively slender point. Cahill had (long before the case against B was prosecuted) called police to say that he believed that he had recognised his assailant in a Gold Maestro car at a nearby public house. The police had attended the scene but had failed to apprehend either the car or its driver. This was never disclosed to B. The Commission made unsuccessful attempts to track down the car and/or its driver but concluded in any event that it was just possible that if this matter had been disclosed closer to the event, B might have been able to use this information to point to another possible culprit. The Court in quashing the conviction implicitly shared the concerns of the Commission about the thinness of the original case against B.

The foregoing catalogue of cases might be taken to imply that the Court is relatively open to reconsidering old cases of suspected miscarriage but that would be too optimistic a formulation. They show that it is *just* possible to get the Court to think again but much depends on some fresh 'angle' and (probably) a favourable constitution of the Court of Appeal. The other face of the Court can be seen in **Stock**, convicted of armed robbery in 1970, who has now been the subject of three unsuccessful appeals, having had his case referred by the Home Office (heard in 1996) and the Commission (heard in 2003). Successive investigations have unraveled almost every part of the case against Stock in a case which has involved a discredited police sergeant, unfair identification procedures and breaches of rules. The case now rests substantially on a single identification obtained in the most unfair of circumstances.

The Court, considering the appeal following the Commission's reference, cited the dictum from **Thomas**, quoted above, and emphasised the requirement for exceptional circumstances and added:

> *Much of the argument upon which the reference was made, and some of the argument advanced by Mr Mansfield on this appeal, was developed and determined in 1996. We accept that Mr Mansfield has developed some new points, which he did not see and therefore did not develop in 1996. We accept that our task is to consider whether, in all the circumstances and taking account of the new points, the appellant's conviction is in our view safe. It is open to us to reconsider and reach a different conclusion on elements of the 1996 decision. But we should give weight to the 1996 judgment and will be very slow to differ from it or its constituent parts, unless we are persuaded to do so by some cogent argument not advanced or properly developed in 1996.*

And it upheld the conviction.

Mr Stock's case has now been (somewhat courageously) referred for a second time to the Court by the Commission. It is important that the Commission should remain willing to send back old cases where there is a strong suspicion of miscarriage and take some courage and support from the authorities discussed above.

Notes

1. The offence had taken place in 1989 and DNA profiling techniques were in their infancy at the time of the investigation of the murder.
2. It should be noted that the forensic exhibit had been retained by the Forensic Science Service since the crime was committed in 1961. The efficiency of the FSS in retaining exhibits over many years has frequently been impressive and has assisted the Commission in the resolution of many cases (not always in the applicant's favour). If the government eventually privatises the FSS the obligation to retain forensic exhibits should be hard-wired into the privatisation arrangements.
3. The remains of Mr Hanratty – who was hanged – were exhumed for this purpose.
4. This investigation was conducted by Bill Skitt, a former Chief Constable of Hertfordshire and Assistant Metropolitan Police Commissioner – and exemplifies the value to the Commission of in-house experience of high-level criminal investigations.
5. Loc cit.
6. [2001] *Crim LR* 506, Case No 9806611 W4 1 November 2000.
7. [2001] EWCA Crim 1096.
8. The Court seems less allergic to allegations of incompetent pre-trial preparation by solicitors!
9. This case was brought to the Commission by the Student Law Office of the University of Northumbria – it is the only referral in the first ten years of the Commission emanating from

the efforts of a student innocence project. A number of similar projects are getting under way at the present time.

10. S78(1) Police and Criminal Evidence Act 1984 provides that:

> *(1) In any proceedings the court may refuse to allow evidence on which the prosecution proposes to rely to be given if it appears to the court that, having regard to all the circumstances in which the evidence was obtained, the admission of the evidence would have such an adverse affect on the fairness of the proceedings that the court ought not to admit it.*

It affords the trial judge discretion, inter alia, to exclude from evidence statements obtained in breach of the relevant Codes of Practice.

11. The Commission's view was that the pictures would not have been admissible in any event.

12. One of a number of cases where the Court has sought to deprive the appellant of any emotional satisfaction from the success of his appeal. It was, in fact, the view of those involved in W's case that his defence had substantive merit.

13. Completely opposite considerations apply when the witness in question is an expert witness. If the Commission considers that there may be any weight in criticisms made of expert evidence given at trial, then it is normally de rigueur for the Commission to ask the expert whether or not he or she stands by the evidence in the light of the criticisms made of it.

14. In the context of the previous discussion about legal representation, it is pertinent to note that, had leading counsel visited the scene, he could almost certainly have cross-examined B to destruction on the matter. Unfortunately, he was so lately instructed that he had apparently had no time to visit the scene.

15. Reading of the judgment as a whole would tend to support the view that criticism *was* intended.

16. This formulation was in *Coffey* (unreported, 7 February 1995), see also *Linegar and Purcell* [2001] EWCA Crim 460, *Tully* [2001] EWCA Crim 1896 and *Godfrey* [2005] EWCA Crim 220 for other examples.

17. Note also the case of **Johnson (Harold)**, discussed in the next chapter, which raises somewhat similar issues.

18. [1969] 1 QB 271.

19. The *Times*, 20 October 1998. Case No 9800893 X3.

20. See for instance *Dookran and Dookran* [2007] UKPC 15 for a recent case in which an appellate court has acknowledged this point.

21. At the time that T's appeal was heard, an appellant was permitted to raise any grounds of appeal irrespective of whether they had formed any part of the grounds for the Commission's reference. The government later amended the law by s315 Criminal Justice Act 2003 to restrict appellants from developing adventitious grounds of appeal: this has been discussed in chapter 1.

22. 'Fiction' in the sense that the argument was more a reformulation of an old point than a genuinely new point.

Chapter 6 - Modern standards of fairness

The Bentley doctrine

Among the many difficult unresolved cases bequeathed to the Commission by the Home Office was the much discussed case of Derek **Bentley**. Bentley, aged 19, was sentenced after his younger confederate, Christopher Craig, shot and killed a policeman. Craig, aged 16, was too young to hang but Bentley was found responsible for the killing under the doctrine of joint enterprise. Much turned on the construction of the words 'Let him have it',[1] which could have been taken either as an incitement to Craig to use the gun or as an appeal to him to surrender it to the police officer.[2] The jury were treated to a one-sided and oppressive summing up by Goddard LJ which most fair-minded observers would say amounted to a direction to convict.

The case was presented to the Commission on the basis of new evidence, relating, inter alia, to Derek Bentley's intellectual functioning and a linguistic analysis of his alleged confession statement, and was referred by the Commission to the Court of Appeal. What did *not* feature large in the referral (or in the subsequent grounds of appeal) was the iniquitous summing up of Goddard LJ. This was because that matter had been raised at Mr Bentley's first-time appeal, when the Court determined that the summing up fell short of a usurpation of the function of the jury and, therefore, did not vitiate the conviction. Bentley's conviction was referred in 1997, and at that early stage of the Commission's history it was thought that the statutory exclusion (exceptional circumstances apart) of 'matters previously raised' precluded this as a primary referral point. In this context, therefore, the eventual judgment of the Court (Bingham LCJ) was as unexpected as it was welcome. Recognising the reality of the impact of the summing up, the Court stated:

> *Where, between conviction and appeal, there have been significant changes in the common law (as opposed to changes effected by statute) or in standards of fairness, the approach indicated requires the court to apply legal rules and procedural criteria which were not and could not reasonably have been applied at the time. **This could cause difficulty in some cases but not, we conclude, in this.*** (Emphasis added)

The judgment provided a clear signal to the Commission that convictions giving rise to concern which had clearly been secured in breach of 'modern standards of fairness', might be quashed by the Court and as such could satisfy the 'real possibility' test. The highlighted words at the end of the passage above signalled that there would be limits to the application to the doctrine, but a trial which was so clearly vitiated by unfairness would be unlikely to be a cause of 'difficulty'.[3]

Bentley considered and re-stated – Hanratty, Hussain and Ashley King

The limits of the **Bentley** doctrine were expressed by the Court of Appeal in the equally famous case of **Hanratty**. H's conviction was referred principally on the basis of numerous affronts to modern standards of fairness in the conduct of the investigation and prosecution. Balancing this was decisive new DNA evidence against Hanratty – which determined the Court's decision to uphold the conviction. On the **Bentley** point the Court stated:

> The non-technical approach is especially important in references by the Commission such as this since standards may have changed because of the passage of time. For understandable reasons, it is now accepted in judging the question of fairness of a trial, and fairness is what rules of procedure are designed to achieve, we apply current standards irrespective of when the trial took place. But this does not mean that because contemporary rules have not been complied with a trial which took place in the past must be judged on the false assumption it was tried yesterday. Such an approach could achieve injustice because the non-compliance with rules does not necessarily mean that a defendant has been treated unfairly. In order to achieve justice, non-compliance with rules which were not current at the time of the trial may need to be treated differently from rules which were in force at the time of trial. If certain of the current requirements of, for example, a summing up are not complied with at a trial which takes place today this can almost automatically result in a conviction being set aside but this approach should not be adopted in relation to trials which took place before the rule was established. The fact that what has happened did not comply with a rule which was in force at the time of trial makes the non-compliance more serious than it would be if there was no rule in force. Proper standards will not be maintained unless this Court can be expected, when appropriate, to enforce the rules by taking a serious view of a breach of the rules at the time they are in force. It is not appropriate to apply this approach to a forty year-old case.

And similarly, in **Hussain**, after citing the discussion in **Hanratty**, the Court stated:

> It will, therefore, often be important in disposing of appeals made by way of references from the CCRC in comparatively old cases for this court to decide whether the facts complained of constitute a breach of rules in force at the time of trial or only of rules and standards that have subsequently become required by law or thought to be desirable. If, moreover, a breach of the rules existing at the time is established, such breach will usually have been brought to the court's attention. If it has been, the court's reaction to such breach and its directions, if any, to the jury will be important matters to which regard should be given. It may be that at the time of trial the breach will have been regarded as less important than it would to-day. In the light of the authorities cited it is the current approach to such breaches that should govern the matter.

The Court in **Hussain** stated that 'the principle set out in **Bentley** cannot be taken too far' and observed:

> The essential question is whether the conviction is safe and it would be surprising if the mere fact that (for example) a "good character" or "lies" direction had not been given in the terms which are conventional today would be enough to enable a court to doubt the safety of a conviction.

The Court has thus signalled to the Commission – in a comprehensible manner – that there has to be some limit to the extent to which aged convictions should be adjudged unsafe on the basis of breach of modern standards of fairness. Clearly, without such limitation the Court would be endlessly engaged in retrying historic cases. The Commission for its part has not encountered undue difficulty in recognising the 'frontier' of the **Bentley** doctrine in deciding which cases should be referred.

Bentley was also no doubt considered, albeit not expressly cited, in the important case of *Ashley King*,[4] who appealed against a 1986 conviction for murder that was based primarily on confession evidence. The confession was made in the course of interview by police officers but was shortly after retracted. King's police interviews had occurred in November 1985, prior to the commencement of PACE, and were not tape-recorded.[5] King was aged 21 at the time, subject to learning difficulties, and had been intensively interviewed by police (ten times in all) in the absence either of a solicitor or of what would now be described as an 'appropriate adult'. As King had not appealed his conviction following trial, the judgment followed an out-of-time appeal and did not come via the Commission.[6] New evidence was brought on appeal of King's vulnerability, affecting the reliability of his confession. Allowing the appeal, the Court stated:

> We were invited by counsel at the outset to consider as a general question what the approach of the court should be in a situation such as this where a crime is investigated and a suspect interrogated and detained at a time when the statutory framework governing investigation, interrogation and detention was different from that now in force. We remind ourselves that our task is to consider whether this conviction is unsafe. If we do so consider it, section 2(1)(a) of the Criminal Appeal Act 1968 obliges us to allow the appeal. We should not (other things being equal) consider a conviction unsafe simply because of a failure to comply with a statute governing police detention, interrogation and investigation, which was not in force at the time. In looking at the safety of the conviction it is relevant to consider whether and to what extent a suspect may have been denied rights which he should have enjoyed under the rules in force at the time and whether and to what extent he may have lacked protections which it was later thought right that he should enjoy. But this court is concerned, and concerned only, with the safety of the conviction. That is a question to be determined in the light of all the material before it, which will include the record of all the evidence in the case and not just an isolated part. **If, in a case where the only evidence against a defendant was his oral confession which he had later retracted, it appeared that such confession was obtained in breach of the rules prevailing at the time and in circumstances which denied the defendant important safeguards later thought necessary to avoid the risk of a miscarriage of justice, there would be at least prima facie grounds for doubting the safety of the conviction** -- a very different thing from concluding that a defendant was necessarily innocent. (Emphasis added)

The Commission's pre-PACE cases

There is no doubt that PACE, although much criticised by civil libertarians at the time, has been a watershed in the advent of modern standards of fairness. It was PACE which for the first time created a statutory presumption against admission of evidence obtained by oppression or rendered unreliable by any circumstances prevailing at the time of interview (section 76); which provided a broad statutory discretion to the trial judge to exclude evidence due to considerations of fairness (section 78); which provided that police interviews should be subject to clear procedural rules and should be tape-recorded; and which provided Codes of Practice clearly defining the rights of suspects to the assistance of a solicitor and (in certain cases) an 'appropriate adult'. Prior to PACE, the protections provided to suspects (by virtue of the Judges' Rules) were fragmentary and imprecise. Moreover, the common law authorities provided that, save in cases of oppression, it was very much within the discretion of judges whether or not to exclude evidence due to procedural irregularities – such discretion being infrequently exercised in practice. As noted in chapter 1, before the coming into force of PACE, a combination of factors increased the likelihood of wrongful convictions based upon dubious confessions. These included the following:

- The absence of tape-recording of interviews made possible the practice of 'verballing'. It also made it possible for police to 'improve' the evidence of what had passed at interviews. It was extremely difficult in practice to challenge the police account of what had passed in the interview room.

- Juries generally had no grasp of the concept of the possibility of coerced or compliant false confessions. Coercion could not be demonstrated in the absence of tape-recording, whilst the concept of compliance was generally not understood.

- The rights of vulnerable suspects to support from solicitors, parents or other adults were fragmentary and ill-observed.

- Judges rarely excluded confession evidence on procedural grounds, to the point – it would seem – that counsel were frequently hesitant to test judicial patience by making applications for such exclusion.

Bentley and *Ashley King* have been applied in a series of pre-PACE cases subsequently referred by the Commission and quashed by the Court of Appeal. These cases have a number of common threads:

- Convictions were substantially or wholly based upon confession evidence.

- The confessions were made at the conclusion of intensive police questioning, lasting many hours or days.

- The interviews took place without the presence of solicitors, parents or other appropriate adults.

- The supporting evidence, whilst possibly impressive to a jury as corroboration of a confession, appears generally flimsy in the absence of a reliable confession to corroborate.

- The convicted persons were mostly young and vulnerable. In a majority of cases, there has been evidence of vulnerability provided by forensic psychologists or psychiatrists.

A question which the Commission has needed to consider in all such pre-PACE cases has been whether the procedures breached not merely *modern* standards of fairness but also *contemporary* standards. As a result, the Commission may well be the only institution where the pre-PACE editions of *Archbold* have been regularly consulted in recent years to determine the likelihood of success of prospective appeals. That said, due to the lack of precision of the legal safeguards for suspects prior to PACE, it has sometimes been difficult for the Commission to come to any clear view as to whether or not contemporary procedures were breached.

Such uncertainties notwithstanding, the Commission (correctly applying the 'real possibility' test) has referred a considerable number of cases falling within *Ashley King* territory. It would be tempting to set out all the facts in full, since these pre-PACE cases are amongst the most emotive ever considered by the Commission and there is a firm sense that 'historic' injustices have been put right. It is as well to emphasise in this context that many of these appellants have been relatively young, in most cases under 50, when their appeals have been allowed following reference by the Commission. Therefore, whilst these cases can be considered 'historic' in terms of the subsequent development of the law, they have concerned appellants with much of their lives still before them. It is important not to overlook, in the exposition of legal principles, the impact of these cases upon the lives of the wrongfully convicted individuals.

English cases

Amongst these pre-PACE cases have been the following:

Peter Fell

Mr Fell's application to the Commission was strongly supported by JUSTICE. He was convicted, in 1982, of two savage murders of women who had been walking their dogs on common land close to Aldershot. He was aged 20 at the time. He had had a disturbed childhood and put himself in the frame by attention-seeking calls to the police implicating himself.[7] The police initially took no interest in Mr Fell as a suspect but returned to him a year after the murders, when all other lines of enquiry had gone cold. He was intensively interviewed by police over three days, during which time he declined any food. He was refused a solicitor and eventually confessed. Exceptionally, the police had chosen to tape-record these interviews although the investigation preceded PACE. Various pieces of supporting evidence were adduced at trial to support the confession evidence. Much of this supporting evidence came from witnesses who had not been asked to make statements setting out their recollection of events until more than a year after the events they described.

The appeal was allowed following fresh evidence of vulnerability (Professors Gudjonsson and Kopelman). The Court concluded that the conduct of the police in refusing Mr Fell a solicitor was reprehensible and considered that his confession evidence should have been excluded. As to the safety of the conviction, the Court stated:

> the longer we listened to the medical evidence, and the longer we reviewed the interviews, the clearer we became that the appellant was entitled to more than a conclusion simply that this verdict is unsafe. There are strange features of the case, not least his failure to support his own alibi, but the alibi exists from an independent source. But more important, since our reading of the interviews and the evidence we have heard leads us to the conclusion that the confession was a false one, that can only mean that we believe that he was innocent of these terrible murders, and he should be entitled to have us say so.

It is a feature of Mr Fell's case that the supporting evidence adduced to bolster the truth of the confession statement, however persuasive it may have appeared at the time of trial, appears flimsy in the extreme once the complete want of reliability of the confession evidence is appreciated. This was recognised by the Court in the passage quoted above.

Paul Blackburn

Mr Blackburn was convicted in December 1978 of attempted murder. He was aged 14 when interviewed and 15 at the time of trial and remained in custody for 25 years (having denied responsibility for the crime) until 2003 when he was released on life licence. His conviction was quashed in 2005. He was convicted on the basis of confession evidence obtained at the conclusion of an interview of over three hours, in which it appeared that officers had exerted pressure on Mr Blackburn by raising the possibility of bringing further charges on an unrelated incident. No solicitor or other adult was present. A confession statement was produced, said by police to have been written by Mr Blackburn without prompting from officers.

It is a testimony to the rigour of the interrogation methods used by police that they had previously obtained confessions from three other youths, not subsequently proceeded against, for the same crime! An attempt at trial to exclude the confession evidence (on the ground that it had been obtained by oppression) was unsuccessful. As in Mr Fell's case, the prosecution put forward a hinterland of evidence said to be corroborative, including the fact that Mr Blackburn had asked to have his hair cut not long after the crime, which was said to evidence a desire to alter his appearance.

The Crown conceded that it appeared that the officers *had* provided prompts to Mr Blackburn as to what to put in his confession statement, contrary to their trial evidence, and contrary also to the Judges' Rules. As the Court of Appeal remarked:

> *once it emerges that these officers did not tell the truth on oath in the witness box in one respect, as must be the case, their whole account of the interview becomes undermined.*

New evidence at trial included evidence from a forensic psychologist, Dr Shepherd, who considered that the circumstances of the interrogation of such a young suspect were liable to lead to a 'coerced compliant confession'.

The Court quashed Mr Blackburn's conviction but, following their usual practice (to which Peter Fell's case provided a notable exception), declined to express a view on Mr Blackburn's responsibility for the offence.

Patrick Nolan

Mr Nolan was convicted of a murder committed in Nottingham in December 1980. He was interviewed in March 1981, one of 6,000 possible suspects interviewed by police, and released. In September he was re-arrested and confessed to the murder in the course of three days of intensive interviewing. No solicitor or other adult was present. Mr Nolan said that he had been denied access to a solicitor and had been abused and hit by interviewing officers. He was aged 19 at the time. The police records of interviews showed a pattern in which Mr Nolan had made a series of partial admissions which he then sought to retract. The police records omitted any record of what had passed during some 25 per cent of the time when he was being interviewed. There was no evidence to support the conviction apart from the confession statement.

The Commission obtained a report (Professor Gudjonsson) that Mr Nolan had had a reading age of seven years nine months, suffered from emotional problems and was easily manipulated and compliant. This evidence was not disputed by the Crown's expert. In quashing the conviction, the Court stated:

> *Even judged by 1982 standards this was a worrying case. Proof of murder depended entirely upon the confession of the 19-year-old illiterate appellant, made in the course of 9 hours of interviews over three days, without a solicitor being present. These interviews were not fully recorded and in them the appellant made, and then more than once retracted, admissions which included things which were obviously untrue.*

> *However, judged by modern standards and in the light of the new evidence, we have no hesitation in saying that this conviction is unsafe. By modern standards the interviews were unfair. The Police and Criminal Evidence Act Codes of Practice require that a detained person is advised of his right to consult with a solicitor on arrival at a police station and his right to free legal advice immediately before any interview. Any interview must now be fully recorded. In 1982 the officers' notes of the interviews should have been offered to the appellant for signature.*

> *But even without these safeguards, if the jury had heard expert evidence of the kind we have admitted, it would have been bound to affect their consideration of the reliability of the appellant's confession.*

Harold Johnson

Johnson is somewhat different from the other modern standards of fairness cases. J was convicted in 1968 of aggravated robbery of post office premises and was unrepresented at trial. The case against him was almost entirely based on the evidence of P, who identified him as the person sitting at the wheel of the getaway car. P's testimony classically showed the dangers of identification evidence. Her first police statement was 'I am willing to help but I don't think I would know him again'. She was also highly uncertain when she picked J out at an identity parade but she then signed a further statement prepared by police that she was 'quite certain' that it was J. She then gave evidence at committal proceedings and finally at trial, becoming progressively more certain of her identification at each iteration. No *Turnbull* warning of the dangers of relying on identification evidence was then required or given and, being unrepresented, J had no counsel to impress upon the jury the dangers of relying upon identification evidence.

The Court of Appeal considered this to be a modern standards of fairness case in that the trial court, applying contemporary standards, had entirely skirted round the difficulties of the identification evidence, and it quashed the conviction. The Court noted that, despite the warnings that had been sounded in some quarters following the decision in **Bentley**, there had been no flood of modern standards of fairness appeals – and, indeed, that remains the case.

Other English pre-PACE cases

In the interests of brevity, the following further pre-PACE cases have been reduced to bare detail in the table which follows. The judgments can for the most part be viewed on the Bailii website. It is a common feature of all of these cases that:

- The appellant's confession formed the lynchpin of the prosecution case.

- The confession was retracted within a short time of being made.

- The interviews were not tape-recorded and records of interviews were sparse.

- There were breaches of Judges' Rules or other contemporary procedures, generally of a serious nature. (For example, Stephen **Downing** was not cautioned for eight hours of interview, in breach of Judges' Rules, on the wholly spurious grounds that he was being interviewed as a witness and not as a suspect.)

- There were differences between the accounts of the interview provided by the defendant and the police.

Name/year convicted	Offence	Age at time of offence	Length of Interviews	Solicitor or other adult present?	New evidence of vulnerability?
Steel 1979	Murder	22	7 interviews over 2 days	No	Yes – IQ 65; borderline compliant
Hussain 1978	Murder	16	3 interviews over 12 hours	In part	Yes[8]
Richardson 1986	GBH with intent	19	9 interviews over 3 days	No	No
Downing 1974	Murder	17	One 8-hour interview	No	No
Pendleton 1986	Murder	25	11 interviews over 3 days	No	Yes

The approach taken to the interviewing of young suspects in the above cases is exemplified in the following summary taken from the Court of Appeal's judgment in Abid **Hussain** – accused at the age of 16 of the murder of his baby brother, Mushtaq:

8.   ... At 12 noon, about the same time as Mushtaq's death, Abid was taken to the police station but not then cautioned by either DC Hirst or DS Richardson. At 12.30 the police officers interviewed Abid for the first time. He was not cautioned and no adult was present. Most of this interview was excluded from the evidence given at the trial ...

9.   At 17.00 the police requested Abid's father, Sabbir, to come to the police station. Sabbir gave evidence that he arrived around 19.00 and was kept waiting before he saw his son.

10. Between 20.00 and 21.05 Abid, who had apparently been alone since the end of the first interview, was interviewed a second time. He was cautioned and the police explained to him in simple terms what the caution meant. Abid was not offered any legal advice nor was any independent adult present. ... At the end of this second interview Abid was informed for the first

time of his right to legal advice. His father requested that a local solicitor be contacted.

....

11. *Abid was then provided with a bed and went to sleep, but at 23.30 he was awoken and interviewed for a third time in the presence of two social workers, Ms Jessie Owens and Mr Brian Mettrick ... At 00.20 on 26th August the third interview ended. Abid was asked if he wanted to make a statement and the police officers left the room so that he could talk to Miss Owens and Mr Mettrick.*

12. *From 00.31 to 01.26 Abid made a written statement under caution to DS Richardson in the presence of Ms Owens and Mr Mettrick ...*

To the foregoing cases must be added that of **Foster**, which has been the only pre-PACE/vulnerable confession case from England and Wales which, to date, has been upheld following reference by the Commission. F, who was described in the Court of Appeal judgment as 'an inadequate 23 years old man of limited intelligence and abnormally suggestible', was arrested on suspicion of murder and interrogated in 1985 prior to the commencement of PACE. He was interviewed by police without support of a legal adviser or appropriate adult ten times over the course of a six-day period. A social worker was brought in at the very final interview *after* F had intimated to police officers that he was ready to make a confession statement. The social worker's statement to the Commission strongly suggested that she had been brought in to 'validate' the confession rather than to give any support or advice to the suspected person. F resiled from his confession not long afterwards. There were unusual features of the case, including the fact that Mr Foster dramatically withdrew his retraction at trial and admitted the offence under cross-examination by prosecution counsel.[9] The (somewhat complex) facts are beyond the scope of brief summary but the judgment is on the Bailii website.

Northern Ireland confession cases

Convictions based upon compliant and unsafe confessions have featured heavily in the Commission's Northern Ireland referrals – but within a very different legal and political context. The modern political troubles in the Province commenced in 1968-9, rapidly escalating into extreme terrorist violence. Emergency legislation was introduced whereby terrorist cases were withdrawn from juries and committed to Diplock judges, who were charged (unlike juries) with giving reasons for their verdicts. An important feature of the emergency legislation was the statutory provision for the drawing of adverse inferences from the failure to answer police questions, preceding by many years somewhat similar provisions introduced in England and Wales by virtue of the Criminal Justice and Public Order Act 1994.

On a practical and operational level, there were also important differences in the Northern Ireland situation. Officers of the Royal Ulster Constabulary (RUC) interrogating persons suspected of terrorist offences were effectively operating in a war situation in which intelligence was vital and there were strong operational imperatives to 'crack' terrorist suspects. Special holding centres were used to interrogate suspects, including the notorious Castlereagh holding centre. It is clear beyond doubt that officers used singularly intensive interrogation methods, often involving the use of pairs of officers to interrogate unrepresented suspects almost continuously during waking hours for up to five days without bringing charge, as permitted by the emergency legislation. Solicitors were almost invariably excluded from interviews to the maximum extent permitted by the emergency legislation. Solicitors were indeed perceived by the security forces as likely vectors of information to paramilitary forces (on both sides of the religious divide) if given access to suspects in detention.

There will, inevitably, be continuing differences of view across the political and religious divide about the extent of oppression routinely (or occasionally) deployed at Castlereagh, as there will be about the justification for such methods. It is beyond question, however, that the conditions of interrogation were harsh. The European Committee for the Prevention of Torture and Inhuman and Degrading Treatment and Punishment (CPT), reporting in 1993, expressed the matter judiciously thus:

> *Even in the absence of overt acts of ill-treatment, there is no doubt that a stay in a holding centre may be – and is perhaps designed to be – a most disagreeable experience. The material conditions of detention are poor (especially at Castlereagh) and important qualifications are, or at least can be, placed upon certain fundamental rights of persons detained by the police (in particular, the possibilities for contact with the outside world are severely limited throughout the whole period of detention and various restrictions can be placed on the right of access to a lawyer). To this must be added the intensive and potentially prolonged character of the interrogation process. The cumulative effect of these factors is to place persons detained at the holding centres under a considerable degree of psychological pressure. The*

CPT must state, in this connection, that to impose upon a detainee such a degree of pressure as to break his will would amount, in its opinion, to inhuman treatment.

It may help to contextualise the above discussion, and to illustrate the interrogation methods used during the Emergency, to draw on the judgment given in the case of Pascal **Mulholland**, who was arrested by police during sectarian riots in Portadown in 1976. He was aged 16 at the time. He was convicted of IRA membership.[10] The facts of his interrogation by police officers following his arrest are set out in the judgment of the Northern Ireland Court of Appeal in the appeal which followed the Commission's reference:

The appellant ... was arrested on 18 October 1976 ... and detained at Portadown Police Station until 20 October 1976 on suspicion of involvement in a gun and petrol bomb attack on an RUC patrol.

The custody log recorded that, on 18 October 1976, [he] was interviewed for over seven hours in total. On 19 October 1976, he was interviewed for nine hours in total, including one interview that lasted for five hours between 7.00 pm and midnight. During the last hour of this interview, the custody log recorded that he had made a statement of admission ...

The appellant spent both nights of 18 October 1976 and 19 October 1976 on a couch in the medical room at the police station. He had been in police custody for some forty hours before he made the statement of admission. During the period of 18 October 1976 to 20 October 1976 he was interviewed for approximately sixteen hours. Throughout all interviews, the only persons in attendance were the appellant and police officers. According to the custody record he arrived at Portadown RUC station at 7.40 am on 18 October 1976 and was not granted access to either his parents or a solicitor or any other appropriate adult until after he had made a statement of admission on 20 October 1976. He first received access to legal advice when he saw a solicitor at 4.45 p.m. on 20 October 1976 after he had been charged at a special court.

He was convicted by a Diplock judge (Lowry LCJ), who rejected an application to exclude the confession evidence. This was notwithstanding the fact that the Children and Young Persons Act (Northern Ireland) 1968 clearly provided that his parents should have been informed and the Judges' Rules stipulated that he should have been allowed legal advice. The judge also rejected as untrue M's allegations of ill-treatment during questioning. M's conviction was quashed following evidence obtained (in a triumph of patient investigation) of misconduct on the part of the interrogating officers in another case. However, the judgment drew heavily on the principles enunciated in **Bentley** and *Ashley King*.

The facts of the Commission's other Northern Ireland sectarian cases are discussed in chapter 13, which deals generally with the Commission's Northern Ireland jurisdiction. However, the bare details of the Commission's modern standards of fairness cases from Northern Ireland are summarised below:[11]

Name/ year convicted	Offence	Age at time of offence where stated	No of Interviews	Solicitor or other adult present?	New evidence of vulnerability?
Hindes 1977	Murder + possession of firearms with intent contrary to s14 Firearms (Northern Ireland) Act 1969	14	8 interviews over 75 hours	Father only present at 7th interview when Hindes made a confession statement.	Yes
Hanna 1977	Ditto	16	4 interviews over 60 hours	Father only present at final interview when Hanna made a confession statement.	Yes
Adams 1977	Murder, false impris- onment, GBH	16	3 interviews over 1½ days	Father only present at final interview when Adams made a confession statement.	Yes
Magee 1990	Conspiracy to murder	24	11 interviews over 54 hours	No.	No

The facts of these cases vary in detail but they are subject to a common pattern of the suspects, generally young and vulnerable, being isolated and continuously interrogated until they provided a confession. It was a common feature of these cases that the suspects were only permitted to be supported by the presence of a parent at the point at which they were ready to sign a confession or had already done so. Applications at trial to exclude evidence of confessions obtained in this fashion were either unsuccessful or were realistically not made by defence

147

counsel on the grounds that the judges were extremely unlikely to agree to them. It is a (creditable) reflection upon the realism of the modern constitution of the Northern Ireland Court of Appeal that it has recognised what had been 'the score' at the time of the Emergency. Thus – in **Magee** – noting that no application was made to exclude confession evidence that was the product of three days of isolation and intensive interviews – the Court observed:

> it is probably fair to say that the appellant's advisers would have been well aware that to attempt at trial to found a case on lack of legal advice or conditions in Castlereagh would have had no chance of success and so did not advance such a ground for exclusion of the statements.

One is reminded of the notice displayed in some retail establishments 'do not ask for credit as a refusal often offends'. Accused persons detained on suspicion of offences were held for extended periods, interrogated with great intensity and denied support and advice (until ready to confess). However, if they raised questions about the fairness of admitting confession evidence they would be 'realistically' advised by their own counsel that there was no point in upsetting the judge by making a song and dance about it when the matter came up to trial.

One further Northern Ireland case deserves mention. Ian **Hay Gordon** was convicted of murder in 1953 – long preceding the recent Troubles. He was found 'guilty but insane', largely on the basis of a confession secured at the conclusion of interrogation in which police officers had used his homosexuality (then illegal and untolerated) to prise a confession out of him. Reference of his case required amending legislation[12] as the 1995 Act did not allow for review of this (long defunct) verdict. The following is drawn from the conclusion of the judgment quashing the verdict:

> It seems to us clear that Detective Superintendent Capstick set out to achieve just this type of sapping of the appellant's will when he conducted the interview on the morning of 15 January 1953 and we think it likely that he succeeded in this object. The phrase "broken down" used by counsel in cross-examination and accepted by Mr Capstick in our view represents the state which he sought to bring about. If the appellant had not been questioned at length about his sexual proclivities on the morning of 15 January, he would not have been so ready to make the confession after lunch that day. We think that the effect on his will to stay silent is likely to have been substantial and that the fear of having his sexual activities revealed to

> *his family and the world would have affected his mind. We therefore would not regard his confession as having been proved to be voluntary in the eyes of the law. It seems to us doubtful whether it could properly have been so regarded in 1953, for the same common law was applicable. But now that the law has been more clearly developed, we have no hesitation in saying that the admission of the confession cannot be sustained by the application of modern standards.*

It should be noted that, despite the age of the verdict, Mr Hay Gordon, who had served a long term for this offence, remained very much alive and concerned at the outcome of his appeal. He contended that his confession had been coerced and false and was anxious that the verdict against him should be quashed.[13]

The current position on modern standards of fairness cases

Most observers would be likely to agree that the Court of Appeal's decision in **Bentley**, and the referrals that have followed from it, represent an important and valuable part of the Commission's achievement in its first ten years. The doctrine of modern standards of fairness denotes, no less, that the criminal justice system will not stand by and allow the perpetuation of unjust convictions based on coerced confessions. The Court of Appeal could have allowed the parrot cry that such convictions were secured in accordance with *contemporary* standards, that all concerned did their reasonable best at the time, and that no one raised serious procedural concerns when the trial took place. No doubt such a position could be pronounced with suitable judicial elegance, but it would have been anathema to the purposes for which the Commission was established.

It is, therefore, of concern to note that the practice of applying modern standards of fairness may not survive the application of new provisions introduced by s44 Criminal Justice and Immigration Act 2008.[14] Section 44 will be discussed in detail in the following chapter dealing with changes in the law but, putting the matter briefly, where the Court of Appeal concludes that:

> *the only ground for allowing [an appeal] would be that there has been a development in the law since the date of the conviction, verdict or finding that is the subject of the appeal,*

the Court *may* dismiss the appeal if it considers that the applicant would have been refused an extension of time to raise the new point of law concerned. Therefore, even if the Commission considers that a modern standards of fairness point should be considered by the Court, the Court may conclude otherwise.[15]

This new formulation potentially strikes at the heart of the proposition posited by **Bentley**, albeit it is important to note that the new section will create a *discretion* rather than a *requirement* for the Court to disregard post-trial developments of the law. The whole saga of the Commission's change-of-law cases, and the rising tide of irritation that such cases have caused the Court, is set out at some length in the following chapter. Cases such as those discussed in this chapter have not apparently lain at the heart of the Court's irritation with change-of-law cases. However, it would seem that at least some of the senior judiciary have come to dislike all change-of-law cases, and persuaded the government to bring in legislation so as to provide the Court with the discretion to close down historic cases.

The judicial suggestion that **Bentley** be repealed emanates from the exasperation of some members of the Court of Appeal with the practical effect of the declaratory and retrospective nature of English common law – the Guy Fawkes 'problem' as it were. The position is nicely summarised in a postscript to the submission of The Council of Her Majesty's Circuit Judges made in response to the *Quashing Convictions* consultation:[16]

> One area worthy of consideration for possible reform arises from the decision in Bentley ... The problem, described at page 310 of Bentley arises when, after conviction, "there have been significant changes in the common law (as opposed to changes of statute) or in standards of fairness". When such a case is referred by the CCRC, the Court of Appeal is required to "apply legal rules and procedural criteria that were not and could not reasonably have been applied at the time".

> Lord Justice Kay, sitting in the Queen's Bench Division on 5 December 2006, expressed the view of the court that it would "now be timely for the legislature to reconsider the approach to changes in the common law expounded" in Bentley *as well as the relationship between the CCRC and the Court of Appeal in change of law cases (paragraph 49,* R (on the application of the Director of Revenue and Customs Prosecutions) v CCRC).[17] *This is an issue of principle and difficulty about what is described as "the declaratory theory of the common law" in the area of criminal justice which would in our view, and in agreement with Kay LJ, repay further consideration.*

The new provisions are clearly designed to do the job proposed by this submission.

The difficulty with this position is that to abolish or limit the retrospective application of the law could affect the position of entirely worthy applicants who are clearly victims of miscarriages of justice – such as discussed in this chapter – along with less worthy applicants who seek to take opportunistic advantage of changes of the law to evade responsibility for their obviously criminal behaviour. One way that this circle might be squared is to deem the doctrine of modern standards of fairness *unnecessary*; this is the position formulated by Judge LJ in the very difficult case of **Cottrell and Fletcher**, a Commission case decided on 31 July 2007 and discussed at greater length in the next chapter. Judge LJ put the position as follows:

> *Cases like these are very different from* R v Bentley ... *where this court applied modern standards of fairness to a notorious conviction. Bentley's conviction would not have been regarded as unsafe if the summing up had been fair and the directions of law adequate.* **It was quashed because by standards in 1952 as well as modern standards, the summing up, in particular in the context of the burden of standard of proof, and the lack of overall balance, deprived the appellant of his "birthright" of a fair trial.** *The decision did not depend on a legal view of the principles governing joint enterprise, and in particular the then recent decision ... in* R v Powell *and* R v English ... *In relation to criticisms of the judge's directions of law,* **the only ground which succeeded was based on the later court's view that the first court had simply failed to grapple with the point. In other words, the defect arose at the time of trial. It was not based on any post-trial change of law.** (Emphases added)

According to this reading of the law, **Bentley** (and possibly by analogy the other cases discussed in this chapter) could have been quashed on the basis of breaches of *contemporary* legal requirements and standards of fairness. On this view, it was not necessary to have recourse to *modern* standards of fairness at all.

The difficulty with this formulation is that the Court has resorted to modern standards of fairness in so many pre-PACE cases precisely because the rights of suspects to protection against oppressive questioning and compliant confessions were formerly sketchy and incomplete; a point which a reading of any pre-PACE edition of *Archbold* will amply confirm. In case after case, pre-PACE convictions were upheld of vulnerable defendants whose will had been plainly broken by persistent police questioning in the harshest of conditions and in the absence of modern protections. It is all very well to take a most extreme case, such as Derek Bentley, and to pronounce that his conviction should have been quashed at the first-time appeal (as indeed it should). It has to be recognised, however, that – by the standards of contemporary legal practices – other cases were not so clear cut. That is why resort to *modern* standards of fairness is sometimes required to resolve miscarriages of justice.

It is also somewhat disconcerting that this particular hare was set running in some measure due to comments of the Commission chairman, Professor Zellick, who suggested that **Bentley** might be due for legislative repeal in an affidavit filed in the case of **R (on the application of the Director of Revenue and Customs Prosecutions) v Criminal Cases Review Commission**. The issues raised by this particular case will be discussed in the following chapter, but they were far removed from the **Bentley** point of law. In his affidavit prepared for the case, Professor Zellick nevertheless called into question whether the **Bentley** doctrine should remain law. As the Court stated in its judgment:

> *Professor Zellick has expressed surprise that* Bentley *is not mentioned in the recent consultation paper on Quashing Convictions. We share his surprise. We do not regard it as beyond dispute that, as a matter of policy, the declaratory theory of the common law should be a trump card in this area of criminal law.*

The postscript to the submission of The Council of Her Majesty's Circuit Judges, therefore, seems to be an indirect consequence of Professor Zellick's affidavit.

The new provisions should not, of course, mean that future modern standards of fairness cases are doomed, nor that the Court of Appeal will feel constrained to uphold convictions in cases of obvious miscarriages of justice such as those discussed in this chapter. Should similar cases arise in the future, the Commission would, no doubt, reason that the Court *might* consider the impact of modern legal developments, notwithstanding the statutory discretion not to do so. There may be cases where it can additionally be argued, as suggested by Judge LJ in **Cottrell and Fletcher**, that there had been a breach of *contemporary* legal standards in any event. In general, the Courts of Appeal, both in England and Wales and in Northern Ireland, have not hesitated to quash unjust convictions such as those discussed in this chapter. It is greatly to be hoped that this will not change in the future.

Finally, the history outlined in the last few paragraphs demonstrates why it is ultimately necessary for pressure groups, such as JUSTICE, to remain vigilant in monitoring miscarriages of justice and not to rely entirely on institutions of government – even non-departmental independent bodies like the Commission – to do so. The **Bentley** decision has served to clear the name of some still relatively young men who were convicted on the basis of thoroughly unreliable confessions obtained by oppressive and unfair means, and it seems most regrettable that the Commission should be seen to have been advocating the repeal of this point of law.[18] There remains an important role in the future, therefore, both for the profession, and for non-governmental organisations such as JUSTICE, to prick the conscience of the government to stand by its commitment to victims of miscarriage of justice and resist any further proposed dismantling of the 1995 Act.

Notes

1. This was also the title of a film about the trial. Other Commission referral cases which have inspired films include *Essex Boys* (loosely based upon the case of **Steele, Whomes and Corry**), and *Dance with a Stranger* (**Ruth Ellis**). Cases not referred include those of Timothy Evans, which inspired *10 Rillington Place*, and *Stafford and Luvaglio* which is said to have provided very loose inspiration for *Get Carter*.

2. Although many will question whether the alleged words were actually said.

3. The necessity of promulgating the doctrine of modern standards of fairness has been challenged by the judgment of Judge LJ in **Cottrell and Fletcher**. This is discussed at the conclusion of this chapter.

4. [2000] 2 Cr App R 391.

5. PACE, although it received Royal Assent in 1984, did not for the most part come into force until 1 January 1986.

6. In granting leave, the Court made the interesting observation that if it refused leave to appeal out of time, the case would surely bounce back to the Court via the Commission.

7. The police are, of course, aware that attention-seeking calls are a feature of many high-profile enquiries.

8. In **Hussain**'s case, the Court of Appeal declined to receive the psychological evidence of vulnerability due to the lapse of time between the interview and his subsequent psychological assessment.

9. A vulnerable defendant, to this day, takes his chances that if he goes into the witness box and gives evidence, he may be torn apart limb by limb by cross-examining prosecution counsel. The cross-examination and capitulation of Mr Foster was witnessed by Professor Gudjonsson who remarked to the author that he said to himself, 'where's the protection in that', as he witnessed this somewhat gladiatorial scene.

10. But was acquitted of a petrol bombing offence.

11. It should also be noted that four of the other Northern Ireland cases referred by the Commission – **Green, Gorman and Mackinney, Latimer,** and **MacDermott and McCartney** – although referred and decided on grounds other than modern standards of fairness, all disclose a very similar pattern of interrogation of suspects to confession. More details of these cases are in chapter 13.

12. The Criminal Cases Review (Insanity) Act 1999.

13. There is illuminating contemporary coverage of this appeal and its impact upon Mr Hay Gordon on the BBC News website which may be found at http://news.bbc.co.uk/1/hi/northern_ireland/1078576.stm.

14. This Act received Royal Assent on 8 May 2008.

15. The practice of the Court, in relation to the grant of leave to appeal in change-of-law cases, is discussed in the succeeding chapter.

16. This submission was not published but a copy was provided to the author by the Ministry of Justice.

17. [2006] EWHC Admin 3064.

18. This somewhat impassioned passage exposes me to the possible charge of hypocrisy in drawing the Commission's pay and then subjecting it to such criticism. Whilst I have generally avoided the first person singular in my account of the Commission's work, I would say in self-defence that I made precisely these points whilst a serving Commissioner.

Chapter 7 - Changes in the law

The Bentley problem

To some degree, the legal proposition established by the Court's judgment in **Bentley** was trite. It is an axiom learned by law students in their first week at college that judges are said not to *create* the common law but to *declare* what it is (and always has been). At one level, therefore, the Court's declaration in **Bentley** that an appellant may be entitled to take the benefit of any clarifications of the common law that have occurred prior to the appeal was an entirely conventional statement of English legal doctrine.[1]

That said, the Court of Appeal has grappled for many years with the difficulty that can arise when applicants seek opportunistically to use changes of legal interpretation in order to overturn old convictions. The division of the Court which decided **Bentley** was well aware – in the words of Lord Bingham – that its judgment 'could cause difficulty in some cases'. **Bentley** has provided the Commission with the legal means of re-opening festering miscarriage of justice cases resulting from procedures which would today be recognised as unfair and unacceptable. That is a point of principle which the Commission should surely be ready to defend. But, on the other hand, the judgment also potentially opened up to review *any* conviction which had been secured upon an understanding of the law that has subsequently changed. At this point, the jibe that the Commission will soon be re-opening the case of Guy Fawkes heaves into view.[2]

Moreover, changes in the law that the Commission is required to take into account are not confined to restatements of the *common* law. The same principle applies in cases where there has been a changed understanding of the effect of *statute* law. As the Court stated in **Bentley**, a statute cannot (as a rule) be applied to convictions predating the commencement of the statute,[3] but where the Court delivers judgment correcting a previous misunderstanding about the effect of a statutory provision, that judgment will relate back to the commencement of the statute. Driven to extremes, the **Bentley** doctrine could be used by vast numbers of applicants, including those very obviously guilty, to seek review of historic convictions on the basis that the understanding of the law has now changed.

This problem can be illustrated by the case of *Preddy*.[4] P had been convicted of a mortgage fraud under s15 Theft Act 1968, which created the offence of obtaining 'property of another' by deception. The species of mortgage fraud practised by P and others had had the effect of inducing the victim (usually a bank or building society) to issue a cheque – a chose in action – in favour of the defendant. The House of Lords concluded that although there had clearly been deception, it could not identify any 'property of another' obtained by the fraud. It ruled that P's conduct in dishonestly causing the building society to issue a cheque was not apt to be prosecuted under that particular section of the Theft Act.

Following this decision, the statute was swiftly revised by the Theft (Amendment) Act 1996, which created a new section 15A to fill the lacuna created by *Preddy*. However, the decision left a door open to sundry others – who had been convicted upon similar facts and under the same section – to seek to re-open their convictions.[5] Those who had not appealed previously applied for leave to appeal out of time. Putting the matter briefly, it was decided in the ensuing decisions of the Court that appellants who had pleaded *not guilty* at trial would achieve only a hollow victory on appeal. In the case of convictions, which had been proved to the jury (following a not guilty plea), the Court was generally able to exercise power under s3 Criminal Appeal Act 1968 to quash the section 15 conviction but to substitute a conviction under an alternative section of the Theft Act carrying the same sentence, leaving the appellant no better off.

However, where appellants had pleaded *guilty*, no such power of substitution at that time existed under the provisions of the Criminal Appeal Act 1968.[6] The Court, therefore, faced the situation that if it heard their appeals it would be bound to quash their convictions without any power of substitution, even though they had pleaded guilty to the criminal course of conduct charged against them. In *Hawkins*,[7] the Court decided that it was not prepared to quash the conviction of an appellant in just that position, and it declined leave to appeal out of time sought by the appellant. This meant that although H's appeal would have inevitably succeeded if he had been given leave, the Court baulked his appeal by refusing to hear it. In doing so, the Court applied the dictum of Lord Lane in *Mitchell*:[8]

> *It should be clearly understood, and this Court wants to make it even more*
> *abundantly clear, that the fact that there has been an apparent change in*
> *the law or, to put it more precisely, that previous misconceptions about the*

> *meaning of a statute have been put right, does not afford a proper ground for*
> *allowing an extension of time in which to appeal against conviction.*

In H's case, the Court noted:

> *That practice may on its face seem harsh. On the other hand, the*
> *consequences of any other rule are equally unattractive. It would mean*
> *that a defendant who had roundly and on advice accepted that he had*
> *acted dishonestly and fraudulently, and pleaded guilty, or who had been*
> *found guilty and chosen not to appeal, could after the event seek to reopen*
> *the convictions. If such convictions were to be readily reopened it would be*
> *difficult to know where to draw the line or how far to go back.*

And it continued:

> *It is plain, as we read the authorities, that there is no inflexible rule on this*
> *subject, but the general practice is plainly one which sets its face against the*
> *reopening of convictions recorded in such circumstances. Counsel submits*
> *-- and in our judgment submits correctly -- that the practice of the court*
> *has in the past, in this and comparable situations, been to eschew undue*
> *technicality and ask whether any substantial injustice has been done.*

This general rule of practice has been applied in many subsequent authorities. For example, in *Benjafield*,[9] the issue was whether an altered understanding of the impact of a statute, due to the coming into force of the Human Rights Act 1998, should open up the possibility of an out-of-time appeal. The Court affirmed its general practice:

> *It is not usual to grant leave to appeal out of time where the grounds of*
> *appeal are based on post-trial changes in the law ... The court would not*
> *wish in this case to do other than confirm the existing practice.*

The general practice has been more recently reaffirmed in *Ballinger*,[10] in which B sought leave to appeal out of time a conviction received in a Naval Court Martial following an earlier decision, which held that the naval system of Courts Martial lacked independence and, therefore, violated the Human Rights Act. The Court declined B leave to appeal his conviction out of time, notwithstanding that his conviction would almost certainly have been quashed had leave been given.

The Court's practice in refusing leave in change-of-law cases to appellants who (not having previously appealed) require leave to bring an out-of-time appeal has been clear. The issue for the Commission is how to deal with similar cases brought to it by applicants who have previously appealed or have been refused leave to appeal and who can only get back before the Court if referred by the Commission. The Commission has a gatekeeper role in relation to such applications, and once a case has been referred by it the Court does not have the option of refusing to hear the appeal. The Commission has, therefore, to decide whether or not it should apply its gatekeeper role to keep change-of-law cases out of the appeal arena. The Commission's dilemma can be clearly seen in the change-of-law cases referred by it.

Preddy cases

Preddy was decided by the House of Lords in 1996 and a number of applications, which came to the Commission in its early days on the back of *Preddy*, were referred.

In **Duncan Smith**, DS had been convicted after a trial, having pleaded not guilty. In the appeal following the Commission's referral, the Court substituted alternative offences apt to the proven facts and, therefore, DS gained nothing from having his conviction quashed. The Court stated that the appropriate approach to be taken by the Commission would be to bear in mind the possibility of substitution and not to refer in cases where substitution could be foreseen. (The Court recognised that the Commission had already adopted this approach by the time DS's appeal was heard.)

In two other early referrals based on *Preddy*, namely **Garner** and **Burke**, the applicants also gained no benefit. In **Burke**, the Court substituted an alternative apt charge for the conviction that was bad due to *Preddy*. In **Garner**, counsel – no doubt recognising that substitution was inevitable – did not pursue the *Preddy* point at all.

In **Kansal**, the Court of Appeal stated that it would have substituted alternative convictions on the *Preddy* point, but allowed the appeal on a separate human rights issue. The Court stated:

> we express the very firm hope that, in exercising the discretion under s9 and the judgment conferred by s13(1)(a), the CCRC may think it right to take into account this court's practice in refusing leave because of a change in

the law just as, in the light of Pearson, *they take the court's practice into account when assessing the possibility of fresh evidence being received.*

On the referral of cases raising human rights issues, the Court noted sardonically:

> *Leaving aside colourful historical examples such as Sir Thomas More, Guy Fawkes and Charles I, all of whom would have benefited from convention rights, until the Criminal Evidence Act 1898, no defendant was permitted to give evidence on his own behalf. That is a clear breach of Article 6. Many examples in the 20th century of other rules and procedures which, viewed with the wisdom of hindsight, were in breach of the Convention could be given. But we resist that temptation lest, by succumbing, we exacerbate the problem to which we are drawing attention.*

In **Clark (Brian)**, the Court adopted a quite different approach. C had been convicted of a number of offences following a guilty plea, three of the convictions being bad due to *Preddy* considerations. The Commission referred, noting that if the *Preddy* convictions were quashed, the criminal bankruptcy order against C would fall to be discharged. Quashing those convictions the Court stated:

> *It will, in our judgment, be only in rare and exceptional cases that reasonableness and fairness will require a reference in relation to conviction because of a change in the law many years after a plea of guilty. In the present case, because of the potential benefit to the appellant if the convictions on counts 4, 5 and 7 are quashed, we regard the Commission's decision to refer the convictions on those counts, if we may say so, as an entirely appropriate exercise of the Commission's discretion.*

By the time **Clark** was decided, the Commission had, however, come to the view that it would not normally refer *Preddy*-type cases in the light of the Court's observations and also in the light of the absence of any discernible interests of justice being served by such referrals. The Commission's practice survived a judicial review challenge in **Saxon (R on the application of) v Criminal Cases Review Commission**.

Hayes (Dennis Francis)

H's case revolved around a very different change of law point. H had been convicted of murder, the circumstances being that he and his confederates had been confronted by the occupant of premises they were burgling. H thrust a handkerchief into the victim's mouth to silence him, which had the result (which in the Commission's judgment he was most unlikely to have foreseen) that the victim's dentures were forced into his throat, resulting in death. The jury had been correctly directed – on the basis of the understanding of the law at time of trial – that they could convict of murder if they were satisfied that the defendant foresaw death or serious injury as the *probable* result of his actions. However, the foresight test had been altered subsequent to the trial in *Nedrick*[11] and *Woollin*[12] in which it was stated that a jury should be directed to convict of murder only if sure that 'death or serious bodily harm was a *virtual certainty* (barring some unforeseen intervention) as a result of a defendant's actions and that the defendant appreciated that such was the case' (emphasis added). The Commission felt that on these very specific facts the jury might well have taken a different view as to whether the offence of murder (as opposed to manslaughter) had been made out if they had been directed to apply the 'virtual certainty' test. The Commission, therefore, referred the conviction.

Upholding the conviction, the Court somewhat disingenuously pronounced itself satisfied that, even if the jury had been directed in terms of 'virtual certainty', the result would have been the same since it was 'quite obvious that at least really serious bodily injury was a virtual certainty as a result of the appellant's actions'. Whilst no criticism was sounded of the Commission, the manner in which the Court stepped round the legal issue clearly indicated that it disliked the change of law point raised by the referral.

Morgan Smith and the provocation cases

The cases raising *Morgan Smith*[13] are discussed at length in chapter 8 dealing with homicide cases. Put very briefly, the House of Lords in *Morgan Smith* ruled that where provocation was raised as a defence to murder, the jury should be directed to consider whether there were any 'personal characteristics' (generally psychological frailties) affecting the susceptibility of the defendant to react to provocative words or conduct and, therefore, the reasonableness of his response to such words or conduct. This was a reversal of previous authority.[14] Seven referrals – **Josephine Smith, Rowland, Farnell, Karimi, James, Moses** and **Hill** – all raised in varying degrees the proposition that the jury, whilst properly directed on the law as understood at the time of trial, had not been correctly directed in the light of *Morgan Smith*. The convictions of the first four were all quashed on the basis of change-of-law considerations, although **Karimi** was re-convicted of murder following a re-trial. In the later cases of **James** and **Moses**, by the time their appeals came to be heard the status quo ante had been restored after *Morgan Smith* was effectively reversed by the later case of *Holley*.[15] Their convictions were upheld. In the case of **Hill**, the Court ruled at a directions hearing that his appeal could not, following *Holley*, succeed in reliance upon *Morgan Smith*, which had been the basis of the Commission's reference. His appeal was pursued on other grounds but was not successful.

It should be noted, finally, that whilst the Court exhibited extreme irritation with the House of Lords for deciding *Morgan Smith* as it had, it was never suggested that the Commission had been at fault for referring the above cases due to the change of law brought about by *Morgan Smith*.

Joint enterprise cases

In *Powell and English*,[16] the House of Lords clarified and amended the test of foresight which is needed to convict B of a crime in a case where B has acted jointly with A in a criminal enterprise but A has escalated the criminal activity by producing and using a more dangerous weapon – for instance by using a gun or a knife in a fight where less offensive weapons (or no weapons at all) were being used.

Mair was referred as a change-of-law case raising this issue. M had participated in a fight in a public house and armed himself with a broken bottle. His confederate, B, then produced a knife which he used to kill. The jury was not directed, as it would have been if the trial had taken place after the judgment in *Powell and English*, as to how they should approach the question of M's foresight of the fact that B would use a knife. Giving judgment on M's appeal the Court stated:

> For the appellant to be guilty upon a joint enterprise of murder the jury would need to be sure either that the appellant knew that B had a knife and in that knowledge participated in the joint enterprise; or that, in the circumstances, a broken glass or bottle was equally dangerous as a small lockknife. These are both questions of fact for the jury. We are satisfied, for the reasons that we have given, that the jury was not directed to consider either of these matters.

The Court – being unable to assess how the jury would have decided those questions – quashed the murder conviction.

Miah was a somewhat similar case. The summing up was described by the Court as 'impeccable' upon the understanding of the law at the time of trial, but the law had been overtaken by the decision in *Powell and English,* in consequence whereof M's co-defendant, *Uddin,*[17] successfully appealed his conviction. The Court noted:

> It is quite clear that the primary basis of the decision of the Court [in Uddin] was the failure of the judge to direct the jury that they must be sure that those taking part were aware that one of their number might use a knife before they could convict, and that must apply whether the offence is one of murder or of manslaughter.

And it quashed M's conviction. **Mair** and **Miah** were, arguably, among the more successful change-of-law referrals. The law of joint enterprise was capable of operating extremely harshly, and *Powell and English* redressed the law to the benefit of those who sought to show that the murderous attack had been due to an unforeseen escalation by the principal assailant.

Compare and contrast **Webb**, where W effectively controlled a gang of young burglars. He had sent them out to burgle knowing that they were tooled up with knives, but the evidence was that he had not been aware that one of them had the handkerchief which was used to kill the occupant of the target house. The Commission was obviously aware that the unforeseen use of a handkerchief could scarcely be characterised as unforeseen escalation in the eyes of Mr Webb, who was aware not only that the young burglars were carrying knives but also that they were prepared to use them if necessary. However, it referred (with a somewhat heavy heart) on the basis that the jury had not been given a direction in the terms of *Powell and English*. The Court agreed with the Commission that the directions had been deficient in that the jury were not given a direction (in terms required by *Powell and English*) to consider whether or not the handkerchief might be regarded as more dangerous than the weapons which W had known about. The Court continued, however:

> We have to ask whether the conviction is unsafe. In our view, in the light of the admissions made by the appellant, a jury would inevitably have convicted if this direction had been given.

The decision clearly shows that the Commission needs to consider whether or not the change in the law is a matter of real significance in relation to the issues in contention at the trial. A very clear distinction can be made between **Mair**, who clearly was entitled to have the jury consider the argument that his confederate's use of a knife represented an escalation of violence unforeseen by him; and **Webb**, where a similar argument applied to the use of a handkerchief would have been extremely unlikely to have impressed the jury.

Richards and Kennedy – assisting self-administration of drugs leading to death

In **Richards**, R had assisted B, a heroin addict, to inject drugs, in consequence of which B died. The jury was directed that the offence was made out if they were satisfied that R had supplied the drug to B – because it was an unlawful act simply to supply the drug and that constituted a sufficient unlawful act for the offence of manslaughter. This direction correctly reflected the law as then understood following the case of *Kennedy (No 1)*.[18] Subsequently, *Kennedy (No 1)* was overruled by *Dias*[19] where it was decided (in brief) that the act causing death was the self-injection, which was not an offence under the Misuse of Drugs Act. The possession and supply of the drug in such circumstances was a separate act – not causative of death. R's conviction was referred by the Commission as a result of the change of law brought about by *Dias* and his conviction was quashed by the Court of Appeal.

In the light of the change of the law encompassed by the decisions in *Dias* and **Richards**, the Commission traced Mr Kennedy and suggested that he might apply to the Commission for review of his conviction. He did so and the Commission referred his conviction. Following referral, the Court of Appeal in **Kennedy (No 2)**, adopting an argument which can only be described as ingenious, concluded that in K's case, the supply of the drug by K to the victim and the fatal self-administration of the drug by the victim could be characterised as one 'combined operation'. This enabled the Court to circumvent the point of law in *Dias* and the conviction was upheld. This decision was, however, overturned upon appeal to the House of Lords and Mr Kennedy's conviction was quashed.

Other change-of-law cases

Bain

Bain is perhaps a case in which the Commission tested the logic of the **Bentley** judgment to destruction. B had been convicted of murder in 1971. The case against him was relatively thin, unless one took account of the many palpable lies he had told police officers investigating the offence – lies which almost certainly helped to persuade the jury that they could be sure that B was guilty of the offence. This conviction occurred well before the case of *Lucas*,[20] in which the Court of Appeal had laid down guidelines about the way juries should be directed to consider the importance of lies (and in particular to be cautious in assuming that lies are evidence of guilt). The jury had not, therefore, been directed in *Lucas* terms. The Commission referred the conviction (not without hesitation) as the significance of B's lies had received so much emphasis in the trial that the absence of a lies direction was a matter of particular significance on the facts of the instant case. The Court dealt adroitly with this case, noting that defence counsel had told the jury in his closing speech that 'people tell lies for all sorts of reasons' and that the judge had referred to this in his summing up, adding that counsel had been 'perfectly right' in making this point. The jury had, therefore, been put on notice of the issue, even though not correctly directed on the basis of a modern understanding of the law, and the conviction was upheld.

Sheehan

S was convicted of two charges of indecent assault in a case which had involved consensual intercourse with an underage girl. A major issue in the trial was whether or not she had, indeed, been aged under 16 when the offences took place. The judge directed the jury that, if they were satisfied that the complainant was under 16 at the relevant time, the offence was made out. Subsequently in *R v K*,[21] the House of Lords ruled that, in an offence of indecent assault on a female under the age of 16, where there is evidence that the complainant consented or may have consented, the prosecution had to prove that the defendant did not have an honest belief that the complainant was aged 16 or over. This had been very much a live issue in S's trial – the evidence being that the complainant (who admitted having worked as a prostitute) may have appeared considerably older than she was. The conviction was referred by the Commission as a change-of-law case and quashed.

Williams

This curious case is worth a brief mention. W – in urgent need of a drink – went to an all-night supermarket outside licensing hours where he demanded, and was refused, a bottle of whisky. He then took a carrier bag containing an empty bottle and tapped it on the counter pointing it at the shop assistant. She apprehended that it might be a gun and gave him a bottle of whisky. He pleaded guilty to carrying an imitation firearm with intent to commit an indictable offence (s18 Firearms Act 1968), and received a life sentence under the 'two-strikes-and-you're-out' legislation, discussed in chapter 12. His case was referred following the later House of Lords decision in *Bentham*[22] that fingers pointed inside a pocket could not constitute an imitation firearm for the purposes of this offence. The Commission considered that *Bentham* afforded at least an arguable defence and that W might have pleaded not guilty had he been aware of it. Expressed briefly, the Court decided that *Bentham* applied to sufficiently different facts for it to conclude that, on the instant facts, the law applicable to W's case had not changed – and it upheld the conviction.

Human Rights Act cases

For a brief period, the possible retrospective effect of the Human Rights Act 1998 (HRA) was a major point of concern for the Commission. The HRA mostly came into force on 2 October 2000 and incorporated provisions of the European Convention on Human Rights into domestic law in respect of criminal proceedings with effect from that date. The issue of concern to the Commission was the correct interpretation of s22(4) HRA. This provided that s7(1)(b) HRA, which entitles a person to rely on his or her Convention rights in any legal proceedings,

> *applies to proceedings brought by or at the instigation of a public authority whenever the act in question took place; but otherwise that subsection does not apply to an act taking place before the coming into force of that section.*

The Commission thought it at least arguable that if it referred a case on the basis that there had been a breach of Convention rights in a case preceding the HRA's commencement, then the ensuing appeal would constitute 'proceedings brought by or at the instigation of a public authority' – such that the HRA would take retrospective effect.

This was no small matter! It was (and is) beyond question the case that – as the Court of Appeal had stated in **Kansal** – many criminal convictions in the past have been secured in circumstances which would have violated the defendant's Convention rights. To give two relevant examples:

1. In Northern Ireland many persons had been convicted of terrorist offences, having been held for questioning for an extended period pursuant to the Emergency legislation and without the benefit of legal assistance. They were also made subject to adverse inferences if they failed to answer police questions. The provision for the drawing of adverse inferences in police interview, where the suspect lacked the protection of access to legal advice, had been specifically declared as violating the suspect's Convention rights by the European Court of Human Rights in *John Murray v United Kingdom*.[23]

2. A number of financial offences were formerly subject to investigation under provisions of the Companies Act, Insolvency Act and other legislation, which required suspected persons (under pain of criminal sanction) to answer questions, and as such breached the suspect's Convention right against self-incrimination.

Point 1 featured in the Commission's reference of **Magee**, the facts of which are more fully dealt with in chapter 13. The self-incrimination issue featured in the referrals of **Kansal** and, later, of **Lyons, Parnes, Ronson and Saunders** – far more famously known as the 'Guinness Four'.

The outcome of these cases was as follows. **Magee's** appeal was allowed upon the basis that section 22(4) *did* give the HRA retrospective effect. So too was that of **Kansal**, albeit the Court excoriated the Commission for making the reference. The Crown was given leave to appeal the decision in **Kansal** to the House of Lords, but before that appeal was heard the House of Lords decided (by a majority) in *Lambert*[24] that the HRA could not be applied retrospectively. Following *Lambert*, the House of Lords allowed the prosecution's appeal in **Kansal** and reinstated K's convictions for Insolvency Act offences.

The convictions of **Lyons et al** were also upheld, the judgment concluding with the following observations:

> For the benefit of those members of the public without the opportunity or inclination to read the full judgment, it amounts to this: the single ground on which the Criminal Cases Review Commission again referred this case to this Court became unarguable because, after the Reference, the House of Lords ruled that the Human Rights Act is not retrospective in a way benefiting the appellants. Without such retrospectivity, the appellants cannot rely on the United Kingdom's obligations in a treaty which was not incorporated into English law until 10 years after their trial.

This judgment brought to a close this chapter in the Commission's legal history as well as forming the final part of the lengthy and famed legal saga that followed the Guinness takeover of Distillers in the 1980s.

Subsequently, the Northern Ireland Court of Appeal stated in **Walsh** and **Latimer** that **Magee** had been wrongly decided and should not be followed. Additionally, the High Court in Northern Ireland (later affirmed by the Northern Ireland Court of Appeal) in a judicial review case named **In the matter of Quinn**

(Dermot) [25] rejected the argument that the HRA has the effect that Convention rights can be read back into an understanding of the pre-existing common law. It was unsuccessfully argued on behalf of Mr Quinn that the general approach required by the Convention should be incorporated – as an underground river as it were – into an understanding of the previously developing state of the common law.

The law is now very clear that the HRA does not have retrospective effect.

Section 34 and 35 cases – misdirection of juries on inferences from silence

A number of the Commission's referrals have been based upon misdirection of juries as to the inferences that may be drawn when a defendant elects not to give evidence in his or her own defence at trial, or when a defendant has failed to mention at police interview facts subsequently relied upon at trial.

These referrals have to a substantial extent been based upon developing judicial interpretation of the effect of ss34 and 35 Criminal Justice and Public Order Act 1994 (CJPOA). The CJPOA brought in highly contentious provisions providing that juries could be directed that they were entitled to draw adverse inferences from silence in certain circumstances, and it has been a matter which has racked judicial ingenuity to devise directions to the jury which reflect both the objectives of the CJPOA and the requirement for fairness of trials. The standard approved form of direction has undergone a continual process of revision in the light of successive authorities and the guidebook issued to judges – the Judicial Studies Board Bench Book – has been revised accordingly. This has opened up the question whether a person convicted after the jury received an 'out of date' direction should be entitled to take the benefit of an up to date direction reflecting the current understanding of the statute.

The commonsense answer to this question – surely – is to ask whether the difference in the direction is relevant to the issues that were raised at trial, and whether it can realistically be said that the different direction might have tipped the balance of the jury's deliberations. This was the approach taken in **Beckles**, which has been discussed in chapter 2, one of only two cases in which the Court has quashed convictions following a reference by the Commission on the basis of an inferences-from-silence point.[26]

The history of the Commission's section 34 and 35 referrals has been outlined in chapter 2 and it is suggested that the Commission has sometimes abandoned the promptings of common sense and adopted an over-academic approach to such cases. This has led to a hardening of judicial responses to such issues, most particularly in **Boyle and Ford**. It now seems likely that the Court will only in the rarest case entertain an appeal based upon changing judicial views as to the terms in which a jury should be directed on the drawing of inferences from silence.

The road to Rizvi

The issue of the correct approach to be taken by the Commission in change-of-law cases resurfaced with a vengeance in a number of linked cases where applicants had been convicted of conspiracy to commit money laundering offences. The substantive offence was defined in s49(2) Drug Trafficking Act 1994. This provided as follows:

> (2)   *A person is guilty of an offence if, knowing or having reasonable grounds to suspect that any property is, or in whole or in part directly or indirectly represents, another person's proceeds of drug trafficking, he - -*
>
> (a)   *conceals or disguises that property, or*
>
> (b)   *converts or transfers that property or removes it from the jurisdiction,*
>
> *for the purpose of assisting any person to avoid prosecution for a drug trafficking offence or the making or enforcement of a confiscation order.*

The substantive law has, subsequently, been replaced by the Proceeds of Crime Act 2002.

All of the cases referred by the Commission have been of persons convicted not of the substantive offence – as defined above – but of *conspiracy* to commit the offence. In *Saik*,[27] the House of Lords considered what matters had to be proved in order to establish the conspiracy offence – a matter which had been the source of conflicting prior authority. Put briefly, the House of Lords concluded that, in order to establish conspiracy, it was necessary for the prosecution to prove *actual* suspicion on the part of the defendant that the moneys being handled were the proceeds of drug trafficking. Previously, prosecutors had believed that it was sufficient to show that *reasonable grounds for belief* existed, and framed indictments accordingly. There existed, therefore, a group of convicted persons (many subject to very long prison sentences) who were in a position to argue that the prosecution had failed to establish all of the elements which it had become clear – following *Saik* – were necessary in order to establish the conspiracy offence.[28]

The case of Amer **Ramzan** – which raised precisely this issue – was referred by the Commission and heard by the Court along with six other appellants pursuing the same point, five of whom were seeking leave to appeal. R had, in effect, received leave by virtue of the Commission's reference. In its judgment, the Court set out at length the restrictive test applied by the Court in deciding whether to give leave in change-of-law cases and it refused leave to the five appellants applying for it. As for the Commission's reference of Mr Ramzan's conviction, the Court stated (clearly for the Commission's guidance) that:

> we would respectfully express the hope that full consideration will be given to the test which is applied in English law when applications of this kind are made.

However, leave having been given (by virtue of the Commission's reference), the Court considered that it had no option but to quash the conviction – the prosecution having failed to persuade the Court that there was an apt substitute offence for the proven conduct. The Court ordered a retrial.

Before **Ramzan** was decided, the Commission referred a further six cases, all based on the point of law in *Saik* and all raising somewhat similar facts. This drew forth a judicial review challenge in **R (on the application of the Director of Revenue and Customs Prosecutions) v Criminal Cases Review Commission** (henceforth referred to as **Rizvi**), challenging the Commission's decision to refer the cases of Mumtaz **Ahmed**, Ussama **El-Kurd**, Gulbir Rana **Singh** and Zafar **Rizvi**. The proposition advanced by the Director was that (as the judgment put it):

> when considering whether or not to refer what we shall call change of law cases, the Commission is "bound to apply an identical filter to that applied by the Court of Appeal when deciding whether or not to grant leave to appeal out of time".

In other words, it was submitted, if the Court of Appeal would refuse leave to appeal a change-of-law case out of time, the Commission was legally bound to do likewise.

The Court recognised that:

At the heart of this litigation there is a tension between the statutory powers of the Commission and the approach of the CACD to appeals based on the subsequent development of the law by judicial decision.

It resolved that point of principle firmly in the Commission's favour. The Court stated that:

the Commission is under no obligation to have regard to, still less to implement, a practice of the CACD which operates at a stage with which the Commission is not concerned.

The Court noted:

- That the Commission's role is to determine whether there is any real possibility that a conviction is 'unsafe' and it is not statutorily bound to the issue of whether or not there had been a miscarriage of justice.

- The Commission had referred other change-of-law cases – as discussed above – without criticism in many cases from the Court of Appeal.

- There was a distinct difference between proving *grounds to believe* that money being handled was drug money, and *actual knowledge*. The Court did not accept the Director's assertion that it was virtually certain that they would have been convicted if they had been indicted and tried on the basis of a correct understanding of the law.

As to the practicalities of dealing with such cases, the Court expressed itself 'relieved' that the issue resolved by *Saik* no longer arose in relation to prosecutions brought since the coming into effect of the Proceeds of Crime Act 2002.

The judgment concluded in the following terms:

One only has to read the judgment of Hughes LJ in Ramzan *and the witness statement of Professor Zellick in this case to appreciate that, whatever had been the outcome of this case, there is a tension between the practice of the CACD and the Commission in cases such as this. It may be a creative tension and, of course, it is accompanied by civility in both institutions. It seems to us that its source is not simply the statutory framework within which the Commission works but is more the result of the way in which the CACD applies the recently developed law to old cases as propounded in Bentley (para 5, above). It is not the job of this Court to express any view on that approach.*

... To an extent, the tension is being addressed because the Commission has recently adopted a new policy document on its discretion not to refer a case despite a finding of real possibility in the context of a change of law. Of particular relevance is paragraph 10 which provides that where an applicant to the Commission has not previously appealed or applied for leave to appeal to the CACD, the Commission will advise him of his right to apply for an extension of time and for leave to appeal. If that application is unsuccessful and he returns to the Commission, he will have to advance a new argument or evidence not previously considered by the CACD or point to exceptional circumstances. Also, where an applicant has previously appealed to the CACD, the Commission, even if it is satisfied as to the real possibility test, will also consider whether the CACD could substitute a verdict or a plea of guilty of another offence under section 3 or 3A of the Criminal Appeal Act 1968. If it could, that "normally will militate against referral", unless the anticipated sentence would be lower than that originally passed, in which case the Commission will consider "any benefit that might accrue to the applicant from a referral, and the public interest" (paragraphs 11 – 12).

For our part we welcome these developments but it cannot be said that they resolve all the problems. In our view it would now be timely for the legislature to reconsider the approach to changes in the common law expounded in the passage from Bentley cited at paragraph 7 above (as Lord Justice Auld invited it to do when recommending its abolition in his Review of the Criminal Courts) and hence the relationship between the Commission and the CACD in change of law cases. Professor Zellick has expressed surprise that Bentley is not mentioned in the recent consultation paper on Quashing Convictions. We share his surprise. We do not regard it as beyond dispute that, as a matter of policy, the declaratory theory of the common law should be a trump card in this area of criminal law.

Following this judgment, the convictions of **Ahmed**, **El-Kurd**, **Singh** and **Rizvi**, together with two further cases referred by the Commission, **Reichwald** and **Sakavickas**, were heard by the Court of Appeal. The convictions were quashed but re-trials were ordered.[29]

The Commission's policy response

As the Court noted in **Rizvi**, the Commission has reviewed its policy on discretion in referrals, and particularly in change-of-law cases. The Commission has promulgated a revised Formal Memorandum on this subject which is published on the Commission's website.[30] The Commission's policy provides that in deciding whether or not to refer convictions that satisfy the real possibility test it will have regard to the following questions.

Benefit resulting from a referral

> The first question is whether any benefit would accrue either to the applicant or to the criminal justice system if the case were referred. In assessing benefit, regard may be had to a variety of factors, including the seriousness of the offence, the nature and severity of the sentence, the age of the conviction and its impact on the applicant – such as loss of job opportunities, loss of reputation, personal sense of injustice, effect on family.

...

Other general considerations

> In addition to possible benefit to the applicant or more generally, the Commission may also have regard to the following factors in considering whether to exercise its discretion not to refer:

> • The public interest in correction of an injustice.

> • The age and seriousness of the conviction.

> • The interests of third parties.

> • Whether the defendant was denied a basic constitutional right.

> • Whether the prosecution constituted an abuse of process or affront to justice.

> This list is expressed to be illustrative and not comprehensive.

Change-of-law cases

> In all change-of-law cases where the development raises a real possibility that the conviction is unsafe or sentence is questionable, the Commission

will have regard to the considerations set out above, as well as the following considerations specific to this type of case:

- *The practice of the Court of Appeal, Criminal Division, in relation to applications for an extension of time in which to appeal based on a change of law.*

- *The public interest in finality to litigation.*

- *The absence of any statutory time limit on applications to the Commission.*

- *The public interest that defendants should not be convicted of offences which they are not proved to have committed (see* Coutts *[2006] UKHL 39, para 12).*

- *The legal significance of the development.*

*Regard will **not** be had to the number of convictions that may be affected by the development of the Court of Appeal's practice.* (Emphasis is in the memorandum)

Change-of-law cases where the applicant has not previously appealed

Where an application is based on a change in the case law relating to the criteria for liability of the substantive offence and the applicant has not previously appealed or applied for leave to appeal, the Commission will advise the applicant of his/her right to apply to the Court of Appeal for an extension of time to apply for leave to appeal in accordance with the procedure outlined by the Court of Appeal in Ramzan *... Where an applicant has been refused an extension of time to apply for leave to appeal under the Court's procedure and then applies to the Commission, a referral will be possible only where there is new argument or evidence not previously considered by the Court of Appeal or there are exceptional circumstances.*

It will be noted from the last of these extracts that applicants who have not previously appealed their convictions are required by the new policy to take their chances by seeking leave of the Court – which is overwhelmingly likely to be refused on the basis of the Court's policy considerations outlined above. Whilst such applicants are free to bring their cases to the Commission *after* the Court has refused them leave, they then face the almost insuperable obstacle that they will be advancing arguments that have previously been deployed, unsuccessfully, in seeking leave. It is hard to see that the Commission is likely in any but the rarest cases to use the exceptional circumstances provision to refer such cases.

It would, perhaps, be fair to say that the Commission – in adopting the new memorandum – moved more than half way to the position desired by the Court of Appeal.

Cottrell and Fletcher

This is not the end of the story for, on 31 July 2007, the Court delivered its judgment in the cases of **Cottrell and Fletcher**. Both appeals raised a change-of-law point following the decision of the House of Lords in *R v J*.[31] The point of law concerned the legality of the practice of charging sexual intercourse with underage girls as indecent assault in cases where the statutory 12-month time limit for bringing a charge of unlawful sexual intercourse has expired. In *R v J*, the House of Lords concluded that, as a matter of statutory construction, this practice, in getting round the time limit imposed by statute, had the impermissible effect of dispensing with or suspending an unequivocal statutory provision and that charges brought in accordance with this practice were bad. There were a large number of potential beneficiaries of this change in the law.

Cottrell had not previously appealed his conviction. In exercise of the new policy, he was advised by the Commission to apply for leave to appeal out of time to the Court. His application for leave was heard together with the case of **Fletcher.** Fletcher's convictions were referred by the Commission on various grounds, including the decision in *R v J*.[32]

Cottrell was (predictably) refused leave by the Court in exercise of the policy considerations already described. Fletcher's appeal was allowed (with gritted teeth) on the *R v J* point. However, the importance of the Court's judgment lies not in those decisions but in the dicta of Lord Justice Judge giving the judgment of the Court. The learned judge made the following observations:

The general objection to change-of-law cases

These cases present issues of great sensitivity and latent tension. Those convicted on the basis of the old law assert that their convictions were based on an erroneous understanding of the criminal law and that they have therefore suffered an injustice. At the same time there is a continuing public imperative that so far as possible there should be finality and certainty in the administration of criminal justice. In reality, society can only operate on the basis that the courts administering the criminal justice system apply the law as it is. The law as it may later be declared or perceived to be is irrelevant. Change of law appeals create quite different problems to those which arise in the normal case where an individual was wrongly convicted on the basis of the law which applied at the date of conviction. (Paragraph 42)

Commentary on the previous practice of the Commission

We are not impressed with the submission that the court has not criticised the Commission for referring a change of law case. No one has suggested that the Commission is subject to a statutory prohibition against making a reference in such cases ... it would be rare for the court to criticise the Commission for referring a case which resulted in the quashing of a conviction ... That does not constitute approval. Thus, for example, we pause to consider the decisions in R v Caley-Knowles *and* R v Iorwerth Jones ... *which were referred to the court following a decision in the House of Lords in* R v Wang *which held that a judge should never direct a jury to convict. Caley-Knowles was convicted in 1972, on the judge's direction of assault occasioning actual bodily harm. The evidence of the complainant was unchallenged. ... The judge directed the jury to convict in circumstances which, in 1972, would have attracted "no possible criticism". Iowerth Jones was convicted more recently, but still, as long ago as 1994 of criminal damage. He admitted the damage alleged, caused as a protest against an incident which had happened in 1983. There was no defence. The judge directed the jury to convict. They did so. His conduct in 1994 was not open to criticism. As the cases were referred directly to the court by the Commission time was abridged. Leave to appeal out of time was not required. On the basis of the judgment which we have read, we have very grave doubts whether, if invited to do so, the court would have extended time in either case.* (Paragraph 47)

Failure of the Runciman Commission or Parliament to foresee the problem of change-of-law cases

The failure to anticipate the problem is unsurprising. At that time, the focus of the Runciman Commission was indeed "old" or historic cases, where the appeal process had been exhausted and the Home Office represented the only, and a hazardous route, to remedy miscarriages of justice in accordance with section 17(1) of the Criminal Appeal Act 1968. Just because so many of the troublesome cases were old and well out of time for any appeal, or further appeal, the normal time limits were disapplied. The Commission may refer a conviction "at any time". With historic cases understandably occupying so much attention, the problem of change of law cases was not directly addressed. At the time, the normal approach of the court to such cases was straightforward and well understood: save exceptionally, any necessary extensions of time would be refused. In short, in relation to these cases, neither the Runciman Commission, nor indeed the legislation, were required to address what was a non-problem. (Paragraph 50)

The true intention of the 1995 Act

If it were intended that the Commission should ignore any aspect of the law and practice of the court, in particular for present purposes, in relation to "change of law" cases, its authority to do so would have been expressly provided in the legislative structure which created it. The legislation was clearly not intended to have this effect. (Paragraph 54)

The duty of the Commission to follow the practice of the Court

Lord Justice Judge considered that the Administrative Court in **Rizvi** had viewed the problem of the Commission's practice in change-of-law cases from too narrow a perspective. He stated, in effect, that the Administrative Court had been wrong both to refer to a 'creative tension' between the Commission and the Court and to suggest that the Commission had any freedom of action to depart from the practice of the Court:

It would indeed be disturbing, and we believe productive of public disquiet, if the Commission were to adopt an approach to change of law cases which conflicted with the approach of the court. We would not see this as a "healthy" tension. ... In our judgment, in these cases, it is not open to the Commission lawfully to apply a policy based on the conclusion of the Divisional Court ... (Paragraphs 56-58)

The possibility of legislative change

The judgment portended the possible amendment of statute:

For the time being the court is bound by what we shall identify as the declaratory principle of the common law. (Paragraph 52. Emphasis added)

Reflections on Cottrell and Fletcher

It will be perfectly clear from the foregoing lengthy citations that Lord Justice Judge sought, once and for all, to restrain the Commission from giving any scope to applications based on changes-of-law taking effect post trial. It might be noted that a proposal to like effect was made by Lord Justice Auld in his *Review of the Criminal Courts of England and Wales*.[33] Auld had recommended simply that:

> on any reference by the Commission to the Court of Appeal or the Crown Court of a conviction or sentence, those courts should apply the law in force at the time of conviction or sentence as the case may be.

Auld's recommendations were disagreed with by JUSTICE, among many others, and it cannot be overlooked that the present government – no slouch when it comes to legislating on criminal justice matters – had not previously chosen to legislate this aspect of the Auld proposals. Lord Justice Judge clearly expressed the consummate wish that Auld's proposal be given the force of statute law, and in the meantime has not hesitated to use the authority of the Court to adjust the law to what he would like it to be. It is somewhat ironic in this context that he vehemently criticised the House of Lords in his judgment for having been guilty of 'judicial legislation' in the case of *R v J*.[34]

The government intervenes

The conclusion to this story can now be told as the government has brought in a compromise measure in the Criminal Justice and Immigration Act 2008. This inserts a new s16C into the Criminal Appeal Act 1968. The new section provides as follows:

(1) *This section applies where there is an appeal under this Part following a reference by the Criminal Cases Review Commission under section 9(1)(a), (5) or (6) of the Criminal Appeal Act 1995 (c. 35) or section 1(1) of the Criminal Cases (Insanity) Act 1999.*

(2) *Notwithstanding anything in section 2, 13 or 16 of this Act, the Court of Appeal may dismiss the appeal if -*

(a) *the only ground for allowing it would be that there has been a development in the law since the date of the conviction, verdict or finding that is the subject of the appeal, and*

(b) *the condition in subsection (3) is met.*

(3) *The condition in this subsection is that if -*

(a) the reference had not been made, and

(b) the appellant had made (and had been entitled to make) an application for an extension of time within which to seek leave to appeal on the ground of the development in the law,

the Court would not think it appropriate to grant the application by exercising the power conferred by section 18(3).

In summary, the new clause 16C provides the Court of Appeal with the power to decide that if the Court itself would not have given the appellant leave for extension of time to appeal (beyond the normal 28-day time limit) to develop a change-of-law point, it may (without more) dismiss the appeal, notwithstanding that the appellant has surmounted the requirement for leave by virtue of the Commission's referral.

The provision appears to be a compromise between the position apparently advocated by Judge LJ in **Cottrell and Fletcher** (who seemed to want to proscribe change-of-law considerations influencing either referrals or appeals) and the existing position following **Bentley**. There can be no doubt that, in the course of time, the Court of Appeal will provide some clarification of the circumstances in which it thinks it '*appropriate*' to allow an appellant extension of time to argue change-of-law points. It is to be hoped that judicial guidance, when it comes, is not overly prescriptive and that it does not curb the Commission's referral of cases where it appears just to have regard to post-trial developments of the law. The nature and the terms of the clarification may depend to some extent on the cases that come up to it by virtue of the Commission's referrals in the future.

Perhaps in this case the word 'appropriate' actually means – or should mean – the same thing as 'just'. It is at least, arguably, just that an appellant should be permitted to take the benefit of changes in the law in – for instance – the following circumstances:

- A young defendant has been convicted, pre-PACE, on the basis of a confession obtained in oppressive circumstances and without modern protections – a modern standards of fairness case.

- A defendant has been convicted of murder after being involved in a mêlée, without the jury being directed to consider whether or not he or she had foresight that one of his or her confederates might escalate the conflict by producing a murderous weapon – a joint enterprise case.

- A man is convicted of indecent assault following consensual sex with a 15-year-old girl of sophisticated appearance without the jury being directed to consider the possibility that the defendant might have honestly believed that the girl was older than she actually was.

On the other hand, it would seem neither appropriate nor just that in a *Preddy*-type case, a defendant, who has been convicted of an obvious mortgage fraud, should be allowed to take opportunistic advantage of an error in the charging or indictment disclosed by subsequent case law. Similarly, in summing up cases, it does not seem unduly difficult to draw a distinction between a case where the summing up error disclosed by subsequent authority goes (or arguably goes) to the justice of the conviction (as in **Beckles**) and a case where it plainly does not (as in **Lowe**).

Providing these distinctions are tolerably clear, and are recognised by the Court, then the discretion provided by the new section 16C to the Court to screen out change-of-law cases may not represent an undue setback to the cause of remedying miscarriages of justice. The Commission for its part will need to exercise care and discrimination in referring future change-of-law cases, articulating why it is appropriate (and just) to grant leave and (of course) exercising the gatekeeper role provided to it by the 'real possibility' test to refer marginal cases for the decision of the Court. If the Court for its part curbs its irritable instincts when faced with such referrals, a just and sensible outcome may well emerge.

Postscript – witness anonymity and *R v Davis*

The House of Lords' decision in *R v Davis*,[35] decided in June 2008, provides an interesting postscript to the discussion in this chapter. Put very briefly, their Lordships decided that in certain circumstances the current practice of granting anonymity to witnesses in criminal trials goes beyond the position allowed either by common law or European Convention law. Although *Davis* is not a clear cut change-of-law case, their Lordships did conclude that prior authorities, in particular the decision of the Court of Appeal in *Taylor and Crabb*,[36] had given undue sanction to the modern practice of granting anonymity to witnesses. As Lord Bingham stated in his opinion:

By a series of small steps, largely unobjectionable on their own facts, the courts have arrived at a position which is irreconcilable with long-standing principle.

Their Lordships stated that it was up to Parliament – if it wished – to change the position by legislation. The government hastened to take up this invitation. Shortly before this book went to press, it brought forward legislation to alter the statute law – as it did following the decision in *Preddy*. The Criminal Evidence (Witness Anonymity) Act 2008 provides for the making of a witness protection order, provided that three conditions are met:

- the order is necessary in order to protect the safety of the witness or another person or to prevent any serious damage to property, or to prevent real harm to the public interest;

- the taking of measures to protect the identity of the witness would be consistent with the defendant receiving a fair trial; and

- it is necessary to make the order in the interests of justice as it appears that it is important that the witness should testify but he or she would not otherwise do so.

Ordinarily, applicants convicted prior to the amending legislation on the basis of a 'misreading' of the law would be entitled to bring cases to the Commission as they did following *Preddy*. In this case, however, the position is affected by section 11 which is designed to make the Act effectively retrospective. This provides that:

(2) *The appeal court—*

(a) *may not treat the conviction as unsafe solely on the ground that the trial court had no power at common law to make the order mentioned in subsection (1)(b), but*

(b) *must treat the conviction as unsafe if it considers—*

(i) *that the order was not one that the trial court could have made if this Act had been in force at the material time, and*

> (ii) *that, as a result of the order, the defendant did not receive a fair trial.*

In the generality of cases, an applicant seeking to launch a fresh appeal on the back of *Davis* is likely to be baulked by section 11(2)(a). However, where an applicant can put up a case that (i) the conditions for the making of an order – as summarised above – would not have been met; and (ii) his or her rights to a fair trial were prejudiced by the granting of anonymity to the witness, then the real possibility test is likely to be satisfied. Moreover, it does not seem particularly likely that the Court would deem it inappropriate for the purposes of section 16C of the 1968 Act to hear an out-of-time appeal on a witness protection point if the conditions of section 11(2)(b) were satisfied. It would seem perverse if – Parliament having stated in terms that the Court of Appeal must allow appeals that satisfy the requirements of section 11(2)(b) – the Court then refused to hear them. Indeed, it may well be the case that by seeking to stop up the flow of retrospective appeals in this way, the Act will lead to more applications to the Commission, and more referrals, than would have been the case, had the Act not sought to deal with appeals at all. Since some practitioners have already announced their intention to launch appeals on the point of law in *Davis*, it seems likely that these issues will shortly come before the Commission for consideration.

Two qualifications need to be made to the foregoing discussion. First – and notwithstanding the tabloid brouhaha that followed *Davis* – no presumption was stated that witnesses should never be granted anonymity. It is a question – as Lord Bingham put it – of the 'impact [of the witness protection measures] on the conduct of the defence' in any instant case. Second, this Act, which was rushed through Parliament as an emergency measure, contains a 'sunset clause' which limits the effect of the legislation to December 2009, and it will, therefore, be subject to review and reconsideration in the coming year.

One further rueful comment may be added. The Criminal Justice and Immigration Act received Royal Assent in May 2008. The Witness Anonymity Act passed through Parliament and received Royal Assent in July 2008. It is a reflection on the tempo of modern criminal justice legislation that the review by the Commission of change-of-law cases should be subject to two statutory interventions within the space of three months.

Notes

1. Although note the observation of Judge LJ in **Cottrell and Fletcher** that 'The declaratory theory of the common law appears remote from the practical realities which should underpin the administration of criminal justice'.

2. In fact, s44A Criminal Appeal Act 1968 requires that any appeal on behalf of a deceased appellant, including any appeal following reference by the Commission, may be brought only by (i) the deceased's widow or widower (ii) the deceased's personal representative or (iii) a person who by reason of family or similar relationship has a substantial interest in the outcome of the appeal. Guy Fawkes' conviction, therefore, appears quite safe from the depredations of the Commission.

3. To give an example, Ruth **Ellis**, who was convicted of murder in 1955, might have benefited from the defence of diminished responsibility had that defence existed at the time. The defence was introduced by the Homicide Act 1957 but, being a new statutory provision, it only applied from the commencement of that Act and cannot be read back into the criminal law that was in force at the time of Miss Ellis's conviction.

4. [1996] AC 815.

5. Many of those convicted of this offence were (until struck off) accountants and solicitors – they were, therefore, better placed than most to keep abreast of beneficial developments of the law!

6. This statutory lacuna was filled by s316 Criminal Justice Act 2003, which provided the power of substitution in cases where conviction had followed a guilty plea.

7. [1997] 1 Cr App R 234.

8. (1977) 65 Cr App R 185.

9. [2001] 3 WLR 75.

10. [2005] EWCA Crim 1060.

11. [1986] 1 WLR 1025.

12. [1999] 1 AC 82.

13. [2001] 1 AC 146.

14. Previous authorities, although not unanimous on the subject, in broad terms provided that a defendant's physical characteristics might be taken into account in assessing the reasonableness of his actions, but not his psychological characteristics.

15. [2005] UKPC 23.

16. [1999] 1 AC 1.

17. [1998] EWCA Crim 999.

18. [1999] *Crim LR* 65.

19. [2001] EWCA Crim 2986.

20. (1981) 73 Crim App R 159.

21. [2001] 3 All ER 897.

22. [2005] UKHL 18.

23. (1997) 23 EHRR 313.

24. [2001] 3 WLR 206.

25. [2005] NIQB 21.

26. See chapter 2 for a discussion of this case.

27. [2006] UKHL 18.

28. The point of law in **Saik** was overruled by the Proceeds of Crime Act 2002 but only with prospective effect.

29. The judgments in **El-Kurd, Singh, Reichwald** and **Sakavickas** were given just outside the ten-year period covered by this study.

30. The Commission's current version of the Memorandum entitled: *Discretion in Referrals (including applications based on a change in the law)* is found via the 'publications' tab on the

home page of the Commission's website. This Memorandum has undergone a number of revisions due to the legal developments discussed in this chapter.

31. [2005] 1 AC 562.

32. It might be added parenthetically that *R v J* was not a major factor in the Commission's decision to refer although this is not readily apparent from the Court of Appeal's judgment!

33. *A Review of the Criminal Courts of England and Wales* by The Right Honourable Lord Justice Auld September 2001. Chapter 12 paras 102-107. The report has no Cmnd number but may be found at www.criminal-courts-review.org.uk/.

34. It should also be added that the constitutionality of the Court of Appeal purporting to overrule the decision of the Administrative Court in **Rizvi** is a questionable matter to say the least.

35. [2008] UKHL 36.

36. Unreported, 22 July 1994.

Chapter 8 - Homicide cases

Overview

Of the Commission's cases considered by the Court of Appeal within the ten-year period of this study, no fewer than 110 – more than one-third of the total – have concerned convictions for murder or manslaughter. This is vastly disproportionate to the incidence of homicide in recorded crime statistics as a whole. The table at page 186 below provides a schematic characterisation of the grounds for referral of the Commission's homicide cases. It will be apparent that the grounds for referral have been extremely varied and there is by no means any unifying theme linking all of the Commission's homicide cases. However, there are a number of partial explanations for the strikingly high incidence of homicide cases in the Commission's caseload.

First, there quite clearly are *some* cases where the police, anxious to clear up a high-profile murder case, have brought charges – and juries have convicted – on the basis of a relatively thin forensic case.[1]

A second factor is the greater commitment of those convicted of homicide to clear their names. As already noted, the **Bentley** doctrine of modern standards of fairness has enabled some applicants convicted of crimes 20 or more years ago to bring their cases back, through the Commission, to appeal. It is scarcely surprising that – amongst the victims of unfair interrogations, 'verbals', and coerced confessions – it has been the subjects of homicide convictions who have been most anxious to seek review of their cases.

A third factor is the existence of multiple alternative defences to murder. Some defences – diminished responsibility and provocation – are partial defences reducing murder to manslaughter; other defences, such as self-defence and accident, are absolute. The Law Commission has been picking away (without – one senses – any great level of support from government) at the state of the law relating to homicide. The experience of the Commission lends significant support to the case that the present state of the law is unsatisfactory and illogical.

Fourth, the appellate courts have been uncommonly active in adjusting the law applicable to homicide cases. In the 1980s, the cases of *Woollin*[2] and *Nedrick*[3] changed the test of foresight necessary for murder – such that death or serious bodily harm had to be foreseen by the defendant as a virtual certainty and no longer only as a probability. In *Powell and English*,[4] the test (again) of foresight was changed in joint enterprise cases. Additionally, the appellate courts have performed a Duke of York act in relation to the relevance of a fragile personality to the provocation defence. In *Morgan Smith*,[5] the House of Lords marched to the top of the hill and declared that 'personal characteristics' are relevant to such a defence. In *Holley*,[6] the Judicial Committee of the Privy Council marched down again and declared that they are not – taking a bit of the British constitution with them in the process.[7] At a humbler level, the question whether a person who assists a drug abuser to inject drugs resulting in death should be convicted of manslaughter has been the subject of recent judicial prevarication. The Commission has at times been buffeted haplessly in this ebb and flow of judicial opinion.

Fifth, some of the forensic disciplines deployed in the investigation and proof of homicide have been and remain contentious. Particularly, the conclusions of pathologists may be matters of subjective judgment, possibly to an extent beyond the appreciation of the juries considering what weight to give to their evidence. The pathology profession has also been riven by charges of insufficiently painstaking professional practice (as outlined in the judgment in Sally **Clark**) and from time to time by charges against individuals of professional incompetence (which feature in the case of **Boreman and Byrne**). Superimposed upon this, there have been very significant divisions of professional opinion in relation to the pathology of shaken baby cases.

Finally, medical science has been astute in establishing new medical explanations for abnormal behaviour – of which homicide is the most extreme example. Commission referrals have entailed diagnoses (inter alia) of Asperger's Syndrome; Dissocial Personality Disorder; and Enduring Personality Change after a Catastrophic Experience – conditions which were not recognised nor raised at the time of trial.

A classification of the Commission's homicide referrals

The table which follows represents an approximate classification of the Commission's homicide referrals. In each case a main ground of referral has been adopted for classification purposes but this does not necessarily reflect the complexity of the considerations leading to referral.

It should be noted that many of the individual cases are referred to in greater detail in other chapters relating to expert evidence (chapter 5); modern standards of fairness (chapter 6); changes in the law (chapter 7); prosecution misconduct (chapter 10); and Northern Ireland cases (chapter 13).

Name	Principal grounds of referral	Outcome
Modern standards of fairness		
Bentley	Modern standards of fairness	Quashed
Downing	Modern standards of fairness	Quashed
Hussain	Modern standards of fairness	Quashed
Fell	Modern standards of fairness Evidence re unreliability of confession	Quashed
Nolan	Modern standards of fairness	Quashed
Steel	Modern standards of fairness	Quashed
Foster	Modern standards of fairness Evidence re unreliability of confession	Upheld
Adams	Modern standards of fairness Coerced confession (NI)	Quashed
Hay Gordon	Modern standards of fairness Coerced confession (NI)	Quashed
Hindes and Hanna	Modern standards of fairness Coerced confession (NI)	Quashed
Magee	Modern standards of fairness + human rights (NI)	Quashed
Change of law		
Mair	Change of law re foresight required for joint enterprise (*Powell and English*)	Quashed
Miah	Ditto	Quashed
Webb	Ditto	Upheld
Hayes (Dennis Francis)	Change of law re foresight of death or serious injury *(Woollin)*	Upheld
Smith (Josephine)	Change of law re relevance of personal characteristics to the defence of provocation (*Morgan Smith*)	Quashed
Rowland	Ditto	Quashed
James	Ditto	Upheld following *Holley*
Moses	Ditto	Upheld following *Holley*
Farnell	Ditto + failure to leave provocation properly to the decision of the jury	Quashed
Karimi	Ditto + new medical diagnosis supporting provocation defence	Quashed – retrial – convicted

Name	Principal grounds of referral	Outcome
Ellis	Development of law – relevance of slow burn provocation	Upheld
Kennedy	Change of law re assisting self-administration of drug causing death	Upheld, but later quashed on appeal to House of Lords
Richards	Ditto	Quashed
Expert evidence – pathology		
Nicholls	Pathology	Quashed
Sally Clark	Pathology (Professor Meadows)	Quashed
Anthony	Pathology (Professor Meadows)	Quashed
Wickens	Pathology	Quashed
Waters	Pathology	Upheld
Boreman and Byrne	Pathology (Dr Heath)	Quashed
Fannin	Pathology	Upheld
Kavanagh	Pathology/ligatures	Upheld
Williams (Harold)	Fresh evidence re time of death (lay witness + pathologist)	Upheld
Expert evidence – reliability of confession		
Green	Confession evidence – fitness for interview due to hypoglycaemic episode (NI)	Quashed
Hall, O'Brien and Sherwood ('Cardiff 3')	Reliability of confession evidence	Quashed
J	Reliability of confession evidence/police conduct	Quashed
James (Albert)	Reliability of confession evidence/breach of PACE	Quashed
Latimer	Reliability of confession evidence (NI)	Upheld
Pendleton	Reliability of confession evidence	Upheld but later quashed on appeal to House of Lords
Expert evidence – other		
Bamber	DNA/firearms analysis	Upheld
Cleeland	Firearms	Upheld
Gilfoyle	Ligatures, possibility of suicide	Upheld
Gorman and Mackinney	ESDA (NI)	Quashed
Jenkins	Bloodspatter	Quashed

Name	Principal grounds of referral	Outcome
Johnson (Frank)	Fitness to plead	Quashed
Maloney	Accident reconstruction	Upheld
May	Sufficiency of scene of crime investigation	Upheld
Probyn	Accident reconstruction	Upheld
Shirley	DNA	Quashed
Wooster	Ballistics evidence re trajectory of bullet	Upheld
Diminished responsibility – fresh medical evidence		
F (M)	Diminished responsibility – post-traumatic stress	Quashed – verdict of diminished responsibility (DR) substituted
Gilfillan	Diminished responsibility – paranoid schizophrenia	Quashed – verdict of DR substituted
Haddon	Diminished responsibility – dissocial personality disorder	Quashed – verdict of DR substituted
Reynolds	Diminished responsibility – Asperger's Syndrome	Quashed – verdict of DR substituted
Samra	Diminished responsibility – personality disorder + learning difficulties	Quashed – verdict of DR substituted
Duggan	Diminished responsibility – psychopathic personality disorder	Quashed – verdict of DR substituted
Ashton	Diminished responsibility – paranoid schizophrenia	Quashed – verdict of DR substituted
Smith (Charlie)	Diminished responsibility – psychopathic personality disorder	Quashed – verdict of DR substituted
Sharp	Diminished responsibility – behavioural disturbance attributed to medication	Upheld
Shickle	Diminished responsibility – evidence of personality disorder	Upheld
Gilbert	Diminished responsibility – paranoid schizophrenia	Upheld
Directions to jury		
Allan (Richard Roy)	S34 – directions to jury on inferences from silence	Quashed
Bain	Omission of lies direction	Upheld
Boyle and Forde	S34 – directions to jury on inferences from silence	Upheld
Serrano	Failure to leave provocation properly to the decision of the jury	Upheld
Legal incompetence		
Adams	Legal incompetence	Quashed

Name	Principal grounds of referral	Outcome
Day	Legal incompetence	Upheld
Kamara	Failure to halt trial	Quashed
Misconduct by investigators		
Brown (Robert)	Discredited officer, coerced confession, linguistic expert evidence, non-disclosure	Quashed
Campbell	Discredited officers (West Midlands Serious Crimes Squad) affecting reliability of evidence	Quashed
Irvine	Discredited officers (West Midlands Serious Crimes Squad) affecting reliability of evidence	Quashed
Twitchell	Discredited officers (West Midlands Serious Crimes Squad) affecting reliability of evidence	Quashed
Willis	Discredited officers (Rigg Approach) affecting reliability of witness evidence	Quashed
Other new evidence/miscellaneous		
Ahmed (Ishtiaq)	Witness reliability	Upheld
Brannan and Murphy	New witness evidence Prosecution non-disclosure	Quashed
Causeley	Reliability of cell confession evidence	Quashed but convicted on re-trial
Christofides	Conduct/course of trial. Defence position affected by unexpected dismissal of prosecution case against co-defendant	Quashed
Craven	Non-disclosure of fingerprint	Upheld
Davis, Rowe and Johnson ('M25 Three')	Non-disclosure/Public Interest Immunity/ human rights	Quashed
Druhan	New statement from witness	Quashed
Dudley and Maynard	Witness retraction evidence Expert evidence re reliability of police account of interview	Quashed
Friend	New evidence re fitness of defendant to give evidence at trial (ADHD)	Quashed
Hanratty	Conduct of investigation/non-disclosure	Upheld
Kelly (George)	Non-disclosure	Quashed
Knighton	Forensic/scene of crimes evidence/non-disclosure	Upheld
Mattan	Fresh evidence re reliability of witness testimony – non-disclosure	Quashed
McCann	Fresh evidence re witness reliability	Upheld

Name	Principal grounds of referral	Outcome
MacDermott and McCartney	Fresh evidence relating to integrity of interrogating police officers (NI)	Quashed
Parsons	Fresh evidence re time of death (electricity consumption)	Upheld
Mackenney and Pinfold	Medical evidence re witness reliability	Quashed
Quinn (Michael)	Fresh evidence (DNA) – evidence relied upon in referral proved to be erroneous on further investigation post-referral	Upheld
Steele and Whomes	New information affecting reliability of key witness	Upheld
Thomas (Ian)	Fresh evidence	Upheld
Underwood	Fresh evidence re previous convictions of witness/non-disclosure	Upheld
Slender new evidence/lurking doubt		
Cooper and McMahon	Doubts about reliability of main prosecution witness + other matters	Quashed
Mills and Poole	Doubts about integrity of police investigation + other matters	Quashed

The new evidence/diminished responsibility cases
The diminished responsibility defence

Section 2 of the Homicide Act 1957 sets out the diminished responsibility defence:

1) *Where a person kills or is a party to the killing of another, he shall not be convicted of murder if he was suffering from such abnormality of mind (whether arising from a condition of arrested or retarded development of mind or any inherent causes or induced by disease or injury) as substantially impaired his mental responsibility for his acts and omissions in doing or being a party to the killing.*

(2) *On a charge of murder, it shall be for the defence to prove that the person charged is by virtue of this section not liable to be convicted of murder.*

(3) *A person who but for this section would be liable, whether as principal or as accessory, to be convicted of murder shall be liable instead to be convicted of manslaughter . . .*

The defence has the following characteristics:

- The first indispensable element of the defence is the existence of an 'abnormality of mind'. This is a matter for expert evidence.

- The second question – whether the mental illness 'substantially impaired responsibility for the killing' – is a further matter for expert medical evidence. However, it is also a matter for juries who may (and sometimes do) find defendants guilty of murder because they do not accept that the abnormality of mind provides any excuse for the defendant's acts.

- The onus lies on the defence to prove diminished responsibility.

- Diminished responsibility is generally an 'all or nothing' defence. A defendant cannot sensibly deny *any* responsibility (for instance by arguing that he or she killed in self-defence or due to accident) and at the same time argue diminished responsibility. A defendant arguing diminished responsibility has to accept that he or she unlawfully killed the victim; that even if the defence succeeds he or she will be convicted of manslaughter; and that he or she may be made subject to lengthy or even lifelong detention. Experienced criminal practitioners are aware that some defendants who have killed are unwilling to accept the unpalatable choices available to them, and may seek to box and cox between alternative narrative accounts according to their perception of their best legal interests.

Diminished responsibility cases on appeal – the new evidence dilemma

A concern always arises for the Court when an appeal is mounted on the basis of a medical/diminished responsibility case that was not put forward at trial. Any such appeal is subject to understandable suspicion on the part of the Court which may wonder (i) whether the defendant has shifted his or her ground after failing to establish some completely different defence (such as accident or self-defence) at trial; and/or (ii) whether the appeal is based upon expert evidence from pliable (or gullible) doctors who are willing to accept the defendant's account of his or her actions in applying a diagnostic label that supports a diminished responsibility defence.

This dilemma came to the Court's attention (prior to the Commission's inception) in the so-called battered wives cases, where expert evidence recognised a syndrome of 'learned helplessness' which might in some cases amount to an 'abnormality of mind'. The Court was torn between the impulse to consider the justice of individual cases and the concern to discourage others from bringing similar appeals on an opportunistic basis. In one such case, *Ahluwalia*,[8] the Court said as follows:

> *Ordinarily, of course, any available defences should be advanced at trial. Accordingly, if medical evidence is available to support a plea of diminished responsibility, it should be adduced at the trial. It cannot be too strongly emphasised that this court would require much persuasion to allow such a defence to be raised for the first time here if the option had been exercised at the trial not to pursue it. Otherwise, as must be clear, defendants might be encouraged to run one defence at trial in the belief that if it fails, this court would allow a different defence to be raised and give the defendant, in effect, two opportunities to run different defences.*

And in *Campbell*,[9] the Court set out to be extremely discouraging in general of 'newly minted' defences raised on appeal:

> *This Court has repeatedly underlined the necessity for defendants in criminal trials to advance their full defence before the jury and call any necessary evidence at that stage. It is not permissible to advance one defence before the jury and when that has failed, to devise a new defence, perhaps many years later, and then to seek to raise the defence on appeal.*

The Court has also had to grapple with a dilemma which is specific to diminished responsibility cases. In such cases a defendant may *accept* that he chose deliberately not to put forward his best defence at appeal, but to argue that the diminished responsibility which he now seeks to rely on should also excuse his failure to advance his best defence at trial. In a case called *Weekes*,[10] the Court set out a somewhat complex menu of considerations that it would apply in deciding whether to accede to arguments of that sort. As will be seen, two of the Commission's cases (by no means amongst the Commission's best referrals) have put the *Weekes* criteria under strain.

The following cases have been referred on the basis of new evidence of diminished responsibility:

Gilfillan

G killed his victim by kicking him with great violence in the course of a fight. The Crown's medical expert, who examined G prior to trial, thought that he might be subject to diminished responsibility, but no evidence of this was put forward at trial and the charge was defended on the basis of self-defence. Subsequently, clear and undisputed evidence emerged from prison doctors that he had been subject to paranoid schizophrenia at the time of the offence. The only question was whether there was any reasonable excuse to explain why evidence to support this defence had not been put up at trial. On this the Court noted:

> *That explanation is to be found in the very mental condition of the appellant which gives rise to the ground of the appeal. A rational person with ordinary insight would no doubt have made full disclosure of his mental condition as apparent to him both to his medical and to his legal advisers, and sought advice as to the availability of any relevant defences. The evidence, however, shows that this appellant was fearful of the possible consequences of a finding that he was mentally ill and, more importantly, did not consider that he was. He accordingly concealed his mental condition from those who examined him and prevailed on his parents similarly to make no relevant disclosure.*

The Court allowed the appeal and substituted an order under the Mental Health Act.

Haddon

Mr Haddon killed his baby daughter in 1980. No medical evidence of diminished responsibility was adduced at trial. He remained incarcerated when the appeal was heard in 2003 (although subject to a tariff of only ten years). The referral was based upon evidence of a number of forms of personality disorder recognised in the International Classification of Diseases (ICD 10) but which had not been medically recognised at the time of trial. The appeal was not opposed by the Crown. However, in view of his continuing dangerousness, Mr Haddon remained subject to life imprisonment for manslaughter. The Court noted, incidentally, that before referring the conviction to the Court:

> *the Criminal Cases Review Commission also, very properly, explored the question of whether or not the doctors might be being manipulated by the appellant in his account of matters, which necessarily, formed a central plank leading to the conclusions of both doctors.*

Reynolds

R had carried out a violent and motiveless killing in 1987. The matter was referred on evidence that the killing was attributable to an autistic disorder, Asperger's Syndrome, which is now well understood but was not medically recognised at the time of trial. As in Mr Haddon's case, no evidence of diminished responsibility was argued at trial. The Crown's expert agreed that R suffered from Asperger's Syndrome and the Crown did not oppose the appeal. However, in view of his continuing dangerousness outside the structured prison environment, R remained subject to life imprisonment for manslaughter.

Duggan

D was convicted of the murder of his co-habitee. Dr Harris, who examined him pre-trial, did not consider that he was subject to diminished responsibility and he was convicted of murder following a guilty plea. He was subsequently transferred to a mental hospital where he was examined by Dr Hunter, who came to the conclusion that he suffered from a psychopathic personality disorder characterised by psychosexual abnormality and sexual sadism. Although Dr Harris, when he re-examined D, adhered to his view that D was not subject to diminished responsibility, the Crown did not oppose D's appeal. He too was sentenced to life imprisonment after being newly convicted of manslaughter.

F (M)

F, then aged 17, had killed the victim, aged 76, whom he described as an 'honorary grandfather'. There was strong evidence that the victim had abused his position of trust to make homosexual advances towards F. Pre-trial, F was seen by a psychiatrist, who ruled out diminished responsibility, and the case was defended on the basis of lack of intent. The case was referred by the Commission and argued at appeal upon the basis of expert opinion from adolescent psychiatrists that F had been suffering from post-traumatic stress, related to his reaction to the unwanted advances, and that he had been subject to diminished responsibility. The Crown expert agreed and the appeal was not opposed. The Court noted:

> *[Crown counsel] helpfully accepted that, had it been the case at the time of trial that there had been a report from a properly qualified psychiatrist, eliciting, as may well have been possible, factual material from the defendant capable of sustaining a defence of diminished responsibility, and had such a psychiatrist concluded that such a defence was available to the defendant, the high probability is that, subject to concurrent views having been obtained*

by the Crown, a plea of guilty to manslaughter on the ground of diminished responsibility would have been accepted by the Crown at trial.

Or, to put it more simply, F had not been assessed by doctors with the appropriate specialised psychiatric experience prior to his trial.

Samra

S, a Sikh, killed his wife by stabbing her with a ceremonial sword which he had seized from the victim's mother. There had been a long history of matrimonial difficulties. He was examined pre-trial by Dr Winton who found no evidence to support diminished responsibility but diagnosed a condition called 'Explosive Personality Disorder'. S defended the case on the basis of provocation but the Court refused to admit evidence of this disorder in support of the provocation defence. The case was referred by the Commission on the basis of evidence that S had been subject to personality disorder combined with learning difficulties – giving rise to an argument for diminished responsibility. The Court noted that an arguable defence had been missed at trial (and there was no suggestion that this had been due to any tactical decision on the part of S). It quashed the verdict and ordered a re-trial. The case is notable for the fact that in this case the Commission suggested, and the Court effectively accepted, that the medical advice obtained by the defence prior to trial had been deficient; the Court is not always so generous in the face of argument based on the inadequacy of expert advice.[11] It is also notable as a case where the expert evidence referred to cultural factors associated with S's (and his wife's) Sikh background, which may have contributed to his mental complexion at the time of the offence.[12]

Ashton

Mr Ashton killed his victim with a butcher's knife in the course of a fight. No medical evidence was put forward of diminished responsibility and the case was defended on the basis of self-defence. Four doctors provided new evidence for the appeal that he had been suffering from paranoid schizophrenia and the appeal was not opposed by the Crown. In its judgment the Court of Appeal noted as follows:

Unfortunately Mr Ashton was only detained in Ashworth Hospital for two weeks prior to his trial. This was an inadequate time period to facilitate a full psychiatric assessment of his mental health and his likely mental state at the time of the alleged offence. Therefore it is unsurprising that a mental illness was not diagnosed and no psychiatric defence was raised at the time of his trial.

With the benefit of hindsight, it can be demonstrated that Mr Ashton's paranoid schizophrenia impaired his ability to consider all available defences to him at the time of his original trial. Mr Ashton's absolute lack of insight at the time led to him instructing his defence team to pursue the defences of self-defence and/or provocation. He would have believed with absolute conviction that he was being persecuted and that therefore he had been provoked and/or was acting in self-defence.

The Court allowed the appeal and substituted an order under the Mental Health Act.

By contrast, the following convictions were upheld following reference.

Gilbert

G killed his common-law wife, irrationally and with great savagery, in 1993. The case was defended on the basis of provocation. Following the killing, G started to complain of hearing 'voices' prompting him to do it but several doctors who saw G pre-trial rejected a diagnosis of schizophrenia and several thought that he was 'putting it on'. The case was referred by the Commission on the basis of new medical evidence that G had indeed been subject to paranoid schizophrenia pre-dating the offence, including evidence that G had been talking about hearing voices before he committed the offence. The appeal was opposed by the Crown. The Court – noting that the onus of proving diminished responsibility is upon the defence – concluded that the new evidence would not have enabled the defence to discharge the burden of proof laid upon it.[13] The Court also questioned the virtue of referring such a case stating:

we doubt if, in a case where it is now accepted that a convicted appellant is suffering from mental illness at the time of a reference and is likely to be continuing so to suffer at the end of any term recommended by the trial judge to be served, it is really in the public interest to incur the considerable expense that is necessarily incurred in references such as the present. It is difficult to see how the appellant's ultimate disposal could differ whatever conclusion this court came to on this reference.

But note that the Court has not expressed sentiments of this sort in any other of the Commission's diminished responsibility cases.

Sharp

S shot and killed his former girlfriend and her husband in 1991. The case was defended (implausibly) on the basis of accident – a struggle followed by the accidental discharge of the firearm. It was referred on new evidence that the killing could have been due to behavioural disturbance caused by S's taking of the drug Halcion. In a somewhat vituperative judgment dismissing the appeal, the Court of Appeal (Buxton LJ):

- Roundly criticised the Commission for failure to consider fully the tactical considerations which had caused S to defend the case on the basis of self-defence rather than (as he now claimed) behavioural disturbance – the dicta from *Ahluwalia* and *Campbell*, quoted previously, were cited.

- Preferred the evidence of the Crown medical expert (Dr Joseph) that S's normal social functioning prior to the offence was incompatible with the picture of his state of mind that was now being presented.

- Stated that where an appellant sought, following the authority of *Weekes*, to rely on a medical diminished responsibility defence not advanced at trial it would be necessary to establish (i) that the availability of the diminished responsibility defence is effectively unchallenged or at least certainly not controversial; and (ii) that there is an explanation in medical terms for any decision by the defendant not to run that diminished responsibility case at the trial.

Shickle

S killed her victim in 1996 through repeated stabbing with a syringe – her defence was denial, with causation of death raised as a separate issue. The case was referred on new evidence of a severe personality disorder. It was stated by doctors, and argued at the appeal that followed the Commission's reference, that the personality disorder impaired her judgment in defending the case at trial. As in the case of **Sharp**, the Crown expert (Dr Joseph) provided a somewhat more cogent analysis of the defendant's mental state than the doctors giving evidence for S. The Court reiterated the dicta in **Sharp** as to the very limited circumstances in which such new medical evidence should be admitted.

Sharp and **Shickle** appear to be relatively poor referrals, which have provoked the Court to take a very restrictive view of new evidence of diminished responsibility. However, the Court took a far more liberal approach in the later case of **Ashton**, suggesting that such cases would be treated on their respective merits.

Subsequently, and outside the period covered by this study, the Court gave judgment in **Diamond**. In brief, the referral and appeal were founded upon fresh medical evidence of diminished responsibility. Diminished responsibility had not been argued at trial. The judgment contains a lengthy review of the principles and the authorities to be applied to such cases. The Court noted, following the authority of *Straw*[14], that:

> *If at the time of plea there was medical evidence that the defendant was fit to plead, and if he was fully advised as to the position in relation to diminished responsibility and fully capable of taking the decision as to how the case was to be put, and decided not to advance a defence of diminished responsibility, then even if the defendant was not a "normal person", it was not permissible for a defendant to change his mind after the verdict.*

The Court concluded:

> *that, on the evidence available to us, the decision made by the appellant to plead not guilty at the trial and not to avail himself of the defence of diminished responsibility was tactical and not made on the basis that a material cause of giving the instructions has been shown to be his mental condition at that time. Because it was a tactical decision not materially caused by his mental condition, there is therefore no reasonable explanation for the failure to adduce the evidence at the trial.*

The judgment is a most helpful guide to the approach likely to be taken by the Court. It should, nevertheless, be emphasised that the line between an appellant like Mr Gilfillan (who could be excused his misconceived stance at trial) and Mr Diamond (who could not) is often far from clear, especially to the legal team advising the defendant at the time of trial.

Finally in this vein, note should be made of **Karimi.** K's conviction was quashed following the decision of the House of Lords in *Morgan Smith* – as discussed below. However, a second main ground of reference was a diagnosis of EPCC – enduring personality change after catastrophic experience – which was not raised at trial.[15] As in the two previous cases, the Court preferred the medical view expressed by Dr Joseph for the Crown and subjected K's trial strategy (and the Commission's reference) to somewhat penetrating criticism.

Diminished responsibility – summary

It will be seen from the above cases that the Court of Appeal has been ready to quash convictions based on new evidence of diminished responsibility, with no rigid distinction between cases (such as **Reynolds**) where the diagnosis of abnormality of mind was *not available* on the basis of medical understanding at the time of trial; and cases (such as **F (M) and Samra**) where the appropriate diagnosis was *missed*. The Court has also generally treated on their merits arguments to the effect that mentally disordered appellants should be excused for failing to put forward their best defence at trial. The Crown for its part has not generally sought to oppose appeals based upon cogent new expert evidence.

In terms of practical outcome, many of these appeals have not improved the prospects for release of the appellants, who have remained subject to a term of life imprisonment. By and large, the Court has expressed no misgivings about the use of the appellate process to substitute the appropriate conviction – even if the practical outcome is the same. Indeed, at a preliminary hearing in the case of **Gilbert**,[16] the Court stated:

> We should add that we have considered [Crown counsel's] further point that the appropriate course would be to allow the matter to be dealt with through the prison service and the parole board who can determine when it will be safe to release the appellant into the community. We recognise that even if an appeal succeeds it may be appropriate, given the appellant's mental condition, to pass an indeterminate sentence. However, a conviction for murder is a serious matter. In our view it is expedient in the interests of justice to receive the evidence, notwithstanding those considerations.

Provocation cases

The statutory defence

The provocation defence is set forth at s3 Homicide Act 1957 as follows:

> Where on a charge of murder there is evidence on which the jury can find that the person charged was provoked (whether by things done or by things said or by both together) to lose his self-control, the question whether the provocation was enough to make a reasonable man do as he did shall be left to be determined by the jury; and in determining that question the jury shall take into account everything both done and said according to the effect which, in their opinion, it would have on a reasonable man.

The defence, therefore, requires two elements:

- Evidence that the accused did actually lose self-control due to the provoking effect of acts done and/or words said (sometimes referred to as the *subjective* condition).

- Evidence that the response to the provocation was in line with the response that might have been made by a *reasonable man* (sometimes referred to as the *objective* condition).

In contrast to the defence of diminished responsibility, the defence of provocation, once raised, has to be disproved by the prosecution.

The defence stands in sharp contrast with the diminished responsibility defence. Putting the matter colloquially, the diminished responsibility defence can apply where the accused 'flipped' for no reason whatever – outside the workings of his (or her) abnormal state of mind. By contrast, the provocation defence requires not only that the defendant 'flipped' for a reason (the provoking words or conduct), but also that his response in so doing was in line with the possible response of a 'reasonable man'. The consequence is that (traditionally) the two defences are quite separate and that, whereas diminished responsibility is to a substantial degree a matter for expert evidence, provocation has generally been seen as a matter entirely for the good sense of the jury.

Against this, common sense suggests that the two defences may elide at the edges – where some extreme form of provocation works upon a volatile personality to produce a homicidal response. This received partial recognition by the House of Lords in *Camplin*,[17] where it was recognised that the susceptibility of a person to provocation, and the reasonableness of his response to it, might be affected by his *physical* characteristics. Thus, for example, it would be more provocative to apply some insulting racial epithets to a black than to a white person. However, authority was divided as to whether non-physical characteristics, such as an emotionally unstable personality, could support a defence of provocation in a case falling short of diminished responsibility.

Morgan Smith

This issue was resolved decisively, but as it proved temporarily, by the House of Lords in the case of *Morgan Smith*, where Lord Hoffman stated:

> *The general principle is that the same standards of behaviour are expected of*
> *everyone, regardless of their individual psychological make-up. In most cases,*
> *nothing more will need to be said. But the jury should in an appropriate case*
> *be told, in whatever language will best convey the distinction, that this is*
> *a principle and not a rigid rule. It may sometimes have to yield to a more*
> *important principle, which is to do justice in the particular case. So the*
> *jury may think that there was some characteristic of the accused, whether*
> *temporary or permanent, which affected the degree of control which society*
> *could reasonably have expected of him and which it would be unjust not to*
> *take into account. If the jury take this view, they are at liberty to give effect*
> *to it.*

Lord Hoffman made a distinction, elsewhere in his speech, between 'personal characteristics' which might support the defence, and mere 'defects of character' which would not.

Morgan Smith had important and immediate ramifications for the Commission:

- In consequence of the new gloss on the statutory concept of the 'reasonable man', it fell to judges to direct juries to consider whether any personal characteristics of the defendant affected the reasonableness of his or her actions. This requirement was rapidly incorporated into the judges' 'bible', the Judicial Studies Board Bench Book, but in the meanwhile persons convicted pre-*Morgan Smith* were able to argue that since the jury had not been directed in these terms, their convictions were based upon wrong directions of law and, accordingly, unsafe. Such considerations were to lead to the quashing of convictions in the cases of **Farnell** and **Karimi**.

- Convicted persons who had argued diminished responsibility unsuccessfully could now raise substantially the same evidence in support of provocation – arguing that although the medical evidence had failed to establish diminished responsibility (in respect of which the onus of proof lay on the defence) it might have been sufficient to support a defence of provocation (where the onus of proof lay on the prosecution). Such considerations were to lead to the quashing of the conviction in the case of **Josephine Smith**.

- The judgment made it open to a convicted person to argue that he or she had failed to bring forward psychiatric evidence relating to his or her personality under the mistaken belief (prior to *Morgan Smith*) that such evidence was not admissible to support a provocation defence. Since the mistaken judgment (that such evidence was inadmissible) was beyond the fault of the defendant, it would only be equitable for the Court to receive such evidence now. Such considerations were to lead to the quashing of the conviction in the case of **Rowland**.

• To make matters more complex, the Court of Appeal in *Weller*[18] stated that the line in the sand that Lord Hoffman had sought to draw between 'personal characteristics' and mere 'defects of character' was impossible to define and could not be sustained. It may possibly be the case that the constitution of the Court of Appeal which decided *Weller* was seeking to exacerbate the practical difficulties of the *Morgan Smith* judgment in order to hasten the moment when it would be overruled!

In summary, whatever the justice of the approach taken by their Lordships in *Morgan Smith*, it stirred up a legal hornets' nest that they could have scarcely foreseen.

The Commission's 'Morgan Smith cases'

As these cases have proved to be of somewhat ephemeral legal significance, they will be touched upon but briefly.

Smith (Josephine)

S was convicted of the murder by shooting of her husband. It was defended as a battered wife/diminished responsibility case with expert evidence of abnormality of mind provided by Dr Eastman. Following *Morgan Smith*, the evidence of Dr Eastman was substantially re-tendered in support of provocation. The appeal was allowed and S was immediately released from prison.

Rowland

R was convicted of the murder of his wife. The case was defended on the basis of provocation – a history of escalating and callous taunting (for which there was some corroboration) – but no medical evidence had been called. Doctors who had seen R pre-trial had considered whether his depressed condition justified a defence of diminished responsibility but considered that the medical evidence did not go that far. The Commission obtained fresh medical reports which supported the case that his depression would have been likely to have affected his response to his wife's taunting. The appeal was allowed and R was also immediately released.

The Court hearing R's appeal expressed its extreme exasperation with the naïveté (as the Court saw it) of the House of Lords in deciding *Morgan Smith* as it had. The richest expressions of the Court's views occurred in untranscribed exchanges during the appeal hearing which are, unfortunately, not preserved for posterity but the heavy irony of the Court is caught in the following comment in its judgment:

> *Thus it seems clear that, in the context of the law of provocation, the reasonable man is now to be regarded as an archetype best left lurking in the statutory undergrowth, lest his emergence should lead the jury down a false trail of reasoning en route to their verdict.*

Farnell and Karimi

In **Farnell** and **Karimi**, both convictions were quashed, simpliciter, on the basis that the jury had not been correctly directed that they should take account of the personal characteristics of the accused in considering the defence of provocation.[19] The directions (in both cases) had been correct when given but were defective in the light of the subsequent restatement of the law in *Morgan Smith*. As such, they are good examples of change-of-law cases, which have given the Commission such difficulty.

The repeal of Morgan Smith

The extreme judicial hostility to *Morgan Smith* led to the taking of steps to overrule it. That objective, however, was subject to the difficulty that – as a decision of the House of Lords – it was considered to be a settled principle that *Morgan Smith* could only be overruled by a later judgment of the same House or by statute. However, an opportunity to review the law came up in *Holley*, an appeal to the Judicial Committee of the Privy Council from a decision of the Court of Appeal in Jersey. The Jersey Court had allowed H's appeal against his conviction for murder on the basis of *Morgan Smith* and the matter reached the Privy Council as an appeal by the Jersey Attorney General. In a neat constitutional device, the Attorney General did not seek to overturn the judgment (since the House of Lords represented the ultimate fount of legal authority) but merely sought clarification of the law. A nine-man constitution of the Privy Council was constituted and decided by a 6-3 majority:

This majority view [in Morgan Smith], if their Lordships may respectfully say so, is one model which could be adopted in framing a law relating to provocation. But their Lordships consider there is one compelling, overriding reason why this view cannot be regarded as an accurate statement of English law. It is this. The law of homicide is a highly sensitive and highly controversial area of the criminal law. In 1957 Parliament altered the common law relating to provocation and declared what the law on this subject should thenceforth be. In these circumstances it is not open to judges now to change ("develop") the common law and thereby depart from the law as declared by Parliament. However much the contrary is asserted, the majority view [in Morgan Smith] does represent a departure from the law as declared in section 3 of the Homicide Act 1957. It involves a significant relaxation of the uniform, objective standard adopted by Parliament.

On this short ground their Lordships, respectfully but firmly, consider the majority view expressed in the Morgan Smith case is erroneous.

The endgame followed in **James and Karimi.** Mr Karimi's conviction had previously been quashed following referral by the Commission (see above) but he was convicted on a retrial and now appealed against that conviction. His case was considered, together with that of Mr James, who was referred by the Commission (prior to the decision of the Privy Council in *Holley*). Both appealed their convictions on the basis of *Morgan Smith.* Characterising the decision of *Morgan Smith* as simply 'erroneous', the Court of Appeal followed *Holley* and dismissed the appeals. Subsequently, in **Moses** (which had also been referred by the Commission at a time when *Morgan Smith* was still thought to be good law), the Court of Appeal followed *Holley* and upheld the conviction for murder.

Reflections

The law on provocation must now be regarded as settled after their Lordships' aberration (as we must now see it) in *Morgan Smith* has been overruled in this unusual way. However, the saga promotes some uncomfortable reflections.

First, it is surely right to recognise the positive and just considerations behind the *Morgan Smith* judgment. Lord Hoffman's speech, as quoted above, recognises that there is a grey area between the defendant who loses his control for no reason at all beyond the workings of his own abnormal mind (diminished responsibility), and the defendant who kills having been so provoked that even the reasonable man on the Clapham omnibus might have been expected to react as he did (provocation). The case of **Rowland** illustrates the point – a man for whom powerfully provoking conduct and mounting depression eventually interacted and overcame his self-control. *Morgan Smith* allowed such a case to be taken (provided the jury accepted the defendant's account) outside the realm of the mandatory life sentence and to be sentenced on the basis of the justice of the individual case. That window of flexibility has now been closed.

Second, this issue is now with the government, who have the Law Commission's report, *Murder, Manslaughter and Infanticide*[20] and must decide whether to bring forward legislation – which is without doubt (as the Privy Council observed in *Holley*) the most satisfactory way to reform unsatisfactory statute law. The political difficulty arises, however, that any 'fix' of the law of homicide requires a more flexible formulation of the circumstances in which the mandatory life sentence should or should not apply. At a time when the government seeks frequently to define its political virility by increasing the numbers of life sentences handed down, it is hard to feel any optimism that the government will grasp this nettle.

Third, one is struck by the rigid 'boxes' in which the defences to murder now sit. Different defences – diminished responsibility, self-defence, provocation, accident – all have their own somewhat rigid definitions and defendants are forced to choose which defence to go for. The point is well illustrated by the case of *Ram*[21] where there was very strong evidence that the defendant had produced a knife and killed the victim only after the latter had advanced on him shouting racist taunts and brandishing a broken wine glass at his face. Simplifying the matter greatly, the case might have been defended on the basis of self-defence 'I stabbed him because it was either him or me' or provocation 'I stabbed him because I lost control at that moment'. Mr Ram's legal difficulties stemmed from the fact that his stance prior to trial had not been consistent and his counsel ended up by advising Mr Ram that he should not go into the witness box at all since he would be 'demolished' in cross-examination due to this inconsistency Realistically, however, one might suppose an account might have been given in the following terms:

> *I really can't say exactly why I lashed out like that – I was scared, petrified, angry – I didn't know what was going to happen next ... I really can't remember exactly what was going on in my mind at the moment*

and so forth. Such a narrative might well – if accepted – have justified a sentence less than life, but under the present law it leaves a defendant in 'no-man's land' between two differing and incompatible defences. Judges and learned counsel expect defendants to provide an account which fits neatly into one or other judicial box, or to fail to do so at their peril. The present state of the law does not provide an answer to this conundrum. It can only be resolved by Parliament.

Farnell and Serrano

In **Farnell**,[22] F, who was suffering from depression, had been subject to loss of sleep due to the barking of a dog owned by his neighbours, Mr and Mrs P. The evidence was that, following a bad night's sleep, F angrily confronted the neighbours about their dog's barking as they were unloading shopping from their car. At a certain point, the neighbours made it clear that they could listen to no more of this and resumed unloading their shopping, following which F, in his frustration, fetched his car jack and swung it at Mr P resulting in P's death. Defence counsel told the jury that the case was being argued on the basis of diminished responsibility and not provocation. The judge in his summing up left the alternative possibility of provocation with the jury but told them that since counsel was disavowing provocation, this defence might not detain them very long. The case was brought to the Commission conjointly on the argument (i) that the evidence of depression supported the provocation case (post *Morgan Smith*) and (ii) the judge by the terms of his summing up had erroneously withdrawn provocation from the jury, contrary to the terms of the Homicide Act 1957, which provided that provocation is a jury issue. At the risk of extreme simplification, the Commission concluded that there was no more real substance in the provocation case after *Morgan Smith* than before and declined to refer. The Administrative Court decided to give the Commission a ticking off for the insufficiency of its legal analysis[23] and allowed the application for judicial review on the point that provocation had not been properly left to the jury. When the case was later referred on this point, the Court of Appeal said that 'if that were the only defect, then the result of this appeal might well have been different'. However, they quashed the verdict because the jury had not been correctly directed in *Morgan Smith* terms.

Subsequently, in **Serrano**, the Commission referred S's conviction for murder on the 'Farnell point' that the judge had failed to leave provocation to the jury. The Court, upholding the conviction, cited authority (ignoring the judgment of the Administrative Court in **Farnell**) to conclude that where provocation was, practically speaking, a 'non-issue' the judge did not need to direct the jury to consider it. The best that can be said of this pair of cases is that the task of deciding when a 'real possibility' does and does not exist will always be interesting!

Ruth Ellis

The Commission also referred – on a provocation point – the conviction of Ruth Ellis, the last woman to be hanged in Britain. The forensic issues raised by the case are complex, but the point of general legal interest is the limit which the Court applied to the concept of 'slow burn provocation'. Miss Ellis had without question been subject to cruel rejection and taunting by her lover, whom she shot and killed on a Sunday evening. The last clearly provocative acts of the victim had been on the previous Tuesday, when he had 'stood her up', and some two weeks prior to the killing, when he had punched her in the stomach whilst she was pregnant almost certainly causing her to miscarry. After standing her up, he had callously avoided her but not committed any 'positively' provoking conduct. The issue raised by the referral was whether subsequent developments of the law, and the recognition of 'slow burn provocation' in battered wives cases, meant that provocation was wrongly withdrawn from the consideration of the jury.[24] On this point the Court ruled:

> *Whilst the Common Law has never sought to impose any time limit between the provocative act and the killing, it could not possibly be said in this case that a loss of self control, even if it did in part relate to the violent act a fortnight before, was a sudden or temporary response to that violence. Any conclusion to the contrary would clearly be wrong.*

The conviction of Miss Ellis for murder was upheld.

Pathology cases

Reference has already been made in chapter 4 to two important Commission cases – Sally **Clark** and **Boreman and Byrne** – which turned on the quality of the pathological evidence. Three further cases are briefly summarised below:

Nicholls

N was convicted of murder and robbery in 1977 and only released, following reference by the Commission, in 1998. The issue at trial was whether N had killed the victim or might have found her dead, which was N's evidence. The victim was an elderly lady with very severe health problems but the pathologist's evidence was decisive – effectively excluding the possibility of death by natural causes. The referral was based on new pathological evidence (Professor Crane) which criticised the pathology report in condemnatory terms. The Court of Appeal concluded its judgment thus:

*We allow this appeal because the pathological evidence that this was an
unlawful killing, and natural causes could be excluded, has now been shown
to be unreliable. In allowing this appeal we wish to express this Court's great
regret that as a result of what has now been shown to be flawed pathological
evidence the appellant was wrongly convicted and has spent such a very long
time in jail.*

Wickens

In this case, dating from 1991, the referral was centred on the insufficiency of
the evidence before the jury about time of death. There were key witnesses for
the prosecution, called Mr and Mrs Wilson, and if their evidence was accepted,
the victim would have died between 11 pm and 12 midnight on a Saturday
night. The pathologist for the Crown did not give an estimated time of death,
and no pathologist was called for the defence. The new pathological evidence
obtained by the Commission (and not disputed by the Crown) suggested that
death within the window of time proposed by the Wilsons' evidence was
unlikely. The Court, applying **Pendleton**, considered that this might well have
affected the jury's verdict and quashed the conviction.

Waters

W's conviction was referred on the basis of new pathological evidence (based
on analysis of stomach contents) that W's baby boy, Aaron, could have been
killed earlier than contended by the Crown and at a time when Aaron's mother
was in the house – it being the Crown's case that Aaron had been killed within
a window of time when W was alone with Aaron. The appeal was dismissed
because the case had been defended by W on the basis that death might have
been *later* than the window of time contended by the Crown, not that it might
have been earlier. The case demonstrates the unwisdom of referring on the basis
of an expert case that does not go with the trial evidence – and lies with **Hakala**
and **Wooster**, which are discussed in chapters 3 and 4 respectively.

Reflections on pathology cases

It is a truism that the evidence of a pathologist is frequently of the greatest
importance in homicide trials and that a wrong-headed pathologist has the
utmost opportunity to wreak a wrongful conviction.[25] It would seem from the
Commission's relatively limited experience that there are three areas of potential
concern about the evidence of pathologists in homicide cases.

First, there have been cases where the extent of pathological investigation – and
the recording of investigation – has not been sufficient, and this applies most

particularly in cases of deaths which are not at first regarded as suspicious. The Court of Appeal has given clear guidelines as to good practice in Sally **Clark**, but it is not apparent whether there has been a systematic inventory of current practice to ensure that those guidelines are being adhered to. It is quite clear that where initial investigation is insufficient, there may be little or nothing that defence experts can do to submit the prosecution case to searching examination.

Second, there has plainly been an issue of competence in a small number of cases. Dr Michael Heath (whose evidence was criticised in **Boreman and Byrne**) resigned as a member of the Royal College of Pathologists after a Disciplinary Tribunal raised concerns about his professional competence. Another experienced forensic pathologist, Dr Paula Lannas, has also been subject to professional criticism. They have both given evidence in many murder cases. It must be emphasised, however, that the evidence of pathologists is only contentious in a small minority of cases. Following **Boreman and Byrne**, the Commission conducted a review[26] of cases in which Dr Heath's evidence had featured but did not identify any in which his evidence had been sufficiently in contention to give rise to concerns about the safety of the conviction.

Third – as the **Faulder** group of 'shaken baby cases' has shown – there can be wide variations of interpretation as to the conclusions that should be drawn from pathological evidence. A reading of the **Faulder** judgment suggests that there are times when pathologists may have expressed themselves in more certain terms than they should have done. To an extent, this appears to be an occupational hazard specific to this profession. Pathologists are regularly pressed forensically to commit themselves to a view – when a person died and how – even where the evidence is not wholly clear cut. Time of death is a particularly difficult issue to be certain about. Pathologists for their part regularly resist attempts to commit them to conclusions where certainty cannot be attained. Nevertheless, it may be that the shades of uncertainty are not always fully exposed to juries.

Homicide – review of the evidence and other cases

The schematic classification of the Commission's homicide cases at the start of this chapter shows that new evidence in some form has informed the majority of the Commission's referrals. Many of the new evidence referrals have been reviewed in this chapter or elsewhere but there are a number of further miscellaneous cases, which are discussed below. They may serve to illustrate the very diverse kinds of cases that the Commission considers.

Causeley

C was convicted of the murder of his wife. She had, in fact, disappeared and her body was never found, but the prosecution averred that she had plainly been murdered by C after he embarked upon a relationship with another woman. The case against C was not the strongest (resting heavily on inferences from circumstances) and the Crown placed considerable reliance on the evidence of three fellow inmates of C (who had been on remand in custody), all of whom gave evidence that C had admitted to the murder. The Commission in its referral had regard to evidence that, in respect of all three cell confession witnesses, there was undisclosed background material which might have affected the weight that the jury gave to their evidence. Most seriously, one such witness, named Murphy, had, 20 years previously whilst on remand in Ireland, given cell confession evidence in suspiciously similar terms against another defendant and had plainly been rewarded by a reduction of the sentence for the offence for which he was then awaiting trial. The judgment contains quite strong and apposite comments on the complete lack of any safeguards (against verballing or invention) which apply to cell confession evidence. C's conviction was quashed, but he was subsequently convicted on a re-trial.

Christofides

C's defence position in relation to a charge of murder went awry when the judge quite unexpectedly threw out the case against his co-defendant midway through trial. The trial continued and C was convicted. The Court of Appeal 'not without considerable hesitation' quashed the conviction due to a 'sense of unease' that the Crown's witnesses had not been fully tested in the light of the dramatic change in the course of the trial.

Dudley and Maynard

The applicants were convicted in 1977 of two particularly revolting East End gangland murders and convicted after a seven-month trial. They were convicted on the basis of disputed confession evidence plus evidence of a criminal associate, named Wild. The senior investigating officer had chosen (pre-PACE) to make a full verbatim written (not tape-recorded) record of the interviews to assure their authenticity. D and M always claimed to have been 'stitched up' by the Metropolitan Police. The referral was based principally on the evidence of a handwriting expert (Dr Hardcastle) showing that it was a physical impossibility for anyone to have written up a verbatim account of critical interviews (when the defendants were said to have confessed to offences) over the time that those interviews were said to have lasted – providing a powerful case that the notes of evidence were not contemporary verbatim accounts at all. Following this evidence, the Commission (after obtaining immunity from prosecution) interviewed Wild, who retracted his evidence against D and M. The Court observed that 'over the years the courts have learned to regard post-trial retractions by persons of Wild's character with a degree of cynicism', but quashed the convictions, due to the doubt placed by Dr Hardcastle's evidence upon the reliability of the police witnesses' account of the interviews in which the confessions were said to have taken place.[27]

J

This is a case which shows the Commission at its investigative best. J – a man with severe learning difficulties – was convicted of manslaughter. As the Court noted, there was not a shred of evidence (apart from J's confession) to connect J with the crime, suspicion having fallen upon him for no better reason than that he helped out from time to time on a market stall where the victim worked. He was interrogated over five interviews to the point of confession by police officers, convicted of manslaughter and made subject to a detention order under the Mental Health Act. No 'appropriate adult' was made available, although this interview took place after the introduction of PACE (which requires that an appropriate adult attend interviews of vulnerable suspects), and no solicitor was present at the first two interviews. J's severe learning difficulties were known at trial but it was argued for the prosecution that (i) no point should be taken against police for failing to summon an appropriate adult as they had been unaware of his mental disability and (ii) the confession should be accepted as reliable notwithstanding those difficulties. The Commission's investigations showed a document in police files describing J as 'MENTAL', affording powerful evidence that the police had been perfectly aware of J's mental disabilities when interviewing him, but had elected to 'press on', despite his obvious vulnerability. This also had some knock-on impact on the integrity of the police officers conducting the investigation and the conviction was quashed.

James (David Ryan)

J, a vet, was convicted of the murder of his wife in a case which attracted a great deal of press publicity at the time. The cause of death was the administration of veterinary drugs and the defence averred that the victim had had access to these drugs and had used them to commit suicide. The jury convicted. The Commission referred on discovery of a note in the victim's hand (confirmed by handwriting analysis) that she was intending to commit suicide. Evidence was also put forward at appeal of the victim's mental state before death and the conviction was quashed.

Johnson (Frank)

J was convicted of murder in 1977. Shortly into the trial, he had dismissed his own legal team and, thereafter, conducted his trial somewhat bizarrely, including recalling prosecution witnesses to put to them an elaborate scenario of conspiracy against him and, later, refusing to submit to cross-examination. Following conviction, he was noted by prison authorities to exhibit paranoia and psychosis, and he was in due course made subject to a Mental Health Act order and transferred to Broadmoor, where he responded to antipsychotic medication. At the appeal, Dr Kopelman (for J) and Dr Joseph (for the Crown) agreed that he had been suffering from psychosis for much of the trial, although they were not in agreement as to when exactly it had begun. In short, although J had been adjudged fit to plead at the start of the trial, there had been an omission to keep his fitness to plead under review when he had begun to exhibit signs of psychosis. Mr J was still in prison (having been discharged back there from Broadmoor) after 26 years and the Court ordered his immediate release.

Mattan

M's case was the first capital case to be referred by the Commission. M was convicted and hanged for a murder committed in the docklands area of Cardiff in 1952. The case depended critically on the evidence of one Cover, a man later convicted of the attempted murder of his own daughter. The conviction was quashed on evidence, which the prosecution failed to disclose: (i) that Cover's witness statement to police was significantly different from his trial evidence; (ii) that Cover had received a reward for his evidence; and (iii) four witnesses, each of whom had seen a man close to the scene of murder at the critical time, had failed to pick out M on an identification parade. The case leaves the strong impression that M, an uneducated and illiterate Somali seaman, had been chosen as a sacrificial victim to expiate a very unpleasant murder. His (Welsh) wife and daughter were in Court when the verdict was given. The Home Office had previously declined to refer this conviction in 1970.

Kelly (George)

K was convicted and hanged in 1950 for the double murder of the manager and assistant manager of the Cameo cinema in Liverpool in the previous year. These murders aroused great public outcry at the time. A man, named Johnson, was charged with being an accessory after the fact to the murders but was acquitted at the direction of the judge (due to the inadmissibility of certain confession statements). He was returned to custody awaiting trial for another offence. A man, named Graham, who was in custody with him made a statement that Johnson had admitted carrying out the murders, but joked that the police could not charge him as he had been tried for the murders and acquitted. Extant (but undisclosed) police documents showed that the police believed Graham's statement and considered that Johnson had got away with it. Following this, the police turned their attention to Kelly and, quite remarkably, obtained a new statement from Graham that Kelly had confessed to the murder. The DPP, in a letter to the Home Secretary following Kelly's conviction stated 'I am of the opinion that but for the evidence that Graham gave before Mr Justice Cassels, Kelly would not have been convicted'. Graham's first statement implicating Johnson was never disclosed. It was accepted by the Court of Appeal that Graham's first statement had been plainly disclosable – even on the relatively scant obligations of disclosure at the time.

Kelly's conviction was quashed following reference by the Commission. Like **Mattan**, his case shows that the gravity of the capital penalty did not prevent the police from acting at times in a manner that was expeditious, unfair and unjust.

Kelly's conviction was referred, along with that of his co-defendant, Connolly, who was convicted of robbery. Connolly's appeal raises quite separate issues, which are considered in chapter 14.

Knighton

Whilst the quashing of Mr Kelly's conviction afforded considerable satisfaction to all concerned, the Court of Appeal expressed no satisfaction whatsoever at the Commission's referral of the considerably older case of **Knighton**, who was convicted of murder in 1929. The Commission referred on the basis of forensic evidence – apparently not disclosed – which it considered might have led the jury to have had doubts about K's guilt. The Court deprecated the significance of the evidence raised by the Commission and deplored the reference:

> We understand that many of the descendants of K are ignorant of this bleak period in their family history. It has now been opened to the public gaze. For them, this appeal will have been profoundly disturbing. More important, in the decision-making process, the CCRC took account of the fact that the conviction resulted in the use of the death penalty or, that, as it was described in an over-emotive comment earlier in the Statement of Reasons, by its verdict the jury had sent the appellant "to the gallows". We do not agree that, of itself, a mandatory sentence of death, a sentence finally abolished nearly 40 years ago, should influence the CCRC's decision whether to refer a conviction. The appellant's execution has had no bearing

*on its safety, or otherwise. There are here no issues of exceptional notoriety,
and therefore public interest, as in* Bentley *... or* Hanratty *... in the present
case, there are no living relatives of the deceased who knew him well, and
for whom the quashing of his conviction would provide real practical benefit,
as well as solace.*

The Court upheld the conviction.

Knighton is a case where the Court has 'indicated' to the Commission in the
most clear and directive terms to 'leave off' a certain category of case. This
judgment was undoubtedly taken to heart by the Commission and is likely to
bear on its consideration of any further 'ancient' cases that come to it in the
future.[28] The Commission subsequently took account of **Knighton** in declining
to refer the case of Timothy *Evans*, wrongfully convicted of the Rillington
Place murders. Evans received a Royal Pardon after it became clear that he was
wholly innocent of the murders, but his convictions have not to this day been
quashed. The Commission declined to refer due to the lack of benefit that would
arise from referral, E having clearly been exonerated in the decision granting
the Royal Pardon. The Commission's decision was challenged in judicial
review proceedings in **R (on the application of Westlake) v CCRC** when the
Administrative Court upheld the Commission's decision not to refer.

The Court also passed extremely waspish comments on the Commission's
referral of the case of Ruth **Ellis**.

It seems unlikely that the Commission will refer any further capital cases in the
future in the absence of very compelling arguments for doing so. There will
be differing views on the justice of this approach as there are without question
unresolved 20th century miscarriages of justice – including some capital cases.
On the other hand, the policy considerations supporting the concentration of
the Commission's resources on more current cases must also be conceded.

Hall, O'Brien and Sherwood (The 'Cardiff 3')

This was an immensely high-profile case, which has been the subject of
continued litigation between the defendants and South Wales police, following
the quashing of the convictions. The three defendants were convicted in 1988 of
the savage murder of a Cardiff newsagent, the lynchpin of the Crown case being
confessions obtained from one of the defendants, Hall, in the course of police
interviews. Hall retracted his confessions some years after trial. There were many
matters raised by the Commission's reference and in the subsequent appeal but

the central matter was new evidence from three experts (Professors Gudjonsson and Kopelman and Dr Thomas-Peter) that Hall (who had been interviewed 9 times over 48 hours) was suggestible, compliant and a wholly unreliable witness. The Court was satisfied that 'Hall is and was a person having traits in his personality of the kind associated with those who make false confessions'.

The Court went on to apply a general rule of thumb to the receipt of psychological evidence of the kind received in this appeal:

> [we] are conscious of the need to have defined limits for the case in which expert evidence of the kind we have heard may be used. First the abnormal disorder must not only be of the type which might render a confession or evidence unreliable, there must also be a very significant deviation from the norm shown. ... Second, there should be a history pre-dating the making of the admissions or the giving of evidence which is not based solely on a history given by the subject, which points to or explains the abnormality or abnormalities.

These guidelines have been cited in subsequent cases.

The 'Cardiff 3' case sits with **J** – outlined above – and also an attempted rape case considered by the Commission, **Smith (Shane Stepon)**, in this important respect. All three are cases in which vulnerable persons were interviewed to confession by police subsequent to the introduction of PACE.[29] In each case, the suspects were not afforded the protection of an appropriate adult and were intensively interviewed until they confessed. The cases serve to show that the safeguards afforded by PACE – the tape-recording of interviews and the provisions of the Codes of Practice – do not *invariably* provide sufficient protection for vulnerable suspects. That said, it is plain that the number of convictions based upon false and unreliable confessions is very much smaller than it was prior to the introduction of PACE.

Parsons

P was convicted of the murder of an old lady, named Ivy Batten, in her bungalow in 1987. The electricity supply to the bungalow had been cut by the intruder(s). Reference was based on evidence that electricity consumption at the bungalow suggested that the victim had been alive and living her normal routine after the time of death put forward by the prosecution, and at a time when P could not have committed the murder. The Court did not find the new evidence based on electricity consumption to be compelling and it upheld the conviction.[30]

Notes

1. It might be ventured that the tabloidisation of news coverage – and the obsessive interest of the media in high-profile murder cases – is placing increasing and perhaps intolerable pressure upon the police to deliver offenders to justice in cases which arouse extreme public reaction. However, the problem is not a new one, and many historic miscarriages of justice concerned offences which aroused great public interest and indignation at the time – see the case of **Kelly (George)**, discussed in this chapter, as a case in point.

2. [1999] 1 AC 82.

3. [1986] 1 WLR 1025.

4. [1997] 1 AC 1.

5. [2001] 1 AC 146.

6. [2005] UKPC 23.

7. The doctrine of judicial precedent has established – since primordial times – that a decision of the House of Lords may not be overruled by an inferior court. Such was the anxiety of the judiciary to reverse *Morgan Smith*, that an (unprecedented) nine-man constitution of the Privy Council was convened in *Holley*, effectively for the purpose of overruling the House of Lords' decision in *Morgan Smith*.

8. (1993) 96 Cr App R 133.

9. [1997] 1 Cr App R 492.

10. (1992) 2 Cr App R 520.

11. See generally the discussion of expert evidence in chapter 4.

12. There have been a small number of other cases submitted to the Commission on the basis that specific cultural factors, not argued at trial, should have formed the basis for a defence based on either diminished responsibility or provocation. No such cases have been referred in the period covered by this study.

13. This case provides an interesting footnote to the discussion of **Pendleton** in chapter 3. The Court in **Gilbert** concluded that the 'jury impact' test should be applied more conservatively in diminished responsibility cases because the onus of proof of diminished responsibility lies on the defence. The logical converse, of course, is that the test should be applied more liberally where the new evidence goes to an issue where the burden of proof is on the prosecution!

14. [1995] 1 All ER 187.

15. In Mr Karimi's case, the medical diagnosis was raised in support of a provocation and not a diminished responsibility defence.

16. The preliminary hearing, which is reported at [2003] EWCA Crim 2385, was held to decide whether it was expedient or necessary in the interests of justice to receive the new evidence of diminished responsibility.

17. [1978] AC 705.

18. [2003] EWCA Crim 815.

19. Both convictions were, in fact, referred primarily for other reasons – in **Karimi**'s case due to fresh medical evidence and in **Farnell**'s case following the outcome of a judicial review application – discussed below.

20. Law Commission Report No 304. The Law Commission's recommendations are summarised in its press release in the following way:

> The Law Commission has previously said that the law of murder is in a mess. The law can be unclear, unfair, or too generous to killers. Juries have too few choices between verdicts to reflect how blameworthy the offender really was. This frequently leads to judges having an inadequate basis on which to sentence offenders. Victims' families also rightly object to the excessive breadth of the different kinds of manslaughter, as compared with the single offence of murder.

The overwhelming majority of our consultees favoured restructuring the law so as to address these serious and persistent problems. We believe that our recommendations, and in particular our recommendation for clearly defined offences of first degree and second degree murder, will go a long way to putting right these injustices and inadequacies in the law.

Responsibility for implementing the Law Commission's proposals would be a matter for the Ministry of Justice.

21. Mr Ram's case was not referred by the Commission but the judgment on his first-time appeal was heard on 7 December 1995 and is briefly reported in *Times Law Reports* 7/12/1995.

22. The discussion which follows relates principally to the judgment in Mr Farnell's judicial review proceedings: [2003] EWHC Admin 835.

23. The following memorable exchange is worth an extended footnote.

Counsel for the Commission (following an extremely erudite submission from Mr Farnell's counsel):

My lords, if the Court expects the Commission to reason its decisions to such a degree, it would need to be very differently constituted. Perhaps your Lordships were not aware that the person who drafted the Statement of Reasons is not a legally qualified person.

His Lordship: *And were any of the Case Committee legally qualified persons?*

Counsel for the Commission: *Mr Elks, who sits behind me, is a solicitor my Lord.*

His Lordship: *Hmm. I see.*

The tone in which this exchange was conducted is left to the imagination of the reader.

24. On this point it should be noted that, prior to the Homicide Act 1957, a judge could withdraw provocation from the jury if he considered that there was no evidence to go with the defence.

25. For an interesting and entertaining account of the role of the pathologist in some of the most famous 20th century murder convictions, see the recent biography by Anthony Rose of the Home Office pathologist, Sir Bernard Spilsbury – Lethal Witness, 2007, The History Press Ltd. Rose argues persuasively that Spilsbury was afforded undue deference as an expert witness and was responsible, in some cases, for miscarriages of justice.

26. Conducted by Commissioner David Jessel.

27. Two co-defendants, Kathleen **Bailey** and Charles **Clarke** (both convicted of conspiracy to cause grievous bodily harm) were also referred, and their convictions were also quashed.

28. This statement requires two qualifications:

1. The Court's objection seems to be to what it might regard as 'academic' referrals of old capital cases. In cases such as **Mattan** and **Kelly (George)**, where there has been obvious miscarriage of justice, the Court's approach has been more favourable.

2. There have been two cases dating back from the 1950s where convictions of living applicants have been quashed – **Hay Gordon**, who was convicted ('guilty but insane') of murder in 1953 and **Quinn (John)** convicted of robbery (theft of scrap metal in Carlisle) in 1957. The Court expressed no resentment of these referrals. Mr Quinn's conviction was quashed – somewhat improbably – on the basis of fresh witness evidence. Now in his 70s, he was a most engaging applicant and his judgment makes entertaining reading.

29. Note also somewhat similar facts in **James (Albert)** albeit it may be said of that case that it occurred so soon after the introduction of PACE that it may have been due to teething problems in giving effect to the new legislation.

30. A number of other issues were also raised in P's appeal.

Chapter 9 - Sexual offences cases

The Commission's caseload and its approach

Just over 25 per cent of all applications made to the Commission are for review of convictions or sentences for sexual offences.[1] Sexual cases, therefore, represent an important element of the Commission's caseload, and the percentage of sex offence cases is disproportionate (along with homicide cases) to the number of convictions for sex offences in the criminal justice statistics 'at large'.

A great number of sexual offence applications raise no issue not previously raised at either trial or appeal and require little or no investigative effort on the part of the Commission. Many applications for review of convictions for sexual offences amount to no more than an assertion that the complainant lied and should have been disbelieved by the jury. Not a few applications suggest distorted thinking, such as a failure to accept the criminality of illegal acts. Whilst it is easy to sense the anguish of these applicants, the Commission can only disabuse them of the idea that it can re-try their cases.

For the period June 2004 to March 2006, the Commission ran a sexual offences 'pilot' scheme consisting of 20 interview cases and 20 control cases. The interview cases were applicants seeking review of convictions for sexual offences against children and were selected on the basis of proximity to the Commission's offices; they were interviewed irrespective of whether their applications raised any issues giving rise to obvious concern. The Commission wanted to establish whether a face to face interview would in any sense sharpen the Commission's appreciation of the issues raised by such applications and/or provide background information helpful to the review of these cases. In the outcome, the interviews yielded insufficient data to conclude that routine interviewing of such applicants would be a justifiable use of Commission casework resources. This pilot scheme (although it may have improved applicants' understanding of the review process) did not add any obvious value to the Commission's deliberations and has been discontinued.

The Commission has clearly recognised, however, that sexual offences trials can lead to miscarriages of justice and should take pride in the fact that a number of clearly wrongful convictions for sexual offences have been set aside following referral. The difficulties that can potentially arise in sexual offences cases include the following:

- An offender may be convicted on the uncorroborated testimony of the complainant, and many sexual offences cases turn on the question whether the jury prefers the testimony of the complainant or the defendant. An unprepossessing defendant may be particularly likely to be disbelieved by the jury. The Criminal Justice and Public Order Act 1994 abrogated the requirement for a trial judge to warn the jury of the dangers of convicting on the uncorroborated evidence of an alleged victim of a sexual offence.

- Medical corroboration – as to whether sexual penetration has taken place, whether it has been recent, or whether it has been rough or violent – can raise more difficult issues of judgment and interpretation than juries necessarily realise.

- Many complainants – particularly in intra-family abuse cases – are emotionally or psychologically damaged – not necessarily as a result of the alleged criminal acts. The Commission has dealt with some cases (discussed below) where it would seem that complaints have been brought by damaged or attention-seeking individuals.

- Sexual abuse charges are sometimes brought long after the complained-of behaviour has ceased. This situation generally arises in one of two situations. First, there are cases where a person says that she (or he) has been a victim during childhood of intra-family abuse but only makes complaint many years later, often in adulthood. Second, there are subjects of alleged abuse in institutional care who make complaint only much later – frequently following publicity about the institution and/or after being contacted by police. There are, of course, very good reasons why complaints may be delayed for many years, and it is one of the pernicious effects of childhood abuse that the abuser may use his or her authority over the victim to make disclosure practically impossible. It is, therefore, clearly right that such complaints should be given the most serious consideration by the prosecuting authorities. On the other hand, there are particular problems for those accused of such offences in mounting an active defence.

Recognising these particular difficulties, the Commission has adopted a number of procedures specific to sexual abuse cases.[2]

Review of social services material

It is the Commission's standard procedure in all cases of intra-family abuse[3] to exercise its statutory powers under section 17 of the 1995 Act to review social services material relating to the complainant. The Commission has power to require the production of files, and generally exercises its powers to require the production of relevant social services material in toto.[4] It is a matter of judgment whether to go beyond social services material to examine the files of other statutory agencies (for instance health visitors, medical practices, counselling services or schools) which may have had contact with the complainant and his or her family. There is no presumption that investigation should go beyond the social services files, but where there are indications that investigations need to be taken further, the Commission should[5] pursue them – see **C (Martin)** below as a case in point.

In many cases, there will have been a prior review of social services material at the time of trial through the making of a third-party disclosure summons against the local authority. It is now normal practice for defendant lawyers acting in the trial of intra-family abuse cases to seek disclosure of 'material' social services documentation. 'Materiality' is defined in well known authorities such as *R v Reading Justices ex p Berkshire County Council*[6] and *Brushett*[7] – which prevent the use of such summonses to carry out 'fishing expeditions' in order to obtain disclosure of matters of peripheral or dubious relevance. Responsibility for disclosure in such cases is typically assigned by the local authority to a social services lawyer (often with no knowledge of the criminal case) who reviews the social services file and flags up 'material' matters for review by the trial judge. It is questionable whether this procedure necessarily elicits all material relevant to the defence case. The Commission's review of social services files ought to be superior to the review carried out for third-party disclosure purposes, in that the file is reviewed comprehensively by a person (the Commission's Case Review Manager) with personal knowledge of the issues raised by the trial. The Commission's review may also, as in **K (Jamie)**, discussed below, take in post-trial material relevant to the complainant's credibility.

Review of Criminal Injuries Compensation Authority (CICA) files

The Commission also routinely reviews CICA files in child sex abuse cases. The rationale for this is set out as follows in the Commission's Formal Memorandum on sex abuse cases:

> *Many victims of child sexual abuse quite properly make an application to the CICA. The Commission will usually use its s17 power to access the*

CICA file and compare the account given by the victim to the CICA with that given to the jury. In a small number of cases the two accounts have been significantly different and this has raised questions about the victim's credibility.

It should be noted that applications by complainants to the CICA are frequently only commenced after the conclusion of the criminal trial and, therefore, any issues as to consistency of accounts generally cannot be explored at trial.

Review of previous complaints recorded by police

This procedure has been adopted as part of the Commission's standard practice following the cases of **Warren** and **Blackwell**, discussed below. In both cases, the complainants had made previous and somewhat similar complaints to other forces which (having been disbelieved) had not resulted in criminal action being taken by police. In **Blackwell**, the complainant had also assumed a number of different identities. The Commission now routinely uses its power under section 17 of the 1995 Act in sex abuse cases to interrogate police records for information about any previous allegations made by the complainant.

All of the foregoing enquiries are conducted 'neutrally' and in the great majority of cases yield no information of assistance to the applicant. They are, however, it is submitted, an entirely appropriate use of the Commission's section 17 powers and – in a small number of cases – they have established significant matters of relevance to the complainant's credibility, going beyond the scope of investigation by the applicant's lawyers at the time of trial.

Social services cases

In the following cases, investigation of social services or other statutory material has led to referral and quashing of convictions.

A (Derek)

A was convicted of offences against his former partner's daughter, who was aged nine at the date of the alleged offences and ten at the time of trial. The relationship had been ended by the mother coincident in time with the allegations. The allegations contained a degree of sexual detail, which a jury would have supposed to have been beyond the knowledge of such a young complainant – unless the complained-of acts had actually taken place. The social services file contained evidence of (i) inappropriate premature sexualisation (making it more likely that she would have known such details); (ii) groundless allegations of sexual misconduct against teachers; and (iii) expressions of great animus on the part of the mother (who had given evidence at trial) against Mr A. The court concluded:

> *If ... there are substantial grounds to question the honesty and reliability of the child and, here, the motivation of the mother -- grounds unknown to the Crown Prosecution Service, prosecution counsel and the defence at the trial, and hence unknown to the jury -- then the safety of a conviction may be thrown into real doubt. In our judgment such is the case here.*

K (Jamie)

The defendant – aged 12 at the time of the alleged offence – was accused of rape of the five-year-old complainant, KJ. KJ's family was extremely troubled and was well known to the local authority social services department, and some disclosure of material relating to the complainant took place prior to trial. The Commission's review of the files included considerable relevant material, which had not been disclosed pre-trial, and also a comprehensive assessment of KJ carried out post trial by a psychologist, all of which raised further serious concerns about her credibility. The Court stated:

> *In the light of these matters, we take the view that, if there had been cross-examination based on the undisclosed pre-trial material to which we have referred, the judge would probably have given a stronger warning about the reliability of KJ ... In any event, with or without such directions, the jury's verdict might have been different. The post-trial material also engenders doubt in this court as to the safety of the conviction in a case which was highly unusual, in view of the ages of the three children and the abnormal sexual background of the two who gave evidence for the prosecution. Accordingly this appeal is allowed and the conviction quashed.*

A significant point arising from this case is that the Commission and the Court were able to take into account material affecting the complainant's credibility, which was not in existence at the time of trial.

C (Martin)

The facts of C have already been referred to in the chapter on expert evidence. In brief, C was convicted on the basis of (i) complaint by his daughter, who would have been aged 6-7 at the time of the alleged offence; (ii) evidence from Dr S that the complainant had been found to have been penetrated when examined in 1993. What was withheld from the defence was the fact that an earlier examination by Dr S in 1991 had found that the child had *not* been penetrated. It was accepted that C had had no possibility of contact with the child since 1990. This provided the strongest case that the complainant had been subject to penetrative assault between 1991 and 1993 by someone other than C. This material was found in the complainant's medical files – after the Commission's review of social services files had suggested to the Case Review Manager that the medical files should be examined. The Court of Appeal, unusually, roundly apologised to C for his wrongful conviction.

B (David)

B was convicted of rape and buggery of two of his partner's children. The children had disclosed abuse when they were placed in the care of a foster parent who ran a children's home. Subsequent to trial, it emerged, following a lengthy judicial enquiry, that the proprietor of this home had a history, inter alia, of (i) encouraging estrangement between children entrusted to her and their natural families; (ii) encouraging allegations of abuse; and (iii) (possibly) appropriating criminal compensation payments. Social services files revealed, inter alia, that the older child had disclosed to her schoolteacher that she had been encouraged to make allegations against her mother. The Commission's investigations also showed that medical evidence that the older child had been penetrated was wrong. The Court of Appeal judgment, unfortunately, fails to set out any detail of the reasons for the quashing of the conviction.

B (Ernest)

The facts of B's case have been discussed in chapter 5.

S (C) and S (O)

Two brothers – then in their 20s – were convicted of a number of offences against a girl with learning disabilities with whom they were acquainted. She was aged 14 at the time of the alleged offences. She continued to socialise with the brothers after the alleged offences and only made complaint two years later. There were numerous discrepancies between the circumstantial detail described in her evidence (such as school attendance dates) and ascertained facts. The jury, however, convicted, and the Court of Appeal in the first-time appeal considered that there had been sufficient evidence to enable the jury to convict. The complainant had said in the course of her evidence at trial that she had seen her doctor due to pain caused by the assaults, but no medical notes were found or disclosed at the time of trial. The Commission (through great persistence) obtained the GP's notes, which indicated that she had not in fact seen her doctor at that time. In its judgment following the Commission's reference, the Court noted the numerous discrepancies between the complainant's evidence and ascertainable facts known to the jury at trial alongside the new information revealed by the Commission's investigations. The Court regarded this new evidence as, in effect, the 'last straw' and allowed the appeals.

Compare and contrast the following cases in which the Court declined to quash convictions on the basis of social services material.

Smith (Allen)

S, aged 35 at the material time, was convicted of rape of the complainant, then aged 19. It was not in dispute that the complainant had invited S home to dinner, had kissed him and that intercourse had taken place – the only issue being consent. Part of the grounds of referral was fresh psychiatric evidence of the complainant's histrionic and unstable personality. This evidence was rejected by the Court as inadmissible (see chapter 4 above). In addition, there was extensive social services material – not disclosed at time of trial – indicating a troubled mental history on the part of the victim, manic depression, self-harm and other matters. The Court considered:

- That much of the material about the complainant was known at time of trial in other ways.

- That much of the material was of such peripheral relevance that the trial judge would not have permitted cross-examination upon it.

- That the defence would have made little headway in pursuing these issues, as the complainant's replies to questioning on 'collateral' matters would have been final.

- That the material did not affect her credibility.

Smith illustrates the limitations placed by the rules of evidence upon the use of social services material, particularly upon the use of evidence of 'collateral' matters. The rule was expressed by Lord Lane in *Edwards*[8] in the following terms:

> *The test is primarily one of relevance, and this is so whether one is considering evidence in chief or questions in cross-examination. To be admissible questions must be relevant to the issue before the court.*

Issues are of varying degrees of relevance or importance. A distinction has to be drawn between, on the one hand, the issue in the case upon which the jury will be pronouncing their verdict and, on the other hand, collateral issues of which the credibility of the witnesses may be one. ...

The distinction between the issue in the case and matters collateral to the issue is often difficult to draw, but it is of considerable importance. Where cross-examination is directed at collateral issues such as the credibility of the witness, as a rule the answers of the witness are final and evidence to contradict them will not be permitted ... The rule is necessary to confine the ambit of a trial within proper limits and to prevent the true issue from becoming submerged in a welter of detail.

Combing through social services material, the Commission's Case Review Managers have to draw distinctions between material, which is relevant and admissible, material which is irrelevant and inadmissible, and material which is 'collateral'. Despite the confidence with which learned judges draw these distinctions, they are not always so apparent when reviewing such material. **Smith** illustrates these difficulties, and is in many ways a harsh and unsatisfactory judgment.

L (Stuart)

In this remarkable judgment, the central issue was the impact of material in undisclosed NSPCC files revealing discrepancies between the allegations made by the complainant, JR (as an adult) at trial, and accounts (potentially exculpatory) given by her as a child and recorded in the NSPCC social work files. The Court of Appeal (Moses LJ) did not question that there were very significant discrepancies, nor that a jury might have found those discrepancies significant. However, in deciding that the convictions against L were safe the Court took into account the following points:

- That the discrepancies might be accounted for by the long interval of time between the two accounts – and did not mean that the trial account was unreliable.

- Whilst the NSPCC files suggested allegations against someone other than L, there might well have been (in a very troubled family) more than one assailant.

- There was reason to suppose that defence counsel had been aware of the NSPCC files and had given them a 'wide berth' – choosing not to seek disclosure or make use of this material at trial because 'it would have revealed the classic signs of a sexually abused child' and it would have been unhelpful to the defendant.

- In relation to other inconsistent allegations which had been made by JR post trial, the Court considered that 'This subsequent history is wholly consistent with the sad picture of an abused child and do (sic) not affect the safety of the verdict in any way.'

L appears to be an extreme application of a post-**Pendleton** approach (see chapter 3) in which the Court clearly took its own view of the guilt of the appellant in dismissing the significance of material in the NSPCC files and disregarding any views that a hypothetical (and perhaps one senses in the Court's judgment – a more gullible) jury might have taken.

New evidence

Another new evidence case, albeit not based upon social services material, was **M (AR)**. The complainants, both young girls, stated that M had committed indecent assaults whilst babysitting them. They had complained to their stepfather, who had immediately gone out and attacked M. M was subsequently arrested and convicted of the offences. The conviction was referred following information from M that he had read a newspaper report that the stepfather had been convicted of assaults against these girls committed over the same period, and also against a third girl. Moreover, in the words of the Court's judgment, 'the nature of the offences alleged against the stepfather bore a striking resemblance to the allegations which had been made in the case of M'. The information was significant, first, because the girls had deposed that no one but M had ever indecently assaulted them, and second the stepfather's proven assaults could have explained how the girls had had the knowledge to give the evidence in support of their complaints. The report, although brief, well illustrates the hazards of sexual offences cases based upon the evidence of young children.

Criminal Injuries Compensation Authority cases
P (Ricardo)

P, aged 27, was convicted of the rape of SB aged 14 – his wife's granddaughter. There were a number of problematic aspects to the evidence and the jury's verdict clearly depended on their belief in the credibility of SB.[9] The Commission referred on the basis of evidence of inconsistent assertions on SB's part in her claim to the CICA. Of this, the Court of Appeal stated in its judgment:

> The account to the CICA included a number of significant features which did not appear in the account of the incident given by the complainant to the police, or to the jury at either of the appellant's trials. In summary, first, she claimed that when she woke to find the appellant on top of her and tried to scream, he held a gun to her head and threatened to kill her. Second, he raped her anally as well as vaginally. Third, he threatened to kill her if she told anyone about the rape. Fourth, she had become pregnant as a result of the rape, and she had then undergone a termination. Fifth, she had also been infected with gonorrhoea and chlamydia.

Two of these claims were manifestly untrue – SB had had a termination some weeks before the alleged rape, having become pregnant by her boyfriend, and she had never been diagnosed as suffering from gonorrhoea.

The judgment continued:

> Part, at least, of the application to the CICA was false. In other respects, it was inconsistent in significant respects with the evidence before the jury. SB's credibility is significantly damaged, damage, we emphasise inextricably linked to the complaint which resulted in the appellant's conviction.

and the conviction was quashed.

Parker and Irwin

By way of contrast, in this case the Court did not consider that inconsistencies in the complainant's CICA form affected the safety of the convictions. It accepted evidence that the inconsistency was due to the haste with which the solicitor had completed the CICA form – paying insufficient attention to the information provided to her. The inconsistency did not, on the facts, undermine the credibility of the complainant's trial account.

Brooke and Siddall

These cases are discussed below.

'Serial complainant' cases

The following 'serial complainant' cases have many common features. They are a reminder that, whilst the great majority of allegations of sexual misconduct are no doubt honestly made, such honesty cannot be taken for granted. At present, there is a great deal of discussion of the need to increase the number of rape cases charged and convicted, and continuing criticism of the police and Crown Prosecution Service for the low number of cases brought to trial. The cases which follow illustrate that there is another side to this story.

Warren

W had been living with his girlfriend, N, but the relationship was failing and they had agreed to separate. Intercourse took place at their flat, which W said was consensual but N said was rape. W's application to the Commission amounted to a simple protestation of innocence (in common with many such applications) and the Commission (in the absence of any new evidence or issues raised by W's application) issued a provisional decision not to refer.[10] The impassioned nature of W's response prompted further enquiry, which revealed that N had made extremely similar allegations in two previous complaints to police in another force area and also somewhat similar allegations in Industrial Tribunal proceedings for unfair dismissal. She had acknowledged to police in one of the previous cases that her allegations had been untrue; and in the second case the police rejected her allegations and recorded them as 'no crime' – a classification which denoted that the complaints were considered to be untrue. These matters could have been ascertained if the prosecution had carried out the pre-trial disclosure review with greater diligence. The conviction was quashed by the Court of Appeal.

Blackwell

B was convicted of an indecent assault on S outside a social club on New Year's eve. She identified B, whom she had met briefly at the club, as her attacker. There was medical evidence of injury consistent with her complaint. B, who had no reason to suspect self-harm, did not dispute the assault but denied being the person responsible for it. The prosecution failed to disclose information about S's psychological history and the Commission's subsequent enquiries showed that S had had a lengthy history of wholly spurious complaints and self-harm. It was clear from this history that it was overwhelmingly likely that the 'attack' was a case of self-harm by S and that B was wholly innocent of the offence, and the conviction was quashed. The facts are considered in greater detail in chapter 14.

K (Jason)

K was convicted of rape and indecent assault against the complainant, who was aged 15 at the time. The complainant said that she had agreed to go out with K in his car but had not consented to intercourse or digital penetration. K's case was that he had not penetrated K, that such sexual activity as occurred was consensual, and that the complainant had conducted a campaign of harassment against him, including sending numerous explicit text messages. The Commission's investigation of police files enabled it to identify the fact that the complainant had made extremely similar allegations against another man, P, who also said that he had been harassed by her. The complainant's close friend, who had been tendered to corroborate the complaint against P, told police, in effect, that the complainant had made up that complaint, which had been marked up as 'no crime' in police records. Although the complaints had both been investigated by Merseyside police, the matters were dealt with by different police divisions and the connection had not been made for disclosure purposes.[11] Although the Court did not put it in quite those terms, the undisclosed information again provided compelling evidence that the complainant was a liar and the convictions were quashed.

To the foregoing there should be added the cases of David **Carrington-Jones** and Dean **Solomon**, whose convictions for rape were both quashed – outside the period of this study – in October 2007. Carrington-Jones was convicted of the rape of two teenage sisters in 2000 and sentenced to ten years' imprisonment. He was denied normal parole, due to the fact that he maintained his innocence. It was later found that one of these sisters, KJ, had made complaints against her brother, fiancé, stepfather and a customer at work and had admitted to police that she had accused her stepfather because she 'did not like him'. After KJ made complaint against Mr Carrington-Jones, her sister had added further complaints of her own. The Court found that the complainants' credibility was 'damaged beyond repair' and quashed the convictions.[12]

The case of **Solomon**, although evoking less sympathy, was even more clear-cut. S was convicted of rape and buggery against two complainants, both aged under 16. Their evidence – plainly believed by the jury – was that the sexual acts had been physically forced by the complainant. Subsequently, the police discovered a video camera at S's premises used for recording indecent images, resulting in further prosecution. The police also, remarkably, recovered a film which captured the events which had led to S's earlier convictions. From this film it was plain that the complainants had consented to all the acts against them and that buggery had not taken place. S had not placed this film in evidence as it would clearly have disclosed indecent assaults against the complainants. The case was referred by the Commission with considerable diffidence as, clearly, S had no 'reasonable explanation' for failing to put forward the evidence of the video film upon which he now relied. On the other hand, it was clear that he had been convicted on perjured evidence. The Court resolved this dilemma, noting that S had served his sentence for the earlier offences. In these unusual circumstances, it was prepared to set the record straight by allowing the appeal.

Historic abuse cases

There have been numerous applications to the Commission for review of convictions for sexual abuse said to have been committed by staff, previously employed at care homes, against children (mostly boys) subject to local authority care orders.[13] The 'care home cases' generally have been of a recurring pattern. Complaints against staff in such homes have been made following allegations (which first emerged in 1991) that Bryn Estyn, a home for adolescent boys in North Wales, was the centre of a paedophile ring. The Bryn Estyn allegations prompted complaints from former residents at other children's homes – most such complaints being made years or decades after the complained-of incidents. The police developed protocols (including the practice sometimes, somewhat tendentiously, described as 'trawling') to approach previous known residents of such homes to ascertain whether or not they had similar allegations to make. The entire process is without question fraught with difficulty and there are a number of active campaigners, mostly associated with the group FACT – Falsely Accused Carers and Teachers – who consider that the investigation and prosecution of such cases has been systemically unfair and that the Commission's efforts in righting injustices has been paltry. Criticism to somewhat similar effect has also been expressed by Claire Curtis-Thomas MP who was previously a member of the Home Affairs Select Committee which has had general Parliamentary oversight of the Commission.

Historic abuse cases are not by any means confined to institutional cases of this sort, and the majority of historic applications to the Commission relate to convictions for intra-family abuse. Typically, the case presented at trial has been that a child subjected to persistent and long-term abuse has only had the practical ability to complain of it after attaining adulthood (or in some cases adolescence) and being no longer subject to the power of the abuser to restrain disclosure.

Before setting out details of the Commission's referrals it will be helpful to set out in barest detail the framing legal context.

Can an historic abuse conviction ever be unsafe simply due to delay in bringing the prosecution?

It is arguable that nobody should be prosecuted – let alone convicted – on the basis of uncorroborated, or barely corroborated, allegations of historic sex abuse. In a typical case of intra-family abuse, a woman in early adulthood discloses that she was regularly abused during childhood by a parent or family member. She made no disclosure at the time, due to being subject to fear or emotional coercion, but now feels able to do so. All the incidents complained of took place at unspecified times in the family home when no other adults were present. Such a case presents a serious dilemma. On the one hand, the serious criminal behaviour, if proved, should be punished. On the other hand, the defendant has probably no means of challenging the truth of the allegations, beyond a bare denial that the events took place. Moreover, to attack the honesty and motives of the complainant – especially if her evidence discloses obvious emotional distress – can simply antagonise the jury.

To put this issue into context, it should be said at once that not very many 'bare' cases are prosecuted or proved,[14] and that most historic abuse cases are framed by some contemporary evidence – such as attempted or partial disclosures made during childhood. However, this corroborating evidence can itself be highly problematical – for instance where witnesses seek to reconstruct fragmentary memories of corroborative details – and again it may be difficult or counter-productive for the defence to mount an effective attack on such evidence.

What if such a case comes to Court and defence counsel seeks a stay of proceedings on the grounds of serious prejudice occasioned by the delay in bringing prosecution? Lord Woolf summed up the prior legal position in giving judgment in the case of *R v B (Brian Selwyn):*[15]

> *In* Attorney General's Reference No 1 of 1990[16] *Lord Lane CJ said that a stay should only be employed in exceptional circumstances. In assessing whether there was likely to be serious prejudice, the power of the judge to regulate the admissibility of evidence, and the trial process, which should ensure that all relevant factual issues arising from delay would be placed before the jury together with the power of the judge to give appropriate directions should be borne in mind.*

And provided that the judge did all these things, a fair trial could ensue. However, at the very conclusion of his judgment Lord Woolf added the following riveting proviso:

Not only does a defendant have difficulty in a trial, but if he is convicted an appellate court has difficulty. The reason the jury convicted was almost inevitably because they felt the complainant was speaking the truth and the defendant was not. No doubt they took into account that generally people do not make allegations of this sort years after the event unless they believe them to be true. However, those who try cases know that sometimes -- and this is in the experience of each member of this court -- honest witnesses can convince themselves that something happened in their youth when it is subsequently shown that what they remember cannot be true. However, having said that, it is difficult to see how this complainant could have made up the details she described unless she was either lying (and that is difficult to conceive having regard to what we know of her), or at one stage in her life she was fantasizing about what had happened. She went into detail in giving her evidence, such as having to remove the semen from her body when her stepfather ejaculated. Nonetheless, there are difficulties in ascertaining where the truth lies in a case of this sort.

One thing is clear: the jury saw the witnesses and we have not. Therefore they were in a better position to judge where the truth lay than this court. Furthermore, the trial process depends upon our confidence in the jury system. We have to have confidence that they made the appropriate allowance here for delay, and we also have to have in mind the intervention of Parliament. Parliament made the decision as to where they considered the right balance between the prosecution and the defence should lie in regard to the question of corroboration. We must not seek to go behind the decision of Parliament. Therefore juries in cases of this sort must be left with the difficult task of determining where the truth lies.

However, there remains in this court a residual discretion to set aside a conviction if we feel it is unsafe or unfair to allow it to stand. This is so even where the trial process itself cannot be faulted. It is a discretion which must be exercised in limited circumstances and with caution. When we exercise that discretion we must be conscious that we are not only involved in deciding where justice lies for the appellant. We must do justice to the prosecution, whose task it is to see that the guilty are brought to justice. We must also do justice to the victim. In this case we are particularly conscious of the position of the victim. If she is right, she was treated in a most disgraceful way by someone whom she should have been entitled to trust: her stepfather. For years, for understandable reasons, as we have already indicated, she felt unable to make public what had happened. She is entitled to justice as well. But we also have to do justice to the appellant. At the heart of our criminal justice system is the principle that while it is important that justice is done to the prosecution and justice is done to the victim, in the final analysis the fact remains that it is even more important that an injustice is not done to a defendant. It is central to the way we administer justice in this country that although it may mean that some guilty people go unpunished, it is more important that the innocent are not wrongly convicted.

B's conviction was quashed by the Court in exercise of this 'residual discretion'. This decision aroused immense interest among practitioners and, had *R v B* been followed in subsequent decisions of the Court, it would have raised a real possibility that many other historic abuse cases would have been quashed. In the outcome, however, the Court, perhaps fearing an opening of the floodgates, drew sharply back from this position. Lord Woolf himself returned to this issue in *Smolinski:*[17]

> *The making of applications to have cases stayed where there has been delay on the basis of abuse of process has become prevalent. ... the court questions whether it is helpful to make applications in relation to abuse of process before any evidence has been given by the complainants in a case of this nature. Clearly, having regard to the period of time which has elapsed, the court expects that careful consideration has been given by the prosecution as to whether it is right to bring the prosecution at all. If, having considered the evidence to be called, and the witnesses having been interviewed on behalf of the prosecution, a decision is reached that the case should proceed, then in the normal way we would suggest that it is better not to make an application based on abuse of process. It will take up the court's time unnecessarily. Unless the case is exceptional, the application will be unsuccessful. That was indicated by this court in* R v B *... which is also referred to in the current edition of Archbold. In that case this court referred to the earlier decision, including* Attorney General's Reference No 1 of 1990 *and suggested that the approach of Lord Lane in that case indicated the general position.*

Lord Woolf added that counsel could consider making an application for stay at the conclusion of the prosecution evidence – if the evidence turned out to be inconsistent or flimsy – but without any specific encouragement that such applications would succeed. The orthodoxy of the Court, however, in *Smolinski* and in sundry other judgments following *R v B*, was that Lord Lane got the position absolutely right in *Attorney General's Reference (No 1)*, and whatever 'residual discretion' existed by reference to *R v B*, the Court wished to hear no more of it.

As a result of the rapid judicial response to 'correct' the disorder threatened by the *R v B* judgment, the Commission has not referred any historic cases on the basis of 'bare' argument that the Court might exercise its residual discretion. In one referral, **G (G)**, (discussed below), the Commission referred to the discretion in *R v B* as a peripheral issue, but without positive outcome.

How should the jury be warned about the approach to be taken in historic abuse cases?

In the case of *Percival*,[18] an historic abuse conviction was successfully appealed on the basis that that jury had not been sufficiently warned about the difficulties faced by a defendant in contesting historic abuse allegations. The Court stated:

> *Before a conviction following such a trial can appear to be safe, it is necessary to be satisfied that the judge has confronted the jury with the fact of delay and its potential impact on the formulation and conduct of the defence and on the Prosecution's fulfillment of the burden of proof.*

As in the case of *R v B*, the Court swiftly became aghast at the opening of the floodgates to further appeals in consequence of this decision. In *M (Brian)*[19] the Court stated:

> *It is apparent that the judgment in* Percival *was directed to the summing-up in that particular case. We find in the judgment no attempt by the court to lay down principles of general application in relation to how judges should sum up in cases of delay and we accordingly would wish to discourage the attempts being made, with apparently increasing frequency, in applications and appeals to this court to rely on* Percival *as affording some sort of blueprint for summings up in cases of delay.*

Before the judgment in *M* was reported, the Commission had referred the case of **P (Michael)**, following *Percival*, on the basis of the insufficiency of the jury warning. The reference received short shrift from the Court of Appeal. Emphasising that 'a summing-up is not a mechanical recitation of formulae taken from the Judicial Studies Board's model directions', the Court stated that the warning required depended on the facts of the instant case – and it dismissed the appeal.

Some years later, in **G** (G), the inadequacy of the jury warning was one of the grounds of referral. The judge had warned the jury in the following terms:

> *How does the prosecution succeed in proving the defendant's guilt? The answer to that is by making you sure of it. Nothing less than that will do, so if after considering all the evidence you are sure the defendant is guilty, you must return a verdict of guilty. If you are not sure your verdict must be not guilty.*
>
> *In this case, Members of the Jury, there has been delay in making these complaints, and that affects the defendant's ability to formulate his defence, to remember events and to find witnesses who have memories of these events. The only way of ensuring a fair trial, fair to the defendant, and of countering any prejudice to him is for you to have a conscientious concern for the burden and standard of proof direction which I have just given you.*

The Commission felt that – in a case which was particularly fraught with complex delay issues – this perfunctory warning (couched in somewhat complex language) appeared to fall far short of 'confronting the jury' with the difficulties faced by Mr G in combating allegations about things said and done some 20 years previously. However, in considering the adequacy of this direction, the Court adopted a 'post-*Percival*' pragmatic approach:

> *The judge thus made it clear that the consequences of delay were to be taken into account in deciding whether the prosecution had discharged the burden of proof and thus whether they were sure of the appellant's guilt. In our judgment, a direction of that kind is sufficient, unless there is or are some particular point or points connected with delay to which the jury's attention should be drawn.*

And the conviction was upheld. It seems in the light of this decision, and the previous authorities, that there are few if any situations in which the adequacy of the jury warning will give rise to a successful appeal of an historic abuse conviction.

Is 'trawling' a problem?

In the care home cases, much of the focus has been on the possible unfairness of the prosecution's 'trawling' for complainants to support the case that abuse by staff at a particular care home had taken place.[20] Where complainants are identified by this method, they not only provide additional counts on the indictment, but their evidence generally provides 'similar fact' evidence, which is capable of bolstering the veracity of the allegations of those who have made earlier complaints. Many of the complainants identified by trawling themselves have criminal records and emotional or drug problems – a sad reflection on the inadequacy of institutional care arrangements in Britain. They are also open to the suspicion that their allegations could be fuelled by the prospect of criminal injuries compensation and/or civil damages claims. The practice of approaching such persons to ask them whether they have any allegations to make is – in the submission of some campaigners – an irredeemably flawed procedure, irrespective of the care that is taken to avoid leading lines of questioning.

Without going further into this somewhat complex problem, it suffices for present purposes to note that the Court of Appeal has declined submissions, simpliciter, that the use of evidence obtained by trawling affects the safety of convictions. The use of such methods is not, therefore, a matter that can of itself assist the applicant. There have been occasions where there have been specific concerns about the trawling methods used,[21] but such issues have generally been raised at trial and are not, therefore, by themselves, likely to be new matters for the Commission to consider.

What if the records go missing?

Following these somewhat unhelpful authorities, an unexpected glimmer of hope for practitioners in this field has emerged in the case of *Anver Sheikh*,[22] which considered the implications of the loss of documentary records which could have been used to put the complainant's allegations to the test. The following hypothetical examples explain this issue:

- Complainant says, 'A buggered me on Saturday night after we watched Match of the Day'. A says, 'I never worked at weekends – only Mondays to Fridays'.

- Complainant says, 'B raped me on a school camping trip in the Lake District'. B says 'I only once went on a school trip to the Lake District and we all stayed in a Youth Hostel'.

- Complainant says, 'My father C assaulted me when I was 13 years old'. C says, 'My daughter had massive psychological problems at that time and has confabulated – this can be supported by obtaining the adolescent counselling records'.

In each case, it is likely that records would have existed at one time which might have helped to establish where the truth lay. However, where allegations are brought many years later, such records almost certainly no longer exist and (if the case is brought) the jury can only decide whether or not they believe the complainant's assertions or the defendant's denials.

In *Sheikh*, the situation resembled the first of these hypothetical scenarios – the defendant said that his annual leave records would prove the impossibility of the allegations against him, but these records proved impossible to trace. The Court stated:

> *In our view the missing documents, in particular the staff rota and the personnel records, were likely to be highly relevant to two issues in this case, first, whether the appellant would have come into contact with MG so as to have the opportunity to win his trust as MG alleged that he had; secondly, whether the appellant had the opportunity to commit these offences against MG ... In these circumstances we have grave doubts whether a judge who properly analysed the consequences of the missing documents would conclude that the trial was fair. If we are wrong, we have no doubt that a judge who carried out such an analysis would not necessarily reach the conclusion that the trial was fair.*

Mr Sheikh's convictions were quashed. It is a matter of significance that the Court placed great emphasis on the specific facts of the case – there was a narrow window of opportunity for the offence to have taken place and the records could have resolved whether the offence could have occurred as described by the complainant. There seems every possibility that the Court will subsequently narrow down the application of this judgment (as they did following *R v B* and *Percival*). Nevertheless, the judgment raises an issue which may well be of assistance to some historic abuse applicants in the future.

The Commission's record in historic abuse cases

The Commission's record in referring historic abuse cases has been intensely disappointing to, and has been much criticised by, a committed group of campaigners. Such criticism appears unfair. The reality is that the case law (at any rate up to *Sheikh*) has been stacked against such cases. It has also to be appreciated that historic abuse cases only reach juries after having passed through two 'sifts'. First, the Crown Prosecution Service must have decided that the strength of the evidence merited prosecution. Second, the case must have survived any challenge made by defence counsel that the prosecution should be stayed (due to delay) as an abuse of process. In addition, the jury (duly warned about the dangers of delay) must have been satisfied that the case was proved. It seems that the Court of Appeal has taken the view that – once a case has successfully passed through these sifts – it will not lend support to the appellate system being used to retry delay issues. Where 'liberal' judgments, such as *R v B* and *Percival* are given, the Court rapidly moves to correct any 'misconceptions' they may have created. *Sheikh* may or may not be subject to 'clarification' in the same way.

Only six historic abuse cases (including two linked pairs of cases) have successfully passed through the Commission's own sift and been heard by the Court of Appeal in the first ten years.

H (J) and G (T)

H is the father of the complainant J. G (who sadly died in prison before his appeal was heard) was her school instrumental music teacher. Both were men of exemplary character. They were accused of sexual abuse by J in very similar terms. The remarkable similarities of the allegations (the two accused men never met) might have put a jury on enquiry, but the two cases were tried separately and neither jury was made aware of the allegations against the other defendant. The allegations made by J against her father contained details of incidents from the age of four upwards. She made the allegations at the age of 19, after she had left home and joined an evangelical Christian group. Referral was based upon new evidence (Professor Conway) that J's detailed evidence about incidents when she was four years old ran far beyond the power of human memory and must have been confabulated. There was also evidence of J's extensive subjection to psychotherapy and information from her medical records (obtained by the Commission in exercise of its powers under section 17 of the 1995 Act) that there were serious inconsistencies between her disclosures to psychotherapists and her evidence in Court.

The Court agreed to receive the evidence of Professor Conway, but in its customary pragmatic mode, warned others against raising hopes based on similar evidence:

> *We would not wish to leave this case without sounding a note of caution about the introduction of evidence of the kind given by Professor Conway in this case. It will only be in the most unusual of circumstances that such evidence will be relevant and admissible at the trial of allegations of child abuse. The evidence would be relevant only in those rare cases in which*

the complainant provides a description of very early events which appears to contain an unrealistic amount of detail. That, in the experience of this court, does not happen often.

The Court quashed H's conviction. It is a somewhat remarkable aspect of this case that the Crown defended H's conviction to the hilt at appeal and persuaded the Court that H should be subject to a retrial. The Crown subsequently, however, abandoned any attempt to stage a retrial and did not oppose the posthumous appeal of G.

G (G)

The facts of **G (G)** were somewhat complex – and reference should be made to the judgment on the Bailii website. In short, the complainant, CA, said she had been regularly assaulted and raped by her father, the incidents starting in 1974 when she was 12 years old. Trial took place in 1999. The only 'incident specific' content of the allegations consisted of evidence that CA had attempted to complain of the conduct against her in 1977. This 'recent complaint' evidence had been raked over at trial – CA had said that she had been so distressed at this time that she had succeeded in getting admitted to hospital (and away from home) by feigning illness. It had been shown at trial that CA had, in fact, been admitted to hospital at this time due to an entirely genuine physical illness. Another matter which might have assisted G's defence was that CA alleged at least 150 incidents of unprotected sex following puberty without becoming pregnant – she had since borne children without gynaecological assistance. Despite these and other difficulties in the prosecution case, the jury convicted.

Referral by the Commission was due to an amalgam of considerations, including counsel's failure to apply for a stay of proceedings; inadequacy of the judge's delay warning to the jury (referred to above); the *R v B* residual discretion issue; and loss of relevant records. The Court upheld the conviction, the core of its reasoning coming at the conclusion of its judgment:

> *In the instant case, we have identified a number of respects in which the appellant was able to challenge the complainant's credibility. This is not a case in which the appellant could only say by way of defence, I have not done it. There was ample material against which the jury was able to test CA's credibility and in the end they believed her. This is not, in our judgment, one of those cases in which this court could properly interfere with their decision.*

The decision is deeply discouraging to others in Mr G's position.

Brooke and Siddall

B and S were workers at two different care homes, convicted at separate trials of sexual offences against RW. RW had, in a 40-page affidavit prepared by investigating police officers, disclosed a lengthy catalogue of abuse from early childhood onwards, said to have been committed by various family members and staff at a number of care homes – subsequently adding further incidents and details. She was apparently an extremely articulate witness in giving evidence. In a lengthy and painstaking investigation, the Commission identified three principal matters supporting referral:

- In a separate trial, RW had accused another care worker, named Jolley, of offences against her. She was cross-examined in that trial about the fact that her allegations to the CICA greatly exceeded the allegations she had made in the criminal case, thereby exposing her to the charge not only of inconsistency but possibly magnifying complaints in order to maximise criminal compensation. After RW had refused to answer questions about this, the trial of J was abandoned.

- RW's allegations to the CICA had also been 'enhanced' in claiming compensation for the injuries said to have been inflicted by B and S.

- The Commission was able to obtain files (not available at trial) from a voluntary body, Nugent Care Homes, which had run one of the care homes where RW had lived. This disclosed information about yet further allegations (including a complaint that she had been raped on one occasion by 12 taxi drivers), which had simply not been taken seriously.[23]

There were other aspects of the case that gave rise to concern. For instance, RW said that the offences against her committed by B were the most traumatic she had ever suffered and had affected her attitude to sex ever since – yet she had made no mention of them at all when she had been originally interviewed by police and given her 40-page affidavit.

The Court noted that the defence case that RW had made up – or confabulated – her allegations appeared far more plausible in the light of the information now known, and it quashed the convictions.

P (Francis)

P was convicted on a re-trial of two offences against his daughter, T, but acquitted of two further offences. The trial was in 2001, and the offences were said to have been committed in 1972-3. Count 4 was a charge that P had assaulted T in a barn. T's evidence was that P had taken her to this barn, owned by a Mr Pope, where her father was rearing calves for market. P said that the allegations had been made for pecuniary motives and there was uncontested evidence at trial that T had committed perjury at previous child care proceedings. There was evidence at trial, which must have been disbelieved by the jury, that P had not owned calves at or close to the time when Count 4 was said to have taken place. The case was referred and quashed on evidence from the diaries of Mr Pope's former wife, who had kept a detailed account of events at the farm. Her diary supported the case that there had been no calves on the farm at or close to this time. The Court refused the Crown's application for a re-trial. The report of the case is interesting as illustrating both (i) the extreme logistical difficulty attending the efforts of the Commission and others in trying to establish (or refute) a link between allegations and external events or circumstances said to have occurred some 30 years previously; and (ii) the diligence and tenacity of the Commission in seeking to ascertain the true facts.

Concluding comments on historic abuse cases

The Commission has taken historic abuse cases very seriously, and examined them thoroughly, recognising the possibility of miscarriages due to false memory, vindictiveness, or the desire for criminal compensation leading to false allegations. It has established a protocol with a panel of specialist solicitors – the Historical Abuse Appeals Panel – for dealing with such cases; it has used its powers diligently (albeit often fruitlessly) to seek out historic documents; and it has sought an extension of the law to enable it to requisition documents from voluntary care bodies.[24] It is probably beyond the power or responsibility of the Commission that the outcome of its efforts, so far, has been disappointing to practitioners and campaigners in this field.

Notes

1. The exact cumulative figure up to December 2007 was 25.3 per cent
2. The Commission's Formal Memorandum on Child Sex Abuse cases, which is available on the Commission's website, provides a helpful overview of the Commission's practices and policies in this area.
3. 'Intra-family' should be given a wide interpretation for this purpose. An allegation by a child against his or her mother's ex-partner, for instance, would be included within this definition.
4. It is sometimes necessary to explain quite painstakingly to social services departments the extent of the Commission's powers and the reasons for them. See an article by the author in

Journal of Local Government Law Issue 2 April 2000, which explains these powers for a local government audience. The article also explains the legal and policy constraints acting on the Commission in making any onward disclosure of social services material.

5. 'Should' is probably the right word (as opposed to 'will'). The Commission has a fixed policy and procedure in relation to the examination of social services files – the question whether to go further and review the files of other relevant statutory agencies is a matter for judgment on a case by case basis. It may possibly be the case that in a volume-driven casework environment, this judgment is not always exercised when it should be.

6. [1996] 1 Cr App R 239.

7. [2001] *Crim LR* 471; [2000] 2 All ER (D) 2432.

8. [1991] 1 WLR 207.

9. At P's first, trial the jury had been unable to agree a verdict, and at the second trial the verdict was 10-2; perhaps an indication of the difficulties of the case. It may be added in passing that the Court of Appeal generally dislikes the Commission giving any weight to such matters or suggesting that a verdict is any more doubtful on account of the fact that there had been a hung jury or majority decision.

10. A point which illustrates the difficulty of the Commission's role. A wholly innocent applicant convicted of a sexual offence says 'I was stitched up by a lying complainant' and 20 perfectly guilty applicants say precisely the same thing. How does the Commission distinguish between such applications in deciding which cases merit in-depth investigation?

11. The Court stated that this was due to inadvertent error rather than conspiracy and like the magistrate in the tale of *The Lion and Albert*, who was called upon to consider why young Albert Ramsbottom had been consumed by a lion in the course of a visit to Blackpool Zoo, concluded that *no one was really to blame*.

12. Note also the telling remark in the Court's judgment: 'The allegations were made in great and no doubt convincing detail. Indeed the officers found her to be, they thought, a convincing complainant.'

13. The care homes themselves have been variously owned and run by local authorities, by voluntary agencies and by private individuals.

14. In a case of 'bare' allegations of historic abuse – without any supporting evidence – defence counsel may seek a stay of the prosecution as an abuse of process. Such applications are frequently successful, a fact which in its turn influences the Crown Prosecution Service in deciding whether or not prosecutions should be brought in such cases.

15. [2003] EWCA Crim 619.

16. (1992) 95 Cr App R 296.

17. [2004] EWCA Crim 1270.

18. [1998] EWCA Crim 2012.

19. 17 June 1999 Case No 984652 Y5.

20. See the article by Professor Di Birch and Claire Taylor, 'People Like Us? Responding to Allegations of Past Abuse in Care' [2003] *Crim LR* 823 for a discussion of concerns expressed by the Home Affairs Select Committee, among others, about the possible dangers of trawling.

21. Trawling – to avoid gross unfairness – must be carefully done and subjects should not be asked any leading questions. The police and prosecution authorities appear to have got better at refining fair trawling procedures as experience of historic institutional care cases has developed.

22. [2006] EWCA Crim 2625.

23. This point raises an important footnote. Nugent Care Homes, not being a government body, was not bound by section 17 to disclose any information to the Commission and it did so voluntarily. Without its co-operation, the referral and appeal case would have been very much weaker. Other voluntary homes have refused similar requests by the Commission,

possibly because of fears that any information provided might subsequently be used in litigation, or be cited as a precedent for other disclosure requests.

24. As a result of the Commission's submissions on this matter, Parliamentary counsel has been briefed to draft a suitable provision, but the Commission has not received intimation as to when such a provision will be brought forward in proposed legislation.

Chapter 10 - Police and prosecution misconduct cases

Police corruption cases – the background

The Commission came into being at a time when the Court of Appeal, the Crown Prosecution Service and police were already engaged in unravelling the consequences of outbreaks of police corruption over the preceding years. The two principal points of concern for the Commission have been convictions based on evidence from members of the West Midlands Serious Crimes Squad (WMSCS) and members of the Metropolitan Police Flying Squad, mostly based at the Rigg Approach police station in North East London. A smaller group of cases has concerned officers of the West Midlands Drugs Squad.

Both the WMSCS and the Rigg Approach squad were charged with investigating the most serious acquisitive crimes and were thus engaged head-to-head with the 'über villains' in their respective patches. Members of both squads fell prey to the belief that, in apprehending individuals believed to be serious criminals, the ends justified the means. Various illegal methods were employed in order to secure convictions. The West Midlands squad appeared given (pre-PACE) to verballing suspects and the use of violence in interrogations. The Rigg Approach squad, on occasions, used fabricated or planted evidence in order to secure convictions.[1]

In the West Midlands, a landmark case, which preceded the inception of the Commission, was the judgment of Mackinnon J in a civil action for damages by Derek *Treadaway*, who complained that he had been assaulted by WMSCS officers who had held a plastic bag over his head during interrogation in order to force a confession. Giving judgment for Mr Treadaway, the judge rejected the evidence of police witnesses whom he found unsatisfactory and untrustworthy. Subsequently, Treadaway's criminal convictions, founded on the evidence of the same officers, were quashed in 1996.[2] By the time of the Commission's inception, a number of WMSCS officers had been found to be unreliable and/or corrupt in earlier decisions of the Court of Appeal. The Commission has referred a number of further cases, mostly going back to the early 1980s, materially founded on the evidence of tainted officers.

Similarly, in the Flying Squad cases, the problem of corruption was known and the Home Office had referred a number of convictions before the Commission's inception, including convictions founded on evidence of officers based at the nearby police station at Stoke Newington. A leading case was *Maxine Edwards*,[3] in which Beldam LJ stated:

> Once the suspicion of perjury starts to infect the evidence and permeate cases in which the witnesses have been involved, and which are closely similar, the evidence on which such convictions are based becomes as questionable as it was in the cases in which the appeals have already been allowed.

Or, as the Court put it following the Commission's reference in **Martin, Taylor and Brown**:

> In practice the precise surgical division between impugned and unimpugned evidence is seldom possible once the jury have experienced what advocates have called the "stench of corruption".

Matters came to a head in relation to the state of affairs at the Rigg Approach station when a Police Complaints Authority enquiry, Operation Goldcard, revealed massive corruption. After two officers had been charged with serious offences, a further 25 officers were either charged with criminal offences or were suspended from duty pending investigation, or would have been suspended had they not already retired. The allegations against them included corruption, dishonesty and perverting the course of justice. Those officers considered to have been clearly corrupt, were referred to as 'A' officers. In addition, evidence emerged concerning a further large group of Flying Squad officers, who became known as 'B' officers. Available information suggested that although 'B' officers had not been proactive in the commission of offences, there was a general awareness among them that a bag containing items, such as an imitation firearm and balaclavas, was available, either to protect the position of an officer who had shot an unarmed suspect in good faith (and thereby to provide a justification for his action) or to enhance a case where the evidence against a defendant was circumstantial but not overwhelming. These 'B' officers were said to have been subject to a 'general taint'.

The task for the Commission

It has not always been a straightforward matter for the Commission to establish which cases emanating from the activities of these squads should be referred as satisfying the 'real possibility' test. The Court of Appeal has drawn attention to the 'bandwagon' effect whereby a person – convicted on ample (or even uncontested) evidence – would opportunistically use evidence of corruption of some officer, that had subsequently come to light, to dispute the safety of his or her conviction. As Judge LJ put it in a Rigg Approach case, called *Crook*:[4]

> *The lamentable history of the operations of the Squad [does not mean] that in every case in which a member of the Squad had given evidence or been involved in an investigation which resulted in a conviction, the conviction should be deemed to be unsafe.*

In *Stephens*,[5] (where the appellant had not originally disputed observation evidence given by Rigg Approach officers), the same judge stated:

> *The problem with [the defence submissions] in the present context can readily be identified. The observation evidence (from witnesses who were not members of the Squad), as well as the remaining evidence from members of the Squad, was unchallenged [at trial] ... The credit-worthiness of Squad officers was not ... in issue at all. To conclude that this conviction is unsafe would be tantamount to accepting that, if the appellant had known the facts, he might then have been able to run a different, but equally false defence at trial to the one rejected by the jury.*

These authorities were drawn to the Commission's attention in the appeal that followed the Commission's referral of **Findlay**. Giving the judgment of the Court, Judge LJ commented as follows:

> *the Commission may wish to consider in the course of investigation of such other cases: first, whether there may at some stage be sufficient evidence when the course of corruption which was to infect the squad actually began; and second, whether there has been, or is to be, any further development in the investigation into the officers in the squad who were regarded in early 2002 as marked by the general, rather than the specific, taint.*

This appeared to be a suggestion that the Commission should avoid casting its net too widely in considering the safety of convictions, and should consider, in particular, whether it might be possible to 'exonerate' from any taint of corruption convictions which either preceded the spread of the canker of corruption or which rested on the evidence of 'B' officers who were not demonstrably corrupt. However, other cases, such as **Murphy and Pope**, of which more later, appear to support the adoption of a more lateral approach in considering the implications of the 'stench of corruption'.

The West Midlands Serious Crime Squad cases

The convictions set out in the table below have been quashed following referral by the Commission. All of the referrals raised, directly or indirectly, the issue of corruption on the part of discredited WMSCS officers. All the cases were pre-PACE and interviews were unrecorded. At the heart of each of the appeals was the proposition that the accused had been verballed by police officers and/ or coerced into making false confessions. In some cases, the disputed verbals consisted of formal confessions; in other cases the accused were said to have let slip damaging admissions at the same time as denying responsibility. With the important exception of John **Brown** (of whom more below), most of the accused had made similar assertions against the police officers at trial. It could not be said, therefore, that they were simply leaping on the bandwagon in seeking to rely on the subsequent discrediting of the officers against whom they had made allegations.

John **Brown** stands out from the cases listed below. Brown not only produced a written confession for police officers, but pleaded guilty at his subsequent trial – his case being that both confession and guilty plea were the result of the terror to which he was subjected by corrupt WMSCS officers. B said that these officers had threatened to expose his informant activities to his more violent criminal associates, who could be expected to operate their own summary justice. As the Commission put it in its Statement of Reasons:

> the information now available about the activities of the officers involved in Operation Cat lends substantial force to the contention that those officers were determined to get confessions, if need be by the use of oppression, from suspects who were arrested on that day.

In its judgment, the Court of Appeal sidestepped the Commission's suggestion that the prosecution amounted to an abuse of process, but stated that if matters now known about the corrupt activities of the officers had been known then:

> ... it is unthinkable that the case against the appellant would have continued or that the appellant would ever therefore have been placed in the position of considering whether to plead guilty.

Only one conviction resulting from referral of a WMSCS case has been upheld – this is the case of Anne **Murray**. In this case, a significant part of the evidence came from a discredited 'supergrass', named Jarvis, who had been handled by corrupt WMSCS officers. It is a measure of Mr Jarvis's activities that when he came up for sentence for his own offending, he asked for 1,501 offences to be taken into account. Subsequent enquiry showed that he could not have been responsible for 203 of these offences, as he had been in custody at the time! In considering the appeal of Mrs Murray, the Court noted that the jury had been made aware that Jarvis was a supergrass and had reason to be wary of relying on Jarvis's evidence alone. The Court concluded, applying **Pendleton**, that there was enough other evidence to convict M, irrespective of the credibility of Jarvis's evidence. The approach is quite contrary to the way **Pendleton** has been applied in other police corruption cases.

Name of appellant	Year convicted	Offence(s)	Corrupt behaviour raised
Brown (John)	1983	Robbery	Confession (leading to guilty plea) coerced by corrupt officers. Reliance upon tainted supergrasses handled by corrupt officers.
Campbell	1985	Murder	Essential plank of Crown case consisted of disputed admissions in C's fourth interview when corrupt officers took over interviewing the suspect.
Cummiskey	1985	Robbery + firearms	Corrupt officers had fabricated damaging admissions in police interviews and forensically tampered with exhibits.
Brown, Brown, Dunne and Gaughan	1983	Robbery + conspiracy to rob (25 counts)	Corrupt officers had fabricated damaging admissions in police interviews. Additionally, large parts of evidence came from tainted 'supergrasses' handled by corrupt officers.
Hagans and Wilson	1983	Robbery + possession of firearm	Corrupt officers had fabricated damaging admissions in police interviews. Additionally, large parts of evidence came from tainted supergrasses handled by corrupt officers. (Linked to **Brown and Brown**)
Irvine	1983	Manslaughter + robbery	Verballed by corrupt officers – co-defendant of **Twitchell.**
Murphy and O'Toole	1978	Robbery	Corrupt officers/fabricated confessions.
Twitchell	1982	Manslaughter and robbery	Confession statement obtained by corrupt officers through 'plastic bagging'.

West Midland Drugs Squad cases

The following cases have been referred by the Commission.

Name of appellant	Year convicted	Offence(s)	Corrupt behaviour raised	Outcome
Deans	1989	Supply of cannabis Supply + possession of cocaine	Evidence given by three officers subsequently found guilty of offences. Failure to maintain proper observation log.	Upheld
Fraser	1993	Possession of cannabis	Case rested on observation evidence of police officers. One officer established as corrupt and a second officer tainted by close association with him.	Quashed
Jamil	1989	Possession of heroin with intent to supply	In a case involving a disputed drugs find, the exhibits officer had subsequently been required to resign for misconduct.	Upheld

The reasoning of the Court in **Deans** is illuminating and the case has been cited by the Court in subsequent decisions. Three of the officers who had given evidence against D had, subsequently, committed disciplinary offences, but the Court considered that this did not affect the safety of the convictions:

> We have given careful consideration to these submissions and to the way in which the case has been set out by the Criminal Cases Review Commission. We deprecate the subsequent misconduct of the officers, particularly Detective Constable Robotham. However in the final analysis we are satisfied that the convictions were and are safe. We certainly accept that police misconduct after the events in issue and after the trial in question can render a conviction unsafe. We also accept that corruption and other reprehensible behaviour by one or more officers may infect a whole investigation notwithstanding the presence of officers against who nothing has been alleged or established. In the present case, however, we attach particular importance to the lapse of time between the events of 1988 and the trial in 1989 on the one hand and the appalling behaviour of Detective Constable Robotham, and to a lesser extent Detective Constable Davis, on the other hand. There is nothing to suggest that either of them acted otherwise than with propriety between 1988 and 1997. We consider it inappropriate to doubt convictions which occurred almost a decade before any known or alleged misbehaviour on the part of these officers. It is clear that the transgressions of Detective

> *Constable Breakwell cover a longer period and go back almost to the time of the events with which this appeal is concerned. However, he was a wholly uncontroversial contributor to the trial of the Appellant. None of his evidence was disputed and no specific allegation of impropriety was made against him. We should add that in none of the cases to which we have been referred was the temporal relationship between the investigation/trial and the subsequent misconduct of police officers in other cases anything like as extensive as in the present case. It sometime (sic) happens that many years pass before the misconduct comes to light. The cases of* Twitchell *... and* Treadaway *... are good examples. [In those cases] when unearthed, the misconduct was contemporaneous or reasonably contemporaneous with the events in dispute in the appeal under consideration.*

In short, not every fallen officer creates an unsafe conviction. If (i) the officer's transgressions occurred long after trial; (ii) the officer's transgressions were trivial; or (iii) the officer's evidence was undisputed, the conviction may be allowed to stand. Somewhat similar considerations applied in **Jamil. Deans** underlines the fact, therefore, that the Commission has to make a carefully calibrated judgment in deciding whether evidence of misconduct by a police officer is a matter of sufficient weight to be capable of disturbing the safety of a conviction.

The Rigg Approach cases

The following cases have been referred by the Commission.

Name of appellant	Year convicted	Offence(s)	Corrupt behaviour raised	Outcome
Christian	1992	Possession of firearm	Discredited officers who had given evidence against C had adopted a practice of planting firearms to secure convictions.	Quashed
Findlay	1989	Conspiracy to rob	Evidence against F came from disputed verbal admissions said to have been made by F (i) when arrested at home and (ii) in police car. Disputed verbal admissions were said to have been made to 'A' officers and were recorded by 'B' officers.	Quashed

Name of appellant	Year convicted	Offence(s)	Corrupt behaviour raised	Outcome
Martin, Taylor and Brown	1995	Robbery, possession of stun gun	Questionable identifications (long after the robbery) alleged to have been contrived by officers; stun gun and palm print alleged to have been planted. 'Officer in the case' + four other officers involved were all 'A' officers.	Quashed
Thomas (Michael)	1994	Robbery, possession of firearm	The case that T had been the perpetrator of an armed robbery of a betting shop (and not an innocent bystander) rested substantially upon the evidence of three 'A' officers.	Quashed
Willis	1995	Murder, robbery	Principal evidence against W consisted of questionable identification given by key witness long after the event. This key witness had been in regular contact with an 'A' officer. Further, according to W's statements a 'B' officer had said 'you're going to get picked out' before the identification parade took place.	Quashed

In both **Findlay** and **Thomas,** the case against the defendants was significantly corroborated by officers who were neither subject to specific taint ('A' officers) nor the general taint ('B' officers).   The Court gave careful consideration in these cases to the question whether there might be sufficient unsullied evidence to enable it to conclude that the convictions were safe, irrespective of the involvement of corrupt officers.   In both cases, the Court concluded that the unsullied evidence was insufficient to sustain the conviction.   To date, no Rigg Approach case referred by the Commission has been upheld by the Court of Appeal.

One Rigg Approach case deserves special mention.   In **Willis,** three robbers entered a jewellery shop, killing a man who was inside the shop at the time. Two of the robbers were clearly identifiable from CCTV stills, but the case that

W was the third robber relied heavily on the evidence of the jeweller, C. C's identification had occurred long after the event (following little more than a fleeting glance) and there were quite strong discrepancies in C's accounts of what he had seen. However, this was all known at trial and C expressed himself certain of his identification. He remained certain when he was interviewed by the Commission and insisted that the police had given him no assistance in making his identification. The Commission, however, felt that knowledge that C had been 'handled' by an 'A' officer raised significant doubts about the identification, and the conviction was quashed following referral.

Other police misconduct cases

Three other London cases can be briefly mentioned.

Guney was convicted of firearms and Class A drug offences. The investigation was carried out by 3 Area Drug Squad, which operated in the same area of North East London as the Rigg Approach officers, but was a separate squad. The grounds of the Commission's referral were contained in a separate confidential annex to the Statement of Reasons, which was withheld from Mr Guney and his legal representatives. The Court of Appeal judgment records:

> Substantial doubt has been cast upon the integrity of persons who were then (but are no longer) police officers, and who played an important part in gathering intelligence. Had the information been available at the time it would have been laid before the trial judge in May 1996 if the Crown was at that time minded to proceed against the appellant. Had it been laid before the trial judge it seems inevitable that disclosure would have been ordered and that in order to protect sources of information the Crown would have offered no evidence. Even if the Crown had been prepared to disclose, the trial would have taken such a different course that we cannot say with confidence that the outcome would have been the same. The reasons which would in May 1996 have motivated the Crown to offer no evidence are still valid. That is why we can say no more, but we have said enough to indicate what led us to allow the appeal.

In other words, intelligence information had been obtained by discredited officers but withheld from the defence and the judge. The Court concluded that, if the Crown had been required to reveal all the withheld information, it might have had to throw in its hand and discontinue the prosecution rather than undergo the disclosure process.

Murphy and Pope concerned three corrupt officers from the South East Regional Crimes Squad (SERCS), which had also been subject to corruption, albeit on a smaller scale than the Rigg Approach squad. M and P were convicted of drugs offences following an investigation in which three corrupt SERCS officers had been involved, working alongside untainted officers. As in **Findlay** and **Thomas,** the issue for the Court was whether the evidence of the untainted officers could sustain the conviction. The Court noted:

> It is the submission of the appellants, and conceded by the Crown, that the fresh material relating to the convictions and disciplinary findings of the three officers mentioned above ... is ... admissible, and that its non-adduction at trial can be reasonably explained, its contents affording a ground of appeal.

> It is also conceded that, in the circumstances of the case, the evidence of other officers given in support of those who have been subsequently convicted, or held by the Crown not to be witnesses of truth, could have been attacked as tainted evidence. As such that material ought properly to be admitted under section 23 of the Criminal Appeal Act in any event on the ground that it is necessary or expedient in the interests of justice.

In other words, in a case where officers who were free from any personal taint of corruption (i) had been working on an investigation alongside demonstrably corrupt officers and (ii) had given evidence at trial that corroborated evidence given by those corrupt officers, their evidence was open to attack as tainted by their association with the corrupt officers.

Finally, **Bashir and Khan** featured an engaging love triangle between a handsome young suspected villain in his 20s; a woman in her 30s besotted with the suspected villain; and a police sergeant in his 40s besotted with the woman and anxious to apprehend the suspected villain. It was a case of real life imitating *The Bill* rather than vice versa. The case shows that even where there is powerful evidence against the convicted person, where a police officer has been engaged in corrupt activities, which are proximate in time and scope to the crime he has investigated, those corrupt activities are likely to render the conviction(s) unsafe.

Customs and Excise cases

Introductory remarks

A detailed exegesis of all that has gone wrong in the detection and prosecution of crimes by the, now defunct, HMCE (Her Majesty's Customs and Excise) is beyond the scope of this study. It should be noted, however, that at the time of the Commission's inception, HMCE took pride in the fact that it managed prosecutions in-house, in contrast with the police whose power of prosecution had long since passed to the Crown Prosecution Service. In a memorable meeting of introduction with senior Customs prosecutors, not long after the Commission's inception, HMCE lawyers informed Commission members with utmost confidence that Customs officers only pursued 'definitely guilty' suspects, and they appeared to take a somewhat Panglossian view of the institutional arrangements then in force. This complacency may well have been HMCE's undoing. Following a string of botched investigations leading to quashed convictions, the prosecution functions were taken into a new authority – the Revenue and Customs Prosecution Office (RCPO) – whilst HMCE itself has been merged into Her Majesty's Revenue and Customs (HMRC).

Without going into undue (or confidential) detail, in its early years the Commission encountered difficulty on a number of occasions in securing active co-operation from HMCE and there were examples – for instance – of HMCE failing to comply with legal orders for the preservation of documents. In one case, **Millen**, where HMCE officials were expressing (legally unjustified) opposition to handing over files to a Case Review Manager, the CRM took unilateral action and walked out of HMCE offices, taking the files with him. Mr Millen's conviction was subsequently quashed by the Court of Appeal and – despite the somewhat grudging observations in the Court's judgment – it appeared to those concerned with the referral that he had been very probably wholly innocent of the charges of which he had been convicted.

London City Bond cases

The Commission came in at the tail end of the London City Bond affair. The leading judgments in this affair, *Villiers*[6] and *Early*,[7] were not the result of Commission references. However, in a follow-up appeal following referral by the Commission, Balbir **Ghuman** had his conviction quashed. In all the London City Bond cases, HMCE had targeted suspected diversion fraud[8] out of bonded warehouses. For the purposes of its investigations, HMCE had recruited the owners and managers of the warehouses as participating informants and actively facilitated criminal activities in order to build up the prosecution case. There was material non-disclosure of contacts between HMCE and informants, and worse, in some cases, trial judges considering the scope of claims for protection from disclosure under Public Interest Immunity were unwittingly misled by prosecuting counsel about the scope of informant contacts. Counsel had in turn been misled by HMCE officials. As the Court put it in *Early*:

> *Judges can only make decisions and counsel can only act and advise on the basis of the information with which they are provided. The integrity of our system of criminal trial depends on judges being able to rely on what they are told by counsel and on counsel being able to rely on what they are told by each other. This is particularly crucial in relation to disclosure and PII hearings. Accordingly, Mr. Gompertz QC, rightly, accepted that when defence counsel advised Rahul, Nilam and Pearcy as to plea, they were entitled to assume that full and proper disclosure had already been made ... in our judgment, if, in the course of a PII hearing or an abuse argument, whether on the voir dire or otherwise, prosecution witnesses lie in evidence to the judge, it is to be expected that, if the judge knows of this, or this court subsequently learns of it, an extremely serious view will be taken. It is likely that the prosecution case will be regarded as tainted beyond redemption, however strong the evidence against the defendant may otherwise be.*

The Court added:

> *Such an approach is consistent with the view expressed by this court, in [Maxine] Edwards*[9]*... where, in a different context, Beldam LJ referred to the suspicion of perjury starting to infect the evidence and permeate other similar cases in which the witnesses are involved.*

The Court had to consider whether it was an obstacle to the appellants' case that some had pleaded guilty at the trial, albeit in ignorance of the material showing the extent of collusion between investigators and participating informants. The Court concluded:

> *We approach the question of safety of these convictions, following pleas of guilty, in accordance with* Mullen *... as approved in* Togher & others *... namely a conviction is generally unsafe if a defendant has been denied a fair trial.*[10]

But contrast the decision following the Commission referral in **Went and Others**. In common with the earlier cases, HMCE had been investigating diversion fraud from a bonded warehouse; the proprietors of the bonded warehouse were enlisted as informants; and there was some non-disclosure of informant contacts. However, in contrast with the London City Bond cases there was no extended course of facilitating illegality, no misleading of the trial judge, and shortcomings in disclosure appeared to be the consequence of bureaucratic and human frailty rather than an active project to mislead. The Court considered that the deficiencies of process did not amount to an abuse of process, nor did they vitiate the convictions.

Controlled delivery cases

The Commission has also been concerned in a number of complex and time-consuming investigations of cases involving 'controlled delivery' of heroin from Pakistan to the UK. In these cases, HMCE had targeted importers of heroin to the UK, using Pakistani informants, who participated in the offences as couriers.

By the time the Commission commenced its involvement in reviewing these convictions, a major police operation, known as 'Operation Brandfield', had been in existence for 18 months. Operation Brandfield was an investigation into suspected corruption of certain Customs officers and participating informants. In April 2006, three Customs officers were convicted of misfeasance in public office. There have been considerable overlaps between the Commission's investigation (of suspected miscarriages of justice) and Operation Brandfield's investigation (of suspected corruption), but the Commission has, rightly, maintained an independent course in its own investigations.

As a result of its investigations, the Commission referred the convictions of **Akhtar** and **Shah** in 2004 on the basis of abuse of process by HMCE. It appeared that the participating informants had acted as agents provocateur to the extent that they may have instigated the offences. There had also been material non-disclosure. These cases were heard by the Court, together with three further (non-Commission) appellants named Choudhery, Ashraf and Ahmed. These cases will be referred to as **Akhtar and Shah**, although it should be noted that Mr Choudhery's name appears as lead appellant in the judgment of the Court of Appeal.

In **Akhtar and Shah**, the Court described what it considered to be a paradigm controlled delivery and listed a number of 'indicators' which might indicate that the participating informant played more than a minor role in the crime and, in turn, might cast doubt on the safety of the conviction(s). In particular, the Court was concerned with evidence that might indicate that the source supplier of the drugs (in Pakistan) knew (or there was a reasonable inference that he must have known) that there was a controlled delivery in operation. If the source supplier had that knowledge, then that might indicate a close alliance between the participating informant and the source supplier, in which event the Court would look closely at the possibility of 'set-up'. The Court observed a tendency in these cases for HMCE officials to be somewhat economical with the truth in providing information to their own counsel about the degree to which the controlled deliveries had been instigated by informants. This lack of candour between HMCE and its own instructed counsel had the consequence that counsel became, unwittingly, party to non-disclosure of relevant material. On the matter of non-disclosure, the Court observed:

> *full disclosure should not be dependent upon the astuteness of prosecuting counsel to ask appropriate questions in any given case ... Nor should the obligations of disclosure be approached by HMCE as if playing a game of hide and seek. We hide it and you seek it ...*

> *... There is, in our judgment, substantial evidence which suggests that there was in existence within HMCE a policy of not disclosing details of the manner in which [controlled deliveries] operated and the role played by [participating informants] not only to the defence but also to members of HMCE's legal department, prosecuting counsel and of course trial judges.*

Of HMCE activities overall, the Court commented:

> *There is, in our view, a strong case for saying that persons employed by HMCE knew that [controlled deliveries] were not being carried out as they ought to have been under the guidelines and that courts were deliberately prevented from knowing the true picture.*

The Court went on to consider each case on its own merits, having particular regard to the defence run at trial, but was willing to quash convictions even where a guilty plea had been entered, and has continued to take that approach subsequently. In **Akhtar and Shah**, the appeals of all five appellants were conceded by the Crown and the convictions were quashed in July 2005. The Crown went on to concede the appeals in the Commission's subsequent referrals of **Nawaz, Latif, Shahzad, Osman and Rasool**, and those convictions were quashed in January 2007.

In a judgment in July 2007, just outside the ten-year period considered in this study, the Court gave judgment on a further 'batch' of Commission referrals. Although most of these cases related to the activities of one participating informant, the appeals had a variety of outcomes. The Court clarified the significance of the paradigm controlled delivery that it had defined in **Akhtar and Shah** and specified two separate 'routes' that might lead to the quashing of convictions in this type of case: (i) significant undisclosed material or fresh evidence and (ii) gross misconduct on the part of investigators or those presenting the case in court. The Crown conceded the appeals of **Ramzan, Ahmed (Nisar) and Ahmed (Rizwan)**, and the Court also quashed the conviction of **Masud** (although contested by the Crown). The Court, however, upheld the convictions of a further six appellants referred by the Commission: **Vernett-Showers, Sabir, Ahmed (Bahktiar), Beg, Ryan and Ahmed (Mumtaz)**.[11]

Regarding **Vernett-Showers, Sabir and Ahmed (Bakhtiar)**, the Court considered that there was 'overwhelming' evidence to suggest that the transaction was genuine and also noted that none of the appellants had run 'set-up' as a defence at trial and the appellants had accepted that heroin had been imported. The Court added that the evidence of the participating informant had 'hardly featured in the summing-up'.

In **Beg**, the appellant had pleaded guilty and the Court commented that 'the strength of the evidence' was 'overwhelming'. There was no evidence of misconduct on the part of prosecutors. Regarding **Ryan**, the Court found that there was nothing in the undisclosed material relied on by the appellant which, had the defence been able to deploy it, might reasonably have affected the jury's decision to convict. Nor was any prosecutorial misconduct established. **Ahmed (Mumtaz)** had also pleaded guilty and had chosen not to run a potentially viable defence of duress. The Court concluded that '[the appellant] has not been able to come anywhere near showing the kind of gross prosecutorial misconduct which might lead to the quashing of the conviction'.

This most recent batch of cases shows (as in **Went**) a more nuanced approach on the part of the Court of Appeal, in which the Court has weighed its general concern about controlled delivery cases against the specifics of the individual cases. It has concluded that absent fresh evidence of (i) non-disclosure, (ii) prosecution misconduct or (iii) other exculpatory matters, the proven participation of the appellant in heroin importation was sufficient to sustain the safety of the conviction.

Notes

1. A succinct account of the travails of the Rigg Approach squad and the ensuing appeal cases can be found in Jeremy Dein, 'Police Conduct Revisited' [2000] *Crim LR* 801.
2. [1996] ECWA Crim 1457.
3. [1996] 2 Cr App R 345.
4. [2003] EWCA Crim 1272.
5. [2003] EWCA Crim 2085.
6. [2001] EWCA Crim 2505.
7. [2002] EWCA Crim 2004.
8. Diversion fraud in this case, expressed very simply, involved avoiding VAT on alcoholic products, by falsely representing that alcoholic products held in bonded warehouses were destined for export and not for the home market.
9. [1996] 2 Cr App R 345.
10. Mr Togher's case was referred by the Commission, albeit at the request of the Court of Appeal.
11. The appeals of these ten appellants are all the subject of one single judgment – [2007] EWCA Crim 1767.

Chapter 11 - The Commission in the magistrates' court

Section 11 of the 1995 Act defines the Commission's jurisdiction to refer convictions and sentences passed in the magistrates' court[1] and is set out below. (Section 12 sets out corresponding provisions for the referral of summary offences and convictions in Northern Ireland.)

11.– (1) Where a person has been convicted of an offence by a magistrates' court in England and Wales, the Commission—

> *(a) may at any time refer the conviction to the Crown Court, and*

> *(b) (whether or not they refer the conviction) may at any time refer to the Crown Court any sentence imposed on, or in subsequent proceedings relating to, the conviction.*

> *(2) A reference under subsection (1) of a person's conviction shall be treated for all purposes as an appeal by the person under section 108(1) of the Magistrates' Courts Act 1980 against the conviction (whether or not he pleaded guilty).*

The effect of section 11(2) is that an appeal against a summary conviction (or sentence) launched by the Commission's referral takes the form of a rehearing of the case by the Crown Court. Such an appeal is *not* a review of the safety of the original conviction (or correctness of the sentence). This contrasts with an appeal heard by the Court of Appeal, which is charged with reviewing the 'correctness' of the conviction or sentence and eschews, in general, a review of the evidence in the case – that being a matter deemed to be within the province of the jury.

In brief, therefore, a referral of a summary conviction or sentence results in a rehearing, whereas a referral of a conviction or sentence tried on indictment is more in the nature of a review. This discrepancy is not confined to Commission cases; it reflects the difference in the two appeal processes.[2] However, the consequences are somewhat odd and it is difficult to avoid the conclusion that sections 11 and 12 passed through the legislature in the slipstream of the 'main' provisions of the 1995 Act and without particularly vigilant Parliamentary scrutiny.

At this point it may be helpful to set out the inherent oddities of the Commission's jurisdiction in summary cases:

First, the Commission's powers of review sit alongside s142(1) Magistrates' Courts Act 1980 which provides that:

> *A magistrates' court may vary or rescind a sentence or other order imposed or made by it when dealing with an offender if it appears to the court to be in the interests of justice to do so; and it is hereby declared that this power extends to replacing a sentence or order which for any reason appears to be invalid by another which the court has power to impose or make.*

Section 142(1) operates without limit of time and is a helpful provision to enable magistrates to correct a slip. Of the cases listed below, a number of the convictions rested upon a misconception on the part of the magistrates as to the relevant facts or law, and one case clearly reflected a misconception on their part as to their sentencing powers. With a certain degree of flexibility, perhaps one half of the Commission's referred summary cases could be dealt with using section 142.

Second, section 13 of the 1995 Act provides that the Commission may refer summary convictions (in the same way as Crown Court convictions) if it determines, upon the basis of evidence or argument not previously raised, that there is a real possibility that the appellate court will find that the conviction is *unsafe*. But since the Crown Court (in its appellate capacity) is charged with rehearing the case – not reviewing the safety of the original conviction – there is an inherent asymmetry between the review process, which is supposed to be carried out by the Commission, and the appeal process that results from referral.

Third, the right to apply for review of summary convictions (and sentences) is without limit of time. Therefore, applicants may, and in a significant number of cases do, bring to the Commission convictions or sentences handed down by magistrates many years ago. In this respect, there is no difference between Crown Court and magistrates' court cases. However, documents are almost invariably – and for understandable reasons – retained for a shorter period in summary cases than in cases tried on indictment, the latter being far fewer in number and inherently more serious. The Commission routinely in summary cases issues section 17 notices[3] to produce files to police, prosecution and the Courts Service. It may also approach defence solicitors for papers. However, in any case heard more than six years prior to receipt of application, it is very unlikely that the Commission will be able to obtain useful documentary records from any source as to what evidence passed at trial. The Commission may, therefore, be left in the position of having only the applicant's account – not always dependable – of what evidence was given at trial. Judging what matters have and have not been 'previously raised' can, therefore, be difficult or impossible.

Fourth, even in more recent cases, where Court files do still exist, there is often scant record of what evidence was given at trial, and how it was put to the test. There is no transcript of proceedings taken in the magistrates' court, nor any summary of evidence akin to a summing up. The notes taken by clerks vary greatly in detail and legibility. If, for instance, the point which the applicant wishes to press on the Commission was raised in evidence and demolished in cross-examination, the Commission would probably have no means of knowing it.

Finally, where the Commission does refer an aged summary case, the Crown is in an even worse position than the Commission. The Commission has at least *one* account of the events leading to the conviction – the applicant's. The Crown may have none at all, if records no longer exist and the details of the case are beyond the recall of police officers and witnesses – always assuming that they can be identified and found. It would also be extremely difficult for the prosecution (in seeking to reconstruct the case), or for the Court (in rehearing it), to have confidence that they could rely upon the accuracy of recall on the part of witnesses giving evidence many years after the event. In such a case, if the matter is referred for a rehearing, the success of the appeal may be not merely a real possibility but a racing certainty – since the Crown has no adequate means of proving its case. This last point has been astutely taken up in an article by Professors Nobles and Schiff.[4] Taking the point that a great many summary cases would be practically incontestable by the Crown – if the Commission were to refer them – they draw the conclusion that the Commission exercises the referral test in summary cases on the basis of policy considerations and not just 'real possibility'.[5] The professors clearly have a point – the Commission considers to the best of its ability the weight of the novel evidence and/or argument in deciding whether to refer summary cases. It does not necessarily address the application from the perspective of whether the prosecution would be in a practical position to reconstitute the Crown's case in the event of referral.

Before considering how the Commission has, in fact, exercised its summary jurisdiction, it may be helpful to consider briefly how summary cases were dealt with in the past, and what were the expectations when reform was mooted. The Home Office did have some limited power to review summary convictions prior to the 1995 Act. In a Discussion Paper published in response to the Runciman report[6] it stated that some 100 cases brought to it each year (out of a total of around 725) concerned convictions made by magistrates. The Discussion Paper stated:

> These range from cases which require significant investigation to others (the majority) in which the only question to be answered is whether late evidence supporting the defendant's case (e.g. a vehicle insurance document) is what it purports to be. There is currently no power to refer summary cases to the Court of Appeal, and the only recourse lies in the exercise of the Royal Prerogative of Mercy.

The Home Office stated that it favoured the introduction of a right for the new Authority to refer such cases:

> Not least in view of the fact that a Free Pardon though it extinguishes all consequences of a conviction does not actually quash it.

It might be noted, in passing, that a document emanating from the Home Office, which expresses concern to clear the names of those wrongly convicted of crimes, reads unfamiliarly at the present time.

For its part, the Runciman Commission's report was limited to discussion of the review of convictions (and sentences) passed by the Court of Appeal, and there is nothing on the record to show that it gave any detailed consideration to summary cases at all. In its response to the Home Office Discussion Paper, JUSTICE assumed that most summary cases raising disputed points of fact would be resolved by a 'first-time' appeal (which all summarily convicted persons are entitled to make – without requirement for leave) whilst noting, without comment, that the new Authority should be able to consider applications where appeals were out of time, or had been unsuccessful.[7]

Cases considered and referred by the Commission

Summary cases accounted for 6.6 per cent of applications to the Commission in the period from inception to December 2007 and approximately 4 per cent of referrals. Within the ten years covered by this study, 11 referrals of summary cases have been considered by the Crown Court. As will be seen from the table below, all but one of these referrals have achieved a result of some sort for the appellant – a 'success' rate of more than 90 per cent.

A significant number of applications to review summary cases have, without question, been turned down in situations where the lack of documentary records has worked to the applicant's detriment. Whilst it is correct (as Professors Nobles and Schiff have pointed out) that the odds would be stacked in the applicant's favour were the conviction to be referred, it is equally the case that the Commission may have no means of deciding that the applicant is putting forward any matters that have not previously been raised. Furthermore, it is sometimes a matter of sensible inference from the applicant's correspondence that the matters he or she is raising are almost certainly matters which *were* pursued at trial. Such cases are likely to be turned down, and the policy considerations (if such they are) appear to be entirely defensible.

The cases which to date have been referred and heard on appeal are summarised below:

Name	Offence + sentence	Grounds of referral	Outcome
Abwnawar, Abwnawar, Nazarian and Sohrabian	Possession of false instrument; attempting to obtain services by deception 3 months' imprisonment	Point of law – s31(8) Immigration and Asylum Act 1999.	Quashed
Borrows	Wilful obstruction of the highway Conditional discharge	New evidence – place where car was parked was not a public highway.	Quashed
Botwright	Assault on a constable in the execution of his duty; using threatening, abusive or insulting words or behaviour likely to cause harassment, alarm or distress 80 hours community service £100 compensation + costs	Failure of defence at trial to raise defence that the constable had been acting outside the execution of his duty.	Upheld

Name	Offence + sentence	Grounds of referral	Outcome
Ealand	Using a prohibited process to make wine (unauthorised flavouring) £2,500 fine + costs	Point of law re interpretation of a European Regulation.	Quashed
Goldsmith	Crossing a continuous solid double white line £115 fine + costs and 3 penalty points on driving licence	Points of evidence + law – absence of warning arrows.	Quashed
F (Mark)	Indecent assault 2 years' supervision order	New evidence that he had been falsely accused of offence by step-relatives.	Quashed
Lamont	Owner allowing a dog to be dangerously out of control in a public place so causing injury £100 fine, £2,552 compensation, destruction of dog + costs	Fresh evidence (animal behaviourist).	Sentence varied – destruction order lifted
Muff	Possession of a firearm contrary to s21 Firearms Act 1968 6 months' imprisonment suspended	Guilty plea (possessing firearm during lifetime ban as a consequence of earlier conviction) entered on incorrect legal and factual basis, because earlier 4-year sentence had been reduced on appeal to less than 3 years, meaning that the lifetime ban did not take effect.	Quashed
Pickavance	Failing to stop after an accident; failing to report an accident £200 total fine + costs and 5 penalty points	Point of law – collision with cyclist had resulted in handlebars being twisted but cyclist was able to fix them with an Allen key – not as a matter of law an accident.	Quashed
Spragg	Driving while disqualified; driving with excess alcohol 5 months consecutive with each other and consecutive with kindred indictable offences – 33 months in total	Point of law – consecutive sentences exceeding 6 months cannot be passed for summary offences.	Sentences reduced to 3 months each consecutive

Name	Offence + sentence	Grounds of referral	Outcome
Wilkinson	Failing to comply with an amended s215 notice under the Town and Country Planning Act 1990 £400 fine + £600 costs	Point of law – amended notice was legally unenforceable.	Quashed

In a number of cases, the prosecution has not sought to defend the convictions, although **Botwright** (which was upheld) and **F (Mark)** (which was quashed) were fully defended by the Crown. The variety of these cases will be helpfully illustrated by setting out the facts of the following in greater detail.

Abwnawar, Abwnawar, Nazarian and Sohrabian

Four linked cases referred by the Commission raised a point of some importance. S31(8) Immigration and Asylum Act 1999, which gives effect to provisions of the Refugee Convention,[8] provides a special statutory defence to certain offences associated with immigration – such as the use of a false passport. The defence applies to a person who has 'come to the United Kingdom directly from a country where his life or freedom was threatened (within the meaning of the Refugee Convention)'. The rationale of the section is that where a person resorts to illegality to enter the UK in order to escape persecution, he or she should not face criminal liability on that account. Mr and Mrs A had fled Libya due to fear of persecution, but spent two years in Denmark before coming to the UK. Their evidence, which the Crown Court accepted, was that they fled Denmark due to threats of violence from Libyan agents in that country. In a highly principled judgment, the Crown Court ruled that their intermediate stay in Denmark, on the facts, did not defeat the availability of the section 31(8) defence.

Borrows

B was inconvenienced and annoyed by the parking of vehicles by workmen carrying out repairs close to his flat. After his remonstrances to them to park elsewhere failed, he parked his own car to block them in, leading to his prosecution for wilful obstruction of the highway, which is an offence under s137 Highways Act 1980. B was convicted and given a conditional discharge. The case was referred on evidence that the private road, within the block of flats where B lived, was not a public highway and, therefore, the offence was not made out. The prosecution offered no evidence and the Court quashed the conviction.

This case had an unexpected aftertow as the *Daily Mail* picked up the story and issued a thundering denunciation of the waste of resources in employing public servants to pursue such trivial matters. The Commission was, subsequently, ambushed by journalists, brandishing the *Mail* report, at the press conference called on the publication of the Commission's following annual report. The hostile response contrasts with the favourable treatment of the 'Dino the Dog' case referred to below.

F (Mark)

F, then aged 16, was convicted in the juvenile court in 1982 of an act of indecent assault against his two-year-old stepsister. He pleaded guilty to the offence. F's case was that his stepmother (with whom he got on badly) had alleged that this offence had taken place (although she did not claim to have been witness to it); that he had been arrested at work on her complaint by two police officers; and that he had then been interrogated to the point of confession by the officers who said that he would be sent to Risley Remand Centre (and be dealt with there as a 'nonce') if he did not confess. No solicitor or other adult was present. He had then signed a confession dictated by the police officer and was dealt with in the juvenile court on the following day.

F's case epitomised all the difficulties faced by the Commission in dealing with aged summary cases, particularly the lack of any extant record of the prosecution or proceedings. Nevertheless, it was investigated in depth by the Commission because F's account appeared to ring strongly true. There were two witnesses, F's grandmother and a probation officer who had been involved at the time of the charge, who were both strongly supportive of F's account. In addition, the Commission was concerned that the matter had been disposed of with undue haste.

Following referral by the Commission, the appeal was heard at the Crown Court by a circuit judge who, in his judgment, concluded that it was necessary as a preliminary step to decide whether F should be permitted to change his guilty plea. The judge, like the Commission, concluded that the evidence suggested F's case had been dealt with in a wholly unsatisfactory way which did not give the appellant any protection against wrongful conviction. The judge's conclusions are worth quoting in full:

> As is so often the case, it all comes down to a matter of impression. I do not consider myself to be given to the naive and unquestioning acceptance of tall stories. The fact is that each of us found F to be a compelling witness.

267

He spoke with a convincing passion about the injustice under which he had laboured these many years. It is difficult to identify the particular fragments of evidence that give credence to a witness's account but two passages come to mind. First, he became upset and emotional but not at those points which would naturally suggest themselves to someone adding spurious drama to his untrue evidence.

Secondly, it is true that many people have difficulty understanding hypothetical questions but when [Crown counsel] tested him at some length with a series of logical questions which were predicated upon his guilt, it was quite clear to us that the appellant was completely unable to understand the proposition from that stand point; this was not a contrivance, it was convincing.

There is, as we have pointed out some confirmation of his account from his grandmother and from [the probation officer]. We accept his evidence. We think that he was knocked about in the police station, causing some injury to him, which his grandmother and [the probation officer] saw. We think that he was threatened with being remanded to Risley. In breach of the Judges' Rules, he was deliberately not allowed an adult to see fair play. The confession was dictated to him; it is entirely unreliable. The perfunctory advice of the duty solicitor was given in disregard of the complete absence of other evidence against the boy. The hurried court hearing, which the officers themselves attended, provided no real safeguard against wrongful conviction. The guilty plea was the inevitable consequence of this oppression. The plea must in the interests of justice be vacated. It would indeed be an affront to justice if it was to stand.

The judge also noted:

The appellant is now aged 37, he now works as a service engineer. He explained the impact that this conviction has had on his life. As lawyers we may know of the continuing legal consequences of such a conviction: he is a Schedule 1 offender; he would be considered unsuitable to work with children, in the education or health service, or in voluntary organisations. He put it in rather more personal terms. He said that although he has always tried to put the conviction behind him, he was always worried on gaining every job and on every promotion that it would come out. It has had a grave impact on his family life; it has been a feature in two failed relationships.

He remains convicted of a paedophile offence; to have that on your name wrongfully, he said, is a terrible thing.

The guilty plea was vacated and the appeal allowed.

Lamont
The facts of this case are helpfully set out in the following report reproduced (with permission) from The *Guardian:*[9]

> **Dino the dog has his day as judge lifts death order**
>
> *After three years, £60,000 in legal fees and the intervention of an animal behaviourist, in the end it was a 12-minute video that saved Dino the dog yesterday.*
>
> *Judge Patrick Eccles QC, lifted a death sentence that had been hanging over Dino since an unfortunate incident in 2001 when he bit a woman in a park after a confrontation with her terrier Ralph. The video suggested that the alsatian was a reformed character.*
>
> *His owner, Bryan Lamont - who turned to the Criminal Cases Review Commission in his fight to save his pet from a lethal injection under the Dangerous Dogs Act - sat with a team of animal experts behind him at Northampton Crown Court as his lawyers fought for a permanent reprieve.*
>
> *In the end, none of them was needed. The short film, made by an animal behaviourist, showed Dino frolicking peacefully with canine pals and was enough to persuade the judge that the dog was more pussy cat than public threat.*
>
> *Judge Eccles was moved to quote Hamlet: "'Every dog will have his day',," said the Bard, "and Mr Lamont's devotion has allowed Dino to have his day." He added: "If a Scotsman with deep pockets and spirit takes on the judiciary to vindicate his dog, the contest is likely to be vigorous and prolonged".*
>
> *Dino, aged seven, was not in court to hear his death sentence lifted. He was where every dog should be while the master is out - guarding the homestead in East Hunsbury, Northampton. The Lamont house is evidence itself of the long and vigorous battle to save Dino's life since he was put under a*

destruction order for biting Elizabeth Coull, who had tried to intervene between him and her terrier.

As well as exhausting all avenues in the courts - including the House of Lords and the European court of Human Rights - Mr Lamont and his wife, Carol, have been determined over the past three years to show that Dino is not a threat to anyone. They built 6ft fences around their home, used padlocks on the gates to ensure Dino could not escape and took him for walks wearing a muzzle.

They engaged animal behaviourists to assess Dino and finally turned to the group responsible for sending potential miscarriages of justice to the appeal court.

In testimony to the Criminal Cases Review Commission, Roger Mugford, an animal behaviourist, said: "We think a death sentence is a bit extreme. The dog is now substantially reformed. He has passed those teenage years."

As a result, the Commission concluded there was "a real possibility that the destruction order ... would not be upheld if it were referred", and it sent Mr Lamont's conviction, for allowing Dino to be out of control in a public place, back to Northampton crown court.

Unlike the case of **Borrows**, this case attracted generally sympathetic press comment, the *Daily Telegraph* going to the length of putting this case (in a kindly – if somewhat tongue in cheek leading article) alongside John Hampden as an example of the judicial defence of individual liberties.

Wilkinson

W was served with a notice under s215 Town and Country Planning Act 1990 requiring him 'to clear disused vehicles, trailers and machinery and the removal of all soil, timber, and pallets brought on to the land to abate the injury caused to the amenity of the area'. He appealed this notice to a bench of magistrates, which ordered the notice to be amended to read, 'The site should be cleared to an acceptable level of tidiness which said level is to be determined by the Council.' The council prosecuted him for failure to comply with the amended notice. W was fined, with costs, and the council took steps to clear the land in default of W's doing so.

The Commission referred the conviction because the amended notice – being more onerous than the original notice – did not comply with the terms of section 217 of the 1990 Act and was, therefore, unenforceable. The Commission's investigations showed that the council had prosecuted W for failure to comply with the amended notice although aware of this defect. The Commission concluded (on the basis of legal authority) that this amounted to an abuse of process on the council's part. The Commission considered whether or not it was right in the exercise of its discretion to refer this matter, but concluded that, although the land had been cleared (making the matter in a sense history), the matter should be referred as W had had to pay a fine and costs.

Reflections

The summary of referred cases set out above shows that the offences – and the consequences of the convictions – have been generally of a lower order than in the Commission's indictable cases. **Wilkinson**, perhaps, represents a low point in terms of the significance of the Commission's referral. In that sense, it is not difficult to understand the *Daily Mail's* critique in the case of **Borrows** that the effort and expense that goes into such cases is disproportionate. It would be easy, on the other hand, to take this matter out of proportion. Summary cases take a small proportion of caseworking time, and few of the cases have required lengthy investigation. There is also some scope for passing 'slip' cases back to the magistrates' court for correction under the section 142 procedure – a matter which may reduce the Commission's summary workload to some extent in the future. The Commission was successful in one recent case in persuading the magistrates (not without some difficulty) to take back an erroneous conviction for correction, as an alternative to a referral by the Commission.

Moreover, it is easy to see that if errors resulting in wrongful convictions (as happened in Mr Borrows' case) remain unresolved, this might draw the equally forceful outrage of the *Daily Mail* that injustices can be perpetrated by incompetent petty officialdom and remain unredressed. The case of **F (Mark)**, which has been quite fully summarised above, would be the acid test for the *Daily Mail* critique. F was wrongly and unfairly convicted of a serious offence and his version of events – if accepted – shows that police officers must have breached the safeguards which should be afforded to defendants. In a stirring speech given on the retirement of Sir Frederick Crawford, the former Lord Chancellor, Lord Falconer, expressed with some passion his admiration of the Commission for referring the case of F, and stressed the importance that such injustices should not go unredressed. If that view is accepted, then it must be correct that the Commission's powers to refer summary cases should continue.

Equally, if the legislation is ever to be reviewed dispassionately – and not from the reactive stance which characterises most modern criminal justice legislation – the case for tidying up might be accepted. The reality is that the Commission, when it refers summary cases, does so because it concludes that there is new evidence or argument which it considers might cause the Crown Court, on rehearing the evidence, to pass down a different verdict or sentence – which is not quite what the present Act says. However, if the legislation remains in its present illogical format, the Commission will no doubt cope – as it has done in the past.

Notes

1. References to the magistrates' court include cases tried in the youth court (previously juvenile court).
2. It is part of the background to this discrepancy that there is an alternative route for appealing a conviction or sentence passed in the magistrates' court – by way of a case stated to the High Court. Broadly, the case stated procedure is more apt where there has been an alleged error of law. An appeal to the Crown Court is generally appropriate where the conclusions to be drawn from the evidence are sought to be put into dispute.
3. See chapter 1.
4. 'The Criminal Cases Review Commission: Establishing a Workable Relationship with the Court of Appeal' [2005] *Crim LR* 173.
5. Nobles and Schiff go on from this to infer that it is probable that the Commission exercises analogous unstated policy considerations throughout its jurisdiction and not merely in summary cases. That is probably a non sequitur and one with which this writer does not agree.
6. Home Office, *Criminal Appeals and the Establishment of a Criminal Cases Review Authority: A Discussion Paper*, 1994 (Ref CB139).
7. JUSTICE discussion paper, *Remedying Miscarriages of Justice*, September 1994.
8. Defined in the 1999 Act as 'the Convention relating to the Status of Refugees done at Geneva on 28 July 1951 and the Protocol to the Convention'.
9. Sandra Laville, Saturday, 16 October 2004.

Chapter 12 - The Commission's sentencing jurisdiction

The extension of the Commission's jurisdiction to include sentences was something of an afterthought. The Home Office did not use the referral process prior to the 1995 Act to send sentences to the Court of Appeal, albeit sentences could (and still can) be remitted by the Home Secretary (but now the Secretary of State for Justice) in exercise of his or her powers under the Royal Prerogative of Mercy. The power for the new independent authority to refer sentences was not a matter raised by the Runciman Commission, and neither was it a matter that had been particularly sought by JUSTICE. It was, however, mooted in the Home Office Discussion Paper issued following the report of the Runciman Commission.[1] This paper noted that 'while it may take account of objective factors [sentence] is ultimately a matter for the judgment and discretion of the courts'. The paper continued:

> It is important that nothing should appear to undermine the judgment of the courts in assessing the gravity of criminal conduct in the individual case and the weight to be given to mitigating factors. Accordingly ... the grounds on which the Authority might refer sentence ... should be confined to where there is reason to doubt the validity of the sentence in law, or where new information ... suggests that the factual basis on which a sentence was calculated was substantially wrong and no other remedy exists.

The Discussion Paper noted that the slip rule (s142 Magistrates' Courts Act 1980) allowed magistrates' courts to rectify sentencing errors without limit of time, whilst the corresponding provision applicable to sentencing slips made by the Crown Court (s47(2) Supreme Act 1981) restricted the Court's power to rectify sentencing errors to sentences corrected within 28 days of sentencing – an anomaly which persists.

JUSTICE, in its response to the Home Office Discussion Paper,[2] stated that the effort of screening sentence applications 'would take up valuable resources which, in our view, should be applied to the organisation's *real* task of reviewing alleged wrongful convictions' (emphasis added). It, nevertheless, supported 'extended rights of appeal in those exceptional circumstances where there remain concerns over the accuracy of a sentence post appeal'.

In the outcome, the 1995 Act provides simply that the Commission may refer a sentence if:

> *The Commission consider that there is a real possibility that the ... sentence would not be upheld ... because of an argument on a point of law, or information not so raised.*

This formulation reflects the views expressed in the Home Office Discussion Paper quoted above. The effective scope of the Commission's jurisdiction depends on what is to be understood by 'an argument on a point of law'. The great majority of sentencing appeals at large are mounted on the basis that the sentence is 'manifestly excessive' having regard to the criminal conduct concerned. Such appeals are invariably mounted on the basis that the sentence is out of line with sentencing authorities, which would appear to be an argument on a point of law. However, this appears not to be the view of the Court of Appeal, as will be apparent from the discussion of tariff cases which follows.

Up to the end of December 2007, some 24.6 per cent of applications received by the Commission concerned both conviction and sentence and a further 13 per cent were sentence-only applications.[3] The great majority of sentence applications are based on the proposition that the applicant has received too long a sentence for the offending behaviour. However, following the decisions of the Court of Appeal in **Graham** and **Robery** – discussed below – the Commission has generally had no locus to consider such cases, and, as a result, most sentence applications are very rapidly resolved as raising no 'real possibility'.

In the relatively small number of cases where applications for review of custodial sentences raise significant investigative issues, and the applicant is in custody at the time the application is received, the Commission will normally prioritise its review, as it would be nugatory for it to refer sentence cases *after* the sentence has been served. Conversely, the Commission normally sees no merit in investigating custodial sentences once expired, since any reduction in the period of sentence achieved by referral would generally be a nullity.

Generally, the concern of JUSTICE that sentence cases would clog up the Commission's activities has not been realised in practice.

Tariff cases

So far as simple tariff cases are concerned, the Court has been swift to step in to impose limitations on the Commission's jurisdiction. In **Graham**, the

Commission referred the sentence for a drugs offence on the grounds that the sentence imposed exceeded the tariff indicated in the subsequent guideline case of *Ronchetti*.[4] It must be conceded that if the appeal had been allowed, it would have had great implications for the workload of the Commission and the Court, as many further sentences for drugs offences would have become eligible for referral. The Court's response was firm and withering:

> *the Commission was established, primarily, so that cases where there had been a possible miscarriage of justice could be referred to this Court. A defendant sentenced lawfully, in accordance with the prevailing tariff, and when all factors relevant to sentence were known to the sentencing judge, can, in our view, hardly be described as the victim of such a miscarriage.*

Therefore, any change in sentencing guidelines should not be a ground for referral. The Court also added that 'an alteration in the statutory maxima or minima penalty (sic) between sentence and reference cannot, in our view, give rise to legitimate grievance'.

The Court concluded by saying:

> *we hope that what we say may be of assistance to the Commission when considering other complaints about sentence.*

Shortly before this judgment was received, the Commission referred the sentence of **Robery**, who was convicted of a street robbery in which he had snatched an old lady's handbag. The guideline cases indicated a tariff of two to five years and all the specifics of the case pointed to a sentence near to the bottom of the tariff, whereas R had been sentenced to an apparently exemplary sentence of 4½ years. The Court, dismissing the appeal, referred to its own dicta in **Graham** and added 'with the greatest of respect to the Commission' that its decision to refer had been flawed.

Graham and **Robery**, whether or not they reflect the intentions of the statute, have, in practical terms, all but eliminated the Commission's scope to review the generality of tariff cases and have had the effect that the Commission is able to deal with the great majority of sentence cases very swiftly. Whatever the merits of those decisions, many will feel that in **Ballard** the Court took the matter too far. The facts were unattractive by any standards. At the conclusion of an evening's drinking, there had been bad feeling between B and his confederates and a rival group, and B took to his car and repeatedly drove it towards the rival group, scattering them. A bystander was killed and B was convicted of manslaughter (having been acquitted of murder) and sentenced to 11 years. The sentence was referred following submissions from David Thomas QC, doyen of sentencing law, that unattractive as the facts were, the sentence did not stand with sentences imposed in the most nearly comparable cases. The Court (Maurice Kay LJ) referred once again to **Graham** and **Robery** adding:

> *A reference [against sentence] cannot be made ... unless ... there is a real possibility that the appeal will be upheld "because of an argument on a point of law or information not ... raised in the proceedings" ... We are at a total loss to identify any such point of law or information in this case. All that we have seen is reference to numerous authorities in the Commission's documents, none of which, in our judgment, can be considered to be "information" in the sense used in the Act ... We are sorry to say that we consider it to have been a misjudgment to refer this case in the circumstances which gave rise to it.*

It is easy to identify with the Court's view that the facts of **Ballard** were grave and sufficiently sui generis to diminish the precedent value of other sentencing cases. However, the judgment appeared to state that the Commission should not refer even clear cases of error in setting tariff, on the basis that sentencing authorities do not constitute either new information or 'an argument on a point of law'. It seems very doubtful whether this reflects the words of the statute quoted above and this may be a case where the Court has looked through the natural meaning of the words contained in the statute to their presumed intention – something which courts are not supposed to do! It is to be hoped that the Commission will not be deterred from referring tariff cases on those vary rare occasions where there has been legal error or oversight in setting tariff which has not been resolved on a first-time appeal.

As a postscript to this discussion, attention should be drawn to two 'successful' referrals of tariff in the cases of **Mohammed** and **Hattersley and Taylor.** In both cases, the applicant's co-defendant had succeeded in getting his sentence reduced on appeal, therefore opening an unacceptable disparity of sentencing between co-defendants. The Court has expressed no objection to redressing such disparities through the mechanism of a Commission referral.

Offen cases

In 1997, the (Conservative) government brought in the 'two strikes and you're out' legislation in the form of s2 Crime (Sentences) Act 1997 (later re-enacted as s109 Powers of the Criminal Courts (Sentencing) Act 2000). In a nutshell, the courts were required to sentence persons convicted of a second violent 'scheduled' offence to an automatic life sentence 'unless the court is of the opinion that there are exceptional circumstances relating to either of the offences or to the offender which justify its not doing so'.

In *Buckland*,[5] Lord Bingham CJ described the rationale of section 2 as reflecting:

> *an assumption that those who have been convicted of two qualifying serious offences present such a serious and continuing danger to the safety of the public that they should be liable to indefinite incarceration and, if released, should be liable indefinitely to recall to prison.*

He added that:

> *If exceptional circumstances are found, and the evidence suggests that an offender does not present a serious and continuing danger to the safety of the public, the Court may be justified in imposing a lesser penalty.*

This judgment presented a more generous view than previously understood of 'exceptional circumstances' and reflected the Court's perception that section 2, as drafted, had caught in its net some offenders who were a great deal less dangerous than the politicians had had in mind when passing it. **Offen**, which was referred by the Commission, was considered by the Court of Appeal following *Buckland*, together with a number of other cases (not referred by the Commission). In its judgment on these cases, the Court set out the approach to be adopted by sentencing judges in deciding whether 'exceptional circumstances' applied.

> *Section 2 establishes a norm. The norm is that those who commit two serious offences are a danger or risk to the public. If in fact, taking into account all the circumstances relating to a particular offender, he does not create an unacceptable risk to the public, he is an exception to this norm. If the offences are of a different kind, or if there is a long period which elapses between the offences during which the offender has not committed other offences, that may be a very relevant indicator as to the degree of risk to the public that he constitutes ... Whether there is significant risk will depend on the evidence which is before the court. ... it will be part of the responsibility of judges to assess the risk to the public that offenders constitute. In many*

cases the degree of risk that an offender constitutes will be established by his record, with or without the assistance of assessments made in reports which are available to the court.

...

This does not mean that we are approaching the passing of an automatic life sentence as though it is no different from the imposition of a discretionary life sentence. ... Section 2 will still mean that a judge is obliged to pass a life sentence in accordance with its terms unless, in all the circumstances, the offender poses no significant risk to the public. ... if the judge decides not to impose a life sentence under section 2, he will have to give reasons as required by section 2(3). Furthermore, the issue of dangerousness will have to be addressed in every case and a decision made as to whether or not to impose a life sentence.

In **Offen**'s case, the Court concluded that 'the appellant is not to be regarded as presenting a significant risk to the public' and substituted a determinate sentence of three years for the life sentence which had been imposed upon him.

Subsequently, **Jackson, Kelly, BJS, Turner** and **Collins** were all referred by the Commission on the basis of **Offen** considerations and all, except **Collins,** had their life sentences quashed and substituted by determinate sentences.[6] Of these cases, **Jackson,** perhaps, represents the most generous application of the exceptional circumstances provision by the Court.

It is unlikely that there will be further referrals based on **Offen** since the **Offen** guidelines were promulgated in 2000 and have, therefore, been known to sentencing judges for some years. However, it remains the case that a somewhat hyperactive Labour government has sought to curb the sentencing options of the courts with increasing frequency, with the 'exceptional circumstances' formulation being used in other legislation.[7] It is, therefore, possible that there will be further instances in the future where broadly drawn legislation becomes subject to subsequent judicial gloss, as occurred in **Offen**, and every possibility that cases, analogous with **Offen**, will come the way of the Commission in the future.

Sentencing errors – credit for time served

The potential for legislators to confuse and bamboozle sentencing judges is shown to further, and almost farcical, lengths in the cases of **Brown (Darren), James**

(Philip), **Keogh**, **Melady**, **Murray (Vincent)** and **Pollard**.　The facts in each case are somewhat similar but, in brief, the court failed in each case to credit the convicted person correctly for time served after he was administratively recalled to prison by the Home Office, due to breach of licence, having previously been released on licence before completing sentence for earlier offences.

Quite apart from the complexity of the sentencing legislation (which gives rise to increasing possibility of sentencing error), it is somewhat absurd that these cases need to be corrected by the mechanism of a Commission reference, a process which involves (i) the prioritisation of the application;[8] (ii) the convening of a case committee of three Commissioners;[9] (iii) the listing and hearing of a formal appeal in the Court of Appeal; and (iv) the instruction of counsel for both parties, the granting of legal aid and so forth.　If the legislation were amended to remove the present 28-day time limit for the rectification of sentencing slips by the Crown Court, such cases could be dealt with more promptly and efficiently. As the Court of Appeal was moved to remark in **Pollard**:

> *The situation that has arisen in this case has taken up the time of the CCRC which could be better used devoted to other work.　It has taken up the time of this Court, which could have heard another appeal.　Indeed, as we have said, it is the first of two such cases in the list today which give rise to this point.　Finally, it is and has been a drain on the legal aid fund which is particularly hard-pressed.*

Sentencing error – extended sentence

The facts of both **Lay** and **Nicholson** are almost ludicrously complicated.　In **Lay**, the case relates to the power of the courts to pass an 'extended sentence' for certain categories of sexual offence.　The period of the extended sentence which the Court may impose is a period during which the convicted person is released on licence (and may, therefore, be recalled in the event of further offending) consecutive to the period he has served in custody.　As the Court pointed out, there are now three different kinds of sentences – all introduced since 2000, and all called 'extended sentences' – which can be passed in different circumstances upon sexual offenders: a fine example of the way politicians have developed a taste for fine-tuning the sentencing powers and duties of judges.　The sentences passed on L by the trial judge had already been corrected by the Court of Appeal at a first time appeal but – as the Court noted:

> *At that stage no one took any point upon the existence of the sentences on the second indictment or upon the fact that those two year sentences were*

consecutive to the sentences on the first indictment, and thus consecutive to the extended sentence on the first indictment. That is the narrow but significant point upon which the Criminal Cases Review Commission now re-refers this case to this court.

L had been sentenced on various counts of indecency, the aggregate of the custodial and the extension periods being 11 years. The point taken by the Commission in its referral was that the aggregate sentence exceeded the statutory maximum for the relevant offences, which was ten years. The Court allowed the appeal but found a way of re-jigging the various sentences to achieve the same result as the sentences passed by the trial judge. The Court also took the opportunity to promulgate guidelines on the use of extended sentences. As with the previous cases, it might make better sense if sentencing slips of this kind could be corrected without recourse to the Commission.

Nicholson was convicted of two counts of possessing indecent photographs of children. The trial judge, believing this to be a 'sexual or violent offence' for the purposes of s85 Powers of Criminal Courts (Sentencing) Act 2000, purported to pass an extended sentence (during which N was released on licence) consecutive to the custodial sentence. N was released from prison having served one half of the sentence, but committed further (similar) offences before the expiry of the period for which he was subject to recall as a result of the extended sentence. As a result, he was subject to administrative recall to serve the unexpired part of his custodial sentence. The problem was that the offence committed was not, in fact, a 'sexual or violent' offence as defined by section 161(2) of the same Act so the purported extended sentence was a nullity; the further offending had, therefore, occurred after N had ceased to be in jeopardy of recall. This was all finally resolved by the Commission's reference. As in **Lay**, a reading of the judgment reveals the extreme complexity of modern sentencing legislation.

Sentencing error – erroneous belief that convicted person in breach of licence

Giacopazzi was a somewhat singular case where the court passed an additional consecutive sentence under the erroneous belief that G had committed the offences at a time when there was a part of the term for a previous sentence still outstanding. It is another example of sentencing mistake and was not opposed by the Crown.

Sample counts

Smith (Peter) and Tovey were cases (heard together) in which the convicted persons had been sentenced on the basis that the counts, which had been either proved (in the case of Smith) or admitted (in the case of Tovey), should be treated as 'specimen' counts. That is to say, the Court passed sentence on the basis that it could take into account other examples of similar conduct even though they were neither proved nor admitted. This was in breach of clear guidance provided by the Court in *Canavan*[10] and *Clark*[11] that a person should only be sentenced for an offence that had either been proved or admitted. Mr Smith's case was referred by the Commission and the two cases were heard together to enable the Court to provide guidance on the use of specimen counts. The Court re-affirmed that the *Canavan* guidelines should have been followed, and in Smith's case, concluded that if he had been sentenced only for the proved counts the sentence passed would have been manifestly excessive, and it, therefore, cut the sentence. In Tovey's case, the Court concluded that even if the sentence had been only for the admitted counts, it would not have been manifestly excessive, and the sentence, therefore, stood.

Sentencing in a defendant's absence

Coleman was sentenced for four years in total for burglary and miscellaneous driving offences – he was already serving a nine-month sentence passed by another court. After C was sentenced and taken down, the judge directed that this four-year sentence be served consecutive to the nine-month sentence that C was already serving. Neither C nor his solicitor was present when this direction was made. The Court considered that this order was made in breach of clear authority that a sentence imposed in the absence of a defendant or legal representative is void. This was another case that was not contested by the Crown, but in the absence of a slip rule for Crown Court sentencing, the matter could only be resolved through a Commission reference.

New information sentence referrals

Section 13(1)(b)(ii) of the 1995 Act provides for referral of sentence on the basis of information not previously raised in trial or appellate proceedings. The inhibition upon tariff referrals propounded in **Graham** and **Robery** does not apply to such new information cases. It should, however, be noted that the Court has a discretion under s23 Criminal Appeal Act 1968 whether or not to receive new evidence relating to sentence. The Court may, therefore, refuse to consider new evidence of mitigation if there is no 'reasonable explanation' for failing to bring forward evidence to support mitigation at the time of trial.[12] The Commission should not, therefore, generally be used as a way of raising sentencing information which was knowingly not put forward at the time of sentencing by the trial judge. This is a matter particularly relevant in confiscation cases – discussed briefly below.

Illness and hardship cases

Cases may arise where, after sentencing, new information comes to light about the health and/or family circumstances of the convicted person which bears on the harshness of the sentence. **Henry** is a case where the sentencing court had not appreciated how limited the arrangements were for the care of the child of H, who was pregnant when sentenced. Following referral by the Commission the Court stated:

> *This Court has jurisdiction to temper just deserts with mercy in appropriate cases. ... We think this to be such a case. This sentence was the right sentence when passed ... but we must ask ourselves ... whether justice requires the fourth year of that term to be served. If it were, it would mean the separation of this young mother from both her children for a further five or six months at a vulnerable stage in their development and in circumstances where it seems that the interim arrangements for those children's care would cause difficulties and might be less than satisfactory.*

H was immediately released, as was **Looker,** whose sentence was referred on the basis of compelling evidence that L had not only committed the criminal act due to the psychological domination of her boyfriend but was also clinically depressed at the time. Both cases caused considerable satisfaction to the Commission. **Henry** and **Looker** were decided in 1999 and 2000 respectively, and it is perhaps surprising that no cases of this kind have been subsequently referred by the Commission. It may well be that legal practitioners are unaware of the Commission's power to refer such cases and have consequently not brought them to its attention.

In a case called Hall, H was sentenced to a long sentence for a drugs mule offence. She became subject to a progressive illness (multiple sclerosis) in prison and there were also difficulties, due to the death of an elderly parent in the West Indies, in the arrangements for the care of her young children. The Prison Service refused to consider early release. The case was referred by the Commission but her appeal was abandoned when she became eligible for parole before her case was heard.

Such cases should properly be a matter for concern. The Court of Appeal in the guideline case of *Bernard*[13] stated that cases where early release is to be considered due to the onset of severe ill-health should generally be dealt with by the Home Office under the Royal Prerogative of Mercy (RPM). The Home Office for its part, in its (limited) dialogue with the Commission on this matter, has expressed utmost reluctance to use the RPM in such cases. It has also expressed constitutional scruples – due to the separation of powers – about treading on the toes of the judiciary in sentencing matters. The position of the Home Office[14] would seem to be that matters, such as reduction of sentence due to ill-health, are properly left to the judiciary, whilst the judiciary has indicated in *Bernard* that such matters should generally be dealt with by the executive under the RPM. It is doubtful whether solicitors with expertise in prison law, acting within the constraints of the legal aid budget, have the resources effectively to deal with such cases of 'pass the parcel'.

The issue is exemplified by drugs mule offences. Young women are habitually sentenced to very lengthy terms for carrying drugs into the United Kingdom. The Court has set out relatively rigid sentencing guidelines, with the result that sentences in such cases are generally fixed by reference to standard tariffs (depending on the identity and the value of the substances carried by the convicted person) and without reference to individual circumstances or hardship. The Court has reasoned that to pass softer sentences on (say) offenders with young children or health problems would send a signal to those who control the drug trafficking trade that it would be advantageous to select the most vulnerable members of the community to commit such offences. Be that as it may, it would seem that sentences may bear particularly harshly on some offenders, as was the case with Ms Hall. It appears that the prison authorities may put such hardship cases in the 'too difficult' drawer, finding it simpler to let such prisoners rot than to consider the exercise of the RPM. It is to be hoped that if similar cases come to the Commission, accompanied by compelling new information, referral of sentence will be seriously considered.

Informant cases

Convicted persons who wish to claim credit (for sentencing purposes) for information provided to the police or prosecuting authorities are generally assisted by means of a secret 'text' supplied to the judge by the informant's police (or customs) handler. It is necessarily a somewhat cloak-and-dagger affair, and there is a good deal of scope for slip-up, whereby the judge is not made aware of the assistance provided by the convicted person to the police or prosecution authorities by the time that sentencing takes place. In a joint trial, there are also concerns on the part of the prisoner claiming credit that any curious disparity in sentencing will lead his or her co-defendants to the view that he or she has been acting as an informant. A leading case, *A and B*[15], sets out guidelines for informant cases but does not deal with cases where the relevant information fails to reach the judge for reasons outside the fault of the convicted person. **S**, **K** and **M** are all cases where credit has been given by the Court in such circumstances following referral by the Commission.

It should be added that the government has now sought to put the sentencing of informants on a clear statutory basis by virtue of the provisions of ss73-4 Serious Organised Crime and Police Act 2005. The provisions of that Act would have been of no assistance in any of the three cases above, all of which reflected something of a breakdown of communication between the convicted person and the judge. It does not seem that the new Act is well adapted to deal with such cases, which may not be uncommon.

Error concerning antecedent offences

Cook and **Maguire** both had their sentences reduced following referral on the ground that the sentences were based upon erroneous information concerning antecedent offences.

Compensation and confiscation cases

The Commission's jurisdiction extends to compensation and confiscation cases. Legal errors and/or new information relevant to the original calculation of compensation or confiscation are matters within the Commission's remit. New information about the convicted person's ability to meet compensation (or confiscation) orders is not a matter for the Commission, but can be the subject of application to the High Court for a Certificate of Inadequacy under s83 Criminal Justice Act 1988.

Applications for review of compensation and confiscation orders are a challenge for the Commission. They are most often made by persons convicted of drugs or fraud offences who have chosen to make the most Byzantine arrangements for the arrangement (and perhaps concealment) of their assets. Where the Commission is presented with new information about these assets, the issue inevitably arises as to whether there is reasonable explanation why these matters were not brought forward at the time of the confiscation hearing. To date, no confiscation or compensation cases have been referred on the basis of new information submitted by the applicant.

Two confiscation cases have been referred on the basis of legal argument. In the colourful case of **Morphy**, M and her husband had been convicted of keeping a disorderly house, a somewhat upmarket establishment in the Home Counties. The confiscation order was quashed by the Court of Appeal on reference by the Commission because it was not clear that the sentencing judge had correctly applied his mind to the question whether the receipts of the 'working girls' could properly be attributed to the keeper of the house. In **Taylor (Alan)**, the confiscation order was upheld following reference on a legal point, and the report of the case nicely illustrates why these cases can be somewhat difficult for the Commission to deal with.

Discretionary life sentences

In discretionary life sentence cases, the sentencing judge is called to carry out a sentencing exercise in which he or she has to stipulate the earliest date that the convicted person can be considered for release. This entails a three-stage process in which the judge is required to:

1. decide the 'notional determinate sentence' which he or she would have passed for the offending behaviour had a life sentence not been imposed;

2. apply a discount to the notional determinate sentence of not more than one half and not less than one third (to reflect the normal entitlement to parole that would have applied had there been a determinate sentence); and

3. give credit for time already served.[16]

The sentencing authorities governing the carrying out of this exercise are somewhat complex and the scope for error is clear. **Jarvis** is a case which was referred, and the date for first consideration of parole was brought forward by the Court, in consequence of error by the trial judge in carrying out this exercise.

Mental health cases

Beatty and **Hempston** both relate to applicants with a history of mental illness who argued, unsuccessfully, following conviction that they should be committed to a mental hospital by an order under the Mental Health Act 1983 (ss37 and 41). Both were sentenced to prison after the sentencing court decided (having considered the psychiatric reports) that they did not fulfil the requirements for such an order. In each case, the sentencing 'problem' was that the defendant did not have the support of statements from two doctors specialising in mental health that the conditions for making an order under the Mental Health Act were satisfied.

In both cases, as a result of observation of their behaviour in prison, they were re-assessed within quite a short time and transferred to mental hospital (where they both now remain), pursuant to the provisions of ss47 and 49 Mental Health Act 1983. Both applications were based on the proposition that an incorrect assessment (in H's case as to whether he was subject to a mental disorder; in B's case as to whether he was treatable) had been made by the doctors at the time of sentencing, and that they should have had a Mental Health Act disposal ab initio.

In broad terms, the legal position is that a convicted person who receives a Mental Health Act disposal ab initio may be entitled to discharge on the basis of his medical condition, whereas a person who is given a life sentence, imprisoned and then subsequently transferred to mental hospital is liable to be discharged back to prison when no longer requiring medical treatment. The Home Office had a long standing extra-statutory practice of treating life sentence prisoners who had been transferred from prison in this way as 'Technical Lifers'. Technical Lifers were treated for practical purposes in the same way as convicted persons who were made subject to a Mental Health Act order ab initio. However, the Technical Lifer status has always been a somewhat precarious administrative device and it was abolished in 2005.[17]

The Court of Appeal in the cases of *Castro*[18] and *De Silva*[19] has stated that it will consider intervening to correct sentencing errors in such circumstances, even if the applicant has subsequently been transferred to mental hospital under sections 47 and 49. The Court has also stated that, in considering whether to allow such appeals, it will have specific regard to the question whether a link can be established between the mental disorder and the circumstances of the index offence. The Court – following these authorities – allowed the appeals of both B and H and substituted a Mental Health Act order ab initio for the terms of life imprisonment passed by the Crown Court.

The judgment in **Beatty** is expressed in quite positive terms, giving encouragement to other prospective applicants who consider themselves to be in the same position. It should be noted, however, from the Court's judgment in **Lomey** that where a person in this situation has sufficiently recovered from his or her illness to be released on licence (and no longer requires treatment), the Court will not intervene to correct the original sentence.

The firm of solicitors which referred the cases of **Beatty** and **Hempston** has intimated that others are likely to follow, and it seems that (where there has been a previous appeal) the Commission is the only route for resolving such cases. The exercise of deciding whether a sentencing error was made in the first instance has not been particularly easy for the Commission, and it may be that a more cost-effective way could be found to deal with such cases.

Notes

1. Home Office, *Criminal Appeals and the Establishment of a Criminal Cases Review Authority A Discussion Paper*, 1994 (Ref CBI39).
2. JUSTICE discussion paper, *Remedying Miscarriages of Justice*, September 1994.
3. It should be noted that (although there are no systematic data to show the point) it has been plain that most of the applicants applying for review of both conviction and sentence have been primarily concerned with review of conviction. Significant numbers of applicants tick the sentence box in the application form (that is to say, request a review of sentence) without making specific submissions with respect to sentence. The bare statistics, therefore, overstate the extent of the Commission's workload concerned with sentence.
4. [1998] 2 Cr App R (S) 100.
5. [2000] 1 WLR 1262.
6. Mr Collins' life sentence was confirmed but his tariff was reduced from 14 to 12 years.
7. See for instance s51A Firearms Act 1968 introduced by the Criminal Justice Act 2003, which requires the Court to pass a minimum five-year sentence for unauthorised possession of certain types of prohibited firearm 'unless there are exceptional circumstances relating to the offence or to the offender which justify not doing so'.
8. Since, if such cases were to wait in the queue for allocation, in many cases the applicant would have served the period for which he or she had been erroneously sentenced before the matter could get back to the Court of Appeal, thereby making the referral a nullity.
9. As the 1995 Act requires any referral decision to be made by a committee consisting of not fewer than three members – see Schedule 1, para 6(3)(a).
10. [1998] 1 Cr App R 70.
11. [1996] 2 Cr App R (S) 351.
12. See s23(2)(d) of the 1968 Act.
13. [1996] EWCA Crim 519.
14. But note that the Ministry of Justice has now assumed responsibility for dealing with the exercise of the RPM. RPM cases are dealt with by the Office for Criminal Justice Reform – the Commission's sponsoring unit.
15. [1999] 1 Cr App R (S) 52.
16. The workings of this formula have attracted somewhat superficial interest within sections of the media pressing the proposition that 'life means life'.
17. The judgment in **Beatty** explains the background to this (somewhat complex) issue.
18. (1985) 7 Cr App R (S) 68.
19. (1994) 15 Cr App R (S) 296.

Chapter 13 - The Commission in Northern Ireland

The history of the Commission's dealings in Northern Ireland would merit a separate study going beyond the legalities of the cases it has referred. By its nature, the Commission deals exclusively with the understanding of events that have occurred in the past, but 'the past' appears (to this writer) to have had a somewhat different resonance in Northern Ireland miscarriage cases. The following points stand out in the Northern Ireland cases considered by the Commission:

- The majority of applications have concerned convictions for terrorist offences.

- The average lapse of time between convictions and applications has been much higher than in the mainland.

- There has been a high concentration of applications from a small number of solicitors' firms.

- A number of applications have been supported by campaigning organisations.

It might also be said that the past is not quite 'another country' in Northern Ireland as on the mainland, since (politically) the interpretation of events in the past continues to influence the approach of communities and politicians to present events and issues. It remains to be seen whether the current political settlement in Northern Ireland will change that situation or affect the Commission's Northern Ireland caseload.

For its part, the Commission's remit in Northern Ireland has been no different from elsewhere – to examine convictions[1] brought to it and consider whether there is any real possibility that they would be found to be unsafe. However, it is perhaps fair to say that the Commission's investigations have shone some new light on the very stringent methods employed in Northern Ireland in dealing with suspected sectarian and paramilitary offences during the Emergency. The Commission cases may possibly promote reflection on the juridical and investigative procedures of that time. Retrospective reflection and juridical detachment cannot, of course, give full account to the pressures and stresses affecting the law enforcement agencies during the Emergency, and it may not be unfair to observe that there have been times when officers of the Royal Ulster Constabulary[2] have wearied of the Commission's persistent enquiries into long-ago cases. That said, the Commission has worked successfully with the law enforcement agencies to resolve a number of historic cases (not always in the applicant's favour) and, indeed, the generally high standard of record-keeping on the part of the police and prosecution authorities in the Province has helped the Commission to resolve the very old cases discussed in this chapter.

The cases that follow need to be considered in the context of distinctive aspects of the Northern Ireland judicial system – at least as applied to terrorist offences during the Emergency:

- Detained persons suspected of terrorist offences were subject to interrogation for extended periods of up to five days.

- Detained persons suspected of terrorist offences were normally denied access to solicitors for a period of 48 hours. Part of the rationale for this was apprehension that solicitors with links to terrorist groups might act as vectors of information helpful to terrorists. But it also gave the police a 'clear run' to interrogate suspects over the first two days of detention.

- Suspects were made subject to the drawing of statutory adverse inferences in the event of failure to respond to police questioning, long before similar provisions were introduced in the mainland by the Criminal Justice and Public Order Act 1994.

In addition, it is well known that Northern Ireland police officers developed a distinctive approach to the questioning of terrorist suspects at Castlereagh and other holding centres. It was standard practice to use the extended period of detention to question suspects intensively, the common pattern being for pairs of officers to work in alternating shifts, sometimes interrogating suspects for 12 or more hours per day over the period allowed for questioning. These methods of detention were seen as necessary in dealing with suspected terrorists thought likely to have been trained to resist police interrogation methods. It is a feature of the Commission's cases that many have concerned persons convicted substantially or wholly on the basis of confessions given after intensive and prolonged interrogation by police officers.

This legal framework has – as is well known – been subject to several adverse judgments of the European Court of Human Rights. A leading case was *John Murray v The United Kingdom*.[3] M alleged breach of his rights under the European Convention on Human Rights (the Convention) having been subject to interrogation in accordance with the provisions of the emergency legislation as outlined above. Put briefly, the European Court of Human Rights,[4] rejected M's complaint (i) that his right to silence had been violated or (ii) that the drawing of adverse inferences from silence violated his right to a fair trial under Article 6 of the Convention. However, the Court considered that M's lack of early access to a lawyer was incompatible with the concept of fairness, as it had placed him in a situation where his rights might be irretrievably prejudiced. In effect, the Court concluded that the 'double whammy' of a suspect being subject to adverse inferences for not answering police questions *and* the lack of a legal adviser to advise him (and to draw attention to the legal dangers of not answering questions) together breached the requirement for a fair trial.

Also notable was the report of the European Committee for the Prevention of Torture and Inhuman and Degrading Treatment and Punishment (CPT) dated July 1993, cited in chapter 6, which noted that the 'intensive and potentially prolonged character of the interrogation process' placed great psychological pressure upon suspects from whom the police were seeking to obtain confessions.

As a result of the judgment in his favour, Mr Murray was awarded damages of £15,000 by the European Court of Human Rights, and a number of others detained and convicted in Northern Ireland also obtained judgments against the United Kingdom (and in some cases damages) upon the principles of the *Murray* judgment. That did not, however, make their convictions unsafe under domestic law. It was a firm principle – until the commencement of the Human Rights Act in October 2000 – that where domestic legislation unambiguously conflicted with Convention rights, the domestic legislation prevailed. Thus, for Mr Murray (and others) the fact that the European Commission or European Court had found that their Article 6 rights had been breached did not alter the fact that they had been duly convicted under domestic laws. Indeed, the Commission has declined to refer convictions of a number of applicants who have had decisions in their favour from the European Commission or Court on the principles of the judgment in *Murray*.

It appeared briefly, following the judgment of the Northern Ireland Court of Appeal (NICA or the Court) in **Magee**, of which more anon, that

Convention rights would be read retrospectively into convictions preceding the commencement of the Human Rights Act. Had that been the case, a very large number of Northern Ireland cases would undoubtedly have been referred and quashed. However, that window of possibility was firmly shut by the decisions of the House of Lords in *Lambert* and **Kansal** (referred to in chapter 7) which ruled against retrospectivity. *Lambert* was cited in the subsequent NICA decisions in **Latimer** and **Walsh** as authority for the proposition that **Magee** had been wrongly decided on this point and should not be followed. In consequence, the Commission continues to be limited to considering the effect of domestic law (in practice an amalgam of English and Northern Ireland case law) in reviewing the safety of the older convictions.

An attempt was made in a judicial review application against the Commission, which appears in the Law Reports as **In the Matter of Quinn (Dermot)**, to argue that even though the Human Rights Act was not retrospective, Convention principles could be properly read back into an understanding of the developing common law. Mr Quinn had previously had judgment from the European Commission on Human Rights that his Convention rights had been breached on the principles of the *Murray* judgment. Mr Quinn's arrest and interrogation had taken place in 1988, so he could only avail himself of this breach of his Convention rights (for the purpose of a domestic appeal) by arguing that Convention principles could be read back into the prior understanding of the law. The matter was heard by the Administrative Court in Northern Ireland and from there appealed to NICA which declined, following the decision of the House of Lords in *In Re McKerr*, to accede to the argument that Convention principles could be applied retrospectively in the manner argued.[5]

The Commission's Northern Ireland referrals of convictions for sectarian offences are considered below in chronological order of referral.

Gorman and McKinney (Quashed)

G was arrested on 24 October 1979 (presumably on the basis of intelligence reports) on suspicion of shooting a police constable some 5½ years earlier. He was taken to Castlereagh and interviewed 11 times between 24 and 26 October. On the eighth interview, according to the testimony of police officers, he said 'Get the paper out and I'll tell you the truth' before making a confession statement. In his final interview, he named McKinney as his accomplice. M was then interviewed nine times from 27 to 29 October and was said to have confessed at the seventh interview. Both men alleged assault which had forced their confessions but the judge, following a voir dire, rejected their evidence and admitted the confessions. The judge found the police officers truthful and reliable witnesses. The convictions were referred on the basis of ESDA evidence that showed some re-writing of interview notes which – if raised at trial – could have been used to put to significant challenge the police officers' evidence about the way the interviews had proceeded and the notes of interviews had been compiled. The Court could not exclude an innocent explanation for the amendments but considered that the information might have affected the judge's assessment of the police officers as reliable witnesses and quashed the convictions.

Green (Quashed)

G was convicted in 1987 of a murder committed the previous year. This was characterised by the Crown as a sectarian rather than a terrorist murder, the victim, a young Catholic, having been beaten up and murdered after going to a bar said to have been frequented by Loyalist paramilitaries.

G was arrested on 20 May 1986 and interviewed by officers 12 times over the next three days. Following the eighth interview, on the evening of 21 May, he was admitted briefly to hospital, due to a hypoglycaemic episode, and the referral was based upon expert evidence obtained by the Commission concerning the effect of this episode upon his fitness for interview, Of this episode the NICA judgment reads as follows:

> At 6.37 pm on 21 May the duty gaoler Reserve Constable Bradley was sitting at his desk in the cell area when he heard a noise of moaning and retching coming from the appellant's cell. He looked into the cell and saw the appellant curled up on the bed holding his chest. He was shaking violently as if having a fit and complained of pains in his chest. R/Con Bradley summoned Sergeant Dove and they held him to keep him from injuring himself until the doctor arrived. When the duty doctor, Mr R Loane FRCS, visited the cell a few minutes later he found the appellant lying quietly and unable to respond to him. His eyes were open and staring. His pupils were equal and reacted to light. His heart rate was 140 per minute (which is very fast) but regular and his blood pressure was 105 over 70 (within normal limits). There was poor air entry to his chest, so that his breathing was shallow. Mr Loane thought it advisable that the appellant should be admitted to hospital, in view of the sudden onset of the condition, and thought that the chest pain might have a cardiac connection. He arranged for the appellant to be transferred to the Ulster Hospital.

At the hospital he was seen by a casualty officer Dr Richard Lawson in the Accident and Emergency Department. He found the appellant in a drowsy and incoherent state, resembling a drunk man, and unable to give a clear history. Chest X-ray and cardiac examination did not show any abnormality. The doctor was informed that the appellant had not eaten anything that day, so he carried out a blood sugar estimation. He found that the blood sugar count was 2.2 mmol/L, well below the normal range of 3.9 to 5.8 mmol/L. He concluded that the low blood sugar would account for the appellant's symptoms and that he had had a hypoglycaemic episode, which was unlikely to recur. He directed that he be given sweetened tea and some toast. He was not diabetic and so the hypoglycaemia condition departed. Dr Lawson considered that when the appellant left him at 9 pm he was "sorted out" and that that was the last he would hear of him. The appellant was accordingly discharged and returned to Castlereagh ...

The appellant was passed fit for interview next morning by Dr Henderson, who had not received any report from the hospital.

G's admissions had been made in the two interviews which preceded and the next interview which followed this episode. G made complaint of mistreatment at his trial and an unsuccessful attempt was made to exclude the confession evidence, which was the only evidence against him. As to the hypoglycaemic episode, the judge decided that it had no bearing on G's fitness for interview, either before or after it took place.

The conviction was quashed on the basis of expert evidence that the hypoglycaemic evidence affected G's fitness for interview both before and after it occurred. The Court accepted that evidence of this nature would have been likely to have led the judge to conclude that the vital confession evidence of G should have been excluded as unreliable. The judgment contains no record as to whether the doctors who saw Mr Green at the time had been moved to question whether he was in fact fit to be interviewed.

Walsh (Upheld)

This was a case of considerable complexity in which the main grounds for reference were not by any means reflected in the grounds of appeal.

W was convicted of the possession of an explosive device (a coffee jar bomb). The main evidence against him came from two paratroopers, Blacklock and Boyce, who said that whilst on patrol they saw W place the coffee jar on a wall. The Commission (very unusually) had the paratroopers re-interviewed by police officers because a visit to the scene by the Commission's Case Review Manager disclosed important discrepancies between the evidence of one of the paratroopers, Boyce, and the physical layout of the surroundings of the crime scene. Boyce very significantly amended his evidence when re-interviewed but adhered to his evidence that he had seen W place the bomb on the wall. The Commission considered that Boyce's credibility would have been unlikely to have survived cross-examination had the discrepancies of his evidence been fully understood at trial.

In addition two witnesses came forward and gave an account to the Commission of having witnessed the incident some five years earlier which was supportive of W's trial account. The Commission thought that these witnesses might well have been highly rehearsed but considered that they were (just) capable of belief and referred the conviction.

At the ensuing appeal, the Court gave no weight to the fact that Boyce had amended his trial evidence and, somewhat unfairly, appeared to criticise the Commission for having re-interviewed the military witnesses, disregarding the fact that the Commission had had them re-interviewed only because of obvious difficulties with the evidence of one of them. The Court considered that the new civilian witness evidence was contrived and lying evidence which undermined rather than supported W's version of events.

In response to a further point raised on W's appeal, the Court found that the trial judge had made an important error in resting his verdict (and rejecting W's evidence) upon the basis of an adverse inference that should not have been drawn. The Court stated that this would have made the conviction unsafe but for the fact that W had, in its view, undermined his own credibility by calling clearly lying eyewitness testimony at the appeal. The Court upheld the conviction.

Mr Walsh's case has been the subject of extensive campaigning and a somewhat one-sided television documentary, perhaps reflecting the polarisation of opinion about events in the past which continues in Northern Ireland. It is the subject of continuing applications to the Northern Ireland courts.

Magee (Quashed)

M was arrested in December 1988 on suspicion of planting a remote controlled roadside bomb. He was intensively interviewed by pairs of officers over the following three days.

M made a verbal confession statement in the sixth interview and a written confession (which he said had been composed for him by police officers) at the seventh interview. He requested a solicitor but the solicitor was withheld for 48 hours in accordance with the emergency legislation. (This was undisputed.) His claims of mistreatment by police, on the other hand, were disputed – a doctor who examined him described his complaints of tenderness as 'subjective'. He claimed that the confession had been worn out of him by the attritional interviewing methods of the police officers.

He complained to the European Court of Human Rights. The European Court in finding in M's favour, quoted the findings of the CPT – set out in chapter 6 – and concluded in M's case that:[6]

> The austerity of the conditions of his detention and his exclusion from outside contact were intended to be psychologically coercive and conducive to breaking down any resolve he may have manifested at the beginning of his detention to remain silent.

Allowing the appeal, the NICA concluded that the HRA had retrospective effect – a decision which, as already noted, has since been overruled. However, the NICA also noted that:

> there were, however, facts in this case which gave more support to the conclusion of the ECHR than might exist in some other cases [including the fact that] M showed symptoms of being materially more distressed and vulnerable than many other suspects in the same position.

The NICA noted that no attempt had been made at trial to exclude the confession evidence due to breach of Judges' Rules. On this point, the judgment noted realistically:

> it is probably fair to say that the appellant's advisers would have been well aware that to attempt at trial to found a case on lack of legal advice or conditions in Castlereagh would have had no chance of success and so did not advance such a ground for exclusion of the statements.

Boyle (Quashed)

B was arrested in May 1976 on suspicion of firearms offences and IRA membership. The only admissible evidence against him of substance consisted of confessions said to have been made in his fifth police interview as recorded in the notes of PCs Briggs and Logan but contested by B. The officers had been adamant that the notes of interview were contemporaneous and true. The case, therefore, turned on the credibility of the conflicting accounts of the course of this interview. The Diplock judge stated in his judgment:

> [B] seems a slippery, evasive and manifestly untruthful witness who was prepared to say anything he thought would assist his case. By contrast I believe in its entirety in the evidence of the two constables, both seem to me completely honest and truthful. If they had been dishonest they could have written down even more damning admissions in a much shorter time.

The case was referred on the basis of ESDA evidence to show that there had been an earlier version of this fifth interview. As the NICA noted, in its judgment that followed referral by the Commission, this could have been used to attack the constables' veracity 'by this side door'. The Court noted that the discrepancies in the deciphered earlier version and the final version were not grave, but as the constables had been emphatic that the notes were exactly as taken down during the course of the interview, their credibility was inevitably cast into doubt. This left no other reliable evidence against B. The similarities to the facts of **Gorman and McKinney** were noted by the Court.

Latimer (Upheld)

L, a UDR member, was arrested on 29 November 1983 on suspicion of a sectarian killing earlier that month. Between his arrest and 5 December he was subject to 29 interviews, typically lasting between two and five hours. His interviews showed a complex history of admissions, retractions and then further admissions eventually leading to confessions of responsibility for the murder. There was significant corroborative eyewitness evidence from a Mrs A supporting part of the narrative of events contended by the prosecution.

At trial and appeal there was considerable discussion and analysis of the reliability both of L's confession evidence and the reliability of the evidence of Mrs A, who was recognised to be a somewhat 'flaky' witness. L's confession evidence was found admissible and he was convicted. Three others were also convicted of responsibility for the murder.

The convictions of all four defendants were referred by the Secretary of State for Northern Ireland in 1991 on presentation of ESDA evidence of re-writing of interview notes. The Court concluded that this evidence significantly undermined the evidence of police officers against L's three co-defendants and quashed their convictions but upheld L's conviction.

L's conviction was referred by the Commission on the basis of psychological evidence (Professor Gudjonsson) of vulnerability affecting the reliability of his confessions. The Crown presented evidence of another psychologist (Dr Heap) disputing vulnerability. The Court rejected Professor Gudjonsson's evidence, citing (inter alia) the 'O'Brien Guidelines' (see chapter 8) and concluding that there was 'insufficient foundation' for Professor Gudjonsson's conclusions. Evidence was also given that Mrs A suffered from a personality disorder that affected the reliability of her evidence, but the Court concluded that Mrs A was unlikely to have invented her evidence and gave little weight to this.

Adams (Robert) (Quashed)

A was convicted in 1977, of murder, false imprisonment, and assault with intent to cause grievous bodily harm. He was 16½ when interviewed and 17 when convicted. He was convicted purely on confession evidence. He was interviewed by police over 1½ days and police records indicated that at other times he had been 'talking' to police officers although not being interviewed by them. His father was permitted to be present at his final interview when he made a confession statement. The prosecution case was that the murder had been a terrorist reprisal killing.

The referral noted, inter alia, that A had been intensively interrogated; he had been denied the support of an adult during interrogation; there were inconsistencies between details of his confession and verifiable facts; and there was evidence of re-writing of notes. As with the previous cases, there had been no challenge at trial to the admissibility of the confession evidence. In addition, there was evidence obtained by the Commission (Professor Gudjonsson) that A was subject to vulnerabilities that would have made him liable to comply with suggestions put to him by police officers and which affected the reliability of his confession.

The NICA applied the judgment in *Ashley King* – which is discussed in chapter 6. The Court stated in its judgment that it considered that the breaches of Judges' Rules that had clearly occurred were a matter for concern (but fell short of stating that the admission of a confession obtained in breach of Judges'

Rules necessarily made a conviction unsafe). In A's case, the absence of an independent adult during interview, the numerous discrepancies between confessions and other known facts, and evidence of re-writing of interviews together led the Court to the conclusion that the conviction was unsafe.

Mulholland (Quashed)

M was arrested by police during riots in Portadown on 18 October 1976. He was 16 years old at the time. He was interviewed for over seven hours in total on that day and for nine hours in total on the following day, including one interview that lasted for five hours between 7.00 pm and midnight. During the last hour of this interview, the custody log recorded that he had made a statement of admission. The statement consisted of an admission of membership of the IRA.

The appellant spent both nights of 18 October 1976 and 19 October 1976 on a couch in the medical room at the police station. He had been in police custody for some 40 hours before he made the statement of admission. He was allowed access to his parents and a solicitor only after he had made his confession statement. At trial, he denied the truth of his confession statement and alleged ill-treatment by officers. His evidence was rejected by the trial judge, who found the confession evidence admissible and found him guilty of the offence of IRA membership. He was acquitted of a second charge of having made a petrol bomb attack on RUC officers.

The referral was based upon the oppressive nature of the interrogation (which, in the Commission's view, should have supported the argument for exclusion of M's confession statement); breaches of Judges' Rules; and, importantly, specific evidence that two of the lead interrogating officers (against whom M had made complaint of maltreatment) had been subject to findings of misconduct – a matter which would have been relevant to the judge's assessment of their credibility.

Quashing the conviction the Court concluded:

- That the principles of the judgment in *Ashley King* should be applied.

- That there had been significant breaches of the Judges' Rules in the interrogation of M which counsel at trial had failed to pursue. The confession evidence should have been excluded due to breach of Judges' Rules.

- That :

  the evidence about the mistreatment of M raised considerable doubt in our minds as to the safety of this conviction. Again, we considered that, had [the trial judge] been aware of the nature of the allegations against the two detective officers in that case, he would have been slow to conclude beyond reasonable doubt that the appellant's allegations about mistreatment were untrue.

Hanna and Hindes (Quashed)

Hanna and Hindes were arrested in 1976 on suspicion of having carried out a murder on behalf of a loyalist paramilitary gang. Hindes, then aged 14 years and 11 months, was interviewed eight times over the space of three days. He was denied the support either of a solicitor or his parents until the seventh interview, when his father was present as he made a confession statement. He named Hanna as his accomplice. Hanna, who was then 16½, was then arrested and interviewed four times. Hanna's father, too, was permitted to be present only at the final interview when Hanna also made a confession statement.

The issues raised by the referral included the length and succession of interviews by teams of officers leading up to confession; the prolonged period of detention in custody; allegations of use of force by interrogating officers and oppressive conduct in questioning; failure to assess fitness for interview; denial of medication; and denial of any supporting adult or legal advice during questioning – in breach of the Judges' Rules then applicable to the interrogation of suspects. (As in **Magee**, no point was taken by trial counsel about breaches of Judges' Rules or other procedures.) In addition the Commission's investigation suggested at the very least:

- That the terms of the boys' confessions had developed and changed – giving rise to doubts about the credibility of the confession evidence.

- That confessions said to have been composed by the boys had apparently been written by police officers and presented to them for signature.

- That significant 'sensitive' information tending to exculpate the boys had been withheld from the defence.

In quashing the convictions, the Court again applied *Ashley King*. The Court concluded that there had been significant failures to observe contemporary

Judges' Rules in denying an independent adult or medical assistance; that the confession statements were inconsistent with each other and evidence from the crime scene; and that there were significant deficiencies in the forensic evidence. In addition, there was evidence from clinical psychologists to suggest that both boys would have been vulnerable in the face of intense questioning – a matter affecting the reliability of their confessions.

MacDermott and McCartney (Quashed)

McCartney and MacDermott, aged 22 and 19 respectively, were arrested in 1977 on suspicion of the murder of an RUC constable and further serious terrorist offences; both were interrogated by teams of RUC officers and confessed to offences, their convictions being substantially based upon confession evidence. Each complained of ill-treatment and was medically examined at various stages during interrogation. In Mr McCartney's case Dr Hendron – one of the examining doctors – stated that injuries found upon examination led him to conclude that 'I had no doubt at all that he had been assaulted'. The judge had also allowed (with some hesitation) medical evidence relating to other suspects who had been held for interrogation in Castlereagh at the same time and who had also complained of assaults. One of the suspects – one Donnelly – had in the view of three doctors suffered injuries during interrogation, which police officers said had occurred when D had put up a struggle and had to be restrained.[7] A DC French was a common factor between the teams of detectives interviewing Donnelly and MacDermott.

Both McCartney and MacDermott were convicted and the trial judge gave no weight to medical evidence supporting McCartney's or Donelly's complaints. In relation to McCartney, the NICA's judgment on the appeal which followed referral reads as follows:

> The judge accepted that Dr Hendron believed that McCartney ... had been assaulted while at Castlereagh but had reached his conclusion having heard only one side of the story. Coloured by this belief his evidence lacked the professional objectivity shown by other medical witnesses.

Neither did the judge at trial accept the account of ill-treatment given by Donnelly (although supported by three doctors) and considered that he was either 'gilding the lily, being inventive or dishonest'.

The convictions were referred upon previously undisclosed evidence that, as a result of the injuries suffered by Donnelly, DC French and another officer had been recommended for prosecution – albeit the Assistant Director of Public Prosecutions for Northern Ireland had declined to act on that recommendation. Evidence that a prima facie case of assault had existed against French strengthened the case that Donnelly, McCartney and MacDermott had been assaulted as they said they were. Applying **Pendleton**, the court concluded 'that the evidence of the police officers might have been discredited by evidence that is now available'. Noting also the striking similarity of the allegations made against French by MacDermott and Donnelly, the Court quashed the convictions.

This case possibly fits with the 'lurking doubt' cases discussed at chapter 5. The new evidence uncovered by the Commission was relatively slender but has to be viewed in the light of the somewhat one-sided view of the evidence taken by the trial judge as tribunal of fact.[8]

Non-sectarian cases
The Commission has made only two referrals of non-sectarian offences in Northern Ireland: **O'Doherty** and **Hay Gordon**. These are discussed briefly at chapters 4 and 8 respectively.

Reflections
Consideration of the Commission's Northern Ireland cases must raise the question whether they represent the tip of an iceberg of wrongful convictions secured on the basis of coerced and unreliable confession evidence. The facts of a case such as **Mulholland** show that police neglected to observe elementary and obvious standards of fairness in questioning a very young man suspected of IRA membership, and that the legal rights available to M were wholly ineffective to protect him. Moreover, a case of this kind cannot be considered in isolation from the extreme sectarian polarisation then existing in Portadown, affecting members of the RUC as it did the wider community. And lest that appears to be a partisan comment, it should be said that Protestant suspects, such as Mr Green and Mr Latimer, appear to have been no less harshly dealt with.

These cases give the sense that the military exigencies of the Emergency; the high volume of serious crimes requiring to be processed by the criminal justice system in the Province; and, not least, the legal framework for the interrogation of suspects established by the emergency legislation engendered a somewhat rough-and-ready approach in which the requirements of justice to individual suspects could be lost to sight. In this context, the attitude of the judge to medical evidence in the case of **MacDermott and McCartney** throws a shaft of light on judicial attitudes at the height of the Troubles. Young terrorist suspects giving evidence in this case had medical support for their claims of assault. The consequence was that the trial judge concluded that a key medical witness lacked 'professional objectivity' whilst a witness who had the support of three doctors for his claims of injury was said to be 'gilding the lily'. Medical witnesses who discounted complaints of assault were rarely found to be lacking in objectivity – a fine example of 'heads we win and tails you lose' justice.

It also appears that in a number of the cases referred by the Commission, defence lawyers made no attempt, or a half-hearted attempt, to use the legal safeguards then in force, such as Judges' Rules, to exclude confession evidence obtained by coercive methods. It is easy to see how, in an emergency situation, judges would have become impatient of legalistic argument advanced on behalf of terrorist suspects, and that counsel in turn would have avoided antagonising judges by refraining from legal applications for exclusion of evidence that were highly unlikely to succeed. This reality was explicitly recognised in the passage in **Magee**, cited above. It is surely a matter to the credit of the NICA that it has recognised the reality of the situation and has been prepared to revisit legal issues that were glossed over at the time of trial.

That said, it should be noted that other confession cases considered by the Commission have involved suspects who were neither particularly young nor vulnerable and who may well have received training from paramilitary organisations to resist interrogation. It is also clearly the case that the RUC frequently conducted investigations on the basis of covert intelligence information which might have given skilled interrogators basis to undermine prepared alibis. Further, in many cases, the judgments of the Diplock judges express perfectly cogent reasons for accepting the reliability of confession statements. It would, therefore, be going too far to say that all convictions based upon uncorroborated (or thinly corroborated) confession evidence are unsafe. Indeed, the Commission has (on different facts) declined to refer convictions of other applicants convicted of terrorist offences substantially on the basis of confession evidence.

The Commission continues to receive a steady flow of applications to review aged convictions for terrorist offences – mostly emanating from a small number of legal firms. Not all of these applications appear to be well-founded, and indeed many of these applications continue to press on the Commission arguments based on the retrospectivity of the Human Rights Act, notwithstanding that those arguments have been dismissed by the NICA in the cases referred to above.

The Commission, for its part, has to continue to apply itself to the specifics and the detail of individual applications, and it seems more likely than not that further cases comparable with those discussed in this chapter will come to light and be referred in due course.

The NICA, for its part, has shown a pragmatic approach to these cases and has not generally attempted to justify indefensible convictions. Moreover, the Commission, as a body standing outside the sectarian divisions of the Province, has secured respect from all sections of the community. The Commission's referrals in Northern Ireland appear to be a valuable part of its achievement to date.

Notes

1. The Commission also has power to refer sentences, but few NI sentence cases have been the subject of application to the Commission and, during the period of this study, no NI sentence case was referred by the Commission.
2. Now the Police Service of Northern Ireland.
3. (1996) 22 EHRR 29.
4. Confirming a decision of the European Commission on Human Rights.
5. [2004] UKHL 12. *McKerr* went up to the House of Lords on appeal from the Court of Appeal in Northern Ireland. It was ruled (per Lord Nicholls of Birkenhead) that the 'free standing positive obligation of ... far reaching character' which counsel argued could be read in the common law from Convention principles would represent a 'development ... far removed from the normal way the common law proceeds'.
6. (2001) 31 EHRR 822.
7. As a result, prosecutors concluded that statements obtained from Donnelly were inadmissible and proceedings against him were discontinued.
8. The judge – sitting as a tribunal of fact in a Diplock court – was required to give reasons for his verdict, something which a jury is – of course – never required to do.

Chapter 14 - Three further topics – non-disclosure, the impact of the Human Rights Act and the significance of plea

Non-disclosure
The introduction of the Criminal Procedure and Investigations Act
The Commission opened for business on the same day, 1 April 1997, that the new disclosure provisions of the Criminal Procedure and Investigations Act 1996 (CPIA), came into force. Expressed briefly, the CPIA sought to limit the prosecution obligations of disclosure which had been greatly expanded as a result of common law authorities in the early 1990s, particularly the case of *Judith Ward*,[1] which was decided in 1993. The prosecution's obligations to disclose potentially undermining material had previously been quite narrowly defined in the Attorney General's Guidelines published in 1982,[2] but in *Ward*, the Court extended the duty of disclosure to all potentially undermining material held by the prosecution.[3] The obligation was expressed by the Court in the following terms:

> those who prepare and conduct prosecutions owe a duty to the courts to ensure that all relevant evidence of help to an accused is either led by them or made available to the defence ... We would emphasise that 'all relevant evidence of help to the accused' is not limited to evidence which will obviously advance the accused's case. It is of help to the accused to have the opportunity of considering all the material evidence which the prosecution have gathered, and from which the prosecution have made their own selection of evidence to be led.

Ward was open to the possible practical objection that it left no margin for the exercise of judgment by the prosecution, and encouraged a 'kitchen sink' approach to disclosure, which potentially slowed down the process (and increased the cost) of criminal justice, by bogging down both prosecution and defence in consideration of volumes of material of possibly marginal (or no) relevance.

In *Keane*,[4] the Court addressed the question of 'relevance', adopting the following dictum:

I would judge to be material in the realm of disclosure that which can be seen on a sensible appraisal by the prosecution: (1) to be relevant or possibly relevant to an issue in the case; (2) to raise or possibly raise a new issue whose existence is not apparent from the evidence the prosecution proposes to use; (3) to hold out a real (as opposed to fanciful) prospect of providing a lead on evidence which goes to (1) or (2).

Keane obviated the need for the prosecution to disclose material in its possession of no conceivable relevance, but still left uncertainty at the margins about how far the obligation of disclosure extended. The politicians acceded to representations from police and prosecutors that clearer limitations needed to be set upon this obligation and the CPIA was the result.

The CPIA scheme of disclosure is complex but, expressed very briefly, the principal features of the original scheme of disclosure established by the CPIA were as follows:

- The CPIA required initial 'primary disclosure' by the prosecutor of unused material 'which in the prosecutor's opinion might undermine the case for the prosecution against the accused' and which had to be disclosed immediately in the interests of justice and fairness in the particular circumstances of the case.

- Following primary disclosure, the defence was required to produce a written statement setting out in general terms the nature of the accused's defence, and indicating the matters on which it took issue with the prosecution, and the reason for doing so.

- The prosecutor was then called upon to make 'secondary disclosure', that is to say, to disclose to the accused any prosecution material (not previously disclosed) which might be reasonably expected to assist the accused's defence as disclosed by the defence statement.

The CPIA scheme was modified by Part 5 Criminal Justice Act 2003 (the 2003 Act). Again, expressed briefly:

- the duty of primary disclosure was amended to take in any material 'which might reasonably be considered capable of undermining the prosecution case or of assisting the case against the accused' – a formulation which removed the much-criticised reference to the 'prosecutor's opinion' in determining the scope of disclosable material.

- The 2003 Act introduced a continuing duty upon the prosecutor to keep under review the question whether undisclosed material 'might reasonably be considered capable of undermining the case for the prosecution against the accused' and to make disclosure as appropriate – this duty ends only when the accused is either acquitted or convicted.

The 2003 Act also provided for considerably ramped-up obligations in respect of disclosure by the defence.

The CPIA has given rise to concern that significant material, which would have been subject to disclosure under the previous common law regime, may now be withheld. A particular concern has been the role of the prosecutor in determining the scope of disclosure, and particularly the fact that the prosecutor might fail to perceive (or even properly to consider) the exculpatory significance of undisclosed material. The amendments to the CPIA effected by the 2003 Act have improved the legislative test and the statutory provisions must also be considered in conjunction with the detailed (and quite exacting) requirements of the CPS Disclosure Manual.[5] Nevertheless, what the new scheme lacks (and the previous 'kitchen sink' disclosure scheme provided), is an overarching ability for the defence to review the entirety of the material and to make its own judgment as to what undisclosed material is helpful and significant. It has been suggested that in these circumstances the Commission, with its special powers of discovery, might have an important role in uncovering non-disclosure and acting as longstop in cases where lack of disclosure has given rise to miscarriages of justice.

Practical considerations

Three limitations upon the Commission's role have to be noted at the outset. First, the CPIA disclosure regime applies to criminal investigations that started on or after 1 April 1997. Clearly, there is a time-lag between the commencement of the investigation and trial and a further time-lag between trial and appeal. It was never anticipated that non-disclosure cases affected by the CPIA would reach the Commission in any numbers until some years after the CPIA commencement date. However, that is a point which is now of essentially historical interest as the CPIA has been in force for over ten years.

Second, the danger of the CPIA from the perspective of defence practitioners is that since they cannot know what material has been withheld, they are generally in no position to complain about non-disclosure. They are reduced to speculating that there *might* be undisclosed relevant material. This clearly affects applications to the Commission. A lawyer drafting an application to the Commission cannot readily make non-disclosure a ground (or at any rate a principal ground) of application where he or she has no evidence of it.

Third, it would be unrealistic to suppose that the Commission *routinely* combs through all of the unused material to see if there has been any breach of disclosure obligations. While the Commission *sometimes* reviews prosecution files – (including police and forensic files) in toto, this only occurs in a minority of cases. If the Commission were to set out to review all the prosecution material in every case, its output would grind to a virtual halt. There is no certainty, therefore, that the Commission's investigations will pick up non-disclosure where it has taken place. .

This last point needs to be put in perspective bearing in mind the following:

- It is an inherent aspect of the Commission's system of triage that a judgment is made as to which files should be called for in exercise of the Commission's powers under section 17 of the 1995 Act.[6] It has already been noted in chapter 9 that in certain sexual offences cases, files held by the social services departments and the Criminal Injuries Compensation Authority are routinely inspected. The Commission now also routinely interrogates police records for evidence of previous complaints by complainants in sexual cases.

- In all cases, a sensible judgment is taken as to what files might be relevant. To give a particularly straightforward example, if the application raises issues about the forensic evidence requiring investigation it would be the Commission's normal practice to review the files of the Forensic Science Service.

- In 'Category C' cases – described in the Commission's 2006/7 annual report as 'those cases which are likely to require a more time-consuming review and typically where the issues are extensive and complex' – it is the normal practice for the Commission to review at least the police and prosecution files.

In principle, the Commission's processes should, therefore, lead it to take a fair and considered view of the extent of review of prosecution material which it needs to make in any particular case.

Disclosure in pre-Ward cases

In principle, the decision of the Court in *Ward* was declaratory and retrospective – the obligations of disclosure lain upon the prosecution being obligations which, arguably, had always existed, although not previously recognised. In *Brown*[7], decided in 1995, the Court stated that 'today the [Attorney General's] Guidelines do not conform to the law of disclosure in a number of critically important respects'. This opened the possibility that an applicant to the Commission for review of a pre-*Ward* case could argue that his or her conviction was vitiated by breach of the prosecution obligations of disclosure, as currently and correctly understood.

This point featured particularly in the appeal of Jeremy **Bamber**, which was referred on other grounds but in which it was argued (with some force) that the extent of disclosure by the prosecution did not meet modern requirements. The Court set limits on the extent to which it would entertain arguments of this nature:

> We have considered whether any documents were not disclosed which should have been so disclosed. The regime of disclosure in 1986 was very different from now and it may be that under the new regime, some of the documents would have been made available to the defence even though they were not at that date. Our conclusion is that the disclosure given at the time was comparable to disclosure in most major cases in 1986 and that there was no evidence of impropriety or want of care in this regard. In so far as we have identified documents that under the modern regime, or even under the regime operating in 1986, should have been made available to the defence, we have considered whether any of these documents might have had an impact upon the jury's verdicts. For the reasons which we have given in detail in our judgment we conclude that they would not.[8]

This formulation leaves it open to the Court to quash pre-*Ward* convictions on the basis of failure to disclose, and non-disclosure features greatly, for instance, in two of the Commission's capital cases: **Mattan** and **Kelly**. However, in practice, it is likely to be necessary to show (i) that *contemporary* obligations of disclosure were breached, and/or (ii) that a specific 'jury impact' issue arises as a result of the undisclosed material. It is very unlikely indeed that the Court would accede, simpliciter, to the argument that failure to comply with later obligations of disclosure affects the safety of a pre-*Ward* conviction.

Non-disclosure referrals made by the Commission

Non-disclosure has been a feature in many Commission referrals without necessarily being the central referral issue in every case. The following table attempts to identify (not necessarily comprehensively) cases in which non-disclosure has been a major referral issue.

Name	Non-disclosed material	Outcome
Akhtar + 15 others	In 16 controlled delivery cases referred by the Commission (discussed in chapter 10) a central issue was non-disclosure by HMCE of methods used by Customs in connection with controlled importations of heroin from Pakistan.	11 quashed, 5 upheld
Bashir and Khan	Information about relationship between investigating officer and a key witness.	Quashed
Blackwell	Psychological material and police records of false complaints affecting reliability of a complainant in a sexual assault case.	Quashed
Brannan and Murphy	Material showing that the police had information to show that the victim of a shooting, named Pollitt, possessed a gun. The question whether or not Pollitt had been armed with a gun at the time he was shot was a major issue at trial.	Quashed
Broughton	Material on police files pointing to a possible alternative suspect.	Quashed
Brown (Robert)	Failure to disclose the presence of a fibre on the deceased's coat which could be linked to an alternative suspect in a murder trial.	Quashed
C (Martin)	Medical report in a rape case to show that the complainant had been a virgin at a time after C had ceased to have any opportunity to commit the offence.	Quashed
Causley	Material affecting the reliability of evidence given by cell confession witnesses.	Quashed
Craven	Potentially exculpatory forensic exhibit (broken beer glass with fingerprint).	Upheld
Davis, Rowe and Johnson	Information that an important prosecution witness was a police informant.	Quashed
Doubtfire	Unspecified material ordered to be protected from disclosure by virtue of an ex parte PII application.	Quashed

Name	Non-disclosed material	Outcome
Ghuman	HMCE material showing the activities of participating informants.	Quashed
Goren and Harrison	Material (unspecified in appeal judgment) not provided to prosecution counsel or disclosed. Judge's rulings on disclosure might have been different if he had been aware of this material.	Quashed
Gray	Undisclosed PII material considered to raise the possibility that other parties might have committed the index offence. Not considered disclosable by the Court.	Upheld
Guney	As in **Doubtfire** an intelligence report had been withheld from disclosure by virtue of a PII application.	Quashed
Hanna and Hindes	'Sensitive' information tending to exonerate defendants of crime of murder to which they had confessed.	Quashed
Iredale	Scene of Crime photograph (showing situation of bloodstains) which could have been helpful to defence.	Quashed
J	Material to show that the police were aware that J was subject to mental disabilities and, therefore, required the protection of an appropriate adult in police interview.	Quashed
K (Jamie)	Social services material affecting the credibility of the complainant in a rape case.	Quashed
K (Jason)	Previous allegation made by a complainant in a rape case – this had been disbelieved by police and recorded as 'no crime'.	Quashed
Kassar	Withholding of unspecified information. Detailed reasons given in confidential annex.	Quashed
Kelly (George)	A key prosecution witness (fellow prisoner on remand) who stated that K had admitted to the offence of murder had made a previous statement that another person had admitted to this offence.	Quashed
McNamee	In a terrorist case, material to show that other individuals were prime makers of explosive devices – contrary to the Crown's position at trial that M had been the prime maker.	Quashed
Martindale	Key prosecution witness was a police informant and had received payments for such from police – both matters denied by witness when giving evidence.	Quashed

Name	Non-disclosed material	Outcome
Mattan	(i) Inconsistency between prosecution witness's trial evidence and prior witness statement (ii) four witnesses had failed to pick out defendant at identity parade.	Quashed
Millen	Non-disclosure by HMCE of information supporting the case that another suspect could have been responsible for importation of drugs.	Quashed
Rowe (Michael)	Unidentified fingerprints on fire door of premises which could have been fingerprints of true robber.	Upheld
Togher	Extensive non-disclosure by HMCE.	Upheld
Underwood	Previous convictions of prosecution witness.	Upheld
Warren	Records of previous complaints made by a complainant in a rape case – including a complaint disbelieved by police and recorded as 'no crime'.	Quashed
Went	HMCE material showing the activities of participating informants.	Upheld

It should be noted that the causes of non-disclosure in the foregoing list are extremely various, and in some cases it is unlikely that either prosecution or police could be considered culpable in the sense of having set out to withhold disclosable material. A few examples will suffice:

- In **C (Martin)** the critical undisclosed medical report may never have come to the notice of the prosecution.

- In **K (Jason)**, where there was disclosable information held by a different division of the Merseyside police, the Court accepted evidence that there was a failure of co-ordination between different police divisions rather than an intent to withhold information.

- In **Underwood** the convictions of a witness were not disclosed because that witness had succeeded in concealing his true identity from the prosecution.

Other cases appear to lie on the margins of culpability. For instance, in **Warren**, the investigating police force (Somerset and Avon) had some information that the complainant had made complaints of sexual assaults to another force (Northamptonshire). The prosecution made limited disclosure – but they failed to 'dig deeper' in order to elicit the full extent of information affecting the reliability of the complainant's evidence. In **Causley**, the full extent of the previous 'form' of cell confession witnesses (in particular the fact that one of them had given evidence of a very similar alleged confession in an Irish court more than 20 years previously) only came to light as a result of a very exacting investigation by the Commission, and may have been beyond the reasonable diligence of the officers charged with disclosure.

It is, perhaps, fair to say that the only clear-cut modern case of deliberate non-disclosure amongst the Commission cases is **Blackwell**,[9] which will be discussed in greater detail below.

The test applied by the Court in non-disclosure cases

It now appears clear that the Court will apply the **Pendleton** jury impact test to non-disclosure cases and, save in the clearest instances of bad faith, is unlikely to enquire closely into the reasons for non-disclosure. For an example of this approach in a modern case, see the non-Commission case of *Heron*,[10] where the non-disclosed material consisted of various mobile telephone records which – if known – might, arguably, have affected the defence strategy at trial. The Court noted of these records:

> They were not disclosed, so it appears, because they were regarded as "sensitive" and in any event not material to be disclosed because it was not considered that the records might undermine the case for the prosecution. There was no PII hearing and it is our view that the records should have been disclosed. The matter does not on the face of it appear to have been properly considered by the prosecuting authorities, but for reasons that will become apparent it is not necessary to go into that issue. There is no suggestion of bad faith.

The Court's approach to this new material was to conduct a detailed analysis as to how the material could have influenced the defence strategy at trial (and taking account of the tactical constraints affecting the defence stance). Applying the **Pendleton** test, the Court concluded that 'the fresh evidence, however introduced, would not reasonably have affected the decision of the jury to convict'. It declined to admit the fresh evidence and dismissed the appeal.

This is quite a striking conclusion in a case where there was clear evidence of a breach both of CPIA requirements and of the requirement to obtain approval of the trial judge for withholding documentation under claims of Public Interest Immunity – a point discussed further in the following sections. However, the

Court pragmatically confined itself to an analysis of the jury impact of the withheld material. Given the approach adopted by the Court in this and other cases, it is plain that 'jury impact' must be at the forefront of the Commission's consideration of the generality of non-disclosure cases.

Public Interest Immunity (PII)

The Commission's investigations not infrequently take it into the realm of material withheld at the time of trial under claims of PII. The Commission's powers under section 17 of the 1995 Act to require disclosure to it of material by public bodies override all contrary claims of confidentiality, and the Commission is, therefore, entitled to call for PII material, and also for transcripts of PII hearings. The Commission naturally takes extreme care to prevent any disclosure of PII material where the sensitivity that attached to such material remains.[11] On the other hand, where it is satisfied that the material has ceased to be sensitive with the lapse of time, the Commission may disclose it.

In broad terms, the judge may only order that material be protected from disclosure under PII having determined:

- that there would be a real risk of prejudice to an important public interest if disclosure were made; and

- that the fairness of the trial process would not be undermined by the withholding of the material.

It has been stated judicially – see in particular *R v H and C*[12] – that the judge is required to carry out a 'balancing exercise' between the requirement to protect the material and the requirement for a fair trial. The process of establishing a PII claim is fraught with danger, particularly if the judge is not put fully in the picture, as was the case in the London City Bond Cases (*Early* et al) and the Controlled Delivery Cases (**Akhtar** et al) which have been discussed in chapter 10. Another danger, which appeared to arise in **Millen**, is that the judge may be rushed through the PII hearing – being asked to grant PII status to complex documents within minutes of first seeing them – without being given the opportunity to understand fully the context of the PII requests. **Millen** was also an HMCE case and the Commission's experience has been that questionable use of PII was very much a practice associated with HMCE when it was a separate prosecuting authority.

In three cases, **Davis, Rowe and Johnson** (better known as the 'M25 Three'), **Guney** and **Doubtfire**, the central issue leading to the quashing of the convictions was that information withheld from disclosure under PII claims might, if disclosed, have led the jury to reach a different verdict. In a fourth case, **Kassar**, the undisclosed confidential information was never disclosed by the prosecution to their own counsel but would have been subject to a PII claim, had matters got that far! In the case of **Davis, Rowe and Johnson** the undisclosed information (the fact that a witness – one Duncan – had been a police informant) was in the open by the time the appeal was heard, and the judgment therefore contains the Court's assessment of its possible significance. In **Guney**,[13] **Doubtfire**, and **Kassar** the undisclosed information continued to be highly sensitive and the Commission, therefore, set out details in a confidential annex that was provided to the Court and prosecution, but not to the applicant or his lawyer. All three convictions were subsequently quashed due to the non-disclosure of the potentially exculpatory information but the applicants remained unaware of what that information consisted of. This was somewhat frustrating to the applicants but the use of the confidential annex achieved the larger purpose of enabling the Court to review the safety of the convictions.

In **Goren and Harrison**, a Class A drugs case (sentences 14 and 15 years), there was also non-disclosure, although the Crown did not accept that this had been deliberate. The judgment reads as follows:

> The respondent takes the view that the disclosure process at trial was flawed and incomplete. It is conceded that there was unused material which ought to have been reviewed by counsel and was not, and that if it had been so reviewed it would have been placed before the trial judge during the PII application. Inevitably it was not ... In the light of the post-trial reflection on the matter by new counsel ... the respondent takes the view that the material which was not seen by the judge falls into a category of material which may have been discloseable but for a ruling on an application for PII. It cannot be said to be insignificant; nor can it be said that it could not possibly have assisted the defence ... The respondent accepts that this court cannot decide whether or not the trial judge's rulings on disclosure would have been different had all the potentially discloseable material been placed before him. The respondent makes it clear that the outcome may have been precisely the same; but, on the other hand, it may not have been. It is therefore conceded that the Court of Appeal could not reach a decision that the trial judge's rulings would not have been different. For this reason the

> *respondent concedes that the convictions are unsafe. Any different ruling on disclosure may have been capable of affecting the outcome of the trial.*

In **Kassar**, the Court quashed the conviction (Class A drug importation – sentence 24 years) due to the withholding of unspecified material. The Court in its 'open' judgment stated that:

> *The nature of that material, coupled with the fact that that material was not disclosed to prosecuting counsel, or the trial judge, and therefore never assessed by either of them, has led the prosecution to conclude that the only proper course available to it is not to contest this appeal.*

And it quashed the conviction, with its more detailed reasons saved to a confidential annex.

In **Gray**, part of the ground for referral was undisclosed intelligence material, protected by claims of PII, which the Commission considered might have promoted the case that other unconnected local villains could have been responsible for the robbery of which G was convicted. The Court, having reviewed this material, considered that it was not subject to the disclosure requirement, and since it related neither to the index offence nor the offender, G would have been unable to have had it admitted at trial. The fact that general intelligence gathered by the police put other known villains in the frame as possible suspects was not a matter capable of assisting the appellant.

Non-disclosure under the CPIA – the case of Warren Blackwell

Blackwell is the only case to date where it can be stated in clear terms that the disclosure provisions of the CPIA worked to create an injustice.[14] The facts of the case are shocking by any standards. Mr Blackwell, a man of good character was introduced to a woman, S, at a New Year's Eve party at a social club and socialised with her briefly. He was unable in the short time he spoke to S to judge that she was psychologically unstable. Some time later, she apparently suffered a horrific sexual assault (with the use of a metal file) a short distance away from the club and she named Mr Blackwell as her attacker. Mr Blackwell was convicted and was given a sentence of three years' imprisonment, later increased to five years after the Attorney General appealed against the sentence as unduly lenient.

The prosecution had in its possession information about S's psychological history which by any standards raised questions about her reliability as a witness and the CPS sought counsel's advice as to the disclosure of this material. Counsel took the view that since Mr Blackwell's defence statement did not put in issue the fact that S had genuinely been the subject of assault, there was no requirement to disclose either the fact that her medical records revealed psychological instability or that she had previous criminal convictions. As a result, neither Mr Blackwell nor the jury had any reason to doubt the credibility of S's complaint that she had been attacked.

In fact, as the Commission's subsequent enquiries later showed, S had had a lengthy history of wholly spurious complaints and self-harm, including complaints containing striking similarities to her allegations against Mr Blackwell. In this light, it was overwhelmingly likely that the 'attack' was in fact a case of self-harm by S and that Mr Blackwell was wholly innocent of the offence, and the conviction was quashed.

Remarkably, Crown counsel (who appeared both at trial and at Mr Blackwell's appeal that followed reference by the Commission) defended the decision not to disclose the information concerning S. Moreover, the Crown did *not* concede the non-disclosure ground of Mr Blackwell's appeal, and the non-disclosure point was, in fact, not considered by the Court after it was conceded by the Crown that the new information about S made the conviction unsafe.

Subsequently, the Principal Legal Advisor of the Crown Prosecution service wrote to the Commission's chairman as follows:

> *I do not think that the decisions concerning non-disclosure were clear cut ... On the evidence available at the time, I can see how the CPS lawyer and independent leading counsel concluded that [S's previous convictions and medical records] should not be disclosed. For example, the complainant's previous convictions were of some considerable age and it was not unreasonable for the prosecution to form the view that the issue in the case was whether her identification was mistaken and to conclude that the convictions did not satisfy the test for disclosure. One can only speculate as to whether, had that material been available to the defence, they would have explored the issue of self harm. It only later became apparent that the complainant had a substantial propensity to fabricate allegations.*

This reply goes to the heart of the issue that concerned practitioners when the CPIA was introduced. It is perfectly correct that the defence *might* have made nothing of the disclosures had they been made. (They might also have taken the tactical decision that to attack a distressed victim at trial as a lying fantasist would have been excessively risky.) However, the mischief presented by the CPIA was that the defence were never able to explore the issue since they were denied the opportunity to do so by prosecuting counsel's decision that the material did not undermine the prosecution case. It would have been more reassuring if the CPS had accepted that, whilst it is unclear whether or not the information would have been put to any good use by the defence, the case for disclosure was absolutely clear on these particular facts.

Having said this, it must be emphasised that the majority of the non-disclosure cases listed above date from prior to the commencement of the CPIA and that **Blackwell** is the *only* case in the first ten years of the Commission where it has been established that the CPIA has been used to withhold possibly undermining material. Taken on balance, the experience of the Commission would give some support to the conclusion that concerns about the CPIA may have been overstated. It is very much to be hoped, however, that the lessons of this case have been taken to heart.

Impact of the Human Rights Act

The Human Rights Act 1998 (HRA) came into force in October 2000, with the result that the provisions of the European Convention on Human Rights (the Convention) are required to be taken into account by the courts in proceedings following commencement. There has already been discussion at chapter 7 of the Commission's travails in establishing whether the HRA applied in any circumstances with retrospective effect. As that chapter has explained, following the decisions of the House of Lords in **Kansal** and *Lambert,* that question has now been decisively answered in the negative.

There remains the important question, however, as to whether the introduction of Convention rights has substantively affected either the test of safety or the way that the Commission is required to carry out its task. The central issue of concern to the Commission has been whether, and in what circumstances, the right to a fair trial guaranteed by Article 6 of the Convention[15] provides any additional layer of protection to criminal defendants over and above the protections provided by domestic common and/or statute law.

This issue was one of intense interest to criminal practitioners in the period that followed the HRA's commencement, and the submissions made on applicants' behalf at that time almost invariably raised human rights issues. The expectation that HRA issues would assist applicants has greatly subsided in later years for reasons which will become clear.

Two early cases gave some basis for belief that the HRA had shifted the goal posts in favour of appellants to some degree. The first was the case of **Davis, Rowe and Johnson**, already referred to in the previous discussion of Public Interest Immunity. The issue here was that, in a trial occurring in 1990, the status of an informant, named Duncan, was withheld by the prosecution without recourse to the judge. By the time of the first-time appeal, the *Judith Ward* case had been decided, where it was ruled that all PII claims asserted by the prosecution should be considered by the trial judge. The Court hearing the first-time appeal was, therefore, aware that the procedure used for establishing PII in this trial had been incorrect. It nevertheless concluded – considering the case as a whole – that the convictions were safe.

By the time of the second appeal, following referral by the Commission, two of the appellants had received a ruling of the European Court of Human Rights that their right to a fair trial under Article 6(1) of the Convention had been violated due to 'the unfairness caused at the trial by the absence of any scrutiny of the withheld information by the trial judge'. One of the issues in the appeal was whether the clarification of this point affected the safety of the conviction. By this time, the HRA had been passed by Parliament, but had yet to come into effect. The Court stated however:

> We are invited to [give judgment] as if the Human Rights Act 1998 were already in force. We accept the invitation ...

and in so doing laid down dicta of considerable importance which have frequently been cited subsequently by the Court.

On the broader issue, the Court ruled that the issue of *fairness* for the purposes of the Convention and *safety* for the purposes of the Criminal Appeal Act 1968 (as amended by the 1995 Act) are separate and distinct:

> The duty of the ECHR is to determine whether or not there has been a violation of the European Convention or in this case, more particularly, of Article 6(1). It is not within the remit of ECHR to comment upon the nature and quality of any breach or upon the impact such a breach might have had upon the safety of the conviction.

...

> *We are satisfied that the two questions must be kept separate and apart. The ECHR is charged with inquiring into whether there has been a breach of a convention right. This court is concerned with the safety of the conviction. That the first question may intrude upon the second is obvious. To what extent it does so will depend upon the circumstances of the particular case. We reject [the] contention that a finding of a breach of Article 6.1 by the ECHR leads inexorably to the quashing of the conviction. Nor do we think it helpful to deal in presumptions. The effect of any unfairness upon the safety of the conviction will vary according to its nature and degree.*

However, the Court was, in practice, willing to look again at the informant point.[16] It concluded that 'at this distance we simply cannot assess the impact which the undisclosed material might have had on the case' and it quashed the convictions partly on this ground. Whilst the Court very explicitly distanced itself from allowing the appeal on any human rights point, it provided some basis for thinking that a human rights point might bolster an appeal ground.

The other case was the much cited case of **Togher**. Lord Woolf reviewed the case law and concluded:

> *Now that the European Convention is part of our domestic law, it would be most unfortunate if the approach identified by the European Court of Human Rights and the approach of this Court continued to differ unless this is inevitable because of the provisions contained in this country's legislation or the state of our case law. As a matter of first principles, we do not consider that either the use of the word "unsafe" in the legislation or the previous cases compel an approach which does not correspond with that of the ECHR. The requirement of fairness in the criminal process has always been a common law tenet of the greatest importance ... Fairness in both jurisdictions is not an abstract concept. Fairness is not concerned with technicalities. If a defendant has not had a fair trial and as a result of that injustice has occurred, it would be extremely unsatisfactory if the powers of this Court were not wide enough to rectify that injustice. If, contrary to our expectations, that has not previously been the position, then it seems to us that this is a defect in our procedures which is now capable of rectification under section 3 of the Human Rights Act 1998 ... The 1998 Act emphasises the desirability of taking a broader rather than narrower approach as to what constitutes an unsafe conviction. In R –v– Johnson, Davis and Rowe,*

this Court acknowledged that there could still be a distinction between its approach and the approach of the ECHR. However, in the later case of R –v– Francom, *this Court indicated ... that we would expect, in the situation there being considered, that the approach of this Court, applying the test of lack of safety would produce the same result as the approach of the ECHR applying the test of lack of fairness. We would suggest that, even if there was previously a difference of approach, that since the 1998 Act came into force, the circumstances in which there will be room for a different result before this Court and before the ECHR because of unfairness based on the respective tests we employ will be rare indeed.* **Applying the broader approach identified by Rose LJ [in Mullen] we consider that if a defendant has been denied a fair trial it will almost be inevitable that the conviction will be regarded as unsafe.** *Certainly, if it would be right to stop a prosecution on the basis that it was an abuse of process, this Court would be most unlikely to conclude that if there was a conviction despite this fact, the conviction should not be set aside.* (Emphasis added)

However, in reverse of **Davis, Rowe and Johnson**, in this case a favourable dictum on the scope of the human rights argument was followed by an unfavourable ruling on the facts of the instant case. In **Togher**, as in many other Customs cases from this period,[17] a series of convictions for major drug importation offences had been marred by systemic non-disclosure by the prosecuting authority. In the final outcome, T had pleaded guilty to the offences with which he was charged in the light of the weight of evidence against him. Having considered all the relevant facts the Court concluded that, grave as they were:

> *the shortcomings on the part of the prosecution are not of the category of misconduct which would justify interfering with the defendants' freely entered pleas of guilty.*

Compare and contrast *Mullen* – previously discussed in chapter 2 – where the illegal activity of the authorities in abducting the defendant to face trial in the UK put the conviction 'beyond the pale'.

Taken together, **Davis** and **Togher** suggested that whilst a human rights point could not be seen as a trump card, there might be circumstances where it could tip the balance of argument in favour of quashing the conviction. Subsequently however, the direction of legal authority on the argumentation of human rights points (from the perspective of applicants) has all been downhill. An important authority has been the decision of the Privy Council in *Brown*[18] where it was noted as follows:

> *The jurisprudence of the European Court very clearly establishes that while the overall fairness of a criminal trial cannot be compromised, the constituent rights comprised, whether expressly or implicitly, within article 6 are not themselves absolute. Limited qualification of these rights is acceptable if reasonably directed by national authorities towards a clear and proper public objective and if representing no greater qualification than the situation calls for. The general language of the Convention could have led to the formulation of hard-edged and inflexible statements of principle from which no departure could be sanctioned whatever the background or the circumstances. But this approach has been consistently eschewed by the Court throughout its history.*

This decision was followed by the decision of the House of Lords in *Forbes*,[19] in which the Court ruled in very broad terms that not every breach of Article 6 would render a conviction unsafe:

> *Reference was made in argument to the right to a fair trial guaranteed by Article 6 of the ECHR. That is an absolute right. But as the Privy Council pointed out in* Brown *the subsidiary rights comprised within that Article are not absolute, and it is always necessary to consider all the facts and the whole history of the proceedings in a particular case to judge whether a defendant's right to a fair trial has been infringed or not. If on such a consideration it is concluded that a defendant's right to a fair trial has been infringed, a conviction will be held to be unsafe within the meaning of section 2 of the Criminal Appeal Act 1968.*

And in *Dundon*[20] the Court ruled as follows:

> *In many cases, breach of an Article 6 Convention right will result in the quashing of a conviction as unsafe. But that is not necessarily the result in all cases ... In every case the outcome depends on the kind of breach and the nature and quality of the evidence in the case. Just and proportionate satisfaction may, in an appropriate case, be provided, for example, by a declaration of breach or a reduction in sentence, rather than the quashing of a conviction. ... And there may be other exceptional cases in which a conviction may not be unsafe, for example if there has been unfairness because of a legal misdirection but the evidence is overwhelming ... or,*

possibly, if the trial is unfair because of inadequate prosecution disclosure on a peripheral issue but compelling evidence of guilt makes the conviction safe.

In the context of the Commission's deliberations, the impact of a breach of Convention rights has been specifically considered by the Administrative Court in a judicial review case, **Dowsett**, where the Administrative Court gave leave to apply so that it could specifically consider the argument that a ruling of the European Court of Human Rights in favour of the applicant obliged the Commission to refer. In the instant case, the European Court had ruled that the prosecution (in a 1987 trial) had breached the applicant's Convention rights by omitting to disclose a document showing that an important prosecution witness, named Gray, who was on remand at the time of trial, had been transferred to another prison and possibly anticipated more favourable treatment in consequence of his agreeing to give evidence for the Crown.

The Commission followed up the information about Gray's treatment in custody and concluded in its Statement of Reasons as follows:

> *Applying that test [that is the* Pendleton *test] to its referral powers, the Commission can only conclude that Document 580 was a letter showing that Mr Gray was being held in isolation from his co-defendants, that the police were facilitating visits for his wife and that he was hopeful for relatively favourable treatment (compared, at least, to his co-defendants) in terms of his life sentence. In the view of the Commission, this new information, taken in any combination with any other frailties in the prosecution case, is not sufficient to lead the Commission to believe that there is a real possibility that any properly directed jury might reasonably have reached a different decision in Mr Dowsett's case.*

The Court for its part noted that:

> *The Commission undertook further enquiries into Gray's imprisonment and discovered that, despite a recommended tariff of 11 years, he was still in prison. It looked for documents before and after document D580 which might have related to it and it found none ... It considered not only document D580 but also the documents that had been listed in a schedule before the hearing before the Court of Appeal but not disclosed either to the court or to the defence. It did so, because of the Strasbourg Court's ... judgment.*

The Court considered that, on the facts of the case, the Commission was 'plainly entitled to reach the view that it did and so refuse to refer'. As Laws LJ stated in his judgment:

> *Unless the finding by the European Court of Human Rights of a violation of Article 6 necessarily entails the conclusion that the verdict is unsafe, the impact of that finding was for the CCRC to evaluate in the course of their consideration of the section 13(1)(a) question.*

The Commission's approach to human rights cases

The Commission's approach to cases raising human rights issues has been guided by the authorities which are now very clear on the following points:

- That lack of fairness cannot necessarily be equated with lack of safety.

- That not every violation of the defendant's Convention rights – even if established by a judgment of the European Court of Human Rights – necessarily gives rise to the conclusion that the conviction is unsafe.

- That in any case of breach of Convention rights the Commission must apply its mind to the real possibility test in the light of the instant facts.

The approach adopted by the Commission in **Dowsett** nicely illustrates the approach to be taken. It is not possible, due to the constraints of confidentiality, to outline the (many) other cases where the Commission has not referred on the basis of breaches of Convention rights, but the judgment of the Northern Ireland Administrative Court in the reported judicial review case of **Quinn (Dermot)** will provide a further illustration of a case where the Commission did not find that an established violation of the defendant's Convention rights (the holding of an interview in the absence of a solicitor combined with the drawing of adverse inferences) affected the safety of the conviction.

In consequence of the approach required to be taken by the Commission, there have been no cases where the Commission has referred purely on the basis of a human rights point. There have, however, been a number of cases where breaches of Convention rights have been a significant background factor to referral.

Beckles – already referred to in chapter 2 – was a case where B had been made subject to the drawing of an adverse inference due to his failure to mention at police interview matters later relied upon at trial. His argument that he had remained silent in the police station due to acceptance of legal advice was unavailing at his first-time appeal. B applied to the European Court of Human Rights, which ruled that his Convention rights had been breached, noting that it could not 'be overlooked that the solicitor's advice appeared in the record of the police interview and was entirely consistent with the [Appellant's] own explanation for his silence' and that B's reliance on 'new matters' at trial went no further than what he had told his solicitor. The Court of Appeal drew well short of saying that the Convention breach made the conviction unsafe but it is probably fair to say that the Convention point influenced both the decision to refer and the decision of the Court to quash the conviction.

In **Friend**, discussed in chapter 4, a central issue considered by the Commission was the fairness of the trial of a child defendant with learning disabilities, and the Statement of Reasons contained considerable discussion of the significance of the judgment of the European Court in *T and V v UK*[21] (the Jamie Bulger case). However, the significance of this legal argument became eclipsed by very strong psychological evidence that F was incapable of following trial proceedings. When the case came to judgment the Court noted:

> *The sixth ground that the appellant did not receive a fair trial as envisaged by Article 6(3) of the European Convention on Human Rights is also not stressed. Effectively, as we see it, any territory which it could cover would be covered by the other grounds.*

In other words, the Court preferred to deal with the safety of the conviction on the specifics of the case and it steered well clear of the Convention points. Likewise, in the case of **K (Jamie)**, a case involving a 12-year-old defendant, the Court completely sidestepped the Commission's discussion of the significance of the *T and V* case and in quashing the conviction, stuck to the specifics of the instant facts.

In a number of the Northern Ireland cases, discussed in chapter 13, there were clear violations of the Convention rights of defendants. These cases have included **Hanna and Hindes, Adams** and **Mulholland**. The original trials all preceded (by many years) the commencement of the HRA so none of the appellants could argue on the basis of the incorporation of Convention rights into domestic law. Nevertheless, the argument could be made (and was referred to in the respective Statements of Reasons) that the breach of Convention rights was a matter to be taken into account in considering the safety of the convictions. In each case, the Northern Ireland Court of Appeal gave Convention points a wide berth. In **Mulholland**, the Convention point was argued by counsel, but the Court, having concentrated on the facts of the case, concluded:

> *In these circumstances we were driven inexorably to the conclusion that the conviction was unsafe and for the reasons that we have given, we quashed it. We do not find it necessary to address the arguments based on article 6 of the convention.*

Finally, in similar vein, note the Commission's many customs cases entailing variously non-disclosure, 'economical' applications for Public Interest Immunity and use of participating informants. Whilst these cases have raised a number of Convention issues, the Court has always identified other factual grounds for quashing the convictions.

Reflections on human rights cases

The Court of Appeal has, without question, tired of human rights points and has developed its jurisprudence in a way which leaves limited scope for developing free-standing human rights arguments. The judges of the Court of Appeal have had well in mind that the Convention, first adopted in 1950, was effectively a gift from the British tradition of common law and fair trials to a European continent still recovering from the ravages of totalitarianism and war. The Court has often shown limited patience when the Convention principles have been sought to be re-exported to the United Kingdom half a century later as somehow representing fundamentally novel principles of fairness. In these circumstances, it has nearly always called upon common law (or occasionally statutory) principles in dealing with fair trial points, and the Commission has been bound to adopt a similar approach in applying the real possibility test.

The Commission must not, on the other hand, adopt a reflexively dismissive approach to human rights points (even if the Court itself occasionally does so). There will be a small number of occasions when a case that has 'done the rounds' to the European Court of Human Rights or the European Commission will promote further reflection in the Court of Appeal – **Davis, Rowe and Johnson** and **Beckles** being cases in point. The Commission will continue to need to give proper consideration to human rights submissions, even though they are not often likely to be decisive.

The significance of plea

It is clear beyond doubt that a conviction may be referred by the Commission and quashed, irrespective of the fact that the applicant pleaded guilty. The applicant will need to overcome the additional hurdle provided by section 13(2) of the 1995 Act, which provides that the Commission may only refer the conviction of an applicant who has not previously appealed (or applied for leave) if there are 'exceptional circumstances which justify the making of [a reference]'. However, that hurdle is not used to prevent the referral of a meritorious case.

Having said this, in respect of cases tried by the Crown Court, the Court of Appeal long ago in the case of *Forde*[22] proposed the following highly restrictive test in the case of appeals tendered following a guilty plea:

> *A plea of Guilty having been recorded, this Court can only entertain an appeal against conviction if it appears (1) that the appellant did not appreciate the nature of the charge or did not intend to admit he was guilty of it, or (2) that upon the admitted facts he could not in law have been convicted of the offence charged.*

This dictum continues to be cited, albeit the Court has applied it with increasing flexibility, in cases where the defendant's freedom of choice of plea has been constrained by factors outside his or her control. The fullest judicial analysis of the exceptions to the rule in *Forde* is in the Commission's case of **Connolly** of which more shortly.

The cases discussed in more detail below have been cases where the Court has been prepared to exercise flexibility. However, it must first be noted that there have been numerous cases put to the Commission where the applicant has asserted that his or her determination to fight the case at trial was overborne by his or her solicitors and/or counsel insisting upon a plea of guilty. In many cases, intuition most strongly suggests that the applicant (grudgingly or otherwise) accepted advice to earn a discount from sentence by pleading guilty, only to dissent from acceptance of that advice by the time of application to the Commission. The case of **Brine**, which was the subject of a judicial review application against the Commission, is an example of such a case. Such arguments must be dealt with by the Commission robustly where necessary.

The following are instructive cases where the Court has shown flexibility:

John Brown

This case has already been discussed in chapter 10. B's was one of the many cases referred due to the misfeasance of the West Midlands Serious Crimes Squad. The Statement of Reasons articulated the grounds why the Commission considered that members of this squad had used threats to expose B's informant activities, not merely to get a confession from him but also to terrify him into pleading guilty at trial. The Court's judgment substantially reproduced the Commission's analysis of this point. The judgment contains some discussion of the relevant legal authorities, but the Court's decision to allow the appeal rested substantially on the concession by Crown counsel that the safety of the conviction could not be defended in the light of all the known facts.

Connolly

C's appeal was considered as part of the judgment of the Court in **Kelly and Connolly** relating to the Cameo Cinema murders, which took place in Liverpool in 1949. K's case has already been discussed in the homicide cases at chapter 8. In short, the Crown secured convictions against K on two counts of murder substantially on the evidence of a fellow remand prisoner, Graham, who stated that K had confessed to these murders. The Crown failed to disclose the fact that Graham had previously stated that another remand prisoner had confessed to those murders – an appalling case of non-disclosure and miscarriage of justice by any standards.

Connolly was also charged with these murders but was due to be tried separately on 13 February 1950, soon after Kelly's conviction. On that day, he was given the opportunity to plead to new charges of robbery and conspiracy to rob. He pleaded guilty, and was sentenced to ten years' imprisonment. The prosecution offered no evidence on the counts of murder, and the jury were directed to acquit. He served just over six years and died in 1997, the appeal being brought by his widow.

The defence solicitor – approached by Mr Connolly many years later – denied that he or counsel had advised Connolly to plead guilty but stated as follows:

> After Kelly had been found guilty by the jury on his re-trial for murder, Counsel for the Crown informed [defence counsel] that the Prosecution would be prepared to seek the approval of the trial Judge, to the addition to the indictment against you of a charge of robbery. Also, if you were prepared to plead guilty to the lesser charge, the Court would be asked to consent to the murder charge being withdrawn. We were informed that this proposal

had been mentioned to the Judge who had indicated his approval of the matter proceeding in that way.

The reality, therefore, was that the Crown, having unfairly and unjustly obtained a conviction against Kelly for offences of which both defendants were in all probability wholly innocent[23] – offered Connolly the choice between a guilty plea to robbery or the likelihood of the death sentence. The Court – in a somewhat dry judgment – conducted an exhaustive review of the authorities before concluding as follows:

> *undue pressure or errors of law or unfairness in the trial process may all be of such an important causative impact on the decision to plead guilty that the conviction which follows on such a plea can, in an appropriate case, be described as unsafe. In our judgment such is this case. Ultimately, as the authorities emphasise, it is a question of fact in each case.*

Holliday

Holliday confessed and pleaded guilty to two robbery offences. In the case of one of these offences, there was no new evidence, in the Commission's view, to throw doubt on the safety of the conviction.[24] However, in respect of the other offence, there came to light the clearest evidence that another man, named Elener, had committed the offence and that Mr Holliday had had nothing whatever to do with it. Apart from Elener's guilty plea, dispassionate analysis showed that elements of Holliday's confession were so clearly wrong that the police might, on reflection, have paused to consider whether the confession was reliable. It appeared that the confession was the product of bravado and fantasy on Mr Holliday's part. The Court was willing in these circumstances (and without discussion of legal authorities) to allow the appeal notwithstanding the previous guilty plea.

Bargery

Bargery was a university student who had obtained summer employment as a security guard at a Butlins holiday camp. He was charged with affray together with a Mr Craggs (C) after a complaint that they had ejected some trouble-makers with undue force. Shortly before trial, the Crown offered a lesser charge of threatening behaviour (s4 Public Order Act 1936) in return for a guilty plea but B told his counsel that he would resist this charge and establish his innocence. It was at this point that things started to go awry.

- First, C told his counsel that he was prepared not only to accept this deal but to assist his own position further by giving evidence against Mr Bargery.

- Second, the judge held a meeting with both counsel in chambers (without a transcript being taken), in which he offered a non-custodial sentence if there were guilty pleas to the section 4 offence but specifically declined to give any such indication if B insisted on standing trial.

This put tremendous pressure on B, who would certainly have lost his university place if sent to prison, and after discussion with his girlfriend he decided to plead guilty to the lesser offence. He was made subject to a Community Service Order and costs and trial counsel's attendance note recorded that he 'appeared to be happy with this outcome'. This also appeared to be counsel's view when taxed by the Commission for his recollection of the case.

The case suggested, putting it mildly, that the Court's invocations against plea-bargaining had not been heeded. Trial judges had been instructed by the Court not to have untranscribed discussions with counsel in chambers concerning sentence and not to offer trade-offs of this kind, but both things had palpably occurred in this case.

There is further interest in this case as to what passed at the appeal hearing that followed the Commission's referral.[25] By the time the appeal came up for hearing, the Court had decided the case of *Nazham and Nazham*,[26] another case where the trial judge had lent himself to a wholly irregular plea bargain. In that case, the Court identified the need for an appellant to show not only that there was an irregularity in the judge's room, but also that the irregularity brought about his subsequent change of plea. In *Nazham and Nazham*, the Court concluded that the first appellant had 'willingly exercised' his choice to plead guilty (and obtain a much shorter sentence), only changing his mind after release from prison. At the appeal hearing, as their Lordships pontificated about B's case, the Court indicated that they felt the case was on all fours with *Nazham and Nazham*. It was at this point that Mr Bargery, present in Court for the appeal and seeing the way things were going, shouted out: 'It wasn't like that at all, you weren't there'. There was an embarrassed silence and a pause for counsel to obtain further instructions before judgment was given. After hearing further submissions the Court finally went on to conclude:

> *... we notice that after the second meeting it took some deliberation and discussion with his girlfriend before he decided to accept the offer. He did so, it seems to us therefore, at that stage rather than in advance or independently; and he did so in circumstances where there were on the table facts which put in front of him a stark choice: fight the affray case, lose and you are going to go to prison, or, accept a plea to section 4, which the Crown Prosecution Service have been suggesting, and you will avoid prison.*

> *That was a choice which, however it came about that it was offered, and as [we] have outlined the circumstances, should not have been one which was put before him.*

And it quashed the conviction. It seems likely that the Court had been on the brink of finding against Mr Bargery and no doubt had it done so its conclusions on the facts would have been quite different!

This description of an unusual appeal hearing is offered to illustrate a point which all experienced advocates well understand: that a Court's findings upon points of fact are frequently nuanced to reflect whatever legal decision it has decided to reach. This emphasises that the Commission's research should always be thorough and its Statements of Reasons should establish a clear and cogent account of the relevant facts. The outcome of Mr Bargery's appeal appears to have been a just one, but it was a very close shave!

Guilty pleas in magistrates' court cases

As discussed in chapter 11, appeals against summary convictions result in a rehearing of the case in the Crown Court, not a review of safety. The decision of the Court of Appeal in *Forde* goes only to the practice of the Court of Appeal, albeit such authority as exists suggests that a Crown Court in its appellate capacity would generally be extremely unlikely to allow an appeal against a summary conviction passed following a plea of guilty.

This issue has come up three times in the Commission's jurisprudence – in the cases of **F (Mark)**, **Abwnawar**, and **Muff**. The facts of the case of **F (Mark)** have been quite fully set out in chapter 11. In that case the defendant, then aged 16, had clearly been denied legal advice and had effectively been harried into a guilty plea as an alternative to being imprisoned as a sex offender. In considering how to deal with the guilty plea, the Court set out the following principles:

1. *The entering of a plea of guilty before a court is not a formality. Most defendants understand that by their plea they admit their guilt before the court ...*

2. *The power to permit a change of plea should be used sparingly and then only when there are clear, cogent and compelling reasons making clear that the interests of justice require the matter to be re-opened ...*

3. *The mere fact that the plea was entered years ago is not, either in itself or in combination with any other circumstance, a reason to doubt its reliability ...*

4. *The fact that the files have now been lost or destroyed is not ... a reason to doubt the reliability of the plea entered ...*

5. *The fact that the defendant continues to protest his innocence after 18 years, is not in itself any reason to doubt the validity of the plea.*

6. *Nor is it a reason to set aside a plea that a defendant was given robust advice that the evidence against him was strong and that a lesser sentence will be passed in the event of a guilty plea; nor that he felt under some pressure at the time ...*

7. *[In summary] the court must be keen to examine the application with particular care and circumspection whilst at the same time avoiding an inflexible rule that such an application can never succeed, for quite obviously there are cases where the interests of justice require that a plea of guilty may be vacated, even after many years. To hold otherwise would be to undermine the whole basis on which the Criminal Appeal Act 1995 was passed. If an injustice has occurred, it is not righted by the passage of time. If we were to come to the conclusion that as a result of oppression or unfairness the appellant was deprived of a real, free and voluntary choice of plea, so that an injustice resulted, then that plea should be set aside. To put it shortly: is it an affront to justice that the plea should be allowed to stand?*

And it ruled that the guilty plea, on the facts, was not a bar either to the Court giving full consideration to the merits of the appeal or to the ultimate success of the appeal.

The dicta summarised above were drawn to the attention of the Court and adopted in **Abwnawar,** where the Court concluded that 'the burden was on the appellants to apply to change their guilty pleas'. In that case, the four appellants pleaded guilty, being unaware that the special defence under s31(8) Immigration and Asylum Act 1999 was available to them.[27] The Court concluded that they had discharged the burden of establishing that their guilty pleas should be vacated on the specific facts.

In **Muff,** M's guilty plea was mistakenly made due to the complexity of modern sentencing legislation. He was charged with violating a lifetime ban on possession of a firearm. However, having successfully had his earlier sentence (for a firearms offence) reduced on appeal from four years to three, one of the preconditions for the making of a lifetime ban had fallen – a point missed by all concerned at the time of trial. The Court was prepared in these circumstances to allow the appeal, notwithstanding the previous guilty plea.

Whilst the dicta set out in **F (Mark)** are not in any sense binding, they appear clear and sensible. Moreover it seems likely that the Commission will cite these dicta in future referrals of summary convictions that have followed guilty pleas. They, therefore, provide a useful guideline as to how the Commission is likely to approach such cases.

Notes

1. [1993] 1 WLR 619.
2. [1982] 1 All ER 734.
3. This term here includes not only the police and CPS but also any other agencies of government (such as the Forensic Science Service) connected with the investigation or the prosecution.
4. [1994] 1 WLR 746.
5. www.cps.gov.uk/legal/section20/chapter_a.html.
6. See chapter 1 for a summary of the Commission's section 17 powers.
7. [1995] 1 Cr App R 191.
8. The above citation is drawn from the Court's summary judgment given on 12 December 2002.
9. Some other of the post-CPIA cases *may* entail deliberate non-disclosure but there appear to be shades of doubt about the degree of deliberation.
10. [2005] EWCA Crim 3245.
11. The Commission must, of course, bear in mind its own obligations of disclosure – that is to say to disclose to applicants any material which would enable them to make their best case against a provisional decision not to refer – see *R v Secretary of State for the Home Department ex p Hickey and Others (No 2)* [1995] 1 All ER 489. In a very few cases the Commission finds itself in possession of sensitive material which it feels it needs to disclose in accordance with the terms of the *Hickey* judgment. Thus far, the Commission has always found it possible to

disclose the gist of the material (which the *Hickey* judgment permits) in a way which avoids disclosure of sensitive information.

12. [2004] UKHL 3.

13. Mr Guney's case is discussed in chapter 10.

14. Disclosure in Mr Blackwell's case followed the requirements of the original CPIA scheme, that is to say, prior to the amendment of the CPIA by the 2003 Act. Disclosure *might* have been dealt with in a more satisfactory manner had the 2003 Act been in force but the matter is not free from doubt.

15. Article 6 reads as follows:

> *ARTICLE 6 RIGHT TO A FAIR TRIAL*
>
> *1 In the determination of his civil rights and obligations or of any criminal charge against him, everyone is entitled to a fair and public hearing within a reasonable time by an independent and impartial tribunal established by law. Judgment shall be pronounced publicly but the press and public may be excluded from all or part of the trial in the interest of morals, public order or national security in a democratic society, where the interests of juveniles or the protection of the private life of the parties so require, or to the extent strictly necessary in the opinion of the court in special circumstances where publicity would prejudice the interests of justice.*
>
> *2 Everyone charged with a criminal offence shall be presumed innocent until proved guilty according to law.*
>
> *3 Everyone charged with a criminal offence has the following minimum rights:*
>
> *(a) to be informed promptly, in a language which he understands and in detail, of the nature and cause of the accusation against him;*
>
> *(b) to have adequate time and facilities for the preparation of his defence;*
>
> *(c) to defend himself in person or through legal assistance of his own choosing or, if he has not sufficient means to pay for legal assistance, to be given it free when the interests of justice so require;*
>
> *(d) to examine or have examined witnesses against him and to obtain the attendance and examination of witnesses on his behalf under the same conditions as witnesses against him;*
>
> *(e) to have the free assistance of an interpreter if he cannot understand or speak the language used in court.*

16. There were also many other issues in this appeal.

17. It should be noted, incidentally, that this was a pre-CPIA investigation.

18. [2001] 2 WLR 817.

19. [2001] 2 WLR 1.

20. [2004] EWCA Crim 621.

21. (2000) 30 EHRR 121.

22. [1923] KB 400.

23. The Court of Appeal – which generally eschews pronouncing on such matters – stated that the Cameo Cinema murders must be regarded as an 'unsolved crime' in the light of the information that emerged at this appeal.

24. Although H's counsel sought unsuccessfully at the appeal which followed the Commission's referral to put the safety of this second conviction in issue.

25. I am grateful to my former colleague, Felix Robinson, for this account.

26. [2004] EWCA Crim 491.

27. The substantive issue has been briefly discussed in chapter 11.

Chapter 15 - Reflections

Evaluation of the success or failure of an institution such as the Commission is not really a matter for an insider who may lack perception of its shortcomings and may be implicated in its failures. The following personal reflections are offered, therefore, with proper (and genuine) diffidence.

Achievements and threats

The overarching achievement of the Commission has been to establish itself as a genuinely independent body committed to carrying out what it was set up to achieve – the investigation and referral of unsafe convictions to the Court of Appeal.[1] The Commission has always sought to investigate cases brought to it without preconceptions and without any political or institutional inhibitions. The Commission takes satisfaction, at both the collective and individual level, each time a well-reasoned referral is made to the Court of Appeal. If the legal or factual premises of the referral challenge received legal or institutional wisdom, the satisfaction of the referral is perhaps all the greater. The Commission was set up as an independent body, it will be recalled, because the Runciman Commission (as well as JUSTICE and many others) considered that the investigation of miscarriages of justice by a part of the executive branch of government created an irreconcilable tension. The Commission, notwithstanding all that follows, has thus far maintained the independence of thought and action that the Runciman Commission intended that it should bring to bear.

The number of cases referred has increased approximately four-fold since the Commission assumed responsibility for reviewing miscarriages. Department C3 referred, typically, ten cases per year. The referrals by the Commission over the first ten years have run as follows:

Year	Referrals	Year	Referrals
1997-8	11	2002-3	35
1998-9	31	2003-4	29
1999-2000	36	2004-5	45
2000-1	45	2005-6	47
2001-2	38	2006-7	39

It will be noted that the rate of referrals has not abated as a result either of the harsher 'post-**Pendleton**' approach to new evidence cases; or the more robust approach taken by the Court to appeals based upon technical irregularities; or the working through of the older pre-PACE cases, which accounted for some of the earlier referrals. The fact that the rate of referrals has held up in these circumstances suggests that the Commission, far from being a compliant institution, has been ruggedly – even obdurately – independent.

It may indeed be the case that this independence of approach has contributed to the Commission's current problems. At present, both the breadth of the Commission's remit and the effectiveness of its activities are in severe danger of becoming undermined, with the threats emanating both from the executive and the judicial branches of government. These threats are four-fold:

First, the Commission has had to endure a difficult relationship with its sponsoring unit: the Office for Criminal Justice Reform (OCJR).[2] The OCJR formerly sat in the Home Office but has been transferred to the Ministry of Justice following the Departmental demerger promoted by John Reid in 2007, albeit without any noticeable immediate change of ethos. The Commission is in an unusual position in that generally, when government devolves functions to an independent agency or quango,[3] the sponsoring ministry views the activities of the hived-off body as desirable, or at least as a necessary evil, even if politicians no longer wish to be answerable for them. The position of the Commission may be different because it has sometimes appeared that the sponsoring unit regards the Commission as an *unnecessary* evil, and this view seems firmly to reflect the current political zeitgeist. This has been an uncomfortable relationship for all concerned, and the Commission has had to endure quite obtrusive regulation involving cuts in funding; reductions in the number and role of Commissioners; and persistent criticisms at times of aspects of the way it performs its business.[4] It must be conceded that the Commission was generously funded in its early years, and that it has been not unreasonable for the OCJR to seek some economies in its operation. What is not acceptable is that a body, such as the Commission, with a critical/review function in relation to the criminal justice system, should be regulated by its sponsoring department from a spirit of underlying hostility – which has sometimes appeared to be the position.[5] The Chairman's foreword to the 2006-7 annual report[6] should perhaps be read in this light.[7]

Second, the executive has clearly shown that it is willing to use legislation to pare down the remit of the Commission, although there is some room for debate as to what extent the provisions of the Criminal Justice and Immigration Bill, discussed earlier at chapters 2, 6 and 7, were brought forward *primarily* to clip the Commission's wings.

Third, the judiciary has also imposed its own limitations upon the Commission (without any assistance from politicians). For example:

- The Commission's remit to deal with sentences was emasculated at a very early stage in the cases of **Graham** and **Robery**.

- The Commission's remit to deal with change-of-law cases has been fiercely attacked in **Cottrell and Fletcher**.

- The Commission has received negative feedback from the Court in a number of referrals, most notably **Day**, based on arguments of legal incompetence.

- The Court has given the Commission very strong indications against referral of old capital cases in **Knighton** and **Ellis**.

- The Court has sought to place limitations on no new evidence/lurking doubt referrals in cases such as **Thomas (Ian)** and **Stock**.[8]

Finally, in new evidence cases, the Court has hauled back the House of Lords' decision in **Pendleton** to a position where it appears to have given itself *more* freedom of action to deprecate the significance of new evidence rather than less, contrary to the clear intention of the majority of their Lordships in **Pendleton**. A senior member of the Court has also gone to the lengths of (discreetly) advising the Commission to be cautious about following the majority opinion in **Pendleton**.[9] There must be concern that some divisions of the Court of Appeal are ready to take a somewhat robust view of the 'jury impact' test, the judgment of Moses LJ in the case **L (Stuart)** being a particularly clear example.

It may be the case that the combined impact of these onslaughts will be inexorably to reduce the scale of the Commission's activities and the number of its referrals. There is without doubt a school of thought both within the executive and judicial branches of government that that might be no bad thing!

The following personal observations are put forward for consideration with this somewhat challenging background position in mind.

Is the Commission still required to perform the task for which it was established?

This question needs to be asked because the legal landscape has changed so much since the unravelling of miscarriages of justice of the 1970s and 1980s engendered the appointment of the Runciman Commission and the establishment of the Commission.

The Runciman Commission was set up after it had become clear that the 'criminal justice system' – taken in its widest sense – had acted indefensibly in seeking to uphold the convictions of the Birmingham Six in the face of mounting evidence that those convictions could not sensibly be defended. However, the original convictions of the Birmingham Six were the product of procedures which had already been overhauled by PACE by the time the Commission was established. Moreover, it is now improbable that any conviction based on confessions that were the product of oppression, violence and 'verbals' would now be sought by the Crown Prosecution Service, let alone succeed if brought to court. The introduction, through PACE, of tape-recorded interviewing of suspects; the implementation of the Codes of Practice; and the overhaul of procedures for pre-trial disclosure following the *Ward* and *Keane* cases, have together transformed the landscape of criminal procedure. It must, therefore, be conceded that much of the 'background noise' which informed the establishment and the deliberations of the Runciman Commission is now of predominantly historical interest.

Tony Blair, in a speech given in 2004, captured the political perspective that it was time to 'move on' in analysing what was in need of change in the criminal justice system:

> All through the 1970s and 1980s, under Labour and Conservative Governments, a key theme of legislation was around the prevention of miscarriages of justice. Meanwhile, some took the freedom without responsibility. The worst criminals became better organised and more violent. The petty criminals were no longer the bungling but wrongheaded villains of old, but drug pushers and drug abusers, desperate and without any residual moral sense. And a society of different lifestyles spawned a group of young people who were brought up without parental discipline, without proper role models and without any sense of responsibility to or

*for others ... here, now today, people have had enough of the 1960s [sic]
consensus.*[10]

The agenda of the government's policy under successive Home Secretaries[11]
has been concerned with 'rebalancing' the focus of the criminal justice system
away from the interests of suspects toward those of victims. In July 2006, the
Home Office issued a consultation paper ambitiously titled *Rebalancing the
criminal justice system in favour of the law-abiding majority. Cutting crime, reducing
reoffending and protecting the public*[12] in which, following a foreword in much the
same vein by Tony Blair, the then Home Secretary, John Reid, wrote as follows:

> *Our criminal justice system, a product of history and piecemeal change,
> has developed in an uneven way. Its unfairness and savagery in Victorian
> times, for example, led to a priority being placed on extra safeguards for the
> accused. These rights are of vital importance. But at times they can now
> seem to overshadow the rights of the victim and the public at large.*
>
> *The immediate improvements we have put in place have given us the
> breathing space needed for a fundamental examination of how the criminal
> justice system is working and, in particular, whether the rights of the
> accused and those of the victim and the community are correctly balanced.
> The reforms and operational changes in this document are the result of this
> thorough audit of the entire system to ensure that we get this balance right.*

What is clear from these pronouncements is that, politically at any rate, the
Commission has a case to answer in terms of defending its relevance, and in
defending the charge that it makes upon public expenditure.[13] The case for the
defence should certainly include at least the following elements:

Expert evidence cases

Whilst many of the causes of miscarriage which occasioned the Commission's
formation have been largely eliminated, new causes of miscarriage have
emerged or have become better appreciated. Foremost among emerging causes
of concern has been the occasional shortcomings of expert evidence. The
Commission's cases have covered instances where:

- the expert science has been questionable (such as the **O'Doherty**
  auditory recognition case);

- the expert's competence has been in question (such as, among others, **Assali** (an explosives expert), **Bacchus** (a facial recognition expert), and **Boreman and Byrne** (a pathologist);

- the expert's objectivity and/or the fairness of his or her evidence has been the subject of criticism (such as **B (Kevin)**, Sally **Clark**);

- the expert case has been marred by non-disclosure (Sally **Clark**, **C (Martin)**);

- the strength of the inferences that can be drawn from the expert evidence has been overstated at trial (such as **McNamee** – fingerprint evidence; **Faulder** – shaken baby evidence; **Kempster** – ear print evidence);

- the expert has drawn unwarranted inferences from the observed facts (such as **F (Reginald)**, and **B (David)** – both involving evidence about the forensic significance of features of the complainant's bodily organs);

- the prosecution case has not been properly tested because the defence expert either lacked appropriate specialist qualifications or failed to give sufficient time to making a proper assessment (such as in the diminished responsibility cases of **Ashton** and **F (M)**).

The diverse range of circumstances leading to shortcomings of expert evidence strongly suggests that the *possibility* of error is systemic rather than isolated. Moreover, as expert science continues to develop, the problem does not diminish. Inevitably, the Crown will seek to put 'cutting edge' expert evidence to the service of convicting suspected criminals. It is inevitable, therefore, that experts will sometimes act and testify at the margins of their competence and of the knowable. Anyone with an interest in this subject should study with care the full judgment in the shaken baby case of **Faulder**.[14] Reading the judgment in this case, it is clear that the trial juries were assailed with the evidence of a battery of experts on all sides, all tendered to show that a jury could – or could not – have been certain that the babies had suffered death or injury due to shaking. What is also clear from the Court of Appeal judgment is that by the time these cases came to appeal the Crown no longer expressed confidence in many of the expert opinions given on its behalf at the respective trials and no longer sought to rely upon them.[15]

The case of Barry **George**, which was heard outside the period considered in this study, very clearly shows the possibility that experts will draw false positive conclusions from forensic evidence and that reservations will not be exposed to the jury.

The Commission has a particularly important continuing role in review of expert cases whether its investigations are prompted by fresh investigative evidence, concerns about individual experts, change in scientific consensus or other matters.

Witness reliability cases

It is an oft-repeated mantra of the Court of Appeal that it is for the jury to assess the reliability of witnesses – having seen and heard them give evidence and assessed the weight to be given to it. The Court of Appeal itself does not have this facility.[16] The Commission's investigations have shown that in a number of cases there may be concerns respecting the reliability of witnesses which juries could not have appreciated. In some cases, such as **A (Derek)** and **K (Jamie)**, important new evidence has been obtained through examination of social services files. In **Warren, Blackwell, K (Jason)** and **Carrington-Jones** there has been information to show that complainants have had a pattern of behaviour which would have undermined their credibility if known to the jury. In **H (J)**, there was evidence to show that a witness must have confabulated memories from early childhood. In **Brooke and Siddall** and **P (Ricardo)** there was evidence of enlarged and contradictory allegations in criminal compensation claims made by witnesses whose credibility lay at the heart of the prosecution case. In **Brooke and Siddall** and **B (Ernest)** there was evidence of additional (and somewhat implausible) allegations made by complainants that were never before the jury. All of the above cases were the outcome of active investigation by the Commission, using its statutory powers to interrogate public files – taking investigations in directions which would never even have been contemplated by the Home Office before the Commission's inception.

There is also the case of **Solomon** where the adventitious discovery of a videotape provided irrefutable evidence that young complainants in a trial for rape and buggery had given a knowingly false account of S's conduct.

All of these cases – it should be added – were convictions for sexual offences. There can scarcely be a worse miscarriage of justice than to be falsely accused of a sexual offence, treated as a 'nonce' in prison, and then to appear on the Sex Offenders Register with the real danger of unemployability or vigilantism. It is important, pace the sentiments of Tony Blair quoted above, that a 'rebalancing' criminal justice agenda does not blind political leaders to the possibility of miscarriages of such kind occurring in the future.

Healing miscarriages from the past

As chapters 6 and 13 in particular have sought to show, the Commission has been able to secure redress for a significant number of applicants both in England and Wales and in Northern Ireland who were victims of miscarriages of justice in the years preceding PACE. These cases have mostly concerned convictions of vulnerable young men who were sentenced to immensely long periods of imprisonment on the basis of coerced confession evidence. The subjects of these miscarriages were still in mid-life at the time that their convictions were quashed following referral by the Commission. In the Northern Ireland cases, the quashing of convictions has provided not merely redress for the individuals but an important acknowledgement of the shortcomings of a harsh interrogation regime introduced in the face of terrorist violence. Whilst such cases will inevitably become fewer in number with the passing of time it is, surely, desirable that the Commission should be available to provide redress for such unjust convictions.

Executive malfeasance

The Commission came into being at a time when customs cases were still prosecuted and investigated by a single 'unitary' authority – Her Majesty's Customs and Excise. In the ensuing years a series of cases has revealed endemic problems of malpractice within HMCE, including non-disclosure, misuse of participating informants and, on occasion, the active promotion of criminality in the interests of law enforcement. The extent of malpractice has, unfortunately, made a number of convictions achieved for very serious offences legally indefensible.

The Commission has played a significant role in bringing to light malpractice, particularly in 'controlled delivery' cases. The Commission's investigations contributed to the acceptance on the part of government that customs prosecutions needed to be placed in the hands of an independent prosecuting authority. This has now been brought about through the establishment of the Revenue and Customs Prosecuting Office (RCPO) by the Commissioners for Revenue and Customs Act 2005.

It is clearly the case that governments of all colours have had a commitment to combat corruption and malfeasance when it comes to light. Indeed, the establishment of the RCPO as an independent prosecution authority is a case in point. However, progress towards institutional propriety and transparency does not always proceed in a straight line and standards can regress as well as advance. This point is illustrated by the eruption of corrupt practice in the Flying Squad at Rigg Approach many years after the problem of such corruption had been highlighted by the former Metropolitan Police Commissioner, Sir Robert Mark – among others. If it is accepted, realistically, that malpractice within the police and prosecution is unlikely ever to be permanently eradicated, it would follow that the Commission has a continuing role in investigating miscarriages arising due to such malpractice.

The dangers of rebalancing

The comments of Tony Blair and John Reid – quoted above – are exemplars of a government pursuing an explicit agenda of paring down safeguards (as well as legal aid budgets) afforded to defendants and refining legislation to facilitate effective prosecution and condign punishment. Mr Blair and Mr Reid have, of course, since moved on and responsibility for criminal justice has shifted from the Home Office to the Ministry of Justice. However, the rebalancing agenda initiated by Mr Blair and Mr Reid appears to have survived the transfer of policy responsibility to the Ministry of Justice. By way of example, the Criminal Justice and Immigration Act 2008, sponsored by the Ministry of Justice, contains a number of provisions based on 'rebalancing' policy proposals originally launched by John Reid.

It is part of the continuing requirement for the Commission that it should act as a 'long stop' when the programme of reforming, or if you prefer rebalancing, the criminal justice legislation has unforeseen or pernicious consequences. Three quite disparate examples will illustrate this point:

In **Warren** (see chapter 9) – a case where the jury were unaware that the complainant had a history of making allegations of sexual offences – the defence had some knowledge that the complainant had previous 'form' in this matter, albeit not to the extent that was later established by the Commission. The defence sought to cross-examine the complainant about her previous sexual *allegations* but the judge disallowed this line of questioning in exercise of his powers under s41 Youth Justice and Criminal Evidence Act 1999, which permits the judge to protect a complainant from being cross-examined about her previous sexual *conduct*. Had the complainant been subject to cross-examination in this case, there is every possibility that Mr Warren would not have been wrongfully convicted and imprisoned. This was a clear case where legislation, designed with the entirely laudable aim of alleviating the ordeal faced by complainants in rape trials, operated in a way which created obvious injustice to the defendant.

In **Blackwell** (see chapter 14) the prosecution failed to disclose information which could have thrown light on the mental instability of the complainant in an indecent assault case. The prosecution took the view that the obligations placed on them by the Criminal Procedure and Investigations Act 1996 did not require them to make disclosure touching on a matter that was not put specifically in issue by the Defence Statement. This was, therefore, a case where a 'rebalancing' statute – aimed to ease the burden upon the prosecution of preparing for trial – led to clear and obvious injustice.

In **Offen** (see chapter 12) and a number of subsequent cases, the subject was the 'two strikes and you're out' legislation – originally the Crime (Sentences) Act 1997 but later re-enacted in the Powers of the Criminal Courts (Sentencing) Act 2000. The Act was intended to ensure that offenders convicted of certain repeat serious offences would be subject to an automatic life sentence. It quite quickly became clear that the legislation caught offenders who could not sensibly be characterised as the kind of dangerous violent individuals with which it was designed to deal, and a number of life sentences were substituted by determinate sentences following references by the Commission. This example has particular resonance as recent governments have shown great penchant for rigid and prescriptive sentencing legislation which may work extremely unjustly in circumstances unforeseen by legislators.

The foregoing examples are just that – *examples* – to show that miscarriages of justice require review even when the most egregious causes of miscarriage that existed in the past no longer apply. Tony Blair's speech quoted above implies that an agenda for the protection of victims requires the curtailment of safeguards or process for the defendant. It is hoped that this discussion will support the conclusion that this is a simplistic and unjustifiable approach.

Has the Commission been sufficiently concerned with genuine 'miscarriages of justice'?

Notwithstanding all that is said above, there remains a case to answer that in pursuing the issue of the *safety* of convictions brought before it, the Commission has, at times, given undue consideration to technical legal considerations in its investigations and referrals. However, the fact that there is such a 'case to answer' is not necessarily a reproach upon the Commission, for two main reasons.

First, the Commission must apply the legislation as it has been enacted, and the 1995 Act unquestionably confers upon the Commission power to refer all *unsafe* convictions, be they unsafe on technical-legal, or factual-evidential grounds. If the Commission had declined 'technical' applications as not meriting its attention this would assuredly have been an unwarranted restriction by it in carrying out its statutory remit, and as such be subject to attack by way of judicial review.

Second, it can be argued that the safeguards of due process established by law are indivisible, and that any person denied due process (such as an appropriate summing up of the relevant law and facts to the jury) has been the victim of a miscarriage of justice. At any rate, it seems wrong in principle that the Commission, acting in its gatekeeper capacity, should as a matter of course deny an appeal to an applicant of a possibly unsafe conviction merely because the appeal raises legal rather than evidential issues.

Most of the Commission's 'technical' referrals have been occasioned either by an error in the summing up or by a changed understanding of the law. Many such cases, indeed, raise both considerations – an error in the legal directions to the jury which has come to light[17] due to a changed understanding of the law. Among such cases have been the post-*Morgan Smith* provocation cases discussed in chapter 8 and the cases relating to the inferences from silence, discussed in chapter 2.

It would be simplistic to draw up any hard and fast approach to the question whether or not summing up/change-of-law cases represent miscarriages of justice. Some of the cases represented by the Commission lack any intrinsic appeal to one's sense of justice. Some cases, on the other hand, do raise genuine concerns as to possible injustice. These include **Mair** (chapter 7 – summing up on foresight of joint enterprise); **Rowland** (chapter 8 – availability of provocation defence); and **Sheehan** (chapter 7 – belief of age of complainant in indecent assault case). It is not a straightforward task to insert a surgical knife to separate 'meritorious' and 'unmeritorious' referrals based upon legal considerations.

Nevertheless, it is arguable that the Commission has in some instances veered to a more technical approach to the question of safety than has strictly been required. It would seem that some of the Commission's referrals of inference-from-silence cases in particular have strained to the limit the *Stirland* test as to whether a correctly directed jury could conceivably have reached a different verdict. It is, in any event, quite a long step from the redress of the kind of miscarriages of justice which prompted the formation of the Commission, to the referral of a conviction upon the ground that the jury should have been warned in slightly different terms about the considerations to be applied in deciding whether to draw any adverse inferences from silence.

Has the Commission been the handmaid of the Court of Appeal?

It is clear that during its first ten years, the Commission's exercise of its powers has been increasingly subject to judicial 'guidance' – sometimes taking the form of indications and sometimes the form of outright direction. At the risk of repetition, the following have been among the more conspicuous examples.

Sentence – tariff cases

The Commission's power to refer sentencing cases has been very clearly curtailed by the cases of **Graham** and **Robery** – both discussed in chapter 12. The Commission had assumed that where an application raised cogent new argument that a convicted person's sentence was 'manifestly excessive', compared with sentencing precedent cases, this could be a matter for reference. The assumption was logical because the 1995 Act included power to refer sentences, and the Court is frequently ready to allow first-time appeals against sentence as being manifestly excessive.[18] The effect of the **Graham** and **Robery** judgments was to give the clearest indication to the Commission that, in the Court's view, the case of a person lawfully sentenced, within the appropriate sentencing bracket, when all relevant information was known to the sentencing judge, is not a miscarriage of justice case with which the Commission should be concerned, or with which the Court would interfere. In the face of such authority, the Commission has had no sensible alternative – in applying the 'real possibility' test – but to refrain from referring cases of that kind.

Change-of-law cases

The Commission has received the clearest possible guidance from the Court of Appeal not to refer cases on the basis of change-of-law considerations in **Cottrell and Fletcher** – discussed at chapter 7.

Inference from silence cases

The Court has given pointed guidance to the Commission on the approach to be taken to such cases, most particularly in **Boyle and Ford** – see chapter 2.

Quite apart from 'guidance' cases of this nature, the Commission is plainly required to apply the appellate case law as it finds it and has little scope for taking an independent view as to how the law should be applied. To give an example, the Commission responded to the House of Lords' judgment in *Morgan Smith* by referring a series of cases on the ground that the point of law in *Morgan Smith* (ie 'personal characteristics' are relevant to the provocation defence to murder) had not been recognised at trial. The referral tap that was turned on by *Morgan Smith* was turned off by the cases of *Holley* and **Karimi and James,** which ruled that *Morgan Smith* had been wrongly decided. As a result, the Commission was, in effect, bound to turn down applications closely resembling cases which it would have referred shortly before. The Commission has had no scope to take its own view of the matter.

One area of contention between the Commission and its critics concerns the approach to be taken to new evidence. There are two distinct criticisms that have been from time to time levelled against the Commission:

- That the Commission has been unduly reluctant to refer cases based upon fresh expert evidence, due to the point of law in *Steven Jones* (chapter 4) in which the Court stated its disposition against allowing appeals based upon the opinion of a 'bigger and better' expert.

- That the Commission is applying the jury impact test unduly restrictively following the authorities of **Hakala** and *Dial and Dottin.*

My personal view – and hope – is that criticisms of this nature are misconceived. If the Commission is confronted with admissible new evidence that appears relevant and significant, then unless it is fanciful to suppose that a jury might have decided the case differently, the Commission's responsibility as gatekeeper is surely to refer the matter to the Court of Appeal.[19] The Court obviously hopes to influence the Commission against too 'liberal' an approach in new evidence cases and, as pointed out in chapter 3, a senior appeal judge has counselled the Commission against 'undue' citation of **Pendleton.** I am not personally aware, however, of any case where the Commission has drawn back from referral of a case in consequence of this guidance.

It may be that the effect of case law is more subtle and pernicious than this discussion allows. The message conveyed by the decision of the Privy Council in *Dial and Dottin*, by the repeated citation of Lord Hobhouse's dicta in **Pendleton**, and by the judgments in Commission cases, such as **Hakala** and **Probyn**, may be that the bar has been raised in new evidence cases. This message could act subliminally upon the Commission, not merely at the decision-making stages but at the investigation and case planning stage. It could be – for instance – that the decision could be made not to commission an accident investigation report because of the Court's negative view of the impact of such a report in **Probyn**, or not to pursue a psychiatric line of enquiry because of the dicta in **Sharp** and **Shickle**.

A hypothesis of this nature is enormously difficult to put to proof one way or the other. The fact, for instance, that the Commission declines to commission an accident investigation report may well reflect a judgment that such a report is incapable of advancing the applicant's case, irrespective of the previous judgments of the Court. It is my personal belief that the Commission correctly defines its line of enquiries by reference to its own assessment of the possible 'jury impact' of any new evidence, without being unduly burdened by the nuances of legal authority at the investigation stage. The Commission should, of course, curtail lines of enquiry which are hopeless, or which are advocated in a **Hakala**-type situation on behalf of an applicant who wishes to develop a case repugnant to the defence put forward at trial.[20] It should not, however, restrict its investigations beyond that for fear of the reaction of the Court of Appeal.

Does the Commission deal properly with 'lurking doubt' cases?

The Court has also given 'guidance' on cases of 'lurking doubt' (ie cases which have been argued out at trial and appeal; where new evidence is scant or lacking; but where there remains a pervasive sense that the verdict may be wrong). Cases of that nature, such as **Cooper and McMahon**, considerably contributed to the recognition of the need for an independent review authority. Furthermore, the legislation specifically allows the Commission to refer cases in the absence of new evidence or argument where it considers that there are exceptional circumstances that justify the making of a reference – a clear statutory 'lurking doubt' exception. But the Court has clearly indicated to the Commission in **Thomas (Ian)** and **Stock** – both discussed in chapter 5 – that it wishes the Commission to be extremely reticent about making such references. Indeed, in **Stock**, the Commission was given something of a judicial wigging for referring a case in which there was plenty of lurking doubt, but limited new evidence.

In the context of this discussion, it is cheering to note that the Commission has recently referred Mr Stock's case for a second time upon the basis that this conviction is permeated from top to bottom with lurking doubt. If the Commission follows legal authority (which it is bound to do), but is also willing to follow its own contrarian convictions, then it will be doing its job correctly. The re-referral of **Stock** is a case in point. The Commission has undergone the occasional judicial browbeating with relative equanimity in the past and will no doubt continue to do so in future.

Has the Commission made sufficient contribution to the criminal justice system?

As noted in chapter 1, the Runciman Commission emphasised the role of the new authority in keeping causes of miscarriage under review and making proposals for preventing miscarriages ex ante as well as ex post. Measured against this expectation, the Commission's contribution has been something of a disappointment in its first ten years.

Clearly, it was unrealistic to expect the Commission to make a significant contribution to the debate in its early years, as its own database of decided cases was too small to make any authoritative contribution based upon its own experience.[21] It would seem, however, that the Commission might have considered making a more significant input in recent years into the numerous debates about the future direction of the criminal justice system.

Among the topics which have been illuminated by the Commission's experiences have been the unfair and illogical state of the law of homicide; the uses and abuses of expert evidence; the limitations, in particular, of pathological evidence; the evidential problems in historic sex abuse cases; and the problem of serial and unreliable complainants in sex offence cases. It would be wrong to say that the Commission has been silent on all of these issues,[22] but its contribution to the debate has often been insubstantial and muted.

This shortfall in the contribution of the Commission may to some extent reflect limitations of its own internal deliberations. There has been very limited debate within the Commission about directions of criminal justice policy and meetings of the Commission members have been predominantly concerned with internal and organisational issues. The fact that the Commission has not had more to say may reflect this lack of internal deliberation. It is a matter which the Commission might reflect upon for the future.

Has an independent Commission represented an improvement on the Home Office?

Whilst it is invidious for a former insider to pass judgment on this point, it is perhaps acceptable, ten years on, to remark upon the dismal state of the files inherited by the Commission at its inception from Department C3 of the Home Office. The enduring impression created by these files was of a department which lacked any systematic means or will to investigate miscarriages of justice in a proactive fashion. It appeared that the political accountability of the department undermined rather than supported the effectiveness of its activities, and that much of its energies went into answering Parliamentary Questions (not always fulsomely) and protecting the Minister from criticism. There appeared to be somewhat less political urgency to resolve possible miscarriages of justice, and many of the files inherited by the Commission had been worked upon without noticeable momentum for many years.

It is to be hoped, therefore, that even the most severe critics of the Commission would concur that it has been a great improvement on what went before, and that it is the independence of the Commission that has been the cornerstone of its success. The Commission was helped to a successful start by its first chairman, Sir Frederick Crawford, who promoted a strong ethos of independence and a non-risk-averse approach to its task. Notwithstanding its various current difficulties, this ethos has continued. There is without doubt some degree of hankering within both the executive and judicial branches of government for a smaller, pared down Commission – one which would, perhaps, deal with a handful of 'obvious miscarriage' cases each year and avoid awkward and challenging referrals. It is hoped that this study will support the case that the Commission 'model' is enormously worth defending at this rather challenging time, even though its friendly critics, such as JUSTICE, should continue to keep a watchful eye on its activities.

Notes
1. And of course, sentences and summary convictions which satisfy the referral test.
2. This unit, under a different name, formerly included Department C3, which had responsibility for reviewing miscarriages before the Commission was established. The OCJR's continuing duties include assessment of the entitlement to compensation of individuals whose convictions are quashed following referral, and advising the Minister on the exercise of the Royal Prerogative of Mercy. The objectives of the OCJR can be viewed at www.cjsonline.gov.uk/the_cjs/departments_of_the_cjs/ocjr/index.html.
3. But now officially termed an NDPB – non-departmental public body.

4. For example, there was a longstanding difference of view between the OCJR and the Commission about the review of 'no appeal' cases. As explained in chapter 1, a Commissioner screens applications from persons who have not previously appealed to determine whether there are issues that merit review, notwithstanding the absence of a previous appeal. Although the time taken to screen these cases has been modest, the OCJR persistently challenged this procedure as an inappropriate use of Commissioners' time. The OCJR has, happily, recently abandoned its opposition to this procedure.

5. It is particularly emphasised that this is a personal observation – the Commission bears no responsibility for this, or any other judgment contained in this chapter.

6. Annual reports may be ordered from the Commission and can be accessed or ordered online at www.ccrc.gov.uk/publications/publications_get.asp.

7. I have, however, been informed by former colleagues still working at the Commission that the working relationship has improved to some extent since I left the Commission.

8. See chapter 5.

9. See the discussion of this matter in chapter 3.

10. Speech given on 19 July 2004 launching the government's five-year strategy for crime. An extract from the speech is on the 10 Downing Street website at http://www.pm.gov.uk/output/Page6129.asp.

11. But note that this mantle has now passed to the head of the Ministry of Justice who bears the impressive title of Lord Chancellor and Secretary of State for Justice.

12. http://www.homeoffice.gov.uk/documents/CJS-review.pdf/CJS-review-english. pdf?view=Binary.

13. Expenditure by the Commission in 2006-7 was approximately £7.5m. The Commission's income and expenditure for each year is set out in its annual reports.

14. Or to give the case its full name, **Harris, Rock, Cherry and Faulder.**

15. On the perils of the very latest forensic techniques, see also the discussion in chapter 4 of the use of Low Copy Number DNA techniques in the Omagh bombing case, *Hoey*.

16. But note the interesting suggestion made by Lord Justice Judge at the Commission's tenth anniversary conference *Miscarriages of Justice: Causes and Remedies*, held at the University of Birmingham on 10 May 2007. Lord Justice Judge ventured that if trial proceedings were recorded, as opposed to being merely transcribed, the Court would have the facility to consider whether evidence had been given by witnesses hesitantly or gabbled – and, therefore, would be better able to make its own assessment of the credibility of the evidence. This suggestion was the subject of a critical article by Marcel Berlins in the *Guardian*, which can be accessed at www.guardian.co.uk/commentisfree/story/0,,2078948,00.html.

17. The words 'come to light' are used to reflect the declaratory and retrospective nature of the common law (and interpretation of statute law). A summing up *appears* to be impeccable on the then current understanding of the law – but subsequent legal authority shows that the understanding of the law and, therefore, the summing up, were in fact flawed.

18. Court of Appeal statistics for 2006 show that there were more than four times as many successful appeals against sentence as against conviction. The great majority of successful sentence applications were on the ground that sentences were 'manifestly excessive'.

19. A possible exception to this statement would arise where the evidence put forward to support the appeal was deliberately not used at trial.

20. This statement requires some qualification – there may be a very few cases where defendants have pursued a lying defence for excusable reasons – such as threats of extreme violence made by co-defendants.

21. Note that there was no continuity of personnel or practice between Department C3 and the Commission. This meant that the Commission inherited no baggage from its predecessor but it also meant that the Commission started with a blank sheet, in terms of its own corporate memory and experience.

22. A submission was made, for instance, in response to the Law Commission's consultation on the reform of the law of homicide.

Appendices

Appendix 1

Commission conviction cases referred to the Court of Appeal

Name	Date of decision	Case reference or neutral citation
A (Derek)	14-Mar-00	998/07511/Y5
Adams (Andrew)	12-Jan-07	[2007] EWCA Crim 1
Adetoro	07-Jun-06	[2006] EWCA Crim 1716
Ahmed (Bakhtiar), Ahmed (Mumtaz), Ahmed (Nisar), Ahmed (Rizwan), Beg, Khan, Masud, Ramzan (Mohammed), Ryan (John), Sabir and Vernett-Showers	18-Jul-07	[2007] EWCA Crim 1767
Ahmed (Ishtiaq)	06-Dec-02	[2002] EWCA Crim 2781
Ahmed (Mumtaz)	14-Feb-07	[2007] EWCA Crim 464
Akhtar and Shah	04-Jul-05	[2005] EWCA Crim 1788
Allan (Richard Roy)	20-Aug-04	[2004] EWCA Crim 2236
Allen (Alexander)	10-Jul-01	[2001] EWCA Crim 1607
Anthony	11-Apr-05	[2005] EWCA Crim 952
Ashton	15-May-06	[2006] EWCA Crim 1267
Assali	19-Jul-05	[2005] EWCA Crim 2031
B (David)	14-Dec-06	[2006] EWCA Crim 3249
B (Ernest)	28-Nov-03	[2002] EWCA Crim 3435
B (Kevin)	22-Jan-04	[2004] EWCA Crim 50
Bacchus	11-Jun-04	[2004] EWCA Crim 1756

Name	Date of decision	Case reference or neutral citation
Bain	09-Mar-04	[2004] EWCA Crim 525
Bamber	12-Dec-02	[2002] EWCA Crim 2912
Bashir and Khan	02-Nov-05	[2005] EWCA Crim 3100
Beckles	12-Nov-04	[2004] EWCA Crim 2766
Benn and Benn	30-Jul-04	[2004] EWCA Crim 2100
Bentley	30-Jul-98	[1998] EWCA Crim 2516 [2001] 1 Cr App R 307
Blackburn	25-May-05	[2005] EWCA Crim 1349
Blackwell	12-Sep-06	[2006] EWCA Crim 2185
Boreman and Byrne	19-Jun-06	[2006] EWCA Crim 2265
Boyle and Ford	25-Aug-06	[2006] EWCA Crim 2101
Brannan and Murphy	25-Jan-02	[2002] EWCA Crim 120
Bromfield	08-Feb-02	[2002] EWCA Crim 195
Brooke and Siddall	15-Jun-06	[2006] EWCA Crim 1353
Broughton	07-Jul-04	[2004] EWCA Crim 2119
Brown, Brown, Dunne and Gaughan	29-Jan-01	[2001] EWCA Crim 169
Brown (John)	15-Feb-06	[2006] EWCA Crim 141
Brown (Robert)	13-Nov-02	[2002] EWCA Crim 2804
Burke	25-Nov-99	95/0123/Z3
Burt	09-Feb-05	[2005] EWCA Crim 315
Burton	14-Mar-02	[2002] EWCA Crim 614

Name	Date of decision	Case reference or neutral citation
C (Anthony Mark)	19-Jul-05	[2005] EWCA Crim 2138
C (Martin)	10-Apr-03	[2003] EWCA Crim 1246
Caley-Knowles and Jones	20-Jun-06	[2006] EWCA Crim 1611
Campbell	14-Oct-99	[1999] EWCA Crim 2264
Carrington-Jones	16-Oct-07	[2007] EWCA Crim 2551
Causley	05-Jun-03	[2003] EWCA Crim 1840
Christian	20-Feb-03	[2003] EWCA Crim 686
Christofides	11-Apr-01	[2001] EWCA Crim 906
Clark (Brian)	05-Apr-01	[2001] EWCA Crim 884
Clark (Sally)	11-Apr-03	[2003] EWCA Crim 1020
Clarke and McDaid (Court of Appeal)	25-May-06	[2006] EWCA Crim 1196
Clarke and McDaid (House of Lords)	06-Feb-08	[2008] UKHL 8
Cleeland	13-Feb-02	[2002] EWCA Crim 293
Cooper and McMahon	31-Jul-03	[2003] EWCA Crim 2257
Cottrell and Fletcher	31-Jul-07	[2007] EWCA Crim 2016
Craven	08-Dec-00	[2001] 2 Cr App R 181
Cummiskey	27-Nov-03	[2003] EWCA Crim 3933
Davis, Rowe and Johnson	17-Jul-00	[2000] EWCA Crim 109 [2001] 1 Cr App R 115
Day	16-Apr-03	[2003] EWCA Crim 1060
Deans	30-Jul-04	[2004] EWCA Crim 2123

Name	Date of decision	Case reference or neutral citation
Diamond	29-Apr-08	[2008] EWCA Crim 923
Doubtfire	19-Dec-00	[2000] EWCA Crim 101 [2001] 2 Cr App R 209
Downing	15-Jan-02	[2002] EWCA Crim 263
Druhan	16-Jul-99	[1999] EWCA Crim 2011
Dudley, Maynard, Bailey and Clarke	31-Jul-02	[2002] EWCA Crim 1942
Duggan	24-Jun-04	[2004] EWCA Crim 1924
Duncan Smith	17-Mar-04	[2004] EWCA Crim 631
El-Kurd, Reichwald, Sakavickas and Singh	27-Apr-07	[2007] EWCA Crim 1888
Ellis	08-Dec-03	[2003] EWCA Crim 3556
F (M)	26-Mar-03	[2003] EWCA Crim 1173
F (Reginald)	14-Feb-02	[2002] EWCA Crim 633
Fannin	18-Jun-99	[1999] EWCA Crim 1697
Farnell	12-Apr-05	[2005] EWCA Crim 1021
Faulder	21-Jul-05	[2005] EWCA Crim 1980
Fell	22-Mar-01	[2001] EWCA Crim 696
Findlay	19-Nov-03	[2003] EWCA Crim 3480
Foster	06-Feb-03	[2003] EWCA Crim 178
Fraser	02-Oct-03	[2003] EWCA Crim 3180
Friend	12-Oct-04	[2004] EWCA Crim 2661
G (G)	22-Jun-05	[2005] EWCA Crim 1792

Name	Date of decision	Case reference or neutral citation
G (T)	31-Mar-06	[2006] EWCA Crim 2271
Garner	29-Apr-02	[2002] EWCA Crim 1166
George	15-Nov-07	[2007] EWCA Crim 2722
Gerald	03-Nov-98	[1998] EWCA Crim 3097
Ghuman	03-Mar-04	[2004] EWCA Crim 742
Gilbert	29-Jul-04	[2004] EWCA Crim 2413
Gilfillan	07-Dec-98	[1998] EWCA Crim 3466
Gilfoyle	20-Dec-00	[2000] EWCA Crim 81
Gore	04-Jul-07	[2007] EWCA Crim 2789
Goren and Harrison	25-Jan-07	[2007] EWCA Crim 308
Gray	28-Mar-07	[2007] EWCA Crim 1063
Guney	23-May-03	[2003] EWCA Crim 1502
H (J) and G (T)	01-Jul-05	[2005] EWCA Crim 1828
Haddon	27-Jan-03	[2003] EWCA Crim 284
Hagans and Wilson	27-Nov-03	[2003] EWCA Crim 3358
Hakala	19-Mar-02	[2002] EWCA Crim 730
Hall, O'Brien and Sherwood	17-Dec-99	(2000) Crim LR 676 [2000] EWCA Crim 3
Hall (Philip)	12-Dec-03	[2003] EWCA Crim 3945
Hanratty	10-May-02	[2002] EWCA Crim 1141
Hayes (Dennis Francis)	01-Aug-02	[2002] EWCA Crim 1945
Hester	03-Dec-98	[1998] EWCA Crim 3442

Name	Date of decision	Case reference or neutral citation
Hill	08-Feb-08	[2008] EWCA Crim 76
Holliday	16-Sep-05	[2005] EWCA Crim 2388
Howard	11-Dec-03	[2003] EWCA Crim 3927
Howell	17-Jan-03	[2003] EWCA Crim 1
Hussain	19-Jan-05	[2005] EWCA Crim 31
Iredale	01-Mar-06	[2006] EWCA Crim 646
Iroegbu	09-Jul-03	[2003] EWCA Crim 2317
Irvine	14-Jan-02	[2002] EWCA Crim 29
Irwin and Parkin	11-Nov-04	[2004] EWCA Crim 2975
J	13-Nov-03	[2003] EWCA Crim 3309
James (David Ryan)	31-Jul-98	[1998] EWCA Crim 2521
James (Albert)	21-May-04	[2004] EWCA Crim 1433
James and Karimi	25-Jan-06	[2006] EWCA Crim 14
Jamil	17-Jul-01	[2001] EWCA Crim 1687
Jenkins	16-Jul-04	[2004] EWCA Crim 2047
Jenkinson	17-Nov-05	[2005] EWCA Crim 3118
Johnson (Frank)	26-Jun-02	[2002] EWCA Crim 1716
Johnson (Harold)	24-Oct-00	[2000] EWCA Crim 102
K (Jamie)	11-Dec-02	[2002] EWCA Crim 2878
K (Jason)	12-Jan-06	[2006] EWCA Crim 67
Kamara	09-May-00	[2000] EWCA Crim 37

Name	Date of decision	Case reference or neutral citation
Kansal (Court of Appeal)	24-May-01	[2001] EWCA Crim 1260 [2001] 3 WLR 751
Kansal (House of Lords)	29-Nov-01	[2002] 1 All ER 257
Karimi	10-Feb-05	[2005] EWCA Crim 369
Kassar	23-Jun-04	[2004] EWCA Crim 1812
Kavanagh	26-Mar-02	[2002] EWCA Crim 904
Kelly (George) and Connolly	28-Oct-03	[2003] EWCA Crim 2957
Kempster	07-May-08	[2008] EWCA Crim 975
Kennedy (Court of Appeal)	17-Mar-05	[2005] EWCA Crim 685
Kennedy (House of Lords)	17-Nov-07	[2007] UKHL 38
Knighton	17-Oct-02	[2002] EWCA Crim 2227
L (Stuart)	08-Dec-05	[2005] EWCA Crim 3119
Latif, Osman, Nawaz, Rasool and Shahzad	18-Jan-07	[2007] EWCA Crim 307
Lowe	12-Mar-07	[2007] EWCA Crim 833
Lyons, Parnes, Ronson and Saunders	21-Dec-01	[2001] EWCA Crim 2860
M (AR)	05-Feb-03	[2003] EWCA Crim 281
M (EM)	13-Oct-05	[2005] EWCA Crim 2683
MacKenney and Pinfold	15-Dec-03	[2003] EWCA Crim 3643
Mair	03-Dec-02	[2002] EWCA Crim 2858
Maloney	20-May-03	[2003] EWCA Crim 1373
Martin, Taylor and Brown	12-Jul-00	[2000] EWCA Crim 104

Name	Date of decision	Case reference or neutral citation
Martindale	01-Jul-03	[2003] EWCA Crim 1975
Mattan	24-Feb-98	[1998] EWCA Crim 676
May	07-Dec-01	[2001] EWCA Crim 2788
McCann	28-Nov-00	[2000] EWCA Crim 105
McNamee	17-Dec-98	[1998] EWCA Crim 3524
Miah	12-May-98	[1998] EWCA Crim 1544 [1999] 1 Cr App R 319
Millen	02-Apr-01	[2001] EWCA Crim 918
Mills and Poole	17-Jun-03	[2003] EWCA Crim 1753
Moseley	21-Apr-99	[1999] EWCA Crim 1089
Moses	28-Jun-06	[2006] EWCA Crim 1721
Mulcahy	26-Oct-00	[2000] EWCA Crim 106
Murphy and O'Toole	25-Feb-06	[2006] EWCA Crim 951
Murphy and Pope	26-Oct-04	[2004] EWCA Crim 2787
Murray (Anne)	24-Jan-03	[2003] EWCA Crim 27
Nicholls	12-Jun-98	[1998] EWCA Crim 1918
Nolan	09-Nov-06	[2006] EWCA Crim 2983
O (Paul)	04-Aug-04	[2004] EWCA Crim 2336
Otoo	31-Jan-00	9906358/Y3
P (Christopher Scott)	13-May-04	[2004] EWCA Crim 1325
P (Ricardo)	01-Nov-05	[2005] EWCA Crim 2910
P (Francis)	24-Jan-07	[2007] EWCA Crim 275

Name	Date of decision	Case reference or neutral citation
P (Michael)	20-Jul-99	[1999] EWCA Crim 2038
P (Peter)	30-Nov-01	[2001] EWCA Crim 2786
Parsons	17-Dec-99	9807595 S2
Pendleton (Court of Appeal)	22-Jun-00	[2000] EWCA Crim 45
Pendleton (House of Lords)	13-Dec-01	[2001] UKHL 66 [2002] 1 All ER 524
Popat	30-Jul-99	[2000] 1 Cr App R 387
Probyn	04-Oct-05	[2005] EWCA Crim 2347
Quinn (John)	12-Nov-04	[2004] EWCA Crim 3026
Quinn (Michael)	02-Feb-06	0501755 C3
R (M)	04-May-07	[2007] EWCA Crim 518
Ramzan	21-Jul-06	[2006] EWCA Crim 1974
Reynolds	08-Jul-04	[2004] EWCA Crim 1834
Richards	12-Dec-02	[2002] EWCA Crim 3175
Richardson	29-Jun-04	[2004] EWCA Crim 1784
Rizvi	14-Feb-07	[2007] EWCA Crim 467
Rowe (Michael)	08-Dec-00	[2000] EWCA Crim 66
Rowland	12-Dec-03	[2003] EWCA Crim 3636
S (C) and S (O)	15-Feb-01	[2001] EWCA Crim 339
Samra	01-Jul-04	[2004] EWCA Crim 1797
Serrano	01-Dec-06	[2006] EWCA Crim 3182
Sharp	18-Dec-03	[2003] EWCA Crim 3870

Name	Date of decision	Case reference or neutral citation
Sheehan	10-Nov-05	[2005] EWCA Crim 3134
Shickle	14-Jul-05	[2005] EWCA Crim 1881
Shirley	29-Jul-03	[2003] EWCA Crim 1976
Smith (Allen)	30-Jul-02	[2002] EWCA Crim 2074
Smith (Charlie)	19-Mar-02	[2002] EWCA Crim 840
Smith (Donald Denzil)	17-Oct-02	[2002] EWCA Crim 2401
Smith (Josephine)	04-Nov-02	[2002] EWCA Crim 2671
Smith (Shane Stepon)	02-Apr-03	[2003] EWCA Crim 927
Solomon	22-Oct-07	[2007] EWCA Crim 2633
Steel	10-Jun-03	[2003] EWCA Crim 1640
Steele, Whomes and Corry	22-Feb-06	[2006] EWCA Crim 195
Stock	26-Aug-04	[2004] EWCA Crim 2238
Such	04-Dec-00	00/3416/W5
Taylor (John Henry)	18-Jun-98	97/8389/S3
Thomas (Ian)	26-Apr-02	[2002] EWCA Crim 941
Thomas (Michael)	07-May-03	[2003] EWCA Crim 1555
Togher	09-Nov-00	[2000] EWCA Crim 111 [2001] 3 All ER 463
Twitchell	26-Oct-99	[2000] 1 Cr App R 373
Underwood	22-May-03	[2003] EWCA Crim 1500
W (CP)	17-Jun-02	[2002] EWCA Crim 1603
Warren	01-Mar-05	[2005] EWCA Crim 659

Name	Date of decision	Case reference or neutral citation
Waters	14-Feb-06	[2006] EWCA Crim 139
Webb	11-Apr-06	[2006] EWCA Crim 962
Went, Brown (Peter) and Walton	23-Nov-05	[2005] EWCA Crim 3212
Whitehead	23-Jun-06	[2006] EWCA Crim 1486
Wickens	17-Jun-03	[2003] EWCA Crim 2196
Williams (Harold)	27-Mar-03	[2003] EWCA Crim 1008
Williams (John)	07-Jun-06	[2006] EWCA Crim 1650
Willis	17-Mar-06	[2006] EWCA Crim 809
Wooster	26-Feb-03	[2003] EWCA Crim 748

Appendix 2

Commission sentence cases referred to the Court of Appeal

Name	Date of Court of Appeal decision	Case reference or neutral citation
Ballard	02-Dec-04	[2004] EWCA Crim 3305
Bargery	19-Mar-04	[2004] EWCA Crim 816
Beatty	17-Oct-06	[2006] EWCA Crim 2359
Brown (Darren)	27-Feb-04	[2004] EWCA Crim 496
Coleman	15-Feb-99	[1999] EWCA Crim 406
Collins	24-Mar-06	[2006] EWCA Crim 1049
Cook	27-Feb-98	[1998] EWCA Crim 728
Giacopazzi	09-Jul-99	[1999] EWCA Crim 1933
Graham	12-Feb-99	[1999] 2 Cr App R (S) 312
Hattersley and Taylor	16-Dec-04	[2004] EWCA Crim 3337
Hempston	30-Oct-06	[2006] EWCA Crim 2869
Henry	12-Oct-99	[1999] EWCA Crim 2265
Jackson	31-Oct-03	[2003] EWCA Crim 3251
James (Philip)	24-Feb-04	[2004] EWCA Crim 453
Jarvis	04-Jul-06	[2006] EWCA Crim 1985
Kelly (Edward)	16-Jul-01	[2001] EWCA Crim 1751
Keogh	25-May-04	[2004] EWCA Crim 1406

Name	Date of Court of Appeal decision	Case reference or neutral citation
K	17-Nov-06	Informant case – no reference provided
Lay	07-Nov-06	[2006] EWCA Crim 2924
Lomey	12-Oct-04	[2004] EWCA Crim 3014
Looker	03-Oct-00	[2000] EWCA Crim 103
M	19-Oct-06	Informant case – no reference provided
Maguire	04-Apr-06	[2006] EWCA Crim 1239
Melady	21-Apr-04	[2004] EWCA Crim 1015
Mohammed	21-Dec-05	[2005] EWCA Crim 3500
Morphy	26-Oct-06	[2006] EWCA Crim 2698
Murray (Vincent)	02-Feb-06	[2006] EWCA Crim 328
Nicholson	26-Oct-04	[2004] EWCA Crim 2840
Offen	09-Nov-00	[2000] EWCA Crim 96 [2000] 1 Cr App R (S) 565
Pollard	28-Oct-05	[2005] EWCA Crim 2938
Robery	13-May-99	[1999] EWCA Crim 1372
S	28-Oct-03	Informant case – no reference provided
BJS	25-Feb-02	[2002] EWCA Crim 542
Taylor (Alan)	09-Mar-06	[2006] EWCA Crim 872
Turner	13-Dec-01	[2001] EWCA Crim 2918

Appendix 3

Commission conviction cases referred to the Northern Ireland Court of Appeal

Name	Date of decision	Case reference or neutral citation
Adams (Robert)	12-Jan-06	[2006] NICA 6
Boyle (John Joseph)	29-Apr-03	CARJ 3677T
Gorman and McKinney	29-Oct-99	CARF 3083
Green	08-Mar-02	[2002] NICA 14
Hanna and Hindes	09-Sep-05	[2005] NICA 36
Hay Gordon	20-Dec-00	[2000] NICA 28
Latimer	09-Feb-04	[2004] NICA 3
MacDermott and McCartney	01-Feb-07	[2007] NICA 10
Magee	06-Apr-01	[2001] NICA 18
Mulholland	10-Jul-06	[2006] NICA 32
O'Doherty	19-Apr-02	[2002] NICA B51
Walsh	11-Jan-02	[2002] NICA 1

Appendix 4

Judicial review cases

Name	Date of decision	Case reference or neutral citation
R v Criminal Cases Review Commission ex p Brine	05-May-99	[1999] EWHC Admin 402
R v Criminal Cases Review Commission ex p Pearson	18-May-99	[1999] EWHC Admin 452
Saxon (R on the application of) v Criminal Cases Review Commission	20-Jun-01	[2001] EWHC Admin 505
Mills and Poole (R on the application of) v Criminal Cases Review Commission	20-Dec-01	[2001] EWHC Admin 1153
Farnell (R on the application of) v Criminal Cases Review Commission	15-Apr-03	[2003] EWHC 835 Admin
Westlake (R on the application of) v Criminal Cases Review Commission	17-Nov-04	[2004] EWHC Admin 2779
In the Matter of Quinn (Dermot)	09-Mar-05	[2005] NIQB 21
Director of Revenue and Customs Prosecutions (R on the application of) v Criminal Cases Review Commission	05-Dec-06	[2006] EWHC Admin 3064
Dowsett (R on the application of) v Criminal Cases Review Commission	08-Jun-07	[2007] EWHC Admin 1923

Appendix 5

Summary cases

Name	Date of appeal decision
Abwnawar, Abwnawar, Nazarian and Sohrabian	28-Oct-05
Borrows	28-Sep-01
Botwright	19-Apr-02
Ealand	03-Sep-99
F (Mark)	11-Oct-02
Goldsmith	23-Oct-01
Lamont	15-Oct-04
Muff	23-Jan-04
Pickavance	28-Feb-03
Spragg	11-Aug-00
Wilkinson	28-Nov-06

Appendix 6

Main cited non-Commission cases

Name	Case reference or neutral citation
R v B	[2003] EWCA Crim 619
Cooper	[1969] 1 QB 267
Dial and Dottin	[2005] UKPC 4
Early and Others	[2003] 1 Cr App R 288
Jones (Steven)	[1997] 1 Cr App R 86
Keane	[1994] 1 WLR 746
King (Ashley)	[2000] 2 Cr App R 391
Lambert	[2002] 2 AC 543
Mullen	[1999] 2 Cr App R 143
Murray (John)`	[1996] 22 EHRR 29
Preddy	[1996] AC 815
Smith (Morgan)	[2001] AC 146
Stafford v DPP	[1974] AC 878
Stirland v DPP	[1944] AC 315
Toohey v Metropolitan Police Commissioner	[1965] AC 595
Ward (Judith)	[1993] 1 WLR 619

Appendix 7

CRIMINAL APPEAL ACT 1995 (C 35)

An Act to amend provisions relating to appeals and references to the Court of Appeal in criminal cases; to establish a Criminal Cases Review Commission and confer functions on, and make other provision in relation to, the Commission; to amend section 142 of the Magistrates' Courts Act 1980 and introduce in Northern Ireland provisions similar to those of that section; to amend section 133 of the Criminal Justice Act 1988; and for connected purposes.

PART II
THE CRIMINAL CASES REVIEW COMMISSION

8 The Commission

(1) There shall be a body corporate to be known as the Criminal Cases Review Commission.

(2) The Commission shall not be regarded as the servant or agent of the Crown or as enjoying any status, immunity or privilege of the Crown; and the Commission's property shall not be regarded as property of, or held on behalf of, the Crown.

(3) The Commission shall consist of not fewer than eleven members.

(4) The members of the Commission shall be appointed by Her Majesty on the recommendation of the Prime Minister.

(5) At least one third of the members of the Commission shall be persons who are legally qualified; and for this purpose a person is legally qualified if--

    (a) he has a ten year general qualification, within the meaning of section 71 of the Courts and Legal Services Act 1990, or

    (b) he is a member of the Bar of Northern Ireland, or solicitor of the Supreme Court of Northern Ireland, of at least ten years' standing.

(6) At least two thirds of the members of the Commission shall be persons who appear to the Prime Minister to have knowledge or experience of any aspect of the criminal justice system and of them at least one shall be a person who appears to him to have knowledge or experience of any aspect of the criminal justice system in Northern Ireland; and for the purposes of this subsection the criminal justice system includes, in particular, the investigation of offences and the treatment of offenders.

(7) Schedule 1 (further provisions with respect to the Commission) shall have effect.

References to court

9 Cases dealt with on indictment in England and Wales

(1) Where a person has been convicted of an offence on indictment in England and Wales, the Commission--

(a) may at any time refer the conviction to the Court of Appeal, and

(b) (whether or not they refer the conviction) may at any time refer to the Court of Appeal any sentence (not being a sentence fixed by law) imposed on, or in subsequent proceedings relating to, the conviction.

(2) A reference under subsection (1) of a person's conviction shall be treated for all purposes as an appeal by the person under section 1 of the 1968 Act against the conviction.

(3) A reference under subsection (1) of a sentence imposed on, or in subsequent proceedings relating to, a person's conviction on an indictment shall be treated for all purposes as an appeal by the person under section 9 of the 1968 Act against--

(a) the sentence, and

       (b) any other sentence (not being a sentence fixed by law) imposed on, or in subsequent proceedings relating to, the conviction or any other conviction on the indictment.

(4) On a reference under subsection (1) of a person's conviction on an indictment the Commission may give notice to the Court of Appeal that any other conviction on the indictment which is specified in the notice is to be treated as referred to the Court of Appeal under subsection (1).

(5) Where a verdict of not guilty by reason of insanity has been returned in England and Wales in the case of a person, the Commission may at any time refer the verdict to the Court of Appeal; and a reference under this subsection shall be treated for all purposes as an appeal by the person under section 12 of the 1968 Act against the verdict.

(6) Where a jury in England and Wales has returned findings that a person is under a disability and that he did the act or made the omission charged against him, the Commission may at any time refer either or both of those findings to the Court of Appeal; and a reference under this subsection shall be treated for all purposes as an appeal by the person under section 15 of the 1968 Act against the finding or findings referred.

10 Cases dealt with on indictment in Northern Ireland

(1) Where a person has been convicted of an offence on indictment in Northern Ireland, the Commission--

       (a) may at any time refer the conviction to the Court of Appeal, and

       (b) (whether or not they refer the conviction) may at any time refer to the Court of Appeal any sentence (not being a sentence fixed by law) imposed on, or in subsequent proceedings relating to, the conviction.

(2) A reference under subsection (1) of a person's conviction shall be treated for all purposes as an appeal by the person under section 1 of the 1980 Act against the conviction.

(3) A reference under subsection (1) of a sentence imposed on, or in subsequent proceedings relating to, a person's conviction on an indictment shall be treated for all purposes as an appeal by the person under section 8 or 9 (as the case may be) of the 1980 Act against--

    (a) the sentence, and

    (b) any other sentence (not being a sentence fixed by law) imposed on, or in subsequent proceedings relating to, the conviction or any other conviction on the indictment.

(4) On a reference under subsection (1) of a person's conviction on an indictment the Commission may give notice to the Court of Appeal that any other conviction on the indictment which is specified in the notice is to be treated as referred to the Court of Appeal under subsection (1).

(5) On a reference under subsection (1) the Court of Appeal may not pass any sentence more severe than that passed by the Crown Court.

(6) Where a finding of not guilty on the ground of insanity has been recorded in Northern Ireland in the case of a person, the Commission may at any time refer the finding to the Court of Appeal; and a reference under this subsection shall be treated for all purposes as an appeal by the person under section 12 of the 1980 Act against the finding.

(7) Where a jury in Northern Ireland has returned a finding that a person is unfit to be tried, the Commission may at any time refer the finding to the Court of Appeal; and a reference under this subsection shall be treated for all purposes as an appeal by the person under section 13A of the 1980 Act against the finding.

11 Cases dealt with summarily in England and Wales

(1) Where a person has been convicted of an offence by a magistrates' court in England and Wales, the Commission--

    (a) may at any time refer the conviction to the Crown Court, and

(b) (whether or not they refer the conviction) may at any time refer to the Crown Court any sentence imposed on, or in subsequent proceedings relating to, the conviction.

(2) A reference under subsection (1) of a person's conviction shall be treated for all purposes as an appeal by the person under section 108(1) of the Magistrates' Courts Act 1980 against the conviction (whether or not he pleaded guilty).

(3) A reference under subsection (1) of a sentence imposed on, or in subsequent proceedings relating to, a person's conviction shall be treated for all purposes as an appeal by the person under section 108(1) of the Magistrates' Courts Act 1980 against--

(a) the sentence, and

(b) any other sentence imposed on, or in subsequent proceedings relating to, the conviction or any related conviction.

(4) On a reference under subsection (1) of a person's conviction the Commission may give notice to the Crown Court that any related conviction which is specified in the notice is to be treated as referred to the Crown Court under subsection (1).

(5) For the purposes of this section convictions are related if they are convictions of the same person by the same court on the same day.

(6) On a reference under this section the Crown Court may not award any punishment more severe than that awarded by the court whose decision is referred.

(7) The Crown Court may grant bail to a person whose conviction or sentence has been referred under this section; and any time during which he is released on bail shall not count as part of any term of imprisonment or detention under his sentence.

12 Cases dealt with summarily in Northern Ireland

(1) Where a person has been convicted of an offence by a magistrates' court in Northern Ireland, the Commission--

    (a) may at any time refer the conviction to a county court, and

    (b) (whether or not they refer the conviction) may at any time refer to a county court any sentence imposed on, or in subsequent proceedings relating to, the conviction.

(2) A reference under subsection (1) of a person's conviction shall be treated for all purposes as an appeal by the person under Article 140(1) of the Magistrates' Courts (Northern Ireland) Order 1981 against the conviction (whether or not he pleaded guilty).

(3) A reference under subsection (1) of a sentence imposed on, or in subsequent proceedings relating to, a person's conviction shall be treated for all purposes as an appeal by the person under Article 140(1) of the Magistrates' Courts (Northern Ireland) Order 1981 against--

    (a) the sentence, and

    (b) any other sentence imposed on, or in subsequent proceedings relating to, the conviction or any related conviction.

(4) On a reference under subsection (1) of a person's conviction the Commission may give notice to the county court that any related conviction which is specified in the notice is to be treated as referred to the county court under subsection (1).

(5) For the purposes of this section convictions are related if they are convictions of the same person by the same court on the same day.

(6) On a reference under this section a county court may not award any punishment more severe than that awarded by the court whose decision is referred.

(7) The High Court may grant bail to a person whose conviction or sentence has been referred to a county court under this section; and any time during which he is released on bail shall not count as part of any term of imprisonment or detention under his sentence.

13 Conditions for making of references

(1)   A reference of a conviction, verdict, finding or sentence shall not be made under any of sections 9 to 12 unless--

   (a)   the Commission consider that there is a real possibility that the conviction, verdict, finding or sentence would not be upheld were the reference to be made,

   (b)   the Commission so consider--

      (i)   in the case of a conviction, verdict or finding, because of an argument, or evidence, not raised in the proceedings which led to it or on any appeal or application for leave to appeal against it, or

      (ii)   in the case of a sentence, because of an argument on a point of law, or information, not so raised, and

   (c)   an appeal against the conviction, verdict, finding or sentence has been determined or leave to appeal against it has been refused.

(2)   Nothing in subsection (1)(b)(i) or (c) shall prevent the making of a reference if it appears to the Commission that there are exceptional circumstances which justify making it.

14 Further provisions about references

(1)   A reference of a conviction, verdict, finding or sentence may be made under any of sections 9 to 12 either after an application has been made by or on behalf of the person to whom it relates or without an application having been so made.

(2)   In considering whether to make a reference of a conviction, verdict, finding or sentence under any of sections 9 to 12 the Commission shall have regard to--

   (a)   any application or representations made to the Commission by or on behalf of the person to whom it relates,

(b) any other representations made to the Commission in relation to it, and

(c) any other matters which appear to the Commission to be relevant.

(3) In considering whether to make a reference under section 9 or 10 the Commission may at any time refer any point on which they desire the assistance of the Court of Appeal to that Court for the Court's opinion on it; and on a reference under this subsection the Court of Appeal shall consider the point referred and furnish the Commission with the Court's opinion on the point.

(4) Where the Commission make a reference under any of sections 9 to 12 the Commission shall--

(a) give to the court to which the reference is made a statement of the Commission's reasons for making the reference, and

(b) send a copy of the statement to every person who appears to the Commission to be likely to be a party to any proceedings on the appeal arising from the reference.

(4A) Subject to subsection (4B), where a reference under section 9 or 10 is treated as an appeal against any conviction, verdict, finding or sentence, the appeal may not be on any ground which is not related to any reason given by the Commission for making the reference.
[Inserted by s315 Criminal Justice Act 2003 as from 4 April 2005]

(4B) The Court of Appeal may give leave for an appeal mentioned in subsection (4A) to be on a ground relating to the conviction, verdict, finding or sentence which is not related to any reason given by the Commission for making the reference.
[Inserted by s315 Criminal Justice Act 2003 as from 4 April 2005]

(5) Where a reference under section 11 or 12 is treated as an appeal against any conviction, verdict, finding or sentence, the appeal may be on any ground relating to the conviction, verdict, finding or sentence

(whether or not the ground is related to any reason given by the Commission for making the reference).

[Amended by s315 Criminal Justice Act 2003 as from 4 April 2005]

(6) In every case in which--

    (a) an application has been made to the Commission by or on behalf of any person for the reference under any of sections 9 to 12 of any conviction, verdict, finding or sentence, but

    (b) the Commission decide not to make a reference of the conviction, verdict, finding or sentence,

the Commission shall give a statement of the reasons for their decision to the person who made the application.

15 Investigations for Court of Appeal

(1) Where a direction is given by the Court of Appeal under section 23A(1) of the 1968 Act or section 25A(1) of the 1980 Act the Commission shall investigate the matter specified in the direction in such manner as the Commission think fit.

(2) Where, in investigating a matter specified in such a direction, it appears to the Commission that-

    (a) another matter (a "related matter") which is relevant to the determination of the case by the Court of Appeal ought, if possible, to be resolved before the case is determined by that Court, and

    (b) an investigation of the related matter is likely to result in the Court's being able to resolve it, the Commission may also investigate the related matter.

(3) The Commission shall--

    (a) keep the Court of Appeal informed as to the progress of the investigation of any matter specified in a direction under section 23A(1) of the 1968 Act or section 25A(1) of the 1980 Act and

    (b) if they decide to investigate any related matter, notify the Court of Appeal of their decision and keep the Court informed as to the progress of the investigation.

(4) The Commission shall report to the Court of Appeal on the investigation of any matter specified in a direction under section 23A(1) of the 1968 Act or section 25A(1) of the 1980 Act when--

    (a) they complete the investigation of that matter and of any related matter investigated by them, or

    (b) they are directed to do so by the Court of Appeal,

whichever happens first.

(5) A report under subsection (4) shall include details of any inquiries made by or for the Commission in the investigation of the matter specified in the direction or any related matter investigated by them.

(6) Such a report shall be accompanied--

    (a) by any statements and opinions received by the Commission in the investigation of the matter specified in the direction or any related matter investigated by them, and

    (b) subject to subsection (7), by any reports so received.

(7) Such a report need not be accompanied by any reports submitted to the Commission under section 20(6) by an investigating officer.

16 Assistance in connection with prerogative of mercy

(1) Where the Secretary of State refers to the Commission any matter which arises in the consideration of whether to recommend the exercise of Her Majesty's prerogative of mercy in relation to a conviction and on which he desires their assistance, the Commission shall--

(a) consider the matter referred, and

(b) give to the Secretary of State a statement of their conclusions on it; and the Secretary of State shall, in considering whether so to recommend, treat the Commission's statement as conclusive of the matter referred.

(2) Where in any case the Commission are of the opinion that the Secretary of State should consider whether to recommend the exercise of Her Majesty's prerogative of mercy in relation to the case they shall give him the reasons for their opinion.

Supplementary powers

17 Power to obtain documents etc

(1) This section applies where the Commission believe that a person serving in a public body has possession or control of a document or other material which may assist the Commission in the exercise of any of their functions.

(2) Where it is reasonable to do so, the Commission may require the person who is the appropriate person in relation to the public body--

(a) to produce the document or other material to the Commission or to give the Commission access to it, and

(b) to allow the Commission to take away the document or other material or to make and take away a copy of it in such form as they think appropriate,

and may direct that person that the document or other material must not be destroyed, damaged or altered before the direction is withdrawn by the Commission.

(3) The documents and other material covered by this section include, in particular, any document or other material obtained or created during any investigation or proceedings relating to--

(a) the case in relation to which the Commission's function is being or may be exercised, or

(b) any other case which may be in any way connected with that case (whether or not any function of the Commission could be exercised in relation to that other case).

(4) The duty to comply with a requirement under this section is not affected by any obligation of secrecy or other limitation on disclosure (including any such obligation or limitation imposed by or by virtue of an enactment) which would otherwise prevent the production of the document or other material to the Commission or the giving of access to it to the Commission.

18 Government documents etc relating to current or old cases

(1) Section 17 does not apply to any document or other material in the possession or control of a person serving in a government department if the document or other material--

(a) is relevant to a case to which this subsection applies, and

(b) is in the possession or control of the person in consequence of the Secretary of State's consideration of the case.

(2) Subsection (1) applies to a case if the Secretary of State--

(a) is, immediately before the day on which the repeal by this Act of section 17 of the 1968 Act or of section 14 of the 1980 Act comes into force, considering the case with a view to deciding whether to make a reference under that section or whether to recommend the exercise of Her Majesty's prerogative of mercy in relation to a conviction by a magistrates' court, or

(b) has at any earlier time considered the case with a view to deciding whether to make such a reference or whether so to recommend.

(3) The Secretary of State shall give to the Commission any document or other material which--

    (a)   contains representations made to him in relation to any case to which this subsection applies, or

    (b)   was received by him in connection with any such case otherwise than from a person serving in a government department,

and may give to the Commission any document or other material which is relevant to any such case but does not fall within paragraph (a) or (b).

(4) Subsection (3) applies to a case if--

    (a)   the Secretary of State is, immediately before the day on which the repeal by this Act of section 17 of the 1968 Act or of section 14 of the 1980 Act comes into force, considering the case with a view to deciding whether to make a reference under that section or whether to recommend the exercise of Her Majesty's prerogative of mercy in relation to a conviction by a magistrates' court, or

    (b)   the Secretary of State has at any earlier time considered the case with a view to deciding whether to make such a reference, or whether so to recommend, and the Commission at any time notify him that they wish subsection (3) to apply to the case.

19 Power to require appointment of investigating officers

(1) Where the Commission believe that inquiries should be made for assisting them in the exercise of any of their functions in relation to any case they may require the appointment of an investigating officer to carry out the inquiries.

(2) Where any offence to which the case relates was investigated by persons serving in a public body, a requirement under this section may be imposed--

(a) on the person who is the appropriate person in relation to the public body, or

(b) where the public body has ceased to exist, on any chief officer of police or on the person who is the appropriate person in relation to any public body which appears to the Commission to have functions which consist of or include functions similar to any of those of the public body which has ceased to exist.

(3) Where no offence to which the case relates was investigated by persons serving in a public body, a requirement under this section may be imposed on any chief officer of police.

(4) A requirement under this section imposed on a chief officer of police may be--

(a) a requirement to appoint a person serving in the police force in relation to which he is the chief officer of police, or

(b) a requirement to appoint a person serving in another police force selected by the chief officer.

(5) A requirement under this section imposed on a person who is the appropriate person in relation to a public body other than a police force may be --

(a) a requirement to appoint a person serving in the public body, or

(b) a requirement to appoint a person serving in a police force, or in a public body (other than a police force) having functions which consist of or include the investigation of offences, selected by the appropriate person.

(6) The Commission may direct--

(a) that a person shall not be appointed, or

(b)   that a police force or other public body shall not be selected,

under subsection (4) or (5) without the approval of the Commission.

(7)   Where an appointment is made under this section by the person who is the appropriate person in relation to any public body, that person shall inform the Commission of the appointment; and if the Commission are not satisfied with the person appointed they may direct that--

(a)   the person who is the appropriate person in relation to the public body shall, as soon as is reasonably practicable, select another person in his place and notify the Commission of the proposal to appoint the other person, and

(b)   the other person shall not be appointed without the approval of the Commission.

20 Inquiries by investigating officers

(1)   A person appointed as the investigating officer in relation to a case shall undertake such inquiries as the Commission may from time to time reasonably direct him to undertake in relation to the case.

(2)   A person appointed as an investigating officer shall be permitted to act as such by the person who is the appropriate person in relation to the public body in which he is serving.

(3)   Where the chief officer of an England and Wales police force appoints a member of the Royal Ulster Constabulary as an investigating officer, the member appointed shall have in England and Wales the same powers and privileges as a member of the police force has there as a constable; and where the Chief Constable of the Royal Ulster Constabulary appoints a member of an England and Wales police force as an investigating officer, the member appointed shall have in Northern Ireland the same powers and privileges as a member of the Royal Ulster Constabulary has there as a constable.

(4) The Commission may take any steps which they consider appropriate for supervising the undertaking of inquiries by an investigating officer.

(5) The Commission may at any time direct that a person appointed as the investigating officer in relation to a case shall cease to act as such; but the making of such a direction shall not prevent the Commission from imposing a requirement under section 19 to appoint another investigating officer in relation to the case.

(6) When a person appointed as the investigating officer in relation to a case has completed the inquiries which he has been directed by the Commission to undertake in relation to the case, he shall--

    (a) prepare a report of his findings,

    (b) submit it to the Commission, and

    (c) send a copy of it to the person by whom he was appointed.

(7) When a person appointed as the investigating officer in relation to a case submits to the Commission a report of his findings he shall also submit to them any statements, opinions and reports received by him in connection with the inquiries which he was directed to undertake in relation to the case.

21 Other powers

Sections 17 to 20 are without prejudice to the taking by the Commission of any steps which they consider appropriate for assisting them in the exercise of any of their functions including, in particular--

    (a) undertaking, or arranging for others to undertake, inquiries, and

    (b) obtaining, or arranging for others to obtain, statements, opinions and reports.

22 Meaning of "public body" etc

(1)   In sections 17, 19 and 20 and this section "public body" means--

    (a)   any police force,

    (b)   any government department, local authority or other body constituted for purposes of the public service, local government or the administration of justice, or

    (c)   any other body whose members are appointed by Her Majesty, any Minister or any government department or whose revenues consist wholly or mainly of money provided by Parliament or appropriated by Measure of the Northern Ireland Assembly.

(2)   In sections 19 and 20 and this section--

    (a)   "police force" includes the Royal Ulster Constabulary and the Royal Ulster Constabulary Reserve, the National Crime Squad and any body of constables maintained otherwise than by a police authority,

    (b)   references to the chief officer of police--

        (i)   in relation to the Royal Ulster Constabulary and the Royal Ulster Constabulary Reserve, are to the Chief Constable of the Constabulary,

        (ii)   in relation to the National Crime Squad, are to the Director General of the Squad, and

        (iii)   in relation to any other police force maintained otherwise than by a police authority, are to the chief constable,

    (c)   references to an England and Wales police force are to a police force maintained under section 2 of the Police Act 1996, the metropolitan police force, the City of London police force or the National Crime Squad.

(d) "police authority" includes the Service Authority for the National Crime Squad, and

(e) references to a person serving in a police force or to a member of a police force, in relation to the National Crime Squad, mean a police member of that Squad appointed under section 55(1)(b) of the Police Act 1997.
[As amended by provisions of the Police Act 1996 and the Police Act 1997]

(3) In section 18 and this section--

(a) references to a government department include a Northern Ireland department and the Office of the Director of Public Prosecutions for Northern Ireland, and

(b) "Minister" means a Minister of the Crown as defined by section 8 of the Ministers of the Crown Act 1975 but also includes the head of a Northern Ireland department.

(4) In sections 17, 19 and 20 "the appropriate person" means -

(a) in relation to a police force, the chief officer of police,

(aa) in relation to the National Criminal Intelligence Service, the Director General of that Service,

(b) in relation to the Crown Prosecution Service, the Director of Public Prosecutions,

(c) in relation to the Office of the Director of Public Prosecutions for Northern Ireland, that Director,

(d) in relation to the Serious Fraud Office, the Director of the Serious Fraud Office,

(e) in relation to the Inland Revenue, the Commissioners of Inland Revenue,

(f) in relation to the Customs and Excise, the Commissioners of Customs and Excise,

(g) in relation to any government department not within any of the preceding paragraphs, the Minister in charge of the department, and

(h) in relation to any public body not within any of the preceding paragraphs, the public body itself (if it is a body corporate) or the person in charge of the public body (if it is not).

[Para (aa) added by the Police Act 1997]

(5) For the purposes of sections 17, 19 and 20--

(a) a justices' chief executive or justices' clerk appointed by, or a member of the staff of, a magistrates' courts committee shall be treated as serving in the committee, ...

(b) ... *[repealed by the Northern Ireland (Emergency Provisions) Act 1996, s 63(7), Sch 7, Part I]*

23 Offence of disclosure

(1) A person who is or has been a member or employee of the Commission shall not disclose any information obtained by the Commission in the exercise of any of their functions unless the disclosure of the information is excepted from this section by section 24.

(2) A person who is or has been an investigating officer shall not disclose any information obtained by him in his inquiries unless the disclosure of the information is excepted from this section by section 24.

(3) A member of the Commission shall not authorise--

(a) the disclosure by an employee of the Commission of any information obtained by the Commission in the exercise of any of their functions, or

    (b) the disclosure by an investigating officer of any information obtained by him in his inquiries,

unless the authorisation of the disclosure of the information is excepted from this section by section 24.

(4) A person who contravenes this section is guilty of an offence and liable on summary conviction to a fine of an amount not exceeding level 5 on the standard scale.

24 Exceptions from obligations of non-disclosure

(1) The disclosure of information, or the authorisation of the disclosure of information, is excepted from section 23 by this section if the information is disclosed, or is authorised to be disclosed--

    (a) for the purposes of any criminal, disciplinary or civil proceedings,

    (b) in order to assist in dealing with an application made to the Secretary of State for compensation for a miscarriage of justice,

    (c) by a person who is a member or an employee of the Commission either to another person who is a member or an employee of the Commission or to an investigating officer,

    (d) by an investigating officer to a member or an employee of the Commission,

    (e) in any statement or report required by this Act,

    (f) in or in connection with the exercise of any function under this Act, or

    (g) in any circumstances in which the disclosure of information is permitted by an order made by the Secretary of State.

(2) The disclosure of information is also excepted from section 23 by this section if the information is disclosed by an employee of the

Commission, or an investigating officer, who is authorised to disclose the information by a member of the Commission.

(3) The disclosure of information, or the authorisation of the disclosure of information, is also excepted from section 23 by this section if the information is disclosed, or is authorised to be disclosed, for the purposes of--

(a) the investigation of an offence, or

(b) deciding whether to prosecute a person for an offence,

unless the disclosure is or would be prevented by an obligation of secrecy or other limitation on disclosure (including any such obligation or limitation imposed by or by virtue of an enactment) arising otherwise than under that section.

(4) Where the disclosure of information is excepted from section 23 by subsection (1) or (2), the disclosure of the information is not prevented by any obligation of secrecy or other limitation on disclosure (including any such obligation or limitation imposed by or by virtue of an enactment)   arising otherwise than under that section.

(5) The power to make an order under subsection (1)(g) is exercisable by statutory instrument which shall be subject to annulment in pursuance of a resolution of either House of Parliament.

25 Consent to disclosure

(1) Where a person on whom a requirement is imposed under section 17 notifies the Commission that any information contained in any document or other material to which the requirement relates is not to be disclosed by the Commission without his prior consent, the Commission shall not disclose the information without such consent.

(2) Such consent may not be withheld unless--

(a) (apart from section 17) the person would have been prevented by any obligation of secrecy or other limitation on disclosure from disclosing the information to the Commission, and

(b) it is reasonable for the person to withhold his consent to disclosure of the information by the Commission.

(3) An obligation of secrecy or other limitation on disclosure which applies to a person only where disclosure is not authorised by another person shall not be taken for the purposes of subsection (2)(a) to prevent the disclosure by the person of information to the Commission unless--

(a) reasonable steps have been taken to obtain the authorisation of the other person, or

(b) such authorisation could not reasonably be expected to be obtained.

SCHEDULE 1
The Commission: Further Provisions

Membership

1. Her Majesty shall, on the recommendation of the Prime Minister, appoint one of the members of the Commission to be the chairman of the Commission.

2. (1) Subject to the following provisions of this paragraph, a person shall hold and vacate office as a member of the Commission, or as chairman of the Commission, in accordance with the terms of his appointment.

(2) An appointment as a member of the Commission may be full-time or part-time.

(3) The appointment of a person as a member of the Commission, or as chairman of the Commission, shall be for a fixed period of not longer than five years.

(4) Subject to sub-paragraph (5), a person whose term of appointment as a member of the Commission, or as chairman of the Commission, expires shall be eligible for re-appointment.

(5) No person may hold office as a member of the Commission for a continuous period which is longer than ten years.

(6) A person may at any time resign his office as a member of the Commission, or as chairman of the Commission, by notice in writing addressed to Her Majesty.

(7) Her Majesty may at any time remove a person from office as a member of the Commission if satisfied--

    (a) that he has without reasonable excuse failed to discharge his functions as a member for a continuous period of three months beginning not earlier than six months before that time,

    (b) that he has been convicted of a criminal offence,

    (c) that a bankruptcy order has been made against him, or his estate has been sequestrated, or he has made a composition or arrangement with, or granted a trust deed for, his creditors, or

    (d) that he is unable or unfit to discharge his functions as a member.

(8) If the chairman of the Commission ceases to be a member of the Commission he shall also cease to be chairman.

Members and employees

3. (1) The Commission shall--

    (a) pay to members of the Commission such remuneration,

    (b) pay to or in respect of members of the Commission any such allowances, fees, expenses and gratuities, and

(c)   pay towards the provision of pensions to or in respect of members of the Commission any such sums,

as the Commission are required to pay by or in accordance with directions given by the Secretary of State.

(2)   Where a member of the Commission was, immediately before becoming a member, a participant in a scheme under section 1 of the Superannuation Act 1972, the Minister for the Civil Service may determine that his term of office as a member shall be treated for the purposes of the scheme as if it were service in the employment or office by reference to which he was a participant in the scheme; and his rights under the scheme shall not be affected by sub-paragraph (1) (c).

(3)   Where--

(a)   a person ceases to hold office as a member of the Commission otherwise than on the expiry of his term of appointment, and

(b)   it appears to the Secretary of State that there are special circumstances which make it right for him to receive compensation,

the Secretary of State may direct the Commission to make to him a payment of such amount as the Secretary of State may determine.

4.   (1)   The Commission may appoint a chief executive and such other employees as the Commission think fit, subject to the consent of the Secretary of State as to their number and terms and conditions of service.

(2)   The Commission shall--

(a)   pay to employees of the Commission such remuneration, and

(b)   pay to or in respect of employees of the Commission any such allowances, fees, expenses and gratuities, as the Commission may, with the consent of the Secretary of State, determine.

(3) Employment by the Commission shall be included among the kinds of employment to which a scheme under section 1 of the Superannuation Act 1972 may apply.

5. The Commission shall pay to the Minister for the Civil Service, at such times as he may direct, such sums as he may determine in respect of any increase attributable to paragraph 3(2) or 4(3) in the sums payable out of money provided by Parliament under the Superannuation Act 1972.

Procedure

6. (1) The arrangements for the procedure of the Commission (including the quorum for meetings) shall be such as the Commission may determine.

(2) The arrangements may provide for the discharge, under the general direction of the Commission, of any function of the Commission--

(a) in the case of a function specified in sub-paragraph (3), by a committee consisting of not fewer than three members of the Commission, and

(b) in any other case, by any committee of, or by one or more of the members or employees of, the Commission.

(3) The functions referred to in sub-paragraph (2)(a) are--

(a) making a reference to a court under any of sections 9 to 12,

(b) reporting to the Court of Appeal under section 15(4),

(c) giving to the Secretary of State a statement under section 16(1)(b), and

(d) requiring the appointment of an investigating officer under section 19.

(4) The validity of any proceedings of the Commission (or of any committee of the Commission) shall not be affected by--

    (a) any vacancy among the members of the Commission or in the office of chairman of the Commission, or

    (b) any defect in the appointment of any person as a member of the Commission or as chairman of the Commission.

(5) Where--

    (a) a document or other material has been produced to the Commission under section 17, or they have been given access to a document or other material under that section, and the Commission have taken away the document or other material (or a copy of it), and

    (b) the person who produced the document or other material to the Commission, or gave them access to it, has notified the Commission that he considers that its disclosure to others may be contrary to the interests of national security,

the Commission shall, after consulting that person, deal with the document or material (or copy) in a manner appropriate for safeguarding the interests of national security.

Evidence

7. A document purporting to be--

    (a) duly executed under the seal of the Commission, or

    (b) signed on behalf of the Commission,

shall be received in evidence and, unless the contrary is proved, taken to be so executed or signed.

Annual reports and accounts

8. (1) As soon as possible after the end of each financial year of the Commission, the Commission shall send to the Secretary of State a report on the discharge of their functions during that year.

    (2) Such a report may include an account of the working of the provisions of sections 9 to 25 and recommendations relating to any of those provisions.

    (3) The Secretary of State shall lay before each House of Parliament, and cause to be published, a copy of every report sent to him under sub-paragraph (1).

9. (1) The Commission shall--

        (a) keep proper accounts and proper records in relation to the accounts, and

        (b) prepare a statement of accounts in respect of each financial year of the Commission.

    (2) The statement of accounts shall contain such information and shall be in such form as the Secretary of State may, with the consent of the Treasury, direct.

    (3) The Commission shall send a copy of the statement of accounts to the Secretary of State and to the Comptroller and Auditor General within such period after the end of the financial year to which the statement relates as the Secretary of State may direct.

    (4) The Comptroller and Auditor General shall--

        (a) examine, certify and report on the statement of accounts, and

        (b) lay a copy of the statement of accounts and of his report before each House of Parliament.

10. For the purposes of this Schedule the Commission's financial year shall be the period of twelve months ending with 31st March; but the first financial year of the Commission shall be the period beginning

with the date of establishment of the Commission and ending with the first 31st March which falls at least six months after that date.

Expenses

11.   The Secretary of State shall defray the expenses of the Commission up to such amount as may be approved by him.